CREEDS, CONFESSIONS,
CATECHISMS, and COVENANTS

CREDO

ENDORSEMENTS

In today's secular and militant culture, it is increasingly difficult for the church to stay the course. That is why this book is an essential help for families and professionals to have at their fingertips the creedal pronouncements of the church that have lasted for centuries. Creeds and confessions are statements of truth founded on Scripture. Most doctrines have been attacked from within and without, but have survived. The church does not need to re-invent the wheel on substantive doctrine. What is more reassuring than knowing that we stand with a long line of believers who believed what we believe? Nogginnose Press has provided us with a valuable resource, perhaps more necessary right now than at any other time.

DR. DEREK W. H. THOMAS
Senior Minister, First Presbyterian Church (Columbia, SC)
Chancellor's Professor, Reformed Theological Seminary
Teaching Fellow, Ligonier Ministries

As the foundations of almost every dimension of our culture are crumbling under the relentless barrage of the world, the flesh, and the devil, there is no timelier moment for a book such as *Credo*. While once-Christian churches and institutions capitulate wholesale to the dogmas of secularism, true believers must return to the unshakeable foundations of biblical doctrine. This book is a critical way to do just that. Every home and church ought to purchase multiple copies of this essential collection of the creeds and confessions of faithful Christians throughout the centuries.

DOUGLAS BOND
Author, *Crown & Covenant Trilogy*, *The Hobgoblins: A Novel on John Bunyan*, and numerous other books of historical fiction, biography, and practical theology (bondbooks.net)

Nogginnose Press has done us all a great service in reintroducing the rich legacy of our faith. *Credo* reminds us of what it is that we believe and why. Highly recommended.

DR. GEORGE GRANT
Pastor, Parish Presbyterian Church (Franklin, TN)
Director, King's Meadow Study Center
Founder, Franklin Classical School & Bannockburn College

The Apostles' Creed contains the confession that we believe in the "holy catholic church." This statement often provokes deep misgivings in the minds of good evangelical Protestants. Why would we call ourselves "catholics"? There are two errors that contribute to this misgiving. The first is simple. The word *catholic* simply means *universal.* To say that the church is catholic is simply to say that God has knit all believers together into one body, his church, which transcends time and space.

But the second error is much more difficult to correct because it is not a matter of correcting a misunderstanding of the meaning of a word. Rather, it has to do with a deep confusion regarding how God has grown his church throughout history. To state it simply, we tend to think that for most of the history of the Christian church, the church was in deep theological error, such that the heritage of the evangelical church goes back no further than the founding of the United States.

This is simply untrue and misses the great work that God has been doing throughout history. We have, in the creeds and confessions contained in this volume, a record of God's faithfulness to his church. As the bride of Christ, we stand firmly on the foundation laid by the apostles and prophets, preserved in the infallible testimony of Scripture. And we have been blessed by centuries of faithful teaching and preaching, built on that one foundation. The spiritual heritage represented here is a great wealth for which we should be tremendously grateful.

BENJAMIN R. MERKLE, D.PHIL
President, New Saint Andrews College (Moscow, ID)

When asked what you believe, the moment you reply "I believe the Bible teaches . . . ," you have made the statement that is *Credo*, or "creed" in Latin. Therefore, every Christian has a creed or confession of Faith and needs to articulate it. God, in his Wisdom, has provided men over the centuries who have done the hard work for us and put Christian belief in easily memorized and understandable form. Every Christian home should have a copy of those systematized truths that help us understand what the Bible teaches. This book provides the sum of centuries of Christian understanding that is practical for families and Christians of all ages, to learn the biblical doctrines that undergird our lives.

BILL POTTER
Historian

The broader evangelical church is innovative in all the wrong ways. She formulates worship after their own preferences, movements grounded in reactionary politics, and yet, the church keeps retreating and refusing to return to tested and tried truths. In light of this present chaos, Nogginnose Press provides fruitful labor to the church. They remind us of the words of our forefathers who were not interested in appealing to the masses, but in formulating creeds and confessions grounded in biblical truth. This repertoire of ecclesiastical documents will reorient the evangelical church back to its roots, but beyond that, it will offer a sobering taste of the articulation of true orthodoxy in a time of ecclesiastical unsavoriness.

REV. DR. URIESOU BRITO

Senior Pastor, Providence Church, CREC (Pensacola, FL)

I have several thousand books in my library but there are a handful that I return to over and over because they provide the valuable service of being a central and accessible resource. I am confident that *Credo: Creeds, Confessions, Catechisms, and Covenants* will take its place among those familiar works on my shelves. Not only does this volume provide a single source for so many clear statements on our faith, but together they demonstrate the historic and geographic unity of God's people through the ages, and I find that to be most encouraging. Every home would benefit from having this collection.

RANDY BOOTH

Pastor, Grace Covenant Presbyterian Church, CREC (Nacogdoches, TX)

CREEDS, CONFESSIONS, CATECHISMS, and COVENANTS

CREDO

Introductions by **RIVERS HOUSEAL**

Foreword by **COLLIN HOUSEAL**

NOGGINNOSE
PRESS

CREDO: CREEDS, CONFESSIONS, CATECHISMS, AND COVENANTS

ISBN 978-1-956611-00-7

Cover design and content layout by Houseal Creative
Edited by Douglas Bond

Cover image: *Luther at the Diet of Worms,* painted in 1877 by Anton von Werner (1843-1915), depicting Martin Luther speaking to Charles V of the Holy Roman Empire at the Diet of Worms, April 1521

Nogginnose Press
PO Box 96
Smithville, AR 72466 USA
nogginnose.com

To the cloud of witnesses behind us,
the brothers and sisters here with us,
and the children of the Covenant
who are yet to come.

To the glory of the God of Ages!

Contents

Foreword

CHRISTIAN, WHAT DO YOU BELIEVE?

As I write these words, there is perhaps no simpler yet more consequential question before the Church. Professing Christians are facing a time of trial and persecution not seen in generations—particularly in the United States, considered by many to be a Christian nation, or at least broadly accepting of Christianity. We're seeing government attempts to regulate worship, lukewarm churchgoers who have abandoned Scripture, and a profane and rebellious society at large.

But these trials are nothing new. Those who say we live in unprecedented times are, frankly, ignorant of history, and Church history in particular.

True enough, today's secular culture seems bound and determined to turn everything upside down and shake it violently, thumbing its collective nose at God and anything remotely traceable to His established order and ordinances. This is disconcerting enough, but perhaps more so is that many Christians are shocked to see this happening, and they appear at a loss how to respond. "Beloved, do not be surprised at the fiery trial when it comes upon you to test you, as though something strange were happening to you" (1 Peter 4:12, ESV).

So, what are we to do? Where do we draw our lines? How do we answer those who confront us with utter nonsense, insisting on "my truth" and "your truth" while casting scorn at God's Truth as hopelessly outdated and irrelevant? How are we to live the life God has called us to amidst such spiritual darkness?

If only we could learn from those who have been here before.

Pastors, parents, children—the creeds, confessions, catechisms, and covenants contained in this volume are, in a literal sense, your spiritual inheritance. All mainstream Protestant denominations, if they were so inclined, would have to trace their roots back to these documents. They are our heritage, the legacy of our spiritual forefathers who when similarly challenged said, "This is what we believe, because this is what the Scriptures principally teach." Contained herein is the wisdom of prior generations who faced down the lies, manipulations, and doctrines of men and responded with the clear exposition of the Word of God, the immovable declaration of the King of kings since time eternal.

> "While, however, ***the Scriptures are from God, the understanding of them belongs to the part of men.*** Men must interpret to the best of their ability each particular part of Scripture separately, and then combine all that the Scriptures teach upon every subject into a consistent whole, and then adjust their teachings upon different subjects in mutual consistency as parts of a harmonious system. Every student of the Bible must do this, and all make it obvious that they do it by the terms they use in their prayers and religious discourse, whether they admit or deny the propriety of human creeds and confessions. If they refuse the assistance afforded by the statements of doctrine slowly elaborated and defined by the Church, they must make out their own creed by their own unaided wisdom. ***The real question is*** not, as often pretended, between the word of God and the creed of man, but ***between the tried and proved faith of the collective body of God's people, and the private judgment and the unassisted wisdom of the repudiator of creeds.***" (A.A. Hodge, 1823-1886; emphasis added)

I was raised in a mainstream denominational church, with solid preaching and the Word of God clearly exposited, yet I was well into my thirties before I became familiar with any of these creeds and confessions. How did such treasures become dusty and hidden away? Likewise, our children were a few years old before my wife and I discovered the value of catechizing them. I have since seen firsthand how effective these creeds and catechisms are to train and encourage the next covenant generation. You are holding the proof of that claim, as my eldest daughter—still in her teens—has worked tirelessly to research and compile this volume, a project born of her heartfelt desire to see her siblings in Christ benefit from these treasures.

Parents, once your children reach an age to begin understanding what they're reading—far earlier than most of us think—you will find them attracted to the substance found here. This is no cartoon Christianity, no mere repetition of trite phrases, no oversimplification of important doctrine and theology. This is meat, not milk—and I'm willing to bet your children are hungry for it. In fact, they will require meat in order to continue their growth as followers of Christ (see Hebrews 5:12-6:2 and 1 Corinthians 3:1-9). If we want men and women of God who are ready to answer for their faith, we cannot raise them on board books, "I Could Sing of Your Love Forever," and the memorization of John 3:16. At some point they need to embrace the passages that come before and after it, and understand their place within the congregation of Christ throughout time—past, present, and future.

These documents are not inspired, as is Scripture—but they are inspiring. They are not inerrant, but they do hold tremendous instructional value. That said, as treasured as they are and ought to be, we must remember that Christianity does not consist of creeds, confessions, catechisms, or covenants. Christianity is Christ. If none of these existed, Christ and His Church still would. Yet all together, throughout Church history these kinds of documents and the truth they contain have been—and remain—a tremendous tool for uniting true followers of Christ. They also serve the essential function of separating the wheat from the chaff, the sheep from the goats.

If your heartfelt desire is to strengthen your own faith, see your children and grandchildren keep to the ancient and narrow path, and together build the Kingdom to the glory of God, I suggest you start here. Saturated with Scripture, formulated by the greatest biblical and theological minds since the Apostles, you will find no better guides to understanding "what the Scriptures principally teach."

Collin Houseal
Smithville, Arkansas
July 2021

Timeline

B.C.–1ST CENTURY A.D. **Creeds in Scripture**

CIRCA 30 A.D. Crucifixion and resurrection of Jesus Christ

3RD–4TH CENTURY **Apostles' Creed**

325 ………… **Nicene Creed**

386 ………… Augustine of Hippo converts to Christianity

451 ………… **Chalcedonian Creed**

5TH CENTURY? **Athanasian Creed**

1384 ………… John Wycliffe dies of a stroke in Lutterworth, England

1415 ………… John Huss is burnt at the stake in Konstanz, Germany

1519 ………… Ulrich Zwingli begins preaching Reformation as a priest in Zürich, Switzerland

1520's ……… Henry VIII breaks with the Church of Rome and the Reformation trickles into England

1521 ………… Martin Luther stands before the Diet of Worms

1526 ………… William Tyndale publishes his first complete translation of the New Testament in English

1528 ………… **Ten Theses of Berne**

1529 ………… **Luther's Small Catechism**

1530 ………… **Augsburg Confession**

1536 ………… John Calvin publishes *Institutes of the Christian Religion* and moves to Geneva

1559 ………… **Gallican Confession**; John Knox leaves Geneva to return to Scotland

1560 ………… **Scots Confession, Calvin's Catechism**; The complete *Geneva Bible* is published, the first English Bible to be entirely translated from original Greek and Hebrew texts

1561 ………… **Belgic Confession**

1563 ………… **Heidelberg Catechism**

1572 .... Thousands of French Huguenots are martyred in the St. Bartholomew's Day Massacre
1603 .... King James VI of Scotland also becomes James I of England
1607 .... Jamestown is founded in the New World
1611 .... The complete *King James Bible* is published in England
1618 .... The Thirty Years' War begins in Europe between Protestants and Roman Catholics
1619 .... **Canons of Dort**
1620 .... The *Mayflower* lands at Plymouth in the New World
1629 .... **First Salem Covenant**
1630 .... **Watertown Covenant, Covenant of the First Church in Boston**
1636 .... **Enlarged Salem Covenant, Dedham Covenant**
1638 .... **Scottish National Covenant**
1642 .... The English Civil Wars begin
1643 .... **Solemn League and Covenant**
1646 .... **Westminster Confession of Faith**
1647 .... **Westminster Shorter Catechism**
1653 .... Oliver Cromwell becomes Lord Protector of England, Scotland, and Ireland
1658 .... **Savoy Declaration**
1660 .... Charles II is restored to the British throne, persecution ramps up for Covenanters in Scotland and Nonconformists in England
1679 .... The "Killing Times" begin for the Scottish Covenanters
1684 .... **The Children's Bond**
1688 .... The "Glorious Revolution" puts William and Mary on the British throne and ends religious persecution in Britain
1689 .... **Second London Baptist Confession**
Keach's Catechism

Documents in **bold** are included in this volume.

CREEDS

It took time for the Early Church to get its doctrinal bearings. Heresies cropped up constantly, as the Apostles had warned. (Matt. 24:4-5, Eph. 4:14, Gal. 1:8-9, 2 Pet. 2:1, etc.) So the Early Church fathers sat down with Scripture and asked one another, "Christians, what do we believe?" They wrote their answers in creeds: Scripture's teachings, distilled into short, easy-to-memorize statements. These creeds were meant to serve the Church in several ways.

The word *creed* comes from the Latin word *credo,* meaning "I believe." Creeds are intended for personal and corporate confessions. When worshipers give voice to a creed, they are vowing before God, "I believe." Creeds are also a teaching tool for new believers: they give the major tenets of Christianity at a glance, as a jumping-off place for deeper study. Creeds are watchdogs against heresy. When we Christians memorize and regularly avow Scriptural doctrine—before God and each other—we are more apt to notice when wolves in sheep's clothing start teaching something contrary to God's Words.

But best of all, creeds unify Christ's people. Though we may differ on secondary doctrines, if you and I can confess the Apostles' Creed together, for example, then we are brethren in Christ—*not because of the creed itself,* but because it represents and summarizes indisputable and essential truths of Scripture. ▪

Creeds in Scripture

Scripture records myriad instances when God's people spontaneously confessed their faith before God. These beautiful declarations of faith are creeds, too.

The selections below are intended to show some examples, but these are certainly not all of the creeds to be found in Scripture.

"In the beginning, God created the heavens and the earth." — GENESIS 1:1 (ESV)

"The LORD is my strength and my song, and he has become my salvation; this is my God, and I will praise him, my father's God, and I will exalt him." — EXODUS 15:2 (ESV)

"Hear, O Israel: The LORD our God, the LORD is one." — DEUTERONOMY 6:4 (ESV)

"The Rock, his work is perfect, for all his ways are justice. A God of faithfulness and without iniquity, just and upright is he." — DEUTERONOMY 32:4 (ESV)

"And when all the people saw it, they fell on their faces and said, 'The LORD, he is God; the LORD, he is God.'" — 1 KINGS 18:39 (ESV)

"Teach me good judgment and knowledge, for I believe in your commandments." — PSALM 119:66 (ESV)

"When he entered the house, the blind men came to him, and Jesus said to them, 'Do you believe that I am able to do this?' They said to him, 'Yes, Lord.'" — MATTHEW 9:28 (ESV)

"He said to them, 'But who do you say that I am?' Simon Peter replied, 'You are the Christ, the Son of the living God.'" — **MATTHEW 16:15-16 (ESV)**

"Nathanael answered him, 'Rabbi, you are the Son of God! You are the King of Israel!'" — **JOHN 1:49 (ESV)**

"Simon Peter answered him, 'Lord, to whom shall we go? You have the words of eternal life, and we have believed, and have come to know, that you are the Holy One of God.'" — **JOHN 6:68-69 (ESV)**

"She said to him, 'Yes, Lord; I believe that you are the Christ, the Son of God, who is coming into the world.'" — **JOHN 11:27 (ESV)**

"Thomas answered him, 'My Lord and my God!'" — **JOHN 20:28 (ESV)**

"Men of Israel, hear these words: Jesus of Nazareth, a man attested to you by God with mighty works and wonders and signs that God did through him in your midst, as you yourselves know—this Jesus, delivered up according to the definite plan and foreknowledge of God, you crucified and killed by the hands of lawless men. God raised him up, loosing the pangs of death, because it was not possible for him to be held by it.... This Jesus God raised up, and of that we all are witnesses. Being therefore exalted at the right hand of God, and having received from the Father the promise of the Holy Spirit, he has poured out this that you yourselves are seeing and hearing.... Let all the house of Israel therefore know for certain that God has made him both Lord and Christ, this Jesus whom you crucified.... Repent and be baptized every one of you in the name of Jesus Christ for the forgiveness of your sins, and you will receive the gift of the Holy Spirit. For the promise is for you and for your children and for all who are far off, everyone whom the Lord our God calls to himself." — **ACTS 2:22-39 (ESV, FRAGMENTED)**

"And they said, 'Believe in the Lord Jesus, and you will be saved, you and your household.'" — **ACTS 16:31 (ESV)**

"If you confess with your mouth that Jesus is Lord and believe in your heart that God raised him from the dead, you will be saved. For with the heart one believes and is justified, and with the mouth one confesses and is saved. For the Scripture says, 'Everyone who believes in him will not be put to shame.' For there is no distinction between Jew and Greek; for the same Lord is Lord of all, bestowing his riches on all who call on him. For 'everyone who calls on the name of the Lord will be saved.'" — **ROMANS 10:9-13 (ESV)**

"For although there may be so-called gods in heaven or on earth—as indeed there are many 'gods' and many 'lords'—yet for us there is one God, the Father, from whom are all things and for whom we exist, and one Lord, Jesus Christ, through whom are all things and through whom we exist." — **1 CORINTHIANS 8:5-6 (ESV)**

"For I delivered to you as of first importance what I also received: that Christ died for our sins in accordance with the Scriptures, that he was buried, that he was raised on the third day in accordance with the Scriptures..." — **1 CORINTHIANS 15:3-4 (ESV)**

"Have this mind among yourselves, which is yours in Christ Jesus, who, though he was in the form of God, did not count equality with God a thing to be grasped, but emptied himself, by taking the form of a servant, being born in the likeness of men. And being found in human form, he humbled himself by becoming obedient to the point of death, even death on a cross. Therefore God has highly exalted him and bestowed on him the name that is above every name, so that at the name of Jesus every knee should bow, in heaven and on earth and under the earth, and every tongue confess that Jesus Christ is Lord, to the glory of God the Father." — **PHILIPPIANS 2:5-11 (ESV)**

"Great indeed, we confess, is the mystery of godliness: he was manifested in the flesh, vindicated by the Spirit, seen by angels, proclaimed among the nations, believed on in the world, taken up in glory." — **1 TIMOTHY 3:16 (ESV)**

Apostles' Creed

In the first few centuries after Christ's coming, the Church needed to be united by clearly stated beliefs, or else schisms and heresies would soon have ripped her apart. To that end, the earliest forms of the Apostles' Creed appeared about the third or fourth century. It was used as a baptismal confession, to make sure new Christians knew the basics of the faith they were embracing. The creed was also called the Apostles' Symbol—a badge of the believer.

Why it was titled the Apostles' *Creed is not certain—perhaps the apostles themselves wrote an early version, or (more historically likely) perhaps it was simply considered a summary of the Apostolic teachings in Scripture. The creed was changed slightly in the eighth century to give us the wording we are familiar with today.*

I believe in God the Father Almighty; Maker of heaven and earth. And in Jesus Christ, His only Son, our Lord; who was conceived by the Holy Ghost and born of the virgin, Mary; suffered under Pontius Pilate, was crucified, dead, and buried; He descended into Hades; the third day He rose from the dead; He ascended into Heaven, and sits at the right hand of God the Father Almighty; from thence He shall come to judge the living and the dead. I believe in the Holy Ghost; the holy catholic[1] Church; the communion of saints; the forgiveness of sins; the resurrection of the body; and the life everlasting. Amen. ▪

1 The word *catholic* is an adjective from the Greek word *katholikos*, which means "universal" or "concerning the whole." It is here referring to the whole Body of Christ, the saints of God worldwide, in the past, present, and future. It does not refer to Roman Catholicism.

Nicene Creed

In the early fourth century, a priest named Arius began to spread a new heresy which taught that Christ was not fully God. To settle the confusion in the Church over this, Emperor Constantine called the First Ecumenical Council to meet in Nicaea in 325. Because the Apostles' Creed does not specifically affirm Christ's "sameness" with God, the First Ecumenical Council (also called the First Council of Nicaea) wrote a new creed to specifically refute Arius' teachings. "...God of God, Light of Light, very God of very God...*" Thus, the Nicene Creed was born.*

Then another heretic, Apollinaris, began teaching that Christ was not fully man. So, in 381 Emperor Theodosius called the Second Ecumenical Council to Constantinople and asked them to reaffirm the Nicene Creed. They re-wrote the creed to also emphasize Christ's sinless humanity, producing the Nicene Creed that we know today—or more specifically, the Niceno-Constantinopolitan Creed (to distinguish it from the first Nicene Creed).

I believe in one God, the Father Almighty, Maker of heaven and earth, and of all things visible and invisible. And in one Lord Jesus Christ, the only-begotten Son of God, begotten of the Father before all worlds, God of God, Light of Light, very God of very God, begotten, not made, being of one substance with the Father; by whom all things were made; who, for us men, and for our salvation, came down from Heaven, and was incarnate by the Holy Ghost of the virgin, Mary, and was made man; and was crucified also for us under Pontius Pilate; He suffered and was buried; and the third day He rose again, according to the Scriptures; and ascended into Heaven, and sits on the right hand of the Father; and He shall come again, with glory, to judge both the living and the dead; whose kingdom shall have no end. And I believe in the Holy Ghost, the Lord, and Giver of Life, who proceeds from the Father and the Son; who with the Father and the Son together is worshiped and glorified; who spoke by the Prophets. And I believe one holy catholic[1] and apostolic Church; I acknowledge one baptism for the remission of sins; and I look for the resurrection of the dead, and the life of the world to come. Amen. ▪

1 The word *catholic* is an adjective from the Greek word *katholikos,* which means "universal" or "concerning the whole." It is here referring to the whole Body of Christ, the saints of God worldwide, in the past, present, and future. It does not refer to Roman Catholicism.

Chalcedonian Creed

In the fifth century, yet another heresy arose about the nature of Christ, called Monophysitism. A priest named Eutyches began teaching that Christ's deity and humanity were mingled together and not distinct, that Christ wasn't God or *Man, but some mixture of both. To rebuke his error, the fourth General Council of Chalcedon met in 451 and wrote the Definition of Chalcedon, or the Chalcedonian Creed. This was the largest of the ancient councils: about 450 bishops working together to defend the Biblical mystery that Christ is both fully man and fully God, simultaneously* and *distinctly.*

Therefore, following the holy fathers, we all with one accord teach men to acknowledge one and the same Son, our Lord Jesus Christ, at once complete in Godhead and complete in manhood, truly God and truly man, consisting also of a reasonable soul and body; of one substance with the Father as regards his Godhead, and at the same time of one substance with us as regards his manhood; like us in all respects, apart from sin; as regards his Godhead, begotten of the Father before the ages, but yet as regards his manhood begotten, for us men and for our salvation, of Mary the virgin, the God-bearer; one and the same Christ, Son, Lord, Only-begotten, recognized in two natures, without confusion, without change, without division, without separation; the distinction of natures being in no way annulled by the union, but rather the characteristics of each nature being preserved and coming together to form one person and subsistence, not as parted or separated into two persons, but one and the same Son and Only-begotten God the Word, Lord Jesus Christ; even as the prophets from earliest times spoke of him, and our Lord Jesus Christ himself taught us, and the creed of the fathers has handed down to us. ▪

Athanasian Creed

Due to its name, it was long believed that the Athanasian Creed was written by Athanasius of Alexandria, who spent his life defending the Biblical doctrine of the Trinity against heresies of all shades. But scholars now believe the creed was more likely a compilation of Athanasius's teaching, written after he died. The earliest record of the creed appears in 633, with the fourth Council of Toledo (260 years after Athanasius died), but it may have existed as early as the fifth century. If it did, its author was probably Vincent of Lérins, or possibly Ambrose of Milan or Augustine of Hippo. It may have been named the Athanasian Creed because it defends the doctrine of the Trinity and reaffirms the statements from Nicaea and Chalcedon, just as Athanasius so faithfully did.

Whoever wants to be saved should above all cling to the catholic[1] faith. Whoever does not guard it whole and inviolable will doubtless perish eternally. Now this is the catholic faith: We worship one God in trinity and the Trinity in unity, neither confusing the persons nor dividing the divine being. For the Father is one person, the Son is another, and the Spirit is still another. But the deity of the Father, Son, and Holy Spirit is one, equal in glory, coeternal in majesty. What the Father is, the Son is, and so is the Holy Spirit. Uncreated is the Father; uncreated is the Son; uncreated is the Spirit. The Father is infinite; the Son is infinite; the Holy Spirit is infinite. Eternal is the Father; eternal is the Son; eternal is the Spirit: And yet there are not three eternal beings, but one who is eternal; as there are not three uncreated and unlimited

1 The word *catholic* is an adjective from the Greek word *katholikos*, which means "universal" or "concerning the whole." It is here referring to the whole Body of Christ, the saints of God worldwide, in the past, present, and future. It does not refer to Roman Catholicism.

beings, but one who is uncreated and unlimited. Almighty is the Father; almighty is the Son; almighty is the Spirit: And yet there are not three almighty beings, but one who is almighty. Thus the Father is God; the Son is God; the Holy Spirit is God: And yet there are not three gods, but one God. Thus the Father is Lord; the Son is Lord; the Holy Spirit is Lord: And yet there are not three lords, but one Lord. As Christian truth compels us to acknowledge each distinct person as God and Lord, so catholic religion forbids us to say that there are three gods or lords. The Father was neither made nor created nor begotten; the Son was neither made nor created, but was alone begotten of the Father; the Spirit was neither made nor created, but is proceeding from the Father and the Son. Thus there is one Father, not three fathers; one Son, not three sons; one Holy Spirit, not three spirits. And in this Trinity, no one is before or after, greater or less than the other; but all three persons are in themselves, coeternal and coequal; and so we must worship the Trinity in unity and the one God in three persons. Whoever wants to be saved should think thus about the Trinity. It is necessary for eternal salvation that one also faithfully believe that our Lord Jesus Christ became flesh. For this is the true faith that we believe and confess: That our Lord Jesus Christ, God's Son, is both God and man. He is God, begotten before all worlds from the being of the Father, and he is man, born in the world from the being of his mother—existing fully as God, and fully as man with a rational soul and a human body; equal to the Father in divinity, subordinate to the Father in humanity. Although he is God and man, he is not divided, but is one Christ. He is united because God has taken humanity into himself; he does not transform deity into humanity. He is completely one in the unity of his person, without confusing his natures. For as the rational soul and body are one person, so the one Christ is God and man. He suffered death for our salvation. He descended into hell and rose again from the dead. He ascended into heaven and is seated at the right hand of the Father. He will come again to judge the living and the dead. At his coming all people shall rise bodily to give an account of their own deeds. Those who have done good will enter eternal life, those who have done evil will enter eternal fire. This is the catholic faith. One cannot be saved without believing this firmly and faithfully. ▪

CONFESSIONS

IN CERTAIN AGES, the issues the Church faced required more answering than would fit into a short creed. At those times, the Church fathers banded together to write *confessions*—thorough summaries of what exactly they believed. Like the creeds, these confessions were never intended to take the place of Scripture, but rather to *confess* and define a faithful and accurate understanding of Scripture. The creeds were distillations of the clear, unquestionable doctrines taught in the Bible. Confessions, too, present these foundational doctrines, but unlike creeds they also include what are considered more secondary doctrinal interpretation.

The confessions were meant to do two things: first, to reaffirm the non-negotiable truths of Scripture, the "essentials," and second, to unite believers who held similar persuasions on secondary doctrines. Though they give much more elaborate answers, the confessions answer the same basic question that the creeds do: "Christians, what do we believe?" ▪

Ten Theses of Berne

In the 1520's, several Reformed pastors were doing their utmost to bring true gospel teaching to the city of Berne in Switzerland: particularly Berthold Haller, Sebastian Meyer, and Francis Kolb, all friends of Ulrich Zwingli.

But the city was not receptive to the Reformation—the Peasant's War in Germany and the Swiss revolutionaries had spooked the Bernese. The city leaders reaffirmed the city's allegiance to Roman Catholicism, and spreading Luther's teachings was forbidden. The city government ordered Berthold Haller to read the mass in his services, upon pain of losing his pulpit. Haller refused. But while the city aligned itself with Rome, the Swiss Council of Two Hundred fearlessly gave Haller and his friends the protection they needed to continue preaching the true gospel.

In 1527 a new city council was elected in Berne. This new council overturned the strict Roman Catholic policies, and called for a disputation on Reformed doctrines. Invitations were sent out. Of the Roman Catholic Swiss cantons, only Lausanne agreed to send men to the debate. But the Reformers' party received delegates from Zurich, Basel, St. Gall, and several cities in South Germany, so that the band of Reformed debaters included Ulrich Zwingli, Berthold Haller, Francis Kolb, Johannes Oecolampadius, Wolfgang Capito, and Martin Bucer.

On the debate's opening day, January 6, 1528, Kolb delivered the Ten Theses of Berne, which had been prepared by Haller and Zwingli. Over the nineteen days of debate, the Ten Theses were thoroughly discussed. By the end, only a few Bernese priests still disagreed with the Reformer. They soon left the city.

The Ten Theses of Berne became a brief confession for the Reformed Church in Berne. The city that had once sold itself to Rome was now permeated with the pure doctrines of the gospel and the Reformation.

1. The holy Christian Church, whose only Head is Christ, is born of the Word of God, and abides in the same, and listens not to the voice of a stranger.

2. The Church of Christ makes no laws and commandments without the Word of God. Hence human traditions are no more binding on us than as far as they are founded in the Word of God.

3. Christ is the only wisdom, righteousness, redemption, and satisfaction for the sins of the whole world. Hence it is a denial of Christ when we confess another ground of salvation and satisfaction.

4. The essential and corporal presence of the body and blood of Christ[1] cannot be demonstrated from the Holy Scripture.

5. The mass as now in use, in which Christ is offered to God the Father for the sins of the living and the dead, is contrary to the Scripture, a blasphemy against the most holy sacrifice, passion, and death of Christ, and on account of its abuses an abomination before God.

6. As Christ alone died for us, so he is also to be adored as the only Mediator and Advocate between God the Father and the believers. Therefore it is contrary to the Word of God to propose and invoke other mediators.

7. Scripture knows nothing of a purgatory after this life. Hence all masses and other offices for the dead are useless.

8. The worship of images is contrary to Scripture. Therefore images should be abolished when they are set up as objects of adoration.

9. Matrimony is not forbidden in the Scripture to any class of men; but fornication and unchastity are forbidden to all.

10. Since, according to the Scripture, an open fornicator must be excommunicated, it follows that unchastity and impure celibacy are more pernicious to the clergy than to any other class.

All to the glory of God and his holy Word. ▪

1 In the Lord's Supper, that is. This was to contradict the Roman doctrine of transubstantiation. (Thesis 5 also.)

Augsburg Confession

In 1530, the Holy Roman Emperor Charles V (who had declared Martin Luther to be an outlaw and a heretic) called the Diet of Augsburg. Among other concerns, the Diet's job was to once again hash out the Reformers' teachings versus Rome's teachings, and hopefully bring settlement to the church in Germany.

As an outlaw already wanted by the emperor, Luther was not at liberty to attend, so his friend, Philipp Melanchthon, went to the Diet in his stead. To represent Lutheran teaching, Melanchthon wrote the Augsburg Confession, drawing from the Articles of Schwabach which he, Luther, and Justus Jonas had drafted a year before. Seven German princes who supported Luther signed Melanchthon's Augsburg Confession, which was simply called an "Apology" at the time, meaning a defense. The emperor did all in his power to prevent the confession from reaching the public until he had seen it first. But when the confession was presented before him on June 25, 1530, the reader dared to read the confession loudly in plain German before he read it again in academic Latin.

In the following years, the Augsburg Confession was published and became the accepted confession of the Lutherans—though Melanchthon continued to make minor adjustments in wording each time it was re-published.

In 1540, Melanchthon made his biggest edit: among other minor changes, he re-wrote Article X, concerning the Lord's Supper. The original version had supported the Lutheran belief in consubstantiation, but the 1540 edition—called the Augsburg Confession Variata—was more vaguely worded, to allow for the Lutheran view and the views of Ulrich Zwingli and John Calvin. Melanchthon was trying to bring unity between the Reformers, and Calvin was grateful—he himself signed the 1540 Augsburg Variata. But strict Lutherans were (and still are) irked with Melanchthon for changing Article X.

The following is the unaltered 1530 edition, but both versions of Article X have been included for comparison.

ARTICLE I: OF GOD

Our Churches, with common consent, do teach that the decree of the Council of Nicaea concerning the Unity of the Divine Essence and concerning the Three Persons, is true and to be believed without any doubting; that is to say, there is one Divine Essence which is called and which is God: eternal, without body, without parts, of infinite power, wisdom, and goodness, the Maker and Preserver of all things, visible and invisible; and yet there are three Persons, of the same essence and power, who also are coeternal, the Father the Son, and the Holy Ghost. And the term "person" they use as the Fathers have used it, to signify, not a part or quality in another, but that which subsists of itself.

They condemn all heresies which have sprung up against this Article, as the Manichaeans, who assumed two principles, one Good and the other Evil—also the Valentinians, Arians, Eunomians, Mohammedans, and all such. They condemn also the Samosatenes, old and new, who, contending that there is but one Person, sophistically and impiously argue that the Word and the Holy Ghost are not distinct Persons, but that "Word" signifies a spoken word, and "Spirit" signifies motion created in things.

ARTICLE II: OF ORIGINAL SIN

Also they teach that since the fall of Adam all men begotten in the natural way are born with sin, that is, without the fear of God, without trust in God, and with concupiscence; and that this disease, or vice of origin, is truly sin, even now condemning and bringing eternal death upon those not born again through Baptism and the Holy Ghost.

They Condemn the Pelagians and others who deny that original depravity is sin, and who, to obscure the glory of Christ's merit and benefits, argue that man can be justified before God by his own strength and reason.

ARTICLE III: OF THE SON OF GOD

Also they teach that the Word, that is, the Son of God, did assume the human nature in the womb of the blessed Virgin Mary, so that there are two natures, the divine and the human, inseparably enjoined in one Person, one Christ, true God and true man, who was born of the Virgin Mary, truly suffered, was crucified, dead, and buried, that He might reconcile the Father unto us, and be a sacrifice, not only for original guilt, but also for all actual sins of men.

He also descended into hell, and truly rose again the third day; afterward He ascended into heaven that He might sit on the right hand of the Father, and forever reign and have dominion over all creatures, and sanctify them that believe in Him, by sending the Holy Ghost into their hearts, to rule, comfort, and quicken them, and to defend them against the devil and the power of sin.

The same Christ shall openly come again to judge the quick and the dead, etc., according to the Apostles' Creed.

ARTICLE IV: OF JUSTIFICATION

Also they teach that men cannot be justified before God by their own strength, merits, or works, but are freely justified for Christ's sake, through faith, when they believe that they are received into favor, and that their sins are forgiven for Christ's sake, who, by His death, has made satisfaction for our sins. This faith God imputes for righteousness in His sight. Rom. 3 and 4.

ARTICLE V: OF THE MINISTRY

That we may obtain this faith, the Ministry of Teaching the Gospel and administering the Sacraments was instituted. For through the Word and Sacraments, as through instruments, the Holy Ghost is given, who works faith; where and when it pleases God, in them that hear the Gospel, to wit, that God, not for our own merits, but for Christ's sake, justifies those who believe that they are received into grace for Christ's sake.

They condemn the Anabaptists and others who think that the Holy Ghost comes to men without the external Word, through their own preparations and works.

ARTICLE VI: OF NEW OBEDIENCE

Also they teach that this faith is bound to bring forth good fruits, and that it is necessary to do good works commanded by God, because of God's will, but that we should not rely on those works to merit justification before God. For remission of sins and justification is apprehended by faith, as also the voice of Christ attests: When ye shall have done all these things, say: We are unprofitable servants. Luke 17:10. The same is also taught by the Fathers. For Ambrose says: It is ordained of God that he who believes in Christ is saved, freely receiving remission of sins, without works, by faith alone.

ARTICLE VII: OF THE CHURCH

Also they teach that one holy Church is to continue forever. The Church is the congregation of saints, in which the Gospel is rightly taught and the Sacraments are rightly administered.

And to the true unity of the Church it is enough to agree concerning the doctrine of the Gospel and the administration of the Sacraments. Nor is it necessary that human traditions, that is, rites or ceremonies, instituted by men, should be everywhere alike. As Paul says: One faith, one Baptism, one God and Father of all, etc. Eph. 4:5-6.

ARTICLE VIII: WHAT THE CHURCH IS

Although the Church properly is the congregation of saints and true believers, nevertheless, since in this life many hypocrites and evil persons are mingled therewith, it is lawful to use Sacraments administered by evil men, according to the saying of Christ: The Scribes and the Pharisees sit in Moses' seat, etc. Matt. 23:2. Both the Sacraments and Word are effectual by reason of the institution and commandment of Christ, notwithstanding they be administered by evil men.

They condemn the Donatists, and such like, who denied it to be lawful to use the ministry of evil men in the Church, and who thought the ministry of evil men to be unprofitable and of none effect.

ARTICLE IX: OF BAPTISM

Of Baptism they teach that it is necessary to salvation, and that through Baptism is offered the grace of God, and that children are to be baptized who, being offered to God through Baptism are received into God's grace.

They condemn the Anabaptists, who reject the baptism of children, and say that children are saved without Baptism.

ARTICLE X: OF THE LORD'S SUPPER

The original version from the "unaltered" 1530 confession:
Of the Supper of the Lord they teach that the Body and Blood of Christ are truly present, and are distributed to those who eat the Supper of the Lord; and they reject those that teach otherwise.

The modified version from the 1540 Variata:
Concerning the Lord's Supper, they teach that with bread and wine are truly exhibited the body and blood of Christ to those that eat in the Lord's Supper.

ARTICLE XI: OF CONFESSION

Of Confession they teach that Private Absolution ought to be retained in the churches, although in confession an enumeration of all sins is not necessary. For it is impossible according to the Psalm: Who can understand his errors? Ps. 19:12.

ARTICLE XII: OF REPENTANCE

Of Repentance they teach that for those who have fallen after Baptism there is remission of sins whenever they are converted and that the Church ought to impart absolution to those thus returning to repentance. Now, repentance consists properly of these two parts: One is contrition, that is, terrors smiting the conscience through the knowledge of sin; the other is faith, which is born of the Gospel, or of absolution, and believes that for Christ's sake, sins are forgiven, comforts the conscience, and delivers it from terrors. Then good works are bound to follow, which are the fruits of repentance.

They condemn the Anabaptists, who deny that those once justified can lose the Holy Ghost. Also those who contend that some may attain to such perfection in this life that they cannot sin.

The Novatians also are condemned, who would not absolve such as had fallen after Baptism, though they returned to repentance.

They also are rejected who do not teach that remission of sins comes through faith but command us to merit grace through satisfactions of our own.

ARTICLE XIII: OF THE USE OF THE SACRAMENTS

Of the Use of the Sacraments they teach that the Sacraments were ordained, not only to be marks of profession among men, but rather to be signs and testimonies of the will of God toward us, instituted to awaken and confirm faith in those who use them. Wherefore we must so use the Sacraments that faith be added to believe the promises which are offered and set forth through the Sacraments.

They therefore condemn those who teach that the Sacraments justify by the outward act, and who do not teach that, in the use of the Sacraments, faith which believes that sins are forgiven, is required.

ARTICLE XIV: OF ECCLESIASTICAL ORDER

Of Ecclesiastical Order they teach that no one should publicly teach in the Church or administer the Sacraments unless he be regularly called.

ARTICLE XV: OF ECCLESIASTICAL USAGES

Of Usages in the Church they teach that those ought to be observed which may be observed without sin, and which are profitable unto tranquility and good order in the Church, as particular holy-days, festivals, and the like.

Nevertheless, concerning such things men are admonished that consciences are not to be burdened, as though such observance was necessary to salvation.

They are admonished also that human traditions instituted to propitiate God, to merit grace, and to make satisfaction for sins, are opposed to the Gospel and the doctrine of faith. Wherefore vows and traditions concerning meats and days, etc., instituted to merit grace and to make satisfaction for sins, are useless and contrary to the Gospel.

ARTICLE XVI: OF CIVIL AFFAIRS

Of Civil Affairs they teach that lawful civil ordinances are good works of God, and that it is right for Christians to bear civil office, to sit as judges, to judge matters by the Imperial and other existing laws, to award just punishments, to engage in just wars, to serve as soldiers, to make legal contracts, to hold property, to make oath when required by the magistrates, to marry a wife, to be given in marriage.

They condemn the Anabaptists who forbid these civil offices to Christians.

They condemn also those who do not place evangelical perfection in the fear of God and in faith, but in forsaking civil offices, for the Gospel teaches an eternal righteousness of the heart. Meanwhile, it does not destroy the State or the family, but very much requires that they be preserved as ordinances of God, and that charity be practiced in such ordinances. Therefore, Christians are necessarily bound to obey their own magistrates and laws save only when commanded to sin; for then they ought to obey God rather than men. Acts 5:29.

ARTICLE XVII: OF CHRIST'S RETURN TO JUDGMENT

Also they teach that at the Consummation of the World Christ will appear for judgment and will raise up all the dead; He will give to the godly and elect eternal life and everlasting joys, but ungodly men and the devils He will condemn to be tormented without end.

They condemn the Anabaptists, who think that there will be an end to the punishments of condemned men and devils.

They condemn also others who are now spreading certain Jewish opinions, that before the resurrection of the dead the godly shall take possession of the kingdom of the world, the ungodly being everywhere suppressed.

ARTICLE XVIII: OF FREE WILL

Of Free Will they teach that man's will has some liberty to choose civil righteousness, and to work things subject to reason. But it has no power, without the Holy Ghost, to work the righteousness of God, that is, spiritual righteousness; since the natural man receiveth not the things of the Spirit of God, 1 Cor. 2:14; but this righteousness is wrought in the heart when the Holy Ghost is received through the Word. These things are said in as many words by Augustine in his *Hypognosticon*, Book III: We grant that all men have a free will, free, inasmuch as it has the judgment of reason; not that it is thereby capable, without God, either to begin, or, at least, to complete aught in things pertaining to God, but only in works of this life, whether good or evil. "Good" I call those works which spring from the good in nature, such as, willing to labor in the field, to eat and drink, to have a friend, to clothe oneself, to build a house, to marry a wife, to raise cattle, to learn divers useful arts, or whatsoever good pertains to this life. For all of these things are not without dependence on the providence of God; yea, of Him and through Him they are and have their being. "Evil" I call such works as willing to worship an idol, to commit murder, etc.

They condemn the Pelagians and others, who teach that without the Holy Ghost, by the power of nature alone, we are able to love God above all things; also to do the commandments of God as touching "the substance of the act." For, although nature is able in a manner to do the outward work, (for it is able to keep the hands from theft and murder,) yet it cannot produce the inward motions, such as the fear of God, trust in God, chastity, patience, etc.

ARTICLE XIX: OF THE CAUSE OF SIN

Of the Cause of Sin they teach that, although God does create and preserve nature, yet the cause of sin is the will of the wicked, that is, of the devil and ungodly men; which will, unaided of God, turns itself from God, as Christ says John 8:44: When he speaketh a lie, he speaketh of his own.

ARTICLE XX: OF GOOD WORKS

Our teachers are falsely accused of forbidding good Works. For their published writings on the Ten Commandments, and others of like import, bear witness that they have taught to good purpose concerning all estates and duties of life, as to what estates of life and what works in every calling be pleasing to God. Concerning these things preachers heretofore taught but little, and urged only childish and needless works, as particular holy-days, particular fasts, brotherhoods, pilgrimages, services in honor of saints, the use of rosaries, monasticism, and such like. Since our adversaries have been admonished of these things, they are now unlearning them, and do not preach these unprofitable works as heretofore. Besides, they begin to mention faith, of which there was heretofore marvelous silence. They teach that we are justified not by works only, but they conjoin faith and works, and say that we are justified by faith and works. This doctrine is more tolerable than the former one, and can afford more consolation than their old doctrine.

Forasmuch, therefore, as the doctrine concerning faith, which ought to be the chief one in the Church, has lain so long unknown, as all must needs grant that there was the deepest silence in their sermons concerning the righteousness of faith, while only the doctrine of works was treated in the churches, our teachers have instructed the churches concerning faith as follows:

First, that our works cannot reconcile God or merit forgiveness of sins, grace, and justification, but that we obtain this only by faith when we believe that we are received into favor for Christs sake, who alone has been set forth the Mediator and Propitiation, 1 Tim. 2:6, in order that the Father may be reconciled through Him. Whoever, therefore, trusts that by works he merits grace, despises the merit and grace of Christ, and seeks a way to God without Christ, by human strength, although Christ has said of Himself: I am the Way, the Truth, and the Life. John 14:6.

This doctrine concerning faith is everywhere treated by Paul, Eph. 2:8: By grace are ye saved through faith; and that not of yourselves; it is the gift of God, not of works, etc.

And lest any one should craftily say that a new interpretation of Paul has been devised by us, this entire matter is supported by the testimonies of the Fathers. For Augustine, in many volumes, defends grace and the righteousness of faith, over against the merits of works. And Ambrose, in his *De Vocatione Gentium,* and elsewhere, teaches to like effect. For in his *De Vocatione Gentium* he says as follows: Redemption by the blood of Christ would become of little value, neither would the preeminence of man's works be superseded by the mercy of God, if justification, which is wrought through grace, were due to the merits going before, so as to be, not the free gift of a donor, but the reward due to the laborer.

But, although this doctrine is despised by the inexperienced, nevertheless God-fearing and anxious consciences find by experience that it brings the greatest consolation, because consciences cannot be set at rest through any works, but only by faith, when they take the sure ground that for Christ's sake they have a reconciled God. As Paul teaches Rom. 5:1: Being justified by faith, we have peace with God. This whole doctrine is to be referred to that conflict of the terrified conscience, neither can it be understood apart from that conflict. Therefore inexperienced and profane men judge ill concerning this matter, who dream that Christian righteousness is nothing but civil and philosophical righteousness.

Heretofore consciences were plagued with the doctrine of works, they did not hear the consolation from the Gospel. Some persons were driven by conscience into the desert, into monasteries hoping there to merit grace by a monastic life. Some also devised other works whereby to merit grace and make satisfaction for sins. Hence there was very great need to treat of, and renew, this doctrine of faith in Christ, to the end that anxious consciences should not be without consolation but that they might know that grace and forgiveness of sins and justification are apprehended by faith in Christ.

Men are also admonished that here the term "faith" does not signify merely the knowledge of the history, such as is in the ungodly and in the devil, but signifies a faith which believes, not merely the history, but also the effect of the history—namely, this:

ARTICLE: the forgiveness of sins, to wit, that we have grace, righteousness, and forgiveness of sins through Christ.

Now he that knows that he has a Father gracious to him through Christ, truly knows God; he knows also that God cares for him, and calls upon God; in a word, he is not without God, as the heathen. For devils and the ungodly are not able to believe this.

ARTICLE: the forgiveness of sins. Hence, they hate God as an enemy, call not upon Him, and expect no good from Him. Augustine also admonishes his readers concerning the word "faith," and teaches that the term "faith" is accepted in the

Scriptures not for knowledge such as is in the ungodly but for confidence which consoles and encourages the terrified mind.

Furthermore, it is taught on our part that it is necessary to do good works, not that we should trust to merit grace by them, but because it is the will of God. It is only by faith that forgiveness of sins is apprehended, and that, for nothing. And because through faith the Holy Ghost is received, hearts are renewed and endowed with new affections, so as to be able to bring forth good works. For Ambrose says: Faith is the mother of a good will and right doing. For man's powers without the Holy Ghost are full of ungodly affections, and are too weak to do works which are good in God's sight. Besides, they are in the power of the devil who impels men to divers sins, to ungodly opinions, to open crimes. This we may see in the philosophers, who, although they endeavored to live an honest life could not succeed, but were defiled with many open crimes. Such is the feebleness of man when he is without faith and without the Holy Ghost, and governs himself only by human strength.

Hence it may be readily seen that this doctrine is not to be charged with prohibiting good works, but rather the more to be commended, because it shows how we are enabled to do good works. For without faith human nature can in no wise do the works of the First or of the Second Commandment. Without faith it does not call upon God, nor expect anything from God, nor bear the cross, but seeks, and trusts in, man's help. And thus, when there is no faith and trust in God all manner of lusts and human devices rule in the heart. Wherefore Christ said, John 16:6: Without Me ye can do nothing; and the Church sings:

Lacking Thy divine favor,
There is nothing found in man,
Naught in him is harmless.

ARTICLE XXI: OF THE WORSHIP OF THE SAINTS

Of the Worship of Saints they teach that the memory of saints may be set before us, that we may follow their faith and good works, according to our calling, as the Emperor may follow the example of David in making war to drive away the Turk from his country; For both are kings. But the Scripture teaches not the invocation of saints or to ask help of saints, since it sets before us the one Christ as the Mediator, Propitiation, High Priest, and Intercessor. He is to be prayed to, and has promised that He will hear our prayer; and this worship He approves above all, to wit, that in all afflictions He be called upon, 1 John 2:1: If any man sin, we have an Advocate with the Father, etc.

This is about the Sum of our Doctrine, in which, as can be seen, there is nothing that varies from the Scriptures, or from the Church Catholic,[1] or from the Church of Rome as known from its writers. This being the case, they judge harshly who insist that our teachers be regarded as heretics. There is, however, disagreement on certain Abuses, which have crept into the Church without rightful authority. And even in these, if there were some difference, there should be proper lenity on the part of bishops to bear with us by reason of the Confession which we have now reviewed; because even the Canons are not so severe as to demand the same rites everywhere, neither, at any time, have the rites of all churches been the same; although, among us, in large part, the ancient rites are diligently observed. For it is a false and malicious charge that all the ceremonies, all the things instituted of old, are abolished in our churches. But it has been a common complaint that some abuses were connected with the ordinary rites. These, inasmuch as they could not be approved with a good conscience, have been to some extent corrected.

ARTICLES IN WHICH ARE REVIEWED THE ABUSES WHICH HAVE BEEN CORRECTED

Inasmuch, then, as our churches dissent in no Article of the faith from the Church Catholic, but only omit some abuses which are new, and which have been erroneously accepted by the corruption of the times, contrary to the intent of the Canons, we pray that Your Imperial Majesty would graciously hear both what has been changed, and what were the reasons why the people were not compelled to observe those abuses against their conscience. Nor should Your Imperial Majesty believe those who, in order to excite the hatred of men against our part, disseminate strange slanders among the people. Having thus excited the minds of good men,

---

1 The word *catholic* is an adjective from the Greek word *katholikos*, which means "universal" or "concerning the whole." It is here referring to the whole Body of Christ, the saints of God worldwide, in the past, present, and future. It does not refer to Roman Catholicism, as this sentence's next phrase clarifies.

they have first given occasion to this controversy, and now endeavor, by the same arts, to increase the discord. For Your Imperial Majesty will undoubtedly find that the form of doctrine and of ceremonies with us is not so intolerable as these ungodly and malicious men represent. Besides, the truth cannot be gathered from common rumors or the revilings of enemies. But it can readily be judged that nothing would serve better to maintain the dignity of ceremonies, and to nourish reverence and pious devotion among the people than if the ceremonies were observed rightly in the churches.

ARTICLE XXII: OF BOTH KINDS IN THE SACRAMENT

To the laity are given Both Kinds in the Sacrament of the Lord's Supper, because this usage has the commandment of the Lord in Matt. 26:27: Drink ye all of it, where Christ has manifestly commanded concerning the cup that all should drink.

And lest any man should craftily say that this refers only to priests, Paul in 1 Cor. 11:27 recites an example from which it appears that the whole congregation did use both kinds. And this usage has long remained in the Church, nor is it known when, or by whose authority, it was changed; although Cardinal Cusanus mentions the time when it was approved. Cyprian in some places testifies that the blood was given to the people. The same is testified by Jerome, who says: The priests administer the Eucharist, and distribute the blood of Christ to the people. Indeed, Pope Gelasius commands that the Sacrament be not divided (dist. II., *De Consecratione*, cap. Comperimus). Only custom, not so ancient, has it otherwise. But it is evident that any custom introduced against the commandments of God is not to be allowed, as the Canons witness (dist. III., cap. Veritate, and the following chapters). But this custom has been received, not only against the Scripture, but also against the old Canons and the example of the Church. Therefore, if any preferred to use both kinds of the Sacrament, they ought not to have been compelled with offense to their consciences to do otherwise. And because the division of the Sacrament does not agree with the ordinance of Christ, we are accustomed to omit the procession, which hitherto has been in use.

ARTICLE XXIII: OF THE MARRIAGE OF PRIESTS

There has been common complaint concerning the examples of priests who were not chaste. For that reason also Pope Pius is reported to have said that there were certain causes why marriage was taken away from priests, but that there were far weightier ones why it ought to be given back; for so Platina writes. Since, therefore, our priests were desirous to avoid these open scandals, they married wives, and taught that it was lawful for them to contract matrimony. First, because Paul says, 1 Cor. 7:2-9: To avoid fornication, let every man have his own wife. Also: It is better to marry than to burn. Secondly Christ says, Matt. 19:11: All men cannot receive this saying, where He teaches that not all men are fit to lead a single life; for God created man for procreation, Gen. 1:28. Nor is it in man's power, without a singular gift and work of God, to alter this creation. [For it is manifest, and many have confessed that no good, honest, chaste life, no Christian, sincere, upright conduct has resulted (from the attempt), but a horrible, fearful unrest and torment of conscience has been felt by many until the end.][2] Therefore, those who are not fit to lead a single life ought to contract matrimony. For no man's law, no vow, can annul the commandment and ordinance of God. For these reasons the priests teach that it is lawful for them to marry wives.

It is also evident that in the ancient Church priests were married men. For Paul says, 1 Tim. 3:2, that a bishop should be chosen who is the husband of one wife. And in Germany, four hundred years ago for the first time, the priests were violently compelled to lead a single life, who indeed offered such resistance that the Archbishop of Mayence, when about to publish the Pope's decree concerning this matter, was almost killed in the tumult raised by the enraged priests. And so harsh was the dealing in the matter that not only were marriages forbidden for the future, but also existing marriages were torn asunder, contrary to all laws, divine and human, contrary even to the Canons themselves, made not only by the Popes, but by most celebrated Synods. [Moreover, many God-fearing and intelligent people in high station are known frequently to have expressed misgivings that such enforced celibacy and depriving men of marriage (which God Himself has instituted and

2 Brackets original, here and following. These bracketed phrases may show where Melanchthon made slight adjustments to his original wording.

left free to men) has never produced any good results, but has brought on many great and evil vices and much iniquity.]

Seeing also that, as the world is aging, man's nature is gradually growing weaker, it is well to guard that no more vices steal into Germany.

Furthermore, God ordained marriage to be a help against human infirmity. The Canons themselves say that the old rigor ought now and then, in the latter times, to be relaxed because of the weakness of men; which it is to be wished were done also in this matter. And it is to be expected that the churches shall at some time lack pastors if marriage is any longer forbidden.

But while the commandment of God is in force, while the custom of the Church is well known, while impure celibacy causes many scandals, adulteries, and other crimes deserving the punishments of just magistrates, yet it is a marvelous thing that in nothing is more cruelty exercised than against the marriage of priests. God has given commandment to honor marriage. By the laws of all well-ordered commonwealths, even among the heathen, marriage is most highly honored. But now men, and that, priests, are cruelly put to death, contrary to the intent of the Canons, for no other cause than marriage. Paul, in 1 Tim. 4:3, calls that a doctrine of devils which forbids marriage. This may now be readily understood when the law against marriage is maintained by such penalties.

But as no law of man can annul the commandment of God, so neither can it be done by any vow. Accordingly, Cyprian also advises that women who do not keep the chastity they have promised should marry. His words are these (Book I, Epistle XI): But if they be unwilling or unable to persevere, it is better for them to marry than to fall into the fire by their lusts; they should certainly give no offense to their brethren and sisters.

And even the Canons show some leniency toward those who have taken vows before the proper age, as heretofore has generally been the case.

ARTICLE XXIV: OF THE MASS

Falsely are our churches accused of abolishing the Mass; for the Mass is retained among us, and celebrated with the highest reverence. Nearly all the usual ceremonies are also preserved, save that the parts sung in Latin are interspersed here and there with German hymns, which have been added to teach the people. For ceremonies are needed to this end alone that the unlearned be taught [what they need to know of Christ]. And not only has Paul commanded to use in the church a language understood by the people, 1 Cor. 14:2-9, but it has also been so ordained by man's law. The people are accustomed to partake of the Sacrament together, if any be fit for it, and this also increases the reverence and devotion of public worship. For none are admitted except they be first examined. The people are also advised concerning the dignity and use of the Sacrament, how great consolation it brings anxious consciences, that they may learn to believe God, and to expect and ask of Him all that is good. [In this connection they are also instructed regarding other and false teachings on the Sacrament.] This worship pleases God; such use of the Sacrament nourishes true devotion toward God. It does not, therefore, appear that the Mass is more devoutly celebrated among our adversaries than among us.

But it is evident that for a long time this also has been the public and most grievous complaint of all good men that Masses have been basely profaned and applied to purposes of lucre. For it is not unknown how far this abuse obtains in all the churches by what manner of men Masses are said only for fees or stipends, and how many celebrate them contrary to the Canons. But Paul severely threatens those who deal unworthily with the Eucharist when he says, 1 Cor. 11:27: Whosoever shall eat this bread, and drink this cup of the Lord, unworthily, shall be guilty of the body and blood of the Lord. When, therefore our priests were admonished concerning this sin, Private Masses were discontinued among us, as scarcely any Private Masses were celebrated except for lucre's sake.

Neither were the bishops ignorant of these abuses, and if they had corrected them in time, there would now be less dissension. Heretofore, by their own connivance, they suffered many corruptions to creep into the Church. Now, when it is too late, they begin to complain of the troubles of the Church, while this disturbance has been occasioned simply by those abuses which were so manifest that they could be borne no longer. There have been great dissensions concerning the Mass, concerning the Sacrament. Perhaps the world is being punished for such long-continued profanations of the Mass as have been tolerated in the churches for so many centuries by the very men who were both able and in duty bound to correct them. For in the Ten Commandments it is written, Ex. 20, 7: The Lord will not hold him guiltless that taketh His name in vain. But since the world began, nothing that God ever ordained seems to have been so abused for filthy lucre as the Mass.

There was also added the opinion which infinitely increased Private Masses, namely that Christ, by His passion, had made satisfaction for original sin, and instituted the Mass wherein an offering should be made for daily sins, venial and mortal. From this has arisen the common opinion that the Mass takes away the sins of the living and the dead by the outward act. Then they began to dispute whether one Mass said for many were worth as much as special Masses for individuals, and this brought forth that infinite multitude of Masses. [With this work men wished to obtain from God all that they needed, and in the mean time faith in Christ and the true worship were forgotten.]

Concerning these opinions our teachers have given warning that they depart from the Holy Scriptures and diminish the glory of the passion of Christ. For Christ's passion was an oblation and satisfaction, not for original guilt only, but also for all other sins, as it is written to the Hebrews, 10, 10: We are sanctified through the offering of Jesus Christ once for all. Also, 10, 14: By one offering He hath perfected forever them that are sanctified. [It is an unheard-of innovation in the Church to teach that Christ by His death made satisfaction only for original sin and not likewise for all other sin. Accordingly it is hoped that everybody will understand that this error has not been reproved without due reason.]

Scripture also teaches that we are justified before God through faith in Christ, when we believe that our sins are forgiven for Christ's sake. Now if the Mass take away the sins of the living and the dead by the outward act justification comes of the work of Masses, and not of faith, which Scripture does not allow.

But Christ commands us, Luke 22:19: This do in remembrance of Me; therefore the Mass was instituted that the faith of those who use the Sacrament should remember what benefits it receives through Christ, and cheer and comfort the anxious conscience. For to remember Christ is to remember His benefits, and to realize that they are truly offered unto us. Nor is it enough only to remember the history; for this also the Jews and the ungodly can remember. Wherefore the Mass is to be used to this end, that there the Sacrament [Communion] may be administered to them that have need of consolation; as Ambrose says: Because

I always sin, I am always bound to take the medicine. [Therefore this Sacrament requires faith, and is used in vain without faith.]

Now, forasmuch as the Mass is such a giving of the Sacrament, we hold one communion every holy-day, and, if any desire the Sacrament, also on other days, when it is given to such as ask for it. And this custom is not new in the Church; for the Fathers before Gregory make no mention of any private Mass, but of the common Mass [the Communion] they speak very much. Chrysostom says that the priest stands daily at the altar, inviting some to the Communion and keeping back others. And it appears from the ancient Canons that some one celebrated the Mass from whom all the other presbyters and deacons received the body of the Lord; for thus the words of the Nicene Canon say: Let the deacons, according to their order, receive the Holy Communion after the presbyters, from the bishop or from a presbyter. And Paul, 1 Cor. 11:33, commands concerning the Communion: Tarry one for another, so that there may be a common participation.

Forasmuch, therefore, as the Mass with us has the example of the Church, taken from the Scripture and the Fathers, we are confident that it cannot be disapproved, especially since public ceremonies, for the most part like those hitherto in use, are retained; only the number of Masses differs, which, because of very great and manifest abuses doubtless might be profitably reduced. For in olden times, even in churches most frequented, the Mass was not celebrated every day, as the *Tripartite History* (Book 9, chap. 33) testifies: Again in Alexandria, every Wednesday and Friday the Scriptures are read, and the doctors expound them, and all things are done, except the solemn rite of Communion.

ARTICLE XXV: OF CONFESSION

Confession in the churches is not abolished among us; for it is not usual to give the body of the Lord, except to them that have been previously examined and absolved. And the people are most carefully taught concerning faith in the absolution, about which formerly there was profound silence. Our people are taught that they should highly prize the absolution, as being the voice of God, and pronounced by God's command. The power of the Keys is set forth in its beauty and they are reminded what great consolation it brings to anxious consciences, also, that God requires faith to believe such absolution as a voice sounding from heaven, and that such faith in Christ truly obtains and receives the forgiveness of sins. Aforetime satisfactions were immoderately extolled; of faith and the merit of Christ and the righteousness of faith no mention was made; wherefore, on this point, our churches are by no means to be blamed. For this even our adversaries must needs concede to us that the doctrine concerning repentance has been most diligently treated and laid open by our teachers.

But of Confession they teach that an enumeration of sins is not necessary, and that consciences be not burdened with anxiety to enumerate all sins, for it is impossible to recount all sins, as the Psalm testifies, 19:13: Who can understand his errors? Also Jeremiah, 17:9: The heart is deceitful; who can know it; But if no sins were forgiven, except those that are recounted, consciences could never find peace; for very many sins they neither see nor can remember. The ancient writers also testify that an enumeration is not necessary. For in the *Decrees*, Chrysostom is quoted, who says thus: I say not to you that you should disclose yourself in public, nor that you accuse yourself before others, but I would have you obey the prophet who says: "Disclose thy self before God." Therefore confess your sins before God, the true Judge, with prayer. Tell your errors, not with the tongue, but with the memory of your conscience, etc. And the *Gloss* (Of Repentance, Distinct. V, Cap. Consideret) admits that Confession is of human right only [not commanded by Scripture, but ordained by the Church]. Nevertheless, on account of the great benefit of absolution, and because it is otherwise useful to the conscience, Confession is retained among us.

ARTICLE XXVI: OF THE DISTINCTION OF MEATS

It has been the general persuasion, not of the people alone, but also of those teaching in the churches, that making Distinctions of Meats, and like traditions of men, are works profitable to merit grace, and able to make satisfactions for sins. And that the world so thought, appears from this, that new ceremonies, new orders, new holy-days, and new fastings were daily instituted, and the teachers in the churches did exact these works as a service necessary to merit grace, and did greatly terrify men's consciences, if they should omit any of these things. From this persuasion concerning traditions much detriment has resulted in the Church.

First, the doctrine of grace and of the righteousness of faith has been obscured by it, which is the chief part of the Gospel, and ought to stand out as the most prominent in the Church, in order that the merit of Christ may be well known, and faith, which believes that sins are forgiven for Christ's sake be exalted far above works. Wherefore Paul also lays the greatest stress on this Article, putting aside the Law and human traditions, in order to show that Christian righteousness is something else than such works, to wit, the faith which believes that sins are freely forgiven for Christ's sake. But this doctrine of Paul has been almost wholly smothered by traditions, which have produced an opinion that, by making distinctions in meats and like services, we must merit grace and righteousness. In treating of repentance, there was no mention made of faith; only those works of satisfaction were set forth; in these the entire repentance seemed to consist.

Secondly, these traditions have obscured the commandments of God, because traditions were placed far above the commandments of God. Christianity was thought to consist wholly in the observance of certain holy-days, rites, fasts, and vestures. These observances had won for themselves the exalted title of being the spiritual life and the perfect life. Meanwhile the commandments of God, according to each one's calling, were without honor namely, that the father brought up his offspring, that the mother bore children, that the prince governed the commonwealth—these were accounted works that were worldly and imperfect, and far below those glittering observances. And this error greatly tormented devout consciences, which grieved that they were held in an imperfect state of life, as in marriage, in the office of magistrate; or in other civil ministrations; on the other hand, they admired the monks and such like, and falsely imagined that the observances of such men were more acceptable to God.

Thirdly, traditions brought great danger to consciences; for it was impossible to keep all traditions, and yet men judged these observances to be necessary acts of worship. Gerson writes that many fell into despair, and that some even took their own lives, because they felt that they were not able to satisfy the traditions, and they had all the while not heard any consolation of the righteousness of faith and grace. We see that the summists and theologians gather the traditions, and seek mitigations whereby to ease consciences, and yet they do not sufficiently unfetter, but sometimes entangle, consciences even more. And with the gathering of these traditions, the schools and sermons have been so much occupied that they have had no leisure to touch upon Scripture, and to seek the more profitable doctrine of faith, of the cross, of hope, of the dignity of civil affairs of consolation of sorely tried consciences. Hence Gerson and some other theologians have grievously complained that by these strivings concerning traditions they were prevented from giving attention to a better kind of doctrine. Augustine also forbids that men's consciences should be burdened with such observances, and prudently advises Januarius that he must know that they are to be observed as things indifferent; for such are his words.

Wherefore our teachers must not be looked upon as having taken up this matter rashly or from hatred of the bishops, as some falsely suspect. There was great need to warn the churches of these errors, which had arisen from misunderstanding the traditions. For the Gospel compels us to insist in the churches upon the doctrine of grace, and of the righteousness of faith; which, however, cannot be understood, if men think that they merit grace by observances of their own choice.

Thus, therefore, they have taught that by the observance of human traditions we cannot merit grace or be justified, and hence we must not think such observances necessary acts of worship. They add hereunto testimonies of Scripture. Christ, Matt. 15:3, defends the Apostles who had not observed the usual tradition, which, however, evidently pertains to a matter not unlawful, but indifferent, and to have a certain affinity with the purifications of the Law, and says, 9: In vain do they worship Me with the commandments of men. He, therefore, does not exact an unprofitable service. Shortly after He adds: Not that which goeth into the mouth defileth a man. So also Paul, Rom. 14:17: The kingdom of God is not meat and drink. Col. 2:16: Let no man, therefore, judge you in meat, or in drink, or in respect of an holy-day, or of the Sabbath-day; also: If ye be dead with Christ from the rudiments of the world, why, as though living in the world, are ye subject to ordinances: Touch not, taste not, handle not! And Peter says, Acts 15:10: Why tempt ye God to put a yoke upon the neck of the disciples, which neither our fathers nor we were able to bear? But we believe that through the grace of the Lord Jesus Christ we shall be saved, even as they. Here Peter forbids to burden the consciences with many rites, either of Moses or of others. And in 1 Tim. 4:1-3 Paul calls the prohibition of meats a doctrine of devils; for it is against the Gospel to institute or to do such works that by them we may merit grace, or as though Christianity could not exist without such service of God.

Here our adversaries object that our teachers are opposed to discipline and mortification of the flesh, as Jovinian. But the contrary may be learned from the writings of our teachers. For they have always taught concerning the cross that it behooves Christians to bear afflictions. This is the true, earnest, and unfeigned mortification, to wit, to be exercised with divers afflictions, and to be crucified with Christ.

Moreover, they teach that every Christian ought to train and subdue himself with bodily restraints, or bodily exercises and labors that neither satiety nor slothfulness tempt him to sin, but not that we may merit grace or make satisfaction for sins by such exercises. And such external discipline ought to be urged at all times, not only on a few and set days. So Christ commands, Luke 21:34: Take heed lest your hearts be overcharged with surfeiting; also Matt. 17:21: This kind goeth not out but by prayer and fasting. Paul also says, 1 Cor. 9:27: I keep under my body and bring it into subjection. Here he clearly shows that he was keeping under his body, not to merit forgiveness of sins by that discipline, but to have his body in subjection and fitted for spiritual things, and for the discharge of duty according to his calling. Therefore, we do not condemn fasting in itself, but the traditions which prescribe certain days and certain meats, with peril of conscience, as though such works were a necessary service.

Nevertheless, very many traditions are kept on our part, which conduce to good order in the Church, as the Order of Lessons in the Mass and the chief holy-days. But, at the same time, men are warned that such observances do not justify before God, and that in such things it should not be made sin if they be omitted without offense. Such liberty in human rites was not unknown to the Fathers. For in the East they kept Easter at another time than at Rome, and when, on account of this diversity, the Romans accused the Eastern Church of schism, they were admonished by others that such usages need not be alike everywhere. And Irenaeus says: Diversity concerning fasting does not destroy the harmony of faith; as also Pope Gregory intimates in Dist. XII, that such diversity does not violate the unity of the Church. And in the *Tripartite History*, Book 9, many examples of dissimilar rites are gathered, and the following statement is made: It was not the mind of the Apostles to enact rules concerning holy-days, but to preach godliness and a holy life [, to teach faith and love].

ARTICLE XXVII: OF MONASTIC VOWS

What is taught on our part concerning Monastic Vows, will be better understood if it be remembered what has been the state of the monasteries, and how many things were daily done in those very monasteries, contrary to the Canons. In Augustine's time they were free associations. Afterward, when discipline was corrupted, vows were everywhere added for the purpose of restoring discipline, as in a carefully planned prison.

Gradually, many other observances were added besides vows. And these fetters were laid upon many before the lawful age, contrary to the Canons.

Many also entered into this kind of life through ignorance, being unable to judge their own strength, though they were of sufficient age. Being thus ensnared, they were compelled to remain, even though some could have been freed by the kind provision of the Canons. And this was more the case in convents of women than of monks, although more consideration should have been shown the weaker sex. This rigor displeased many good men before this time, who saw that young men and maidens were thrown into convents for a living. They saw what unfortunate results came of this procedure, and what scandals were created, what snares were cast upon consciences! They were grieved that the authority of the Canons in so momentous a matter was utterly set aside and despised. To these evils was added such a persuasion concerning vows as, it is well known, in former times displeased even those monks who were more considerate. They taught that vows were equal to Baptism; they taught that by this kind of life they merited forgiveness of sins and justification before God. Yea, they added that the monastic life not only merited righteousness before God but even greater things, because it kept not only the precepts, but also the so-called "evangelical counsels."

Thus they made men believe that the profession of monasticism was far better than Baptism, and that the monastic life was more meritorious than that of magistrates, than the life of pastors, and such like, who serve their calling in accordance with God's commands, without any man-made services. None of these things can be denied; for they appear in their own books. [Moreover, a person who has been thus ensnared and has entered a monastery learns little of Christ.]

What, then, came to pass in the monasteries? Aforetime they were schools of theology and other branches, profitable to the Church; and thence pastors and bishops were obtained. Now it is another thing. It is needless to rehearse what is known to all. Aforetime they came together to learn; now they feign that it is a kind of life instituted to merit grace and righteousness; yea, they preach that it is a state of perfection, and they put it far above all other kinds of life ordained of God. These things we have rehearsed without odious exaggeration, to the end that the doctrine of our teachers on this point might be better understood.

First, concerning such as contract matrimony, they teach on our part that it is lawful for all men who are not fitted for single life to contract matrimony, because vows cannot annul the ordinance and commandment of God. But the commandment of God is 1 Cor. 7:2: To avoid fornication, let every man have his own wife. Nor is it the commandment only, but also the creation and ordinance of God, which forces those to marry who are not excepted by a singular work of God, according to the text Gen. 2:18: It is not good that the man should be alone. Therefore they do not sin who obey this commandment and ordinance of God.

What objection can be raised to this? Let men extol the obligation of a vow as much as they list, yet shall they not bring to pass that the vow annuls the commandment of God. The Canons teach that the right of the superior is excepted in every vow; [that vows are not binding against the decision of the Pope;] much less, therefore, are these vows of force which are against the commandments of God.

Now, if the obligation of vows could not be changed for any cause whatever, the Roman Pontiffs could never have given dispensation for it is not lawful for man to annul an obligation which is simply divine. But the Roman Pontiffs have prudently judged that leniency is to be observed in this obligation, and therefore we read that many times they have dispensed from vows. The case of the King of Aragon who was called back from the monastery is well known, and there are also examples in our own times. [Now, if dispensations have been granted for the sake of securing temporal interests, it is much more proper that they be granted on account of the distress of souls.]

In the second place, why do our adversaries exaggerate the obligation or effect of a vow when, at the same time, they have not a word to say of the nature of the vow itself, that it ought to be in a thing possible, that it ought to be free, and chosen spontaneously and deliberately? But it is not unknown to what extent perpetual chastity is in the power of man. And how few are there who have taken the vow spontaneously and deliberately! Young maidens and men, before they are able to judge, are persuaded, and sometimes even compelled, to take the vow. Wherefore it is not fair to insist so rigorously on the obligation, since it is granted by all that it is against the nature of a vow to take it without spontaneous and deliberate action.

Most canonical laws rescind vows made before the age of fifteen; for before that age there does not seem sufficient judgment in a person to decide concerning a perpetual life. Another Canon, granting more to the weakness of man, adds a few years; for it forbids a vow to be made before the age of eighteen. But which of these two Canons shall we follow? The most part have an excuse for leaving the monasteries, because most of them have taken the vows before they reached these ages.

Finally, even though the violation of a vow might be censured, yet it seems not forthwith to follow that the marriages of such persons must be dissolved. For Augustine denies that they ought to be dissolved (XXVII. Quaest. I, Cap. Nuptiarum), and his authority is not lightly to be esteemed, although other men afterwards thought otherwise.

But although it appears that God's command concerning marriage delivers very many from their vows, yet our teachers introduce also another argument concerning vows to show that they are void. For every service of God, ordained and chosen of men without the commandment of God to merit justification and grace, is wicked, as Christ says Matt. 16:9: In vain do they worship Me with the commandments of men. And Paul teaches everywhere that righteousness is not to be sought from our own observances and acts of worship, devised by men, but that it comes by faith to those who believe that they are received by God into grace for Christ's sake.

But it is evident that monks have taught that services of man's making satisfy for sins and merit grace and justification. What else is this than to detract from the glory of Christ and to obscure and deny the righteousness of faith? It follows, therefore, that the vows thus commonly taken have been wicked services, and, consequently, are void. For a wicked vow, taken against the commandment of God, is not valid; for (as the Canon says) no vow ought to bind men to wickedness.

Paul says, Gal. 5:4: Christ is become of no effect unto you, whosoever of you are justified by the Law, ye are fallen from grace. To those, therefore, who want to be justified by their vows Christ is made of no effect, and they fall from grace. For also these who ascribe justification to vows ascribe to their own works that which properly belongs to the glory of Christ.

Nor can it be denied, indeed, that the monks have taught that, by their vows and observances, they were justified, and merited forgiveness of sins, yea, they invented still greater absurdities, saying that they could give others a share in their works. If any one should be inclined to enlarge on these things with evil intent, how many things could he bring together whereof even the monks are now ashamed! Over and above this, they persuaded men that services of man's making were a state of Christian perfection. And is not this assigning justification to works? It is no light offense in the Church to set forth to the people a service devised by men, without the commandment of God, and to teach that such service justifies men. For the righteousness of faith, which chiefly ought to be taught in the Church, is obscured when these wonderful angelic forms of worship, with their show of poverty, humility, and celibacy, are cast before the eyes of men.

Furthermore, the precepts of God and the true service of God are obscured when men hear that only monks are in a state of perfection. For Christian perfection is to fear God from the heart, and yet to conceive great faith, and to trust that for Christ's sake we have a God who has been reconciled, to ask of God, and assuredly to expect His aid in all things that, according to our calling, are to be done; and meanwhile, to be diligent in outward good works, and to serve our calling. In these things consist the true perfection and the true service of God. It does not consist in celibacy, or in begging, or in vile apparel. But the people conceive many pernicious opinions from the false commendations of monastic life. They hear celibacy praised above measure; therefore they lead their married life with offense to their consciences. They hear that only beggars are perfect; therefore they keep their possessions and do business with offense to their consciences. They hear that it is an evangelical counsel not to seek revenge; therefore some in private life are not afraid to take revenge, for they hear that it is but a counsel, and not a commandment. Others judge that the Christian cannot properly hold a civil office or be a magistrate.

There are on record examples of men who, forsaking marriage and the administration of the Commonwealth, have hid themselves in monasteries. This they called fleeing from the world, and seeking a kind of life which would be more pleasing to God. Neither did they see that God ought to be served in those commandments which He Himself has given and not in commandments devised by men. A good and perfect kind of life is that which has for it the commandment of God. It is necessary to admonish men of these things.

And before these times, Gerson rebukes this error of the monks concerning perfection, and testifies that in his day it was a new saying that the monastic life is a state of perfection.

So many wicked opinions are inherent in the vows, namely, that they justify, that they constitute Christian perfection, that they keep the counsels and commandments, that they have works of supererogation. All these things, since they are false and empty, make vows null and void.

ARTICLE XXVIII: OF ECCLESIASTICAL POWER

There has been great controversy concerning the Power of Bishops, in which some have awkwardly confounded the power of the Church and the power of the sword. And from this confusion very great wars and tumults have resulted, while the Pontiffs, emboldened by the power of the Keys, not only have instituted new services and burdened consciences with reservation of cases and ruthless excommunications, but have also undertaken to transfer the kingdoms of this world, and to take the Empire from the Emperor. These wrongs have long since been rebuked in the Church by learned and godly men. Therefore our teachers, for the comforting of men's consciences, were constrained to show the difference between the power of the Church and the power of the sword, and taught that both of them, because of God's commandment, are to be held in reverence and honor, as the chief blessings of God on earth.

But this is their opinion, that the power of the Keys, or the power of the bishops, according to the Gospel, is a power or commandment of God, to preach the Gospel, to remit and retain sins, and to administer Sacraments. For with this commandment Christ sends forth His Apostles, John 20:21 sqq.: As My Father hath sent Me, even so send I you. Receive ye the Holy Ghost. Whosesoever sins ye remit, they are remitted unto them; and whosesoever sins ye retain, they are retained. Mark 16:15: Go preach the Gospel to every creature.

This power is exercised only by teaching or preaching the Gospel and administering the Sacraments, according to their calling either to many or to individuals. For thereby are granted, not bodily, but eternal things, as eternal righteousness, the Holy Ghost, eternal life. These things cannot come but by the ministry of the Word and the Sacraments, as Paul says, Rom. 1:16: The Gospel is the power of God unto salvation to every one that believeth. Therefore, since the power of the Church grants eternal things, and is exercised only by the ministry of the Word, it does not interfere with civil government; no more than the art of singing interferes with civil government. For civil government deals with other things than does the Gospel. The civil rulers defend not minds, but bodies and bodily things against manifest injuries, and restrain men with the sword and bodily punishments in order to preserve civil justice and peace.

Therefore the power of the Church and the civil power must not be confounded. The power of the Church has its own commission to teach the Gospel and to administer the Sacraments. Let it not break into the office of another; Let it not transfer the kingdoms of this world; let it not abrogate the laws of civil rulers; let it not abolish lawful obedience; let it not interfere with judgments concerning civil ordinances or contracts; let it not prescribe laws to civil rulers concerning the form of the Commonwealth. As Christ says, John 18:33: My kingdom is not of this world; also Luke 12:14: Who made Me a judge or a divider over you? Paul also says, Phil. 3:20: Our citizenship is in heaven; 2 Cor. 10:4: The weapons of our warfare are not carnal, but mighty through God to the casting down of imaginations.

After this manner our teachers discriminate between the duties of both these powers, and command that both be honored and acknowledged as gifts and blessings of God.

If bishops have any power of the sword, that power they have, not as bishops, by the commission of the Gospel, but by human law having received it of kings and emperors for the civil administration of what is theirs. This, however, is another office than the ministry of the Gospel.

When, therefore, the question is concerning the jurisdiction of bishops, civil authority must be distinguished from ecclesiastical jurisdiction. Again, according to the Gospel or, as they say, by divine right, there belongs to the bishops as bishops, that is, to those to whom has been committed the ministry of the Word and the Sacraments, no jurisdiction except to forgive sins, to judge doctrine, to reject doctrines contrary to the Gospel, and to exclude from the communion of the Church wicked men, whose wickedness is known, and this without human force, simply by the Word. Herein the congregations of necessity and by divine right must obey them, according to Luke 10:16: He that heareth you heareth Me. But when they teach or ordain anything against the Gospel, then the congregations have a commandment of God prohibiting obedience, Matt. 7:15: Beware of false prophets; Gal. 1:8: Though an angel from heaven preach any other gospel, let him be accursed; 2 Cor. 13:8: We can do nothing against the truth, but for the truth. Also: The power which the Lord hath given me to edification, and not to destruction. So, also, the Canonical Laws command (II. Q. VII. Cap., Sacerdotes, and Cap. Oves). And Augustine (*Contra Petiliani Epistolam*): Neither must we submit to Catholic bishops if they chance to err, or hold anything contrary to the Canonical Scriptures of God.

If they have any other power or jurisdiction, in hearing and judging certain cases, as of matrimony or of tithes, etc., they have it by human right, in which matters princes are bound, even against their will, when the ordinaries fail, to dispense justice to their subjects for the maintenance of peace.

Moreover, it is disputed whether bishops or pastors have the right to introduce ceremonies in the Church, and to make laws concerning meats, holy-days, and grades, that is, orders of ministers, etc. They that give this right to the bishops refer to this testimony John 16:12-13: I have yet many things to say unto you, but ye cannot bear them now. Howbeit when He, the Spirit of Truth, is come, He will guide you into all truth. They also refer to the example of the Apostles, who commanded to abstain from blood and from things strangled, Acts 15:29. They refer to the Sabbath-day as having been changed into the Lord's Day, contrary to the Decalog, as it seems. Neither is there any example whereof they make more than concerning the changing of the Sabbath-day. Great, say they, is the power of the Church, since it has dispensed with one of the Ten Commandments!

But concerning this question it is taught on our part (as has been shown above) that bishops have no power to decree anything against the Gospel. The Canonical Laws teach the same thing (Dist. IX) . Now, it is against Scripture to establish or require the observance of any traditions, to the end that by such observance we may make satisfaction for sins, or merit grace and righteousness. For the glory of Christ's merit suffers injury when, by such observances, we undertake to merit justification. But it is manifest that, by such belief, traditions have almost infinitely multiplied in the Church, the doctrine concerning faith and the righteousness of faith being meanwhile suppressed. For gradually more holy-days were made, fasts appointed, new ceremonies and services in honor of saints instituted, because the authors of such things thought that by these works they were meriting grace. Thus in times past the Penitential Canons increased, whereof we still see some traces in the satisfactions.

Again, the authors of traditions do contrary to the command of God when they find matters of sin in foods, in days, and like things, and burden the Church with bondage of the law, as if there ought to be among Christians, in order to merit justification a service like the Levitical, the arrangement of which God had committed to the Apostles and bishops. For thus some of them write; and the Pontiffs in some measure seem to be misled by the example of the law of Moses. Hence are such burdens, as that they make it mortal sin, even without offense to others, to do manual labor on holy-days, a mortal sin to omit the Canonical Hours, that certain foods defile the conscience, that fastings are works which appease God that sin in a reserved case cannot be forgiven but by the authority of him who reserved it; whereas the Canons themselves speak only of the reserving of the ecclesiastical penalty, and not of the reserving of the guilt.

Whence have the bishops the right to lay these traditions upon the Church for the ensnaring of consciences, when Peter, Acts 15:10, forbids to put a yoke upon the neck of the disciples, and Paul says, 2 Cor. 13:10, that the power given him was to edification not to destruction? Why, therefore, do they increase sins by these traditions?

But there are clear testimonies which prohibit the making of such traditions, as though they merited grace or were necessary to salvation. Paul says, Col. 2:16-23: Let no man judge you in meat, or in drink, or in respect of an holy-day, or of the new moon, or of the Sabbath-days. If ye be dead with Christ from the rudiments of the world, why, as though living in the world, are ye subject to ordinances (touch not; taste not; handle not, which all are to perish with the using) after the commandments and doctrines of men! which things have indeed a show of wisdom. Also in Titus 1:14 he openly forbids traditions: Not giving heed to Jewish fables and commandments of men that turn from the truth.

And Christ, Matt. 15:14-13, says of those who require traditions: Let them alone; they be blind leaders of the blind; and He rejects such services: Every plant which My heavenly Father hath not planted shall be plucked up.

If bishops have the right to burden churches with infinite traditions, and to ensnare consciences, why does Scripture so often prohibit to make, and to listen to, traditions? Why does it call them "doctrines of devils"? 1 Tim. 4:1. Did the Holy Ghost in vain forewarn of these things?

Since, therefore, ordinances instituted as things necessary, or with an opinion of meriting grace, are contrary to the Gospel, it follows that it is not lawful for any bishop to institute or exact such services. For it is necessary that the doctrine of Christian liberty be preserved in the churches, namely, that the bondage of the Law is not necessary to justification, as it is written in the Epistle to the Galatians, 5:1: Be not entangled again with the yoke of bondage. It is necessary that the chief Article of the Gospel be preserved, to wit, that we obtain grace freely by faith in Christ, and not for certain observances or acts of worship devised by men.

What, then, are we to think of the Sunday and like rites in the house of God? To this we answer that it is lawful for bishops or pastors to make ordinances that things be done orderly in the Church, not that thereby we should merit grace or make satisfaction for sins, or that consciences be bound to judge them necessary services, and to think that it is a sin to break them without offense to others. So Paul ordains, 1 Cor. 11:5, that women should cover their heads in the congregation, 1 Cor. 14:30, that interpreters be heard in order in the church, etc.

It is proper that the churches should keep such ordinances for the sake of love and tranquillity, so far that one do not offend another, that all things be done in the churches in order, and without confusion, 1 Cor. 14:40; comp. Phil. 2:14; but so that consciences be not burdened to think that they are necessary to salvation, or to judge that they sin when they break them without offense to others; as no one will say that a woman sins who goes out in public with her head uncovered provided only that no offense be given.

Of this kind is the observance of the Lord's Day, Easter, Pentecost, and like holy-days and rites. For those who judge that by the authority of the Church the observance of the Lord's Day instead of the Sabbath-day was ordained as a thing necessary, do greatly err. Scripture has abrogated the Sabbath-day; for it teaches that, since the Gospel has been revealed, all the ceremonies of Moses can be omitted. And yet, because it was necessary to appoint a certain day, that the people might know when they ought to come together, it appears that the Church designated the Lord's Day for this purpose; and this day seems to have been chosen all the more for this additional reason, that men might have an example of Christian liberty, and might know that the keeping neither of the Sabbath nor of any other day is necessary.

There are monstrous disputations concerning the changing of the law, the ceremonies of the new law, the changing of the Sabbath-day, which all have sprung from the false belief that there must needs be in the Church a service like to the Levitical, and that Christ had given commission to the Apostles and bishops to devise new ceremonies as necessary to salvation. These errors crept into the Church when the righteousness of faith was not taught clearly enough. Some dispute that the keeping of the Lord's Day is not indeed of divine right, but in a manner so. They prescribe concerning holy-days, how far it is lawful to work. What else are such disputations than snares of consciences? For although they endeavor to modify the traditions, yet the mitigation can never be perceived as long as the opinion remains that they are necessary, which must needs remain where the righteousness of faith and Christian liberty are not known.

The Apostles commanded (Acts 15:20) to abstain from blood. Who does now observe it? And yet they that do it not sin not; for not even the Apostles themselves wanted to burden consciences with such bondage; but they forbade it for a time, to avoid offense. For in this decree we must perpetually consider what the aim of the Gospel is.

Scarcely any Canons are kept with exactness, and from day to day many go out of use even among those who are the most zealous advocates of traditions. Neither can due regard be paid to consciences unless this mitigation be observed, that we know that the Canons are kept without holding them to be necessary, and that no harm is done consciences, even though traditions go out of use.

But the bishops might easily retain the lawful obedience of the people if they would not insist upon the observance of such traditions as cannot be kept with a good conscience. Now they command celibacy; they admit none unless they swear that they will not teach the pure doctrine of the Gospel. The churches do not ask that the bishops should restore concord at the expense of their honor; which, nevertheless, it would be proper for good pastors to do. They ask only that they would release unjust burdens which are new and have been received contrary to the custom of the Church Catholic. It may be that in the beginning there were plausible reasons for some of these ordinances; and yet they are not adapted to later times. It is also evident that some were adopted through erroneous conceptions. Therefore it would be befitting the clemency of the Pontiffs to mitigate them now, because such a modification does not shake the unity of the Church. For many human traditions have been changed in process of time, as the Canons themselves show. But if it be impossible to obtain a mitigation of such observances as cannot be kept without sin, we are bound to follow the apostolic rule, Acts 5:29, which commands us to obey God rather than men.

Peter, 1 Pet. 5:3, forbids bishops to be lords, and to rule over the churches. It is not our design now to wrest the government from the bishops, but this one thing is asked, namely, that they allow the Gospel to be purely taught, and that they relax some few observances which cannot be kept without sin. But if they make no concession, it is for them to see how they shall give account to God for furnishing, by their obstinacy, a cause for schism.

CONCLUSION

These are the chief Articles which seem to be in controversy. For although we might have spoken of more abuses, yet, to avoid undue length, we have set forth the chief points, from which the rest may be readily judged. There have been great complaints concerning indulgences, pilgrimages, and the abuse of excommunications. The parishes have been vexed in many ways by the dealers in indulgences. There were endless contentions between the pastors and the monks concerning the parochial right, confessions, burials, sermons on extraordinary occasions, and innumerable other things. Issues of this sort we have passed over so that the chief points in this matter, having been briefly set forth, might be the more readily understood. Nor has anything been here said or adduced to the reproach of any one. Only those things have been recounted whereof we thought that it was necessary to speak, in order that it might be understood that in doctrine and ceremonies nothing has been received on our part against Scripture or the Church Catholic. For it is manifest that we have taken most diligent care that no new and ungodly doctrine should creep into our churches.

The above Articles we desire to present in accordance with the edict of Your Imperial Majesty, in order to exhibit our Confession and let men see a summary of the doctrine of our teachers. If there is anything that any one might desire in this Confession, we are ready, God willing, to present ampler information according to the Scriptures.

Your Imperial Majesty's faithful subjects:
John, Duke of Saxony, Elector.
George, Margrave of Brandenburg.
Ernest, Duke of Lueneberg.
Philip, Landgrave of Hesse.
John Frederick, Duke of Saxony.
Francis, Duke of Lueneburg.
Wolfgang, Prince of Anhalt.
Senate and Magistracy of Nuremburg.
Senate of Reutlingen. ▪

Gallican Confession

During the persecution and upheaval of the French Church in the mid-16th century, the Huguenots (French Reformed Christians) wished for a confession of faith that would unite them. They consulted Geneva on the matter, and John Calvin, possibly with the help of Theodore Beza and Pierre Viret, drafted thirty-five articles of faith and sent them to the French Christians.

With those thirty-five articles in hand, twenty French church leaders secretly met in Paris. Among them was Antoine de Chandieu, a student of Calvin. Their meeting was the first National Synod of the Reformed Church of France, representing seventy-two French congregations, and the synod officially adopted Calvin's articles as the Gallican Confession (also called the French Confession). They also wrote a preface for it, and presented their new confession to King Francis II in 1560, appealing for the persecution of Huguenots to stop. In 1561, when Charles IX succeeded Francis II as king of France, Theodore Beza brought the confession before him, too.

In 1571, when the confession was twelve years old, the seventh National Synod met in La Rochelle, expanded the confession to forty articles, and signed it again, giving it yet another name: the La Rochelle Confession. This was done in the presence of Theodore Beza and Jean d'Albret, who was both the Queen of Navarre and a Huguenot.

French Bibles printed after this often included a copy of the Gallican Confession. It served as the defining confession of the Reformed Church in France into the 19th century—and still does for the growing number of French Reformed congregations today.

Confession of Faith, made in one accord by the French people, who desire to live according to the purity of the Gospel of our Lord Jesus Christ.

1. We believe and confess that there is but one God, who is one sole and simple essence, spiritual, eternal, invisible, immutable, infinite, incomprehensible, ineffable, omnipotent; who is all-wise all-good, all-just, and all-merciful.

II. As such this God reveals himself to men; firstly, in his works, in their creation, as well as in their preservation and control. Secondly, and more clearly, in his Word, which was in the beginning revealed through oracles, and which was afterward committed to writing in the books which we call the Holy Scriptures.

III. These Holy Scriptures are comprised in the canonical books of the Old and New Testaments, as follows: the five books of Moses, namely: Genesis, Exodus, Leviticus, Numbers, Deuteronomy; then Joshua, Judges, Ruth, the first and second books of Samuel, the first and second books of the Kings, the first and second books of the Chronicles, otherwise called Paralipomenon, the first book of Ezra; then Nehemiah, the book of Esther, Job, the Psalms of David, the Proverbs or Maxims of Solomon; the book of Ecclesiastes, called the Preacher, the Song of Solomon; then the book of Isaiah, Jeremiah, Lamentations of Jeremiah, Ezekiel, Daniel, Hosea, Joel, Amos, Obadiah, Jonah, Micah, Nahum, Habakkuk, Zephaniah, Haggai, Zechariah, Malachi; then the Holy Gospel according to St. Matthew, according to St. Mark, according to St. Luke, according to St. John; then the second book of St. Luke, otherwise called the Acts of the Apostles; then the Epistles of St. Paul: one to the Romans, two to the Corinthians, one to the Galatians, one to the Ephesians, one to the Philippians, one to the Colossians, two to the Thessalonians, two to Timothy, one to Titus, one to Philemon; then the Epistle to the Hebrews, the Epistle of St. James, the first and second Epistles of St. Peter, the first, second, and third Epistles of St. John, the Epistle of St. Jude; and then the Apocalypse, or Revelation of St. John.

IV. We know these books to be canonical, and the sure rule of our faith, not so much by the common accord and consent of the Church, as by the testimony and inward illumination of the Holy Spirit, which enables us to distinguish them from other ecclesiastical books upon which, however useful, we can not found any articles of faith.

V. We believe that the Word contained in these books has proceeded from God, and receives its authority from him alone, and not from men. And inasmuch as it is the rule of all truth, containing all that is necessary for the service of God and for our salvation, it is not lawful for men, nor even for angels, to add to it, to take away from it, or to change it. Whence it follows that no authority, whether of antiquity, or custom, or numbers, or human wisdom, or judgments, or proclamations, or edicts, or decrees, or councils, or visions, or miracles, should be opposed to these Holy Scriptures, but, on the contrary, all things should be examined, regulated, and reformed according to them. And therefore we confess the three creeds, to wit: the Apostles', the Nicene, and the Athanasian, because they are in accordance with the Word of God.

VI. These Holy Scriptures teach us that in this one sole and simple divine essence, whom we have confessed, there are three Persons: the Father, Son, and the Holy Spirit. The Father, first cause, principle, and origin of all things. The Son, his Word and eternal wisdom. The Holy Spirit, his virtue, power, and efficacy. The Son begotten from eternity by the Father. The Holy Spirit proceeding eternally from them both; the three persons not confused, but distinct, and yet not separate, but of the same essence, equal in eternity and power. And in this we confess that which has been established by the ancient councils, and we detest all sects and heresies which were rejected by the holy doctors, such as St. Hilary, St. Athanasius, St. Ambrose, and St. Cyril.

VII. We believe that God, in three co-working persons, by his power, wisdom, and incomprehensible goodness, created all things, not only the heavens and the earth and all that in them is, but also invisible spirits, some of whom have fallen away and gone into perdition, while others have continued in obedience. That the first, being corrupted by evil, are enemies of all good, consequently of the whole Church. The second, having been preserved by the grace of God, are ministers to glorify God's name, and to promote the salvation of his elect.

VIII. We believe that he not only created all things, but that he governs and directs them, disposing and ordaining by his sovereign will all that happens in the world; not that he is the author of evil, or that the guilt of it can imputed to him, as his will is the sovereign and infallible rule of all right and justice; but he has wonderful means of so making use of devils and sinners that he can turn to good the evil which they do, and of which they are guilty. And thus, confessing that the providence of God orders all things, we humbly bow before the secrets which are hidden to us, without questioning what is above our understanding; but rather making use of what is revealed to us in Holy Scripture for our peace and safety, inasmuch as God, who has all things in subjection to him, watches over us with a Father's care, so that not a hair of our heads shall fall without his will. And yet he restrains the devils and all our enemies, so that they can not harm us without his leave.

IX. We believe that man was created pure and perfect in the image of God, and that by his own guilt he fell from the grace which he received, and is thus alienated from God, the fountain of justice and of all good, so that his nature is totally corrupt. And being blinded in mind, and depraved in heart, he has lost all integrity, and there is no good in him. And although he can still discern good and evil, we say, notwithstanding, that the light he has becomes darkness when he seeks for God, so that he can in nowise approach him by his intelligence and reason. And although he has a will that incites him to do this or that, yet it is altogether captive to sin, so that he has no other liberty to do right than that which God gives him.

X. We believe that all the posterity of Adam is in bondage to original sin, which is an hereditary evil, and not an imitation merely, as was declared by the Pelagians, whom we detest in their errors. And we consider that it is not necessary to inquire how sin was conveyed from one man to another, for what God had given Adam was not for him alone, but for all his posterity; and thus in his person we have been deprived of all good things, and have fallen with him into a state of sin and misery.

XI. We believe, also, that this evil is truly sin, sufficient for the condemnation of the whole human race, even of little children in the mother's womb, and that God considers it as such; even after baptism it is still of the nature of sin, but the condemnation of it is abolished for the children of God, out of his mere free grace and love. And further, that it is a perversity always producing fruits of malice and of rebellion, so that the most holy men, although they resist it, are still stained with many weaknesses and imperfections while they are in this life.

XII. We believe that from this corruption and general condemnation in which all men are plunged, God, according to his eternal and immutable counsel, calls those whom he has chosen by his goodness and mercy alone in our Lord Jesus Christ, without consideration of their works, to display in them the riches of his mercy; leaving the rest in this same corruption and condemnation to show in them his justice. For the ones are no better than the others, until God discerns them according to his immutable purpose which he has determined in Jesus Christ before the creation of the world. Neither can any man gain such a reward by his own virtue, as by nature we can not have a single good feeling, affection, or though, except God has first put it into our hearts.

XIII. We believe that all that is necessary for our salvation was offered and communicated to us in Jesus Christ. He is given to us for our salvation, and "is made unto us wisdom, and righteousness, and sanctification, and redemption": so that if we refuse him, we renounce the mercy of the Father, in which alone we can find a refuge.

XIV. We believe that Jesus Christ, being the wisdom of God and his eternal Son, has put on our flesh, so as to be God and man in one person; man, like unto us, capable of suffering in body and soul, yet free from all stain of sin. And as to his humanity, he was the true seed of Abraham and of David, although he was conceived by the secret power of the Holy Spirit. In this we detest all the heresies that have of old troubled the Church, and especially the diabolical conceits of Servetus, which attribute a fantastical divinity to the Lord Jesus, calling him the idea and pattern of all things, and the personal or figurative Son of God, and, finally, attribute to him a body of three uncreated elements, thus confusing and destroying the two natures.

XV. We believe that in one person, that is, Jesus Christ, the two natures are actually and inseparably joined and united, and yet each remains in its proper character; so that in this union the divine nature, retaining its attributes, remained uncreated, infinite, and all-pervading; and the human nature remained finite, having its form, measure, and attributes; and although Jesus Christ, in rising from the dead, bestowed immortality upon his body, yet he did not take from it the truth of its nature, and we so consider him in his divinity that we do not despoil him of his humanity.

XVI. We believe that God, in sending his Son, intended to show his love and inestimable goodness towards us, giving him up to die to accomplish all righteousness, and raising him from the dead to secure for us the heavenly life.

XVII. We believe that by the perfect sacrifice that the Lord Jesus offered on the cross, we are reconciled to God, and justified before; for we cannot be acceptable to him, nor become partakers of the grace of adoption, except as he pardons all our sins, and blots them out. Thus we declare that through Jesus Christ we are cleansed and made perfect; by his death we are fully justified, and through him only can we be delivered from our iniquities and transgressions.

XVIII. We believe that all our justification rests upon the remission of our sins, in which also is our only blessedness, as says the Psalmist (Psa. 32:2). We therefore reject all other means of justification before God, and without claiming any virtue or merit, we rest simply in the obedience of Jesus Christ, which is imputed to us as much to blot out all our sins as to make us find grace and favor in the sight of God. And, in fact, we believe that in falling away from this foundation, however slightly, we could not find rest elsewhere, but should always be troubled. Forasmuch as we are never at peace with God till we resolve to be loved in Jesus Christ, for of ourselves we are worthy of hatred.

XIX. We believe that by this means we have the liberty and privilege of calling upon God, in full confidence that he will show himself a Father to us. For we should have no access to the Father except through this Mediator. And to be heard in his name, we must hold our life from him as from our chief.

XX. We believe that we are made partakers of this justification by faith alone, as it is written: "He suffered for our salvation, that whosoever believes on him should not perish." And this is done inasmuch as we appropriate to our use the promises of life which are given to us through him, and feel their effect when we accept them, being assured that we are established by the Word of God and shall not be deceived. Thus our justification through faith depends upon the free promises by which God declares and testifies his love to us.

XXI. We believe that we are enlightened in faith by the secret power of the Holy Spirit, that it is a gratuitous and special gift which God grants to whom he will, so that the elect have no cause to glory, but are bound to be doubly thankful that they have been preferred to others. We believe also that faith is not given to the elect only to introduce them into the right way, but also to make them continue in it to the end. For as it is God who has begun the work, he will also perfect it.

XXII. We believe that by this faith we are regenerated in newness of life, being by nature subject to sin. Now we receive by faith grace to live holily and in the fear of God, in accepting the promise which is given to us by the Gospel, namely: that God will give us his Holy Spirit. This faith not only does not hinder us from holy living, or turn us from the love of righteousness, but of necessity begets in us all good works. Moreover, although God works in us for our salvation, and renews our hearts, determining us to that which is good, yet we confess that the good works which we do proceed from his Spirit, and can not be accounted to us for justification, neither do they entitle us to the adoption of sons, for we should always be doubting and restless in our hearts, if we did not rest upon the atonement by which Jesus Christ has acquitted us.

XXIII. We believe that the ordinances of the law came to an end at the advent of Jesus Christ; but although the ceremonies are no more in use, yet their substance and truth remain in the person of him in whom they are fulfilled. And, moreover, we must seek aid from the law and the prophets for the ruling of our lives, as well as for our confirmation in the promises of the gospel.

XXIV. We believe, as Jesus Christ is our only advocate, and as he commands us to ask of the Father in his name, and as it is not lawful for us to pray except in accordance with the model God has taught us by his Word, that all imaginations of men concerning the intercession of dead saints are an abuse and a device of Satan to lead men from the right way of worship. We reject, also, all other means by which men hope to redeem themselves before God, as derogating from the sacrifice and passion of Jesus Christ.

Finally, we consider purgatory as an illusion proceeding from the same shop, from which have also sprung monastic vows, pilgrimages, the prohibition of marriage, and of eating meat, the ceremonial observance of days, auricular confession, indulgences, and all such things by which they hope to merit forgiveness and salvation. These things we reject, not only for the false idea of merit which is attached to them, but also because they are human inventions imposing a yoke upon the conscience.

XXV. Now as we enjoy Christ only through the gospel, we believe that the order of the Church, established by his authority, ought to be sacred and inviolable, and that, therefore, the Church can not exist without pastors for instruction, whom we should respect and reverently listen to, when they are properly called and exercise their office faithfully. Not that God is bound to such aid and subordinate means, but because it pleases him to govern us by such restraints. In this we detest all visionaries who would like, so far as lies in their power, to destroy the ministry and preaching of the Word and sacraments.

XXVI. We believe that no one ought to seclude himself and be contented to be alone; but that all jointly should keep and maintain the union of the Church, and submit to the public teaching, and to the yoke of Jesus Christ, wherever God shall have established a true order of the Church, even if the magistrates and their edicts are contrary to it. For if they do not take part in it, or if they separate themselves from it, they do contrary to the Word of God.

XXVII. Nevertheless we believe that it is important to discern with care and prudence which is the true Church, for this title has been much abused. We say, then, according to the Word of God, that it is the company of the faithful who agree to follow his Word, and the pure religion which it teaches; who advance in it all their lives, growing and becoming more confirmed in the fear of God according as they feel the want of growing and pressing onward. Even although they strive continually, they can have no hope save in the remission of their sins. Nevertheless we do not deny that among the faithful there may be hypocrites and reprobates, but their wickedness can not destroy the title of the Church.

XXVIII. In this belief we declare that, properly speaking, there can be no Church where the Word of God is not received, nor profession made of subjection to it, nor use of the sacraments. Therefore we condemn the papal assemblies, as the pure Word of God is banished from them, their sacraments are corrupted, or falsified, or destroyed, and all superstitions and idolatries are in them. We hold, then, that all who take part in those acts, and commune in that Church, separate and cut themselves off from the body of Christ. Nevertheless, as some trace of the Church is left in the papacy, and the virtue and substance of baptism remain, and as the efficacy of baptism does not depend upon the person who administers it, we confess that those baptized in it do not need a second baptism. But, on account of its corruptions, we can not present children to be baptized in it without incurring pollution.

XXIX. As to the true Church, we believe that it should be governed according to the order established by our Lord Jesus Christ. That there should be pastors, overseers, and deacons, so that true doctrine may have its course, that errors may be corrected and suppressed, and the poor who are in affliction may be helped in their necessities; and that assemblies may be held in the name of God, so that great and small may edified.

XXX. We believe that all true pastors, wherever they may be, have the same authority and equal power under one head, one only sovereign and universal bishop, Jesus Christ; and that consequently no Church shall claim any authority or dominion over any other.

XXXI. We believe that no person should undertake to govern the Church upon his own authority, but that this should be derived from election, as far as it is possible, and as God will permit. And we make this exception especially, because sometimes, and even in our own days, when the state of the Church has been interrupted, it has been necessary for God to raise men in an extraordinary manner to restore the Church which was in ruin and desolation. But, notwithstanding, we believe that this rule must always be binding: that all pastors, overseers, and deacons should have evidence of being called to their office.

XXXII. We believe, also, that it is desirable and useful that those elected to be superintendents devise among themselves what means should be adopted for the government of the whole body, and yet that they should never depart from that which was ordained by our Lord Jesus Christ. Which does not prevent there being some special ordinances in each place, as convenience may require.

XXXIII. However, we reject all human inventions, and all laws which men may introduce under the pretense of serving God, by which they wish to bind consciences; and we receive only that which conduces to concord and holds all in obedience, from the greatest to the least. In this we must follow that which the Lord Jesus Christ declared as to excommunication, which we approve and confess to be necessary with all its antecedents and consequences.

XXXIV. We believe that the sacraments are added to the Word for more ample confirmation, that they may be to us pledges and seals of the grace of God, and by this means aid and comfort our faith, because of the infirmity which is in us, and that they are outward signs through which God operates by his Spirit, so that he may not signify any thing to us in vain. Yet we hold that their substance and truth is in Jesus Christ, and that of themselves they are only smoke and shadow.

XXXV. We confess only two sacraments common to the whole Church, of which the first, baptism, is given as a pledge of our adoption; for by it we are grafted into the body of Christ, so as to be washed and cleansed by his blood, and then renewed in purity of life by his Holy Spirit. We hold, also, that although we are baptized only once, yet the gain that it symbolizes to us reaches over our whole lives and to our death, so that we have a lasting witness that Jesus Christ will always be our justification and sanctification. Nevertheless, although it is a sacrament of faith and penitence, yet as God receives little children into the Church with their fathers, we say, upon the authority of Jesus Christ, that the children of believing parents should be baptized.

XXXVI. We confess that the Lord's Supper, which is the second sacrament, is a witness of the union which we have with Christ, inasmuch as he not only died and rose again for us once, but also feeds and nourishes us truly with his flesh and blood, so that we may be one in him, and that our life may be in common. Although he be in heaven until he come to judge all the earth, still we believe that by the secret and incomprehensible power of his Spirit he feeds and strengthens us with the substance of his body and of his blood. We hold that this is done spiritually, not because we put imagination and fancy in the place of fact and truth, but because the greatness of this mystery exceeds the measure of our senses and the laws of nature. In short, because it is heavenly, it can only be apprehended by faith.

XXXVII. We believe, as has been said, that in the Lord's Supper, as well in baptism, God gives us really and in fact that which he there sets forth to us; and that consequently with these signs is given the true possession and enjoyment of that which they present to us. And thus all who bring a pure faith, like a vessel, to the sacred table of Christ, receive truly that of which it is a sign; for the body and the blood of Jesus Christ give food and drink to the soul, no less than bread and wine nourish the body.

XXXVIII. Thus we hold water, being a feeble element, still testifies to us in truth the inward cleansing of our souls in the blood of Jesus Christ by the efficacy of his Spirit, and that the bread and wine given to us in the sacrament serve to our spiritual nourishment, inasmuch as they show, as to our sight, that the body of Christ is our meat, and his blood our drink. And we reject the Enthusiasts and Sacramentarians who will not receive such signs and marks, although our Savior said: "This is my body, and this cup is my blood."

XXXIX. We believe that God wishes to have the world governed by laws and magistrates, so that some restraint may be put upon its disordered appetites. And as he has established kingdoms, republics, and all sorts of principalities, either hereditary or otherwise, and all that belongs to a just government, and wishes to be considered as their Author, so he has put the sword into the hands of magistrates to suppress crimes against the first as well as against the second table of the Commandments of God. We must therefore, on his account, not only submit to them as superiors, but honor and hold them in all reverence as his lieutenants and officers, whom he has commissioned to exercise a legitimate and holy authority.

XL. We hold, then, that we must obey their laws and statutes, pay customs, taxes, and other dues, and bear the yoke of subjection with a good and free will, even if they are unbelievers, provided that the sovereign empire of God remain intact. Therefore we detest all those who would like to reject authority, to establish community and confusion of property, and overthrow the order of justice. ▪

Scots Confession

It came halting and bloody, but by 1560 the Reformation had definitely taken hold in Scotland. In August 1560 the Scottish Parliament agreed to reform the state church (or Kirk), breaking from Roman Catholicism in favor of Presbyterianism—but to accomplish this reform, there needed to be a clear definition of what the new Kirk of Scotland actually believed.

The Scottish Parliament commissioned the Six Johns—John Knox, overseeing John Winram, John Spottiswood, John Willock, John Douglas, and John Row—to write a confession for the Kirk. The Six Johns wrote the Scots Confession in four days. Parliament approved and adopted the confession on August 17, 1560. It wouldn't be accepted by the monarchy for seven years, however, until Roman Catholic Mary was overthrown. The Scots Confession was the official confession of the Scottish Kirk until the Westminster Confession replaced it in 1647.

Because Parliament passed it as the Confession of Faith Ratification Act 1560, the Scots Confession is still Scottish law. Yet very few ministers of the Church of Scotland have read it, let alone believe it.

PREFACE

The Estates of Scotland, with the inhabitants of Scotland who profess the holy Evangel of Jesus Christ, to their fellow countrymen and to all other nations who confess the Lord Jesus with them, wish grace, mercy, and peace from God the Father of our Lord Jesus Christ, with the Spirit of righteous judgment, for salvation.

Long have we thirsted, dear brethren, to have made known to the world the doctrine which we profess and for which we have suffered abuse and danger; but such has been the rage of Satan against us, and against the eternal truth of Christ now recently reborn among us, that until this day we have had neither time nor opportunity to set forth our faith, as gladly we would have done. For how we have been afflicted until now the greater part of Europe, we suppose, knows well.

But since by the infinite goodness of our God (who never suffers His afflicted to be utterly confounded) we have received unexpected rest and liberty, we could not do other than set forth this brief and plain Confession of that doctrine which is set before us, and which we believe and confess; partly to satisfy our brethren whose hearts, we suspect, have been and are grieved by the slanders against us; and partly to silence impudent blasphemers who boldly condemn that which they have not heard and do not understand.

We do not suppose that such malice can be cured merely by our Confession, for we know that the sweet savour of the Gospel is, and shall be, death to the sons of perditions; but we are considering chiefly our own weaker brethren, to whom we would communicate our deepest thoughts, lest they be troubled or carried away by the different rumours which Satan spreads against us to defeat our godly enterprise, protesting that if any man will note in our Confession any chapter or sentence contrary to God's Holy Word, that it would please him of his gentleness and for Christian charity's sake to inform us of it in writing; and we, upon our honour, do promise him that by God's grace we shall give him satisfaction from the mouth of God, that is, from Holy Scripture, or else we shall alter whatever he can prove to be wrong. For we call on God to record that from our hearts we abhor all heretical sects and all teachers of false doctrine, and that with all humility we embrace the purity of Christ's Gospel, which is the one food of our souls and therefore so precious to us that we are determined to suffer the greatest worldly dangers, rather than let our souls be defrauded of it. For we are completely convinced that whoever denies Christ Jesus, or is ashamed of Him in the presence of men, shall be denied before the Father and before His holy angels. Therefore by the aid of the mighty Spirit of our Lord Jesus Christ we firmly intend to endure to the end in the confession of our faith, as in the following chapters.

1. GOD

We confess and acknowledge one God alone, to whom alone we must cleave, whom alone we must serve, whom only we must worship, and in whom alone we put our trust. Who is eternal, infinite, immeasurable, incomprehensible, omnipotent, invisible; one in substance and yet distinct in three persons, the Father, the Son, and the Holy Ghost. By whom we confess and believe all things in heaven and earth, visible and invisible to have been created, to be retained in their being, and to be ruled and guided by his inscrutable providence for such end as his eternal wisdom, goodness, and justice have appointed, and to the manifestation of his own glory.

2. THE CREATION OF MAN

We confess and acknowledge that our God has created man, i.e.., our first father, Adam, after his own image and likeness, to whom he gave wisdom, lordship, justice, free will, and self-consciousness, so that in the whole nature of man no imperfection could be found. From this dignity and perfection man and woman both fell; the woman being deceived by the serpent and man obeying the voice of the woman, both conspiring against the sovereign majesty of God, who in clear words had previously threatened death if they presumed to eat of the forbidden tree.

3. ORIGINAL SIN

By this transgression, generally known as original sin, the image of God was utterly defaced in man, and he and his children became by nature hostile to God, slaves to Satan, and servants to sin. And thus everlasting death has had, and shall have, power and dominion over all who have not been, are not, or shall not be born from above. This rebirth is wrought by the power of the Holy Ghost creating in the hearts of God's chosen ones an assured faith in the promise of God revealed to us in his Word; by this faith we grasp Christ Jesus with the graces and blessings promised in him.

4. THE REVELATION OF THE PROMISE

We constantly believe that God, after the fearful and horrible departure of man from his obedience, did seek Adam again, call upon him, rebuke and convict him of his sin, and in the end made unto him a most joyful promise, that "the seed of the woman should bruise the head of the serpent," that is, that he should destroy the works of the devil. This promise was repeated and made clearer from time to time; it was embraced with joy, and most constantly received by all the faithful from Adam to Noah, from Noah to Abraham, from Abraham to David, and so onwards to the incarnation of Christ Jesus; all (we mean the believing fathers under the law) did see the joyful day of Christ Jesus, and did rejoice.

5. THE CONTINUANCE, INCREASE, AND PRESERVATION OF THE KIRK

We most constantly believe that God preserved, instructed, multiplied, honored, adorned, and called from death to life his Kirk in all ages since Adam until the coming of Christ Jesus in the flesh. For he called Abraham from his father's country, instructed him, and multiplied his seed, he marvelously preserved him, and more marvelously delivered his seed from the bondage and tyranny of Pharaoh; to them he gave his laws, constitutions, and ceremonies; to them he gave the land of Canaan; after he had given them judges, and afterwards Saul, he gave David to be king, to whom he gave promise that of the fruit of his loins should one sit forever upon his royal throne. To this same people from time to time he sent prophets, to recall them to the right way of their God, from which sometimes they strayed by idolatry. And although, because of their stubborn contempt for righteousness he was compelled to give them into the hands of their enemies, as had previously been threatened by the mouth of Moses, so that the holy city was destroyed, the temple burned with fire, and the whole land desolate for seventy years, yet in mercy he restored them again to Jerusalem, where the city and the temple were rebuilt, and they endured against all temptations and assaults of Satan till the Messiah came according to the promise.

6. THE INCARNATION OF JESUS CHRIST

When the fullness of time came God sent his Son, his eternal wisdom, the substance of his own glory, into this world, who took the nature of humanity from the substance of a woman, a virgin, by means of the Holy Ghost. And so was born the "just seed of David," the "Angel of the great counsel of God," the very Messiah promised, whom we confess and acknowledge to be Emmanuel, true God and true man, two perfect natures united and joined in one person. So by our Confession, we condemn the damnable and pestilent heresies of Arius,[1] Marcion, Eutyches,[2] Nestorius, and such others as did either deny the eternity of his Godhead, or the truth of his humanity, or confounded them, or else divided them.

7. WHY THE MEDIATOR HAD TO BE TRUE GOD AND TRUE MAN

We acknowledge and confess that this wonderful union between the Godhead and the humanity in Christ Jesus did arise from the eternal and immutable decree of God from which all our salvation springs and depends.

8. ELECTION

That same eternal God and Father, who by grace alone chose us in his Son Christ Jesus before the foundation of the world was laid, appointed him to be our head, our brother, our pastor, and the great bishop of our souls. But since the opposition between the justice of God and our sins was such that no flesh by itself could or might have attained unto God, it behooved the Son of God to descend unto us and take himself a body of our body, flesh of our flesh, and bone of our bone, and so become the Mediator between God and man, giving power to as many as believe in him to be the sons of God; as he himself says, "I ascend to my Father and to your Father, to my God and to your God." By this most holy brotherhood whatever we have lost in Adam is restored to us again. Therefore we are not afraid to call God our Father, not so much because he has created us, which we have in common with the reprobate, as because he has given unto us his only Son to be our brother, and given us grace to acknowledge and embrace him as our only Mediator. Further, it behooved the Messiah and Redeemer to be true God and true man, because he was able to undergo the punishment of our transgressions and to present himself in the presence of his Father's judgment, as in our stead, to suffer for our transgression and disobedience, and by death to overcome him that was the author of death. But because the Godhead alone could not suffer death,

---

1 See page 13.
2 See page 15.

and neither could manhood overcome death, he joined both together in one person, that the weakness of one should suffer and be subject to death—which we had deserved—and the infinite and invincible power of the other, that is, of the Godhead, should triumph, and purchase for us life, liberty, and perpetual victory. So we confess, and most undoubtedly believe.

9. CHRIST'S DEATH, PASSION, AND BURIAL

That our Lord Jesus offered himself a voluntary sacrifice unto his Father for us, that he suffered contradiction of sinners, that he was wounded and plagued for our transgressions, that he, the clean innocent Lamb of God, was condemned in the presence of an earthly judge, that we should be absolved before the judgment seat of our God; that he suffered not only the cruel death of the cross, which was accursed by the sentence of God; but also that he suffered for a season the wrath of his Father which sinners had deserved. But yet we avow that he remained the only, well beloved, and blessed Son of his Father even in the midst of his anguish and torment which he suffered in body and soul to make full atonement for the sins of his people. From this we confess and avow that there remains no other sacrifice for sin; if any affirm so, we do not hesitate to say that they are blasphemers against Christ's death and the everlasting atonement thereby purchased for us.

10. THE RESURRECTION

We undoubtedly believe, since it was impossible that the sorrows of death should retain in bondage the Author of life, that our Lord Jesus crucified, dead, and buried, who descended into hell, did rise again for our justification, and the destruction of him who was the author of death and its bondage. We know that his resurrection was confirmed by the testimony of his enemies, and by the resurrection of the dead, whose sepulchers did open, and they did rise and appear to many within the city of Jerusalem. It was also confirmed by the testimony of his angels, and by the senses and judgment of his apostles and of others, who had conversation, and did eat and drink with him after his resurrection.

11. THE ASCENSION

We do not doubt but that the selfsame body which was born of the virgin, was crucified, dead, and buried, and which did rise again, did ascend into the heavens, for the accomplishment of all things, where in our name and for our comfort he has received all power in heaven and earth, where he sits at the right hand of the Father, having received his kingdom, the only advocate and mediator for us. Which glory, honor, and prerogative, he alone amongst the brethren shall possess till all his enemies are made his footstool, as we undoubtedly believe they shall be in the Last Judgment. We believe that the same Lord Jesus shall visibly return for this Last Judgment as he was seen to ascend. And then, we firmly believe, the time of refreshing and restitution of all things shall come, so that those who from the beginning have suffered violence, injury, and wrong, for righteousness' sake, shall inherit that blessed immortality promised them from the beginning. But, one the other hand, the stubborn, disobedient, cruel persecutors, filthy persons, idolaters, and all sorts of the unbelieving, shall be cast into the dungeon of utter darkness, where their worm shall not die, nor their fire be quenched. The remembrance of that day, and of the Judgment to be executed in it, is not only a bridle by which our carnal lusts are restrained but also such inestimable comfort that neither the threatening of worldly princes, nor the fear of present danger or of temporal death, may move us to renounce and forsake that blessed society which we, the members, have with our Head and only Mediator, Christ Jesus: whom we confess and avow to be the promised Messiah, the only Head of his Kirk, our just Lawgiver, our only High Priest, Advocate, and Mediator. To which honors and offices, if man or angel presume to intrude themselves, we utterly detest and abhor them, as blasphemous to our sovereign and supreme Governor, Christ Jesus.

12. FAITH IN THE HOLY GHOST

Our faith and its assurance do not proceed from flesh and blood, that is to say, from natural powers within us, but are the inspiration of the Holy Ghost; whom we confess to be God, equal with the Father and with his Son, who sanctifies us, and brings us into all truth by his own working, without whom we should remain forever enemies to God and ignorant of his Son, Christ Jesus. For by nature we are so dead, blind, and perverse, that neither can we feel when we are pricked, see the light when it shines, nor assent to the will of God when it is revealed, unless the Spirit of the Lord Jesus quicken that which is dead, remove the darkness from our minds, and bow our stubborn hearts to the obedience of his blessed will. And so, as we confess that God the Father created us when we were not, as his Son our Lord Jesus redeemed us when we were enemies to him, so also do we confess that the Holy Ghost does sanctify and regenerate us, without respect to any merit proceeding from us, be it before or after our regeneration. To put this even more plainly; as we willingly disclaim any honor and glory from our own creation and redemption, so do we willingly also for our regeneration and sanctification; for by ourselves we are not capable of thinking one good thought, but he who has begun the work in us alone continues us in it, to the praise and glory of his undeserved grace.

13. THE CAUSE OF GOOD WORKS

The cause of good works, we confess, is not our free will, but the Spirit of the Lord Jesus, who dwells in our hearts by true faith, brings forth such works as God has prepared for us to walk in. For we most boldly affirm that it is blasphemy to say that Christ abides in the hearts of those in whom is no spirit of sanctification. Therefore we do not hesitate to affirm that murderers, oppressors, cruel persecutors, adulterers, filthy persons, idolaters, drunkards, thieves, and all workers of iniquity, have neither true faith nor anything of the Spirit of the Lord Jesus, so long as they obstinately continue in wickedness. For as soon as the Spirit of the Lord Jesus, whom God's chosen children receive by true faith, takes possession of the heart of any man, so soon does he regenerate and renew him, so that he begins to hate what before he loved, and to love what he hated before. Thence comes that continual battle which is between the flesh and Spirit in God's children, while the flesh and the natural man, being corrupt, lust for things pleasant and delightful to themselves, are envious in adversity and proud in prosperity, and every moment prone and ready to offend the majesty of God. But the Spirit of God, who bears witness to our spirit that we are the sons of God, makes us resist filthy pleasures and groan in God's presence for deliverance from this bondage of corruption, and finally to triumph over sin so that it does not reign in our mortal bodies. Other men do not share this conflict since they do not have God's Spirit, but they readily follow and obey sin and feel no regrets, since they act as the devil and their corrupt nature urge. But the sons of God fight against sin; sob and mourn when they find themselves tempted to do evil; and, if they fall, rise again with earnest and unfeigned repentance. They do these things, not by their own power, but by the power of the Lord Jesus, apart from whom they can do nothing.

14. THE WORKS WHICH ARE COUNTED GOOD BEFORE GOD

We confess and acknowledge that God has given to man his holy law, in which not only all such works as displease and offend his godly majesty are forbidden, but also those which please him and which he has promised to reward are commanded. These works are of two kinds. The one is done to the honor of God, the other to the profit of our neighbor, and both have the revealed word of God as their assurance. To have one God, to worship and honor him, to call upon him in all our troubles, to reverence his holy Name, to hear his Word and to believe it, and to share in his holy sacraments, belong to the first kind. To honor father, mother, princes, rulers, and superior powers; to love them, to support them, to obey their orders if they are not contrary to the commands of God, to save the lives of the innocent, to repress tyranny, to defend the oppressed, to keep our bodies clean and holy, to live in soberness and temperance, to deal justly with all men in word and deed, and, finally, to repress any desire to harm our neighbor, are the good works of the second kind, and these are most pleasing and acceptable to God as he has commanded them himself. Acts to the contrary are sins, which always displease him and provoke him to anger, such as, not to call upon him alone when we have need, not to hear his Word with reverence, but to condemn and despise it, to have or worship idols, to maintain and defend idolatry, lightly to esteem the reverend name of God, to profane, abuse, or condemn the sacraments of Christ Jesus, to disobey or resist any whom God has placed in authority, so long as they do not exceed the bounds of their office, to murder, or to consent thereto, to bear hatred, or to let innocent blood be shed if we can prevent it. In conclusion, we confess and affirm that the breach of any other commandment of the first or second kind is sin, by which God's anger and displeasure are kindled against the proud, unthankful world. So that we affirm good works to be those alone which are done in faith and at the command of God who, in his law, has set forth the things that please him. We affirm that evil works are not only those expressly done against God's command, but also, in religious matters and the worship of God, those things which have no other warrant than the invention and opinion of man. From the beginning God has rejected such, as we learn from the words of the prophet Isaiah and of our master, Christ Jesus, "In vain do they worship me, teaching the doctrines and commandments of men."

15. THE PERFECTION OF THE LAW AND THE IMPERFECTION OF MAN

We confess and acknowledge that the law of God is most just, equal, holy, and perfect, commanding those things which, when perfectly done, can give life and bring man to eternal felicity; but our nature is so corrupt, weak, and imperfect, that we are never able perfectly to fulfill the works of the law. Even after we are reborn, if we say that we have no sin, we deceive ourselves and the truth of God is not in us. It is therefore essential for us to lay hold on Christ Jesus, in his righteousness and his atonement, since he is the end and consummation of the Law and since it is by him that we are set at liberty so that the curse of God may not fall upon us, even though we do not fulfill the Law in all points. For as God the Father beholds us in the body of his Son Christ Jesus, he accepts our imperfect obedience as if it were perfect, and covers our works, which are defiled with many stains, with the righteousness of his Son. We do not mean that we are so set at liberty that we owe no obedience to the Law—for we have already acknowledged its place—but we affirm that no man on earth, with the sole exception of Christ Jesus, has given, gives, or shall give in action that obedience to the Law which the Law requires. When we have done all things we must fall down and unfeignedly confess that we are unprofitable servants. Therefore, whoever boasts of the merits of his own works or puts his trust in works of supererogation, boasts of what does not exist, and puts his trust in damnable idolatry.

16. THE KIRK

As we believe in one God, Father, Son, and Holy Ghost, so we firmly believe that from the beginning there has been, now is, and to the end of the world shall be, one Kirk, that is to say, one company and multitude of men chosen by God, who rightly worship and embrace him by true faith in Jesus Christ, who is the only Head of the Kirk, even as it is the body and spouse of Christ Jesus. This Kirk is catholic, that is, universal, because it contains the chosen of all ages, of all realms, nations, and tongues, be they of the Jews or be they of the Gentiles, who have communion and society with God the Father, and with his Son, Christ Jesus, through the sanctification of his Holy Spirit. It is therefore called the communion, not of profane persons, but of saints, who, as citizens of the heavenly Jerusalem, have the fruit of inestimable benefits, one God, one Lord Jesus, one faith, and one baptism. Out of this Kirk there is neither life nor eternal felicity. Therefore we utterly abhor the blasphemy of those who hold that men who live according to equity and justice shall be saved, no matter what religion they profess. For since there is neither life nor salvation without Christ Jesus; so shall none have part therein but those whom the Father has given unto his Son Christ Jesus, and those who in time come to him, avow his doctrine, and believe in him. (We include the children with the believing parents.) This Kirk is invisible, known only to God, who alone knows whom he has chosen, and includes both the chosen who are departed, the Kirk triumphant, those who yet live and fight against sin and Satan, and those who shall live hereafter.

17. THE IMMORTALITY OF SOULS

The chosen departed are in peace, and rest from their labors; not that they sleep and are lost in oblivion as some fanatics hold, for they are delivered from all fear and torment, and all the temptations to which we and all God's chosen are subject in this life, and because of which we are called the Kirk militant. On the other hand, the reprobate and unfaithful departed have anguish, torment, and pain which cannot be expressed. Neither the one nor the other is in such sleep that they feel no joy or torment, as is testified by Christ's parable in St. Luke XVI, his words to the thief, and the words of the souls crying under the altar, "O Lord, thou that art righteous and just, how long shalt thou not revenge our blood upon those that dwell in the earth?"

18. THE NOTES BY WHICH THE TRUE KIRK SHALL BE DETERMINED FROM THE FALSE, AND WHO SHALL BE JUDGE OF DOCTRINE

Since Satan has labored from the beginning to adorn his pestilent synagogue with the title of the Kirk of God, and has incited cruel murderers to persecute, trouble, and molest the true Kirk and its members, as Cain did to Abel, Ishmael to Isaac, Esau to Jacob, and the whole priesthood of the Jews to Christ Jesus himself and his apostles after him. So it is essential that the true Kirk be distinguished from the filthy synagogues by clear and perfect notes lest we, being deceived, receive and embrace, to our own condemnation, the one for the other. The notes, signs, and assured tokens whereby the spotless bride of Christ is known from the horrible harlot, the false Kirk, we state, are neither antiquity, usurped title, lineal succession, appointed place, nor the numbers of men approving an error. For Cain was before Abel and Seth in age and title; Jerusalem had precedence above all other parts of the earth, for in it were priests lineally descended from Aaron, and greater numbers followed the scribes, Pharisees, and priests, than unfeignedly believed and followed Christ Jesus and his doctrine, and yet no man of judgment, we suppose, will hold that any of the forenamed were the Kirk of God. The notes of the true Kirk, therefore, we believe, confess, and avow to be: first, the true preaching of the Word of God, in which God has revealed himself to us, as the writings of the prophets and apostles declare; secondly, the right administration of the sacraments of Christ Jesus, with which must be associated the Word and promise of God to seal and confirm them in our hearts; and lastly, ecclesiastical discipline uprightly ministered, as God's Word prescribes, whereby vice is repressed and virtue nourished. Then wherever these notes are seen and continue for any time, be the number complete or not, there, beyond any doubt, is the true Kirk of Christ, who, according to his promise, is in its midst. This is not that universal Kirk of which we have spoken before, but particular Kirks, such as were in Corinth, Galatia, Ephesus, and other places where the ministry was planted by Paul and which he himself called Kirks of God. Such

Kirks, we the inhabitants of the realm of Scotland confessing Christ Jesus, do claim to have in our cities, towns, and reformed districts because of the doctrine taught in our Kirks, contained in the written Word of God, that is, the Old and New Testaments, in those books which were originally reckoned as canonical. We affirm that in these all things necessary to be believed for the salvation of man are sufficiently expressed. The interpretation of Scripture, we confess, does not belong to any private or public person, nor yet to any Kirk for pre-eminence or precedence, personal or local, which it has above others, but pertains to the Spirit of God by whom the Scriptures were written. When controversy arises about the right understanding of any passage or sentence of Scripture, or for the reformation of any abuse within the Kirk of God, we ought not so much to ask what men have said or done before us, as what the Holy Ghost uniformly speaks within the body of the Scriptures and what Christ Jesus himself did and commanded. For it is agreed by all that the Spirit of God, who is the Spirit of unity, cannot contradict himself. So if the interpretation or opinion of any theologian, Kirk, or council, is contrary to the plain Word of God written in any other passage of the Scripture, it is most certain that this is not the true understanding and meaning of the Holy Ghost, although councils, realms, and nations have approved and received it. We dare not receive or admit any interpretation which is contrary to any principal point of our faith, or to any other plain text of Scripture, or to the rule of love.

19. THE AUTHORITY OF THE SCRIPTURES

As we believe and confess the Scriptures of God sufficient to instruct and make perfect the man of God, so do we affirm and avow their authority to be from God, and not to depend on men or angels. We affirm, therefore, that those who say the Scriptures have no other authority save that which they have received from the Kirk are blasphemous against God and injurious to the true Kirk, which always hears and obeys the voice of her own Spouse and Pastor, but takes not upon her to be mistress over the same.

20. GENERAL COUNCILS, THEIR POWER, AUTHORITY, AND THE CAUSE OF THEIR SUMMONING

As we do not rashly condemn what good men, assembled together in general councils lawfully gathered, have set before us; so we do not receive uncritically whatever has been declared to men under the name of the general councils, for it is plain that, being human, some of them have manifestly erred, and that in matters of great weight and importance. So far then as the council confirms its decrees by the plain Word of God, so far do we reverence and embrace them. But if men, under the name of a council, pretend to forge for us new articles of faith, or to make decisions contrary to the Word of God, then we must utterly deny them as the doctrine of devils, drawing our souls from the voice of the one God to follow the doctrines and teachings of men. The reason why the general councils met was not to make any permanent law which God had not made before, nor yet to form new articles for our belief, nor to give the Word of God authority; much less to make that to be his Word, or even the true interpretation of it, which was not expressed previously by his holy will in his Word; but the reason for councils, at least of those that deserve that name, was partly to refute heresies, and to give public confession of their faith to the generations following, which they did by the authority of God's written Word, and not by any opinion or prerogative that they could not err by reason of their numbers. This, we judge, was the primary reason for general councils. The second was that good policy and order should be constitutes and observed in the Kirk where, as in the house of God, it becomes all things to be done decently and in order. Not that we think any policy of order of ceremonies can be appointed for all ages, times, and places; for as ceremonies which men have devised are but temporal, so they may, and ought to be, changed, when they foster superstition rather than edify the Kirk.

21. THE SACRAMENTS

As the fathers under the Law, besides the reality of the sacrifices, had two chief sacraments, that is, circumcision and the Passover, and those who rejected these were not reckoned among God's people; so do we acknowledge and confess that now in the time of the gospel we have two chief sacraments, which alone were instituted by the Lord Jesus and commanded to be used by all who will be counted members of his body, that is, Baptism and the Supper or Table of the Lord Jesus, also called the Communion of His Body and Blood. These sacraments, both of the Old Testament and of the New, were instituted by God not only to make a visible distinction between his people and those who were without the Covenant, but also to exercise the faith of his children and, by participation of these sacraments, to seal in their hearts the assurance of his promise, and of that most blessed conjunction, union, and society, which the chosen have with their Head, Christ Jesus. And so we utterly condemn the vanity of those who affirm the sacraments to be nothing else than naked and bare signs. No, we assuredly believe that by Baptism we are engrafted into Christ Jesus, to be made partakers of his righteousness, by which our sins are covered and remitted, and also that in the Supper rightly used, Christ Jesus is so joined with us that he becomes the very nourishment and food for our souls. Not that we imagine any transubstantiation of bread into Christ's body, and of wine into his natural blood, as the Romanists have perniciously taught and wrongly believed; but this union and conjunction which we have with the body and blood of Christ Jesus in the right use of the sacraments is wrought by means of the Holy Ghost, who by true faith carries us above all things that are visible, carnal, and earthly, and makes us feed upon the body and blood of Christ Jesus, once broken and shed for us but now in heaven, and appearing for us in the presence of his Father. Notwithstanding the distance between his glorified body in heaven and mortal men on earth, yet we must assuredly believe that the bread which we break is the communion of Christ's body and the cup which we bless the communion of his blood. Thus we confess and believe without doubt that the faithful, in the right use of the Lord's Table, do so eat the body and drink the blood of the Lord Jesus that he remains in them and they in him; they are so made flesh of his flesh and bone of his bone that as the eternal Godhood has given to the flesh of Christ Jesus, which by nature was corruptible and mortal, life and immortality, so the eating and drinking of the flesh and blood of Christ Jesus does the like for us. We grant that this is neither given to us merely at the time nor by the power and virtue of the sacrament alone, but we affirm that the faithful, in the right use of the Lord's Table, have such union with Christ Jesus as the natural man cannot apprehend. Further we affirm that although the faithful, hindered by negligence and human weakness, do not profit as much as they ought in the actual moment of the Supper, yet afterwards it shall bring forth fruit, being living seed sown in good ground; for the Holy Spirit, who can never be separated from the right institution of the Lord Jesus, will not deprive the faithful of the fruit of that mystical action. Yet all this, we say again, comes of that true faith which apprehends Christ Jesus, who alone makes the sacrament effective in us. Therefore, if anyone slanders us by saying that we affirm or believe the sacraments to be symbols and nothing more, they are libelous and speak against the plain facts. On the other hand we readily admit that we make a distinction between Christ Jesus in his eternal substance and the elements of the sacramental signs. So we neither worship the elements, in place of that which they signify, nor yet do we despise them or undervalue them, but we use them with great reverence, examining ourselves diligently before we participate, since we are assured by the mouth of the apostle that "whoever shall eat this bread, and drink this cup of the Lord, unworthily, shall be guilty of the body and blood of the Lord."

22. THE RIGHT ADMINISTRATION OF THE SACRAMENTS

Two things are necessary for the right administration of the sacraments. The first is that they should be ministered by lawful ministers, and we declare that these are men appointed to preach the Word, unto whom God has given the power to preach the gospel, and who are lawfully called by some Kirk. The second is that they should be ministered in the elements and manner which God has appointed. Otherwise they cease to be the sacraments of Christ Jesus. This is why we abandon the teaching of the Roman Church and withdraw from its sacraments; firstly, because their ministers are not true ministers of Christ Jesus (indeed they even allow women, whom the Holy Ghost will not permit to preach in the congregation, to baptize) and, secondly, because they have so adulterated both the sacraments with their own additions that no part of Christ's original act remains in its original simplicity. The addition of oil, salt, spittle, and such like in baptism, are merely human additions. To adore or venerate the sacrament, to carry it through streets and towns in procession, or to reserve it in a special case, is not the proper use of Christ's sacrament but an abuse of it. Christ Jesus said, "Take ye, eat ye," and, "Do this in remembrance of me." By these words and commands he sanctified bread and wine to be the sacrament of his holy body and blood, so that the one should be eaten and that all should drink of the other, and not that they should be reserved for worship or honored as God, as the Romanists do. Further, in withdrawing one part of the sacrament—the blessed cup—from the people, they have committed sacrilege. Moreover, if the sacraments are to be rightly used it is essential that the end and purpose of their institution should be understood, not only by the minister but also by the recipients. For if the recipient does not understand what is being done, the sacrament is not being rightly used, as is seen in the case of the Old Testament sacrifices. Similarly, if the teacher teaches false doctrine which is hateful to God, even though the sacraments are his own ordinance, they are not rightly used, since wicked men have used them for another end than what God had commanded. We affirm that this has been done to the sacraments in the Roman Church, for there the whole action of the Lord Jesus is adulterated in form, purpose, and meaning. What Christ Jesus did, and commanded to be done, is evident from the Gospels and from St. Paul; what the priest does at the altar we do not need to tell. The end and purpose of Christ's institution, for which it should be used, is set forth in the words, "Do this in remembrance of Me," and "For as often as ye eat this bread and drink this cup ye do show"—that is, extol, preach, magnify, and praise—"the Lord's death, till He come." But let the words of the mass, and their own doctors and teachings witness, what is the purpose and meaning of the mass; it is that, as mediators between Christ and his Kirk, they should offer to God the Father, a sacrifice in propitiation for the sins of the living and of the dead. This doctrine is blasphemous to Christ Jesus and would deprive his unique sacrifice, once offered on the cross for the cleansing of all who are to be sanctified, of its sufficiency; so we detest and renounce it.

23. TO WHOM SACRAMENTS APPERTAIN

We hold that baptism applies as much to the children of the faithful as to those who are of age and discretion, and so we condemn the error of the Anabaptists, who deny that children should be baptized before they have faith and understanding. But we hold that the Supper of the Lord is only for those who are of the household of faith and can try and examine themselves both in their faith and their duty to their neighbors. Those who eat and drink at that holy table without faith, or without peace and goodwill to their brethren, eat unworthily. This is the reason why ministers in our Kirk make public and individual examination of those who are to be admitted to the table of the Lord Jesus.

24. THE CIVIL MAGISTRATE

We confess and acknowledge that empires, kingdoms, dominions, and cities are appointed and ordained by God; the powers and authorities in them, emperors in empires, kings in their realms, dukes and princes in their dominions, and magistrates in cities, are ordained by God's holy ordinance for the manifestation of his own glory and for the good and well being of all men. We hold that any men who conspire to rebel or to overturn the civil powers, as duly established, are not merely enemies to humanity but rebels against God's will. Further, we confess and acknowledge that such persons as are set in authority are to be loved, honored, feared, and held in the highest respect, because they are the lieutenants of God, and in their councils God himself doth sit and judge. They are the judges and princes to whom God has given the sword for the praise and defense of good men and the punishment of all open evildoers. Moreover, we state the preservation and purification of religion is particularly the duty of kings, princes, rulers, and magistrates. They are not only appointed for civil government but also to maintain true religion and to suppress all idolatry and superstition. This may be seen in David, Jehoshaphat, Hezekiah, Josiah, and others highly commended for their zeal in that cause.

Therefore we confess and avow that those who resist the supreme powers, so long as they are acting in their own spheres, are resisting God's ordinance and cannot be held guiltless. We further state that so long as princes and rulers vigilantly fulfill their office, anyone who denies them aid, counsel, or service, denies it to God, who by his lieutenant craves it of them.

25. THE GIFTS FREELY GIVEN TO THE KIRK

Although the Word of God truly preached, the sacraments rightly ministered, and discipline executed according to the Word of God, are certain and infallible signs of the true Kirk, we do not mean that every individual person in that company is a chosen member of Christ Jesus. We acknowledge and confess that many weeds and tares are sown among the corn and grow in great abundance in its midst, and that the reprobate may be found in the fellowship of the chosen and may take an outward part with them in the benefits of the Word and sacraments. But since they only confess God for a time with their mouths but not with their hearts, they lapse, and do not continue to the end. Therefore they do not share the fruits of Christ's death, resurrection, and ascension. But such as unfeignedly believe with the heart and boldly confess the Lord Jesus with their mouths shall certainly receive his gifts. Firstly, in this life, they shall receive remission of sins and that be faith in Christ's blood alone; for though sin shall remain and continually abide in our mortal bodies, yet it shall not be counted against us, but be pardoned, and covered with Christ's righteousness. Secondly, in the general judgment, there shall be given to every man and woman resurrection of the flesh. The seas shall give up her dead, and the earth those who are buried within her. Yea, the Eternal, our God, shall stretch out his hand on the dust, and the dead shall arise incorruptible, and in the very substance of the selfsame flesh which every man now bears, to receive according to their works, glory or punishment. Such as now delight in vanity, cruelty, filthiness, superstition, or idolatry, shall be condemned to the fire unquenchable, in which those who now serve the devil in all abominations shall be tormented forever, both in body and in spirit. But such as continue in well doing to the end, boldly confessing the Lord Jesus, shall receive glory, honor, and immortality, we constantly believe, to reign forever in life everlasting with Christ Jesus, to whose glorified body all his chosen shall be made like, when he shall appear again in judgment and shall render up the Kingdom to God his Father, who then shall be and ever shall remain, all in all things, God blessed forever. To whom, with the Son and the Holy Ghost, be all honor and glory, now and ever. Amen.

Arise, O Lord, and let thine enemies be confounded; let them flee from thy presence that hate thy godly Name. Give thy servants strength to speak thy Word with boldness, and let all nations cleave to the true knowledge of thee. Amen.

These acts and articles were read in the face of the Parliament and ratified by the Three Estates at Edinburgh the 17th day of August the year of God, 1560 years. ▪

Belgic Confession

The Belgic Confession comes from the Reformed Church in the Lowlands, or "Nether-lands," of Western Europe, now called Belgium. The confession was initially written in French in 1561 by French pastor Guido de Brès, who had studied under John Calvin in Geneva. A number of other pastors helped to revise the confession in the following years. The Belgic Confession was not written to correct any specific error—it is an overview of the Reformed faith, generally elaborating on the three main points of the Apostles' Creed. Its hoped-for purpose was to create peace for the church by reassuring outsiders that the Reformers' teachings were biblical, not heretical, and were not even new—that the Reformation was simply a return to the teaching of the early Church.

To that end, shortly after it was written the confession was presented to Philip II of Spain for approval. Philip denounced it. Nevertheless, the Belgic Confession was approved by Geneva and many Reformed churches in the region. Theodore Beza created the first Latin translation. In 1618–19 the Synod of Dort revised and approved the confession, and had the revised version translated into Dutch, German, and Latin. The Belgic Confession, the Heidelberg Catechism, and the Canons of Dort together became the Three Forms of Unity, the defining confessions of the Continental Reformed Church.

---

1. THAT THERE IS ONE ONLY GOD

We all believe with the heart, and confess with the mouth, that there is one only simple and spiritual Being, which we call God; and that he is eternal, incomprehensible invisible, immutable, infinite, almighty, perfectly wise, just, good, and the overflowing fountain of all good.

2. BY WHAT MEANS GOD IS MADE KNOWN UNTO US

We know him by two means; first, by the creation, preservation and government of the universe; which is before our eyes as a most elegant book, wherein all creatures, great and small, are as so many characters leading us to contemplate the invisible things of God, namely His power and divinity, as the apostle Paul says, Rom. 1:20. All which things are sufficient to convince men, and leave them without excuse. Secondly, he makes himself more clearly fully known to us by his holy and divine Word, that is to say, as far as is necessary for us to know in this life, to his glory and our salvation.

3. OF THE WRITTEN WORD OF GOD

We confess that this Word of God was not sent, nor delivered by the will of man, but that holy men of God spoke as they were moved by the Holy Ghost, as the apostle Peter says. And that afterwards God, from a special care, which he has for us and our salvation, commanded his servants, the prophets and apostles, to commit his revealed word to writing; and he himself wrote with his own finger, the two tables of the law. Therefore we call such writings holy and divine Scriptures.

4. CANONICAL BOOKS OF THE HOLY SCRIPTURE

We believe that the Holy Scriptures are contained in two books, namely, the Old and New Testament, which are canonical, against which nothing can be alleged. These are thus named in the Church of God. The books of the Old Testament are, the five books of Moses, viz.: Genesis, Exodus, Leviticus, Numbers, Deuteronomy; the books of Joshua, Ruth, Judges, the two books of Samuel, the two of the Kings, two books of the Chronicles, commonly called Paralipomenon, the first of Ezra, Nehemiah, Esther, Job, the Psalms of David, the three books of Solomon, namely, the Proverbs, Ecclesiastes, and the Song of Songs; the four great prophets Isaiah, Jeremiah, Ezekiel and Daniel; and the twelve lesser prophets, namely, Hosea, Joel, Amos, Obadiah, Jonah, Micah, Nahum, Habakkuk, Zephaniah, Haggai, Zechariah, and Malachi.

Those of the New Testament are the four evangelists, viz.: Matthew, Mark, Luke, and John; the Acts of the Apostles; the fourteen epistles of the apostle Paul, viz.: one to the Romans, two to the Corinthians, one to the Galatians, one to the Ephesians, one to the Philippians, one to the Colossians, two to the Thessalonians, two to Timothy, one to Titus, one to Philemon, and one to the Hebrews; the seven epistles of the other apostles, namely, one of James, two of Peter, three of John, one of Jude; and the Revelation of the apostle John.

5. FROM WHENCE THE HOLY SCRIPTURES DERIVE THEIR DIGNITY AND AUTHORITY

We receive all these books, and these only, as holy and canonical, for the regulation, foundation, and conformation of our faith; believing without any doubt, all things contained in them, not so much because the Church receives and approves them as such, but more especially because the Holy Ghost witnesses in our hearts, that they are from God, whereof they carry the evidence in themselves. For the very blind are able to perceive that the things foretold in them are fulfilling.

6. THE DIFFERENCE BETWEEN THE CANONICAL AND APOCRYPHAL BOOKS

We distinguish those sacred books from the apocryphal, viz.: the third book of Esdras, the books of Tobias, Judith, Wisdom, Jesus Syrach, Baruch, the appendix to the book of Esther, the Song of the three Children in the Furnace, the history of Susannah, of Bell and the Dragon, the prayer of Manasses, and the two books of the Maccabees. All of which the Church may read and take instruction from, so far as they agree with the canonical books; but they are far from having such power and efficacy, as that we may from their testimony confirm any point of faith, or of the christian religion; much less detract from the authority of the other sacred books.

7. THE SUFFICIENCY OF THE HOLY SCRIPTURES TO BE THE ONLY RULE OF FAITH

We believe that those Holy Scriptures fully contain the will of God, and that whatsoever man ought to believe, unto salvation, is sufficiently taught therein. For, since the whole manner of worship, which God requires of us, is written in them at large, it is unlawful for any one, though an apostle, to teach otherwise than we are now taught in the Holy Scriptures: nay, though it were an angel from heaven, as the apostle Paul says. For, since it is forbidden, to add unto or take away anything from the word of God, it does thereby evidently appear, that the doctrine thereof is most perfect and complete in all respects. Neither do we consider of equal value any writing of men, however holy these men may have been, with those divine Scriptures, nor ought we to consider custom, or the great multitude, or antiquity, or succession of times and persons, or councils, decrees or statutes, as of equal value with the truth of God, for the truth is above all; for all men are of themselves liars, and more vain than vanity itself. Therefore, we reject with all our hearts, whatsoever does not agree with this infallible rule, which the apostles have taught us, saying, Try the spirits whether they are of God. Likewise, if there come any unto you; and bring not this doctrine, receive him not into your house.

8. THAT GOD IS ONE IN ESSENCE, YET NEVERTHELESS DISTINGUISHED IN THREE PERSONS

According to this truth and this Word of God, we believe in one only God, who is the one single essence, in which are three persons, really, truly, and eternally distinct, according to their incommunicable properties; namely, the Father, and the Son, and the Holy Ghost. The Father is the cause, origin and beginning of all things visible and invisible; the Son is the word, wisdom, and image of the Father; the Holy Ghost is the eternal power and might, proceeding from the Father and the Son. Nevertheless God is not by this distinction divided into three, since the Holy Scriptures teach us, that the Father, and the Son, and the Holy Ghost, have each his personality, distinguished by their properties; but in such wise that these three persons are but one only God. Hence then, it is evident, that the Father is not the Son, nor the Son the Father, and likewise the Holy Ghost is neither the Father nor the Son. Nevertheless these persons thus distinguished are not divided, nor intermixed: for the Father has not assumed the flesh, nor has the Holy Ghost, but the Son only. The Father has never been without his Son, or without his Holy Ghost. For they are all three coeternal and co-essential. There is neither first nor last: for they are all three one, in truth, in power, in goodness, and in mercy.

9. THE PROOF OF THE FOREGOING ARTICLE OF THE TRINITY OF PERSONS IN ONE GOD

All this we know, as well from the testimonies of holy writ, as from their operations, and chiefly by those we feel in ourselves. The testimonies of the Holy Scriptures, that teach us to believe this Holy Trinity are written in many places of the Old Testament, which are not so necessary to enumerate, as to choose them out with discretion and judgment. In Genesis, chap. 1:26, 27, God says: Let us make man in our image, after our likeness, etc. So God created man in his own image, male and female created he them. And Gen. 3:22. Behold the man is become as one of us. From this saying, let us make man in our image, it appears that there are more persons than one in the Godhead; and when he says, God created, he signifies the unity. It is true he does not say how many persons there are, but that, which appears to us somewhat obscure in the Old Testament, is very plain in the New. For when our Lord was baptized in Jordan, the voice of the Father was heard, saying, This is my beloved Son: the Son was seen in the water, and the Holy Ghost appeared in the shape of a dove. This form is also instituted by Christ in the baptism of all believers. Baptize all nations, in the name of the Father, and of the Son, and of the Holy Ghost. In the Gospel of Luke, the angel Gabriel thus addressed Mary, the mother of our Lord, the Holy Ghost shall come upon thee, and the power of the Highest shall overshadow thee, therefore also that holy thing, which shall be born of thee, shall be called the Son of God: likewise, the grace of our Lord Jesus Christ, and the love of God, and the communion of the Holy Ghost be with you. And there are three that bear record in heaven, the Father, the Word, and the Holy Ghost, and these three are one. In all which places we are fully taught, that there are three persons in one only divine essence. And although this doctrine far surpasses all human understanding, nevertheless, we now believe it by means of the Word of God, but expect hereafter to enjoy the perfect knowledge and benefit thereof in Heaven. Moreover, we must observe the particular offices and operations of these three persons towards us. The Father is called our Creator, by his power; the Son is our Saviour and Redeemer, by his blood; the Holy Ghost is our Sanctifier, by his dwelling in our hearts. This doctrine of the Holy Trinity, has always been defended and maintained by the true Church, since the time of the apostles, to this very day, against the Jews, Mohammedans, and some false christians and heretics, as

Marcion, Manes, Praxeas, Sabellius, Samosatenus, Arius, and such like, who have been justly condemned by the orthodox fathers. Therefore, in this point, we do willingly receive the three creeds, namely, that of the Apostles,[1] of Nicea,[2] and of Athanasius[3]: likewise that, which, conformable thereunto, is agreed upon by the ancient fathers.

10. THAT JESUS CHRIST IS TRUE AND ETERNAL GOD

We believe that Jesus Christ, according to his divine nature, is the only begotten Son of God, begotten from eternity, not made nor created (for then he should be a creature), but co-essential and coeternal with the Father, the express image of his person, and the brightness of his glory, equal unto him in all things. He is the Son of God, not only from the time that he assumed our nature, but from all eternity, as these testimonies, when compared together, teach us. Moses says, that God created the world; and John says, that all things were made by that Word, which he calls God. And the apostle says, that God made the worlds by his Son; likewise, that God created all things by Jesus Christ. Therefore it must needs follow, that he, who is called God, the Word, the Son, and Jesus Christ, did exist at that time, when all things were created by him. Therefore the prophet Micah says, His goings forth have been from of old, from everlasting. And the apostle: He has neither beginning of days, nor end of life. He therefore is that true, eternal, and almighty God, whom we invoke, worship and serve.

11. THAT THE HOLY GHOST IS TRUE AND ETERNAL GOD

We believe and confess also, that the Holy Ghost, from eternity, proceeds from the Father and Son; and therefore neither is made, created, nor begotten, but only proceeds from both; who in order is the third person of the Holy Trinity; of one and the same essence, majesty and glory with the Father, and the Son: and therefore, is the true and eternal God, as the Holy Scriptures teach us.

---

1 See page 12.
2 See page 13.
3 See page 17.

12. OF THE CREATION

We believe that the Father, by the Word, that is, by his Son, has created of nothing, the heaven, the earth, and all creatures, as it seemed good unto him, giving unto every creature its being, shape, form, and several offices to serve its Creator. That he does also still uphold and govern them by his eternal providence, and infinite power, for the service of mankind, to the end that man may serve his God. He also created the angels good, to be his messengers and to serve his elect; some of whom are fallen from that excellency, in which God created them, into everlasting perdition; and the others have, by the grace of God, remained steadfast and continued in their primitive state. The devils and evil spirits are so depraved, that they are enemies of God and every good thing, to the utmost of their power, as murderers, watching to ruin the Church and every member thereof, and by their wicked stratagems to destroy all; and are, therefore, by their own wickedness, adjudged to eternal damnation, daily expecting their horrible torments. Therefore we reject and abhor the error of the Sadducees, who deny the existence of spirits and angels: and also that of the Manichees, who assert that the devils have their origin of themselves, and that they are wicked of their own nature, without having been corrupted.

13. OF DIVINE PROVIDENCE

We believe that the same God, after he had created all things, did not forsake them, or give them up to fortune or chance, but that he rules and governs them according to his holy will, so that nothing happens in this world without his appointment: nevertheless, God neither is the author of, nor can be charged with, the sins which are committed. For his power and goodness are so great and incomprehensible, that he orders and executes his work in the most excellent and just manner, even then, when devils and wicked men act unjustly. And, as to what he does surpassing human understanding, we will not curiously inquire into, farther than our capacity will admit of; but with the greatest humility and reverence adore the righteous judgments of God, which are hid from us, contenting ourselves that we are disciples of Christ, to learn only those things which he has revealed to us in his Word, without transgressing these limits. This doctrine affords us unspeakable consolation, since we are taught thereby that nothing can befall us by chance, but by the direction of our most gracious and heavenly Father; who watches over us with a paternal care, keeping all creatures so under his power, that not a hair of our head (for they are all numbered), nor a sparrow, can fall to the ground, without the will of our Father, in whom we do entirely trust; being persuaded, that he so restrains the devil and all our enemies, that without his will and permission, they cannot hurt us. And therefore we reject that damnable error of the Epicureans, who say that God regards nothing, but leaves all things to chance.

14. OF THE CREATION AND FALL OF MAN, AND HIS INCAPACITY TO PERFORM WHAT IS TRULY GOOD

We believe that God created man out of the dust of the earth, and made and formed him after his own image and likeness, good, righteous, and holy, capable in all things to will, agreeably to the will of God. But being in honour, he understood it not, neither knew his excellency, but willfully subjected himself to sin, and consequently to death, and the curse, giving ear to the words of the devil. For the commandment of life, which he had received, he transgressed; and by sin separated himself from God, who was his true life, having corrupted his whole nature; whereby he made himself liable to corporal and spiritual death. And being thus become wicked, perverse, and corrupt in all his ways, he has lost all his excellent gifts, which he had received from God, and only retained a few remains thereof, which, however, are sufficient to leave man without excuse; for all the light which is in us is changed into darkness, as the Scriptures teach us, saying: The light shineth in darkness, and the darkness comprehendeth it not: where St. John calls men darkness. Therefore we reject all that is taught repugnant to this, concerning the free will of man, since man is but a slave to sin, and has nothing of himself, unless it is given from heaven. For who may presume to boast, that he of himself can do any good, since Christ says, No man can come to me, except the Father, which hath sent me, draw him? Who will glory in his own will, who understands, that to be carnally minded is enmity against God? Who can speak of his knowledge, since the natural man receiveth not the things of the spirit of God? In short, who dare suggest any thought, since he knows that we are not sufficient of ourselves to think anything as of ourselves, but that our sufficiency is of God? And therefore what the apostle says ought justly to be held sure and firm, that God worketh in us both to will and to do of his good pleasure. For there is no will nor understanding, conformable to the divine will and understanding, but that Christ has wrought in man; which he teaches us, when he says, Without me ye can do nothing.

15. OF ORIGINAL SIN

We believe that, through the disobedience of Adam, original sin is extended to all mankind; which is a corruption of the whole nature, and a hereditary disease, wherewith infants themselves are infected even in their mother's womb, and which produces in man all sorts of sin, being in him as a root thereof; and therefore is so vile and abominable in the sight of God, that it is sufficient to condemn all mankind. Nor is it by any means abolished or done away by baptism; since sin always issues forth from this woeful source, as water from a fountain; notwithstanding it is not imputed to the children of God unto condemnation, but by his grace and mercy is forgiven them. Not that they should rest securely in sin, but that a sense of this corruption should make believers often to sigh, desiring to be delivered from this body of death. Wherefore we reject the error of the Pelagians, who assert that sin proceeds only from imitation.

16. OF ETERNAL ELECTION

We believe that all the posterity of Adam being thus fallen into perdition and ruin, by the sin of our first parents, God then did manifest himself such as he is; that is to say, merciful and just: Merciful, since he delivers and preserves from this perdition all, whom he, in his eternal and unchangeable counsel of mere goodness, has elected in Christ Jesus our Lord, without any respect to their works: Just, in leaving others in the fall and perdition wherein they have involved themselves.

17. OF THE RECOVERY OF FALLEN MAN

We believe that our most gracious God, in his admirable wisdom and goodness, seeing that man had thus thrown himself into temporal and eternal death, and made himself wholly miserable, was pleased to seek and comfort him, when he trembling fled from his presence, promising him that he would give his Son, who should be made of a woman, to bruise the head of the serpent, and would make him happy.

18. OF THE INCARNATION OF JESUS CHRIST

We confess, therefore, that God did fulfill the promise, which he made to the fathers, by the mouth of his holy prophets, when he sent into the world, at the time appointed by him, his own, only-begotten and eternal Son, who took upon him the form of a servant, and became like unto man, really assuming the true human nature, with all its infirmities, sin excepted, being conceived in the womb of the blessed Virgin Mary, by the power of the Holy Ghost, without the means of man, and did not only assume human nature as to the body, but also a true human soul, that he might be a real man. For since the soul was lost as well as the body, it was necessary that he should take both upon him, to save both. Therefore we confess (in opposition to the heresy of the Anabaptists, who deny that Christ assumed human flesh of his mother) that Christ is become a partaker of the flesh and blood of the children; that he is a fruit of the loins of David after the flesh; made of the seed of David according to the flesh; a fruit of the womb of the Virgin Mary, made of a woman, a branch of David; a shoot of the root of Jesse; sprung from the tribe of Judah; descended from the Jews according to the flesh; of the seed of Abraham, since he took on him the seed of Abraham, and became like unto his brethren in all things, sin excepted, so that in truth he is our Immanuel, that is to say, God with us.

19. OF THE UNION AND DISTINCTION OF THE TWO NATURES IN THE PERSON OF CHRIST

We believe that by this conception, the person of the Son is inseparably united and connected with the human nature; so that there are not two Sons of God, nor two persons, but two natures united in one single person: yet, that each nature retains its own distinct properties. As then the divine nature has always remained untreated, without beginning of days or end of life, filling heaven and earth: so also has the human nature not lost its properties, but remained a creature, having beginning of days, being a finite nature, and retaining all the properties of a real body. And though he has by his resurrection given immortality to the same, nevertheless he has not changed the reality of his human nature; forasmuch as our salvation and resurrection also depend on the reality of his body. But these two natures are so closely united in one person, that they were not separated even by his death. Therefore that which he, when dying, commended into the hands of his Father, was a real human spirit, departing from his body. But in the meantime the divine nature always remained united with the human, even when he lay in the grave. And the Godhead did not cease to be in him, any more than it did when he was an infant, though it did not so clearly manifest itself for a while. Wherefore we confess, that he is very God, and very Man: very God by his power to conquer death; and very man that he might die for us according to the infirmity of his flesh.

20. THAT GOD HAS MANIFESTED HIS JUSTICE AND MERCY IN CHRIST

We believe that God, who is perfectly merciful and just, sent his Son to assume that nature, in which the disobedience was committed, to make satisfaction in the same, and to bear the punishment of sin by his most bitter passion and death. God therefore manifested his justice against his Son, when he laid our iniquities upon him; and poured forth his mercy and goodness on us, who were guilty and worthy of damnation, out of mere and perfect love, giving his Son unto death for us, and raising him for our justification, that through him we might obtain immortality and life eternal.

21. OF THE SATISFACTION OF CHRIST, OUR ONLY HIGH PRIEST, FOR US

We believe that Jesus Christ is ordained with an oath to be an everlasting High Priest, after the order of Melchisedec; and that he has presented himself in our behalf before the Father, to appease his wrath by his full satisfaction, by offering himself on the tree of the cross, and pouring out his precious blood to purge away our sins; as the prophets had foretold. For it is written: He was wounded for our transgressions, he was bruised for our iniquities: the chastisement of our peace was upon him, and with his stripes we are healed. He was brought as a lamb to the slaughter, and numbered with the transgressors, and condemned by Pontius Pilate as a malefactor, though he had first declared him innocent. Therefore: he restored that which he took not away, and suffered, the just for the unjust, as well in his body as in his soul, feeling the terrible punishment which our sins had merited; insomuch that his sweat became like unto drops of blood falling on the ground. He called out, my God, my God, why hast thou forsaken me? and has suffered all this for the remission of our sins. Wherefore we justly say with the apostle Paul: that we know nothing, but Jesus Christ, and him crucified; we count all things but loss and dung for the excellency of the knowledge of Christ Jesus our Lord, in whose wounds we find all manner of consolation. Neither is it necessary to seek or invent any other means of being reconciled to God, than this only sacrifice, once offered, by which believers are made perfect forever. This is also the reason why he was called by the angel of God, Jesus, that is to say, Saviour, because he should save his people from their sins.

22. OF FAITH IN JESUS CHRIST

We believe that, to attain the true knowledge of this great mystery, the Holy Ghost kindles in our hearts an upright faith, which embraces Jesus Christ, with all his merits, appropriates him, and seeks nothing more besides him. For it must needs follow, either that all things, which are requisite to our salvation, are not in Jesus Christ. or if all things are in him, that then those who possess Jesus Christ through faith, have complete salvation in him. Therefore, for any to assert, that Christ is not sufficient, but that something more is required besides him, would be too gross a blasphemy: for hence it would follow, that Christ was but half a Saviour. Therefore we justly say with Paul, that we are justified by faith alone, or by faith without works. However, to speak more clearly, we do not mean, that faith itself justifies us, for it is only an instrument with which we embrace Christ our Righteousness. But Jesus Christ, imputing to us all his merits, and so many holy works which he has done for us, and in our stead, is our Righteousness. And faith is an instrument that keeps us in communion with him in all his benefits, which, when become ours, are more than sufficient to acquit us of our sins.

23. OF JUSTIFICATION

We believe that our salvation consists in the remission of our sins for Jesus Christ's sake, and that therein our righteousness before God is implied: as David and Paul teach us, declaring this to be the happiness of man, that God imputes righteousness to him without works. And the same apostle says, that we are justified freely by his grace, through the redemption which is in Jesus Christ. And therefore we always hold fast this foundation, ascribing all the glory to God, humbling ourselves before him, and acknowledging ourselves to be such as we really are, without presuming to trust in any thing in ourselves, or in any merit of ours, relying and resting upon the obedience of Christ crucified alone, which becomes ours, when we believe in him. This is sufficient to cover all our iniquities, and to give us confidence in approving to God; freeing the conscience of fear, terror and dread, without following the example of our first father, Adam, who, trembling, attempted to cover himself with fig-leaves. And verily if we should appear before God, relying on ourselves, or on any other creature, though ever so little, we should, alas! be consumed. And therefore every one must pray with David: O Lord, enter not into judgment with thy servant: for in thy sight shall no man living be justified.

24. OF MAN'S SANCTIFICATION AND GOOD WORKS

We believe that this true faith being wrought in man by the hearing of the Word of God, and the operation of the Holy Ghost, does regenerate and make him a new man, causing him to live a new life, and freeing him from the bondage of sin. Therefore it is so far from being true, that this justifying faith makes men remiss in a pious and holy life, that on the contrary without it they would never do anything out of love to God, but only out of self-love or fear of damnation. Therefore it is impossible that this holy faith can be unfruitful in man: for we do not speak of a vain faith, but of such a faith, which is called in Scripture, a faith that worketh by love, which excites man to the practice of those works, which God has commended in his Word. Which works, as they proceed from the good root of faith, are good and acceptable in the sight of God, forasmuch as they are all sanctified by his grace: howbeit they are of no account towards our justification. For it is by faith in Christ that we are justified, even before we do good works; otherwise they could not be good works, any more than the fruit of a tree can be good, before the tree itself is good. Therefore we do good works, but not to merit by them, (for what can we merit?) nay, we are beholden to God for the good works we do, and not he to us, since it is he that works in us both to will and to do of his good pleasure. Let us therefore attend to what is written: when ye shall have done all those things which are commended you, say, we are unprofitable servants; we have done that which was our duty to do. In the meantime, we not deny that God rewards our good works, but it is through his grace that he crowns his gifts. Moreover, though we do good works, we do not found our salvation upon them; for we do no work but what is polluted by our flesh, and also punishable; and at though we could perform such works, still the remembrance of one sin is sufficient to make God reject them. Thus then we would always be in doubt, tossed to and fro without any certainty, and our poor consciences continually vexed, if they relied not on the merits of the suffering and death of our Saviour.

25. OF THE ABOLISHING OF THE CEREMONIAL LAW

We believe, that the ceremonies and figures of the law ceased at the coming of Christ, and that all the shadows are accomplished; so that the use of them must be abolished amongst Christians; yet the truth and substance of them remain with us in Jesus Christ, in whom they have their completion. In the meantime, we still use the testimonies taken out of the law and the prophets, to confirm us in the doctrine of the gospel, and to regulate our life in all honesty, to the glory of God, according to his will.

26. OF CHRIST'S INTERCESSION

We believe that we have no access unto God, but alone through the only Mediator and Advocate, Jesus Christ the righteous, who therefore became man, having united in one person the divine and human natures, that we men might have access to the divine majesty, which access would otherwise be barred against us. But this Mediator, whom the Father has appointed between him and us, ought in no wise to affright us by his majesty, or cause us to seek another according to our infancy. For there is no creature either in heaven or on earth who loveth us more than Jesus

Christ; who, though he was in the form of God, yet made himself of no reputation, and took upon him the form of a man, and of a servant for us, and was made like unto his brethren in all things. If then we should seek for another Mediator, who would be well affected towards us, whom could we find, who loved us more than he, who laid down his life for us, even when we were his enemies? And if we seek for one who has power and majesty, who is there that has so much of both as he who sits at the right hand of his Father, and who has all power in heaven and on earth? And who will sooner be heard than the own well beloved Son of God? Therefore it was only through distrust that this practice of dishonouring, instead of honouring the saints, was introduced, doing that, which they never have done, nor required, but have on the contrary steadfastly rejected according to their bounden duty, as appears by their writings. Neither must we plead here our unworthiness; for the meaning is not that we should offer our prayers to God on the ground of our own worthiness but only on the ground of the excellency and worthiness of the Lord Jesus Christ, whose righteousness is become ours by faith. Therefore the apostle, to remove this foolish fear, or rather mistrust from us, justly says, that Jesus Christ was made like unto his brethren in all things, that he might be a merciful and faithful High Priest, to make reconciliation for the sins of the people. For in that he himself has suffered, being tempted, he is able to succour them that are tempted; and further to encourage us, he adds, seeing then that we have a great High Priest, that is passed into the heavens, Jesus the Son of God, let us hold fast our profession. For we have not a high priest which cannot be touched with the feeling of our infirmities; but was in all points tempted like as we are, yet without sin. Let us therefore come boldly unto the throne of grace, that we may obtain mercy, and find grace to help in time of need. The same apostle says, having boldness to enter into the holiest, by the blood of Jesus; let us draw near with a true heart in full assurance of faith, etc. Likewise, Christ has an unchangeable priesthood, wherefore he is able also to save them to the utter most, that come unto God by him, seeing he ever liveth to make intercession for them. What more can be required? since Christ himself says, I am the way and the truth, and the life: no man cometh unto the Father but by me. To what purpose should we then seek another advocate, since it has pleased God, to give us his own Son as an advocate? Let us not forsake him to take another, or rather to seek after another, without ever being able to find him; for God well knew, when he gave him to us, that we were sinners. Therefore according to the command of Christ, we call upon the heavenly Father through Jesus Christ our own Mediator, as we are taught in the Lord's prayer; being assured that whatever we ask of the Father in his name, will be granted us.

27. OF THE CATHOLIC CHRISTIAN CHURCH

We believe and profess, one catholic[4] or universal Church, which is a holy congregation, of true Christian believers, all expecting their salvation in Jesus Christ, being washed by his blood, sanctified and sealed by the Holy Ghost. This Church has been from the beginning of the world, and will be to the end thereof; which is evident from this, that Christ is an eternal King, which, without subjects, cannot be. And this holy Church is preserved or supported by God, against the rage of the whole world; though she sometimes (for a while) appears very small, and in the eyes of men, to be reduced to nothing; as during the perilous reign of Ahab, the Lord reserved unto him seven thousand men, who had not bowed their knees to Baal. Furthermore, this holy Church is not confined, bound, or limited to a certain place or to certain persons, but is spread and dispersed over the whole world; and yet is joined and united with heart and will, by the power of faith, in one and the same spirit.

28. THAT EVERY ONE IS BOUND TO JOIN HIMSELF TO THE TRUE CHURCH

We believe, since this holy congregation is an assembly of those who are saved, and that out of it there is no salvation, that no person of whatsoever state or condition he may be, ought to withdraw himself, to live in a separate state from it; but that all men are in duty bound to join and unite themselves with it; maintaining the unity of the Church; submitting themselves to the doctrine and discipline thereof; bowing their necks under the yoke of Jesus Christ; and as mutual members of the same body, serving to the edification of the brethren, according to the talents God

---

4 The word *catholic* is an adjective from the Greek word *katholikos*, which means "universal" or "concerning the whole." It is here referring to the whole Body of Christ, the saints of God worldwide, in the past, present, and future. It does not refer to Roman Catholicism.

has given them. And that this may be the more effectually observed, it is the duty of all believers, according to the word of God, to separate themselves from all those who do not belong to the Church, and to join themselves to this congregation, wheresoever God has established it, even though the magistrates and edicts of princes were against it, yea, though they should suffer death or any other corporal punishment. Therefore all those, who separate themselves from the same, or do not join themselves to it, act contrary to the ordinance of God.

29. OF THE MARKS OF THE TRUE CHURCH, AND WHEREIN SHE DIFFERS FROM THE FALSE CHURCH

We believe, that we ought diligently and circumspectly to discern from the Word of God which is the true Church, since all sects which are in the world assume to themselves the name of the Church. But we speak not here of hypocrites, who are mixed in the Church with the good, yet are not of the Church, though externally in it; but we say that the body and communion of the true Church must be distinguished from all sects, who call themselves the Church. The marks, by which the true Church is known, are these: if the pure doctrine of the gospel is preached therein; if she maintains the pure administration of the sacraments as instituted by Christ; if church discipline is exercised in punishing of sin: in short, if all things are managed according to the pure Word of God, all things contrary thereto corrected, and Jesus Christ acknowledged as the only Head of the Church. Hereby the true Church may certainly be known from which no man has a right to separate himself. With respect to those, who are members of the Church, they may be known by the marks of Christians: namely, by faith; and when they have received Jesus Christ the only Saviour, they avoid sin, follow after righteousness, love the true God and their neighbour, neither turn aside to the right or left, and crucify the flesh with the works thereof. But this is not to be understood, as if there did not remain in them great infirmities; but they fight against them through the Spirit, all the days of their life, continually taking their refuge in the blood, death, passion and obedience of our Lord Jesus Christ, "in whom they have remission of sins, through faith in him." As for the false Church, she ascribes more power and authority to herself and her ordinances than to the Word of God, and will not submit herself to the yoke of Christ. Neither does she administer the sacraments as appointed by Christ in his Word, but adds to and takes from them, as she thinks proper; she relies more upon men than upon Christ; and persecutes those, who live holily according to the Word of God, and rebuke her for her errors, covetousness, and idolatry. These two Churches are easily known and distinguished from each other.

30. CONCERNING THE GOVERNMENT OF, AND OFFICES IN THE CHURCH

We believe, that this true Church must be governed by that spiritual policy which our Lord has taught us in his Word; namely, that there must be ministers or pastors to preach the Word of God, and to administer the sacraments; also elders and deacons, who, together with the pastors, form the council of the Church: that by these means the true religion may be preserved, and the true doctrine everywhere propagated, likewise transgressors punished and restrained by spiritual means: also that the poor and distressed may be relieved and comforted, according to their necessities. By these means everything will be carried on in the Church with good order and decency, when faithful men are chosen, according to the rule prescribed by St. Paul in his Epistle to Timothy.

31. OF THE MINISTERS, ELDERS, AND DEACONS

We believe, that the ministers of God's Word, and the elders and deacons, ought to be chosen to their respective offices by a lawful election by the Church, with calling upon the name of the Lord, and in that order which the Word of God teaches. Therefore every one must take heed, not to intrude himself by indecent means, but is bound to wait till it shall please God to call him; that he may have testimony of his calling, and be certain and assured that it is of the Lord. As for the ministers of God's Word, they have equally the same power and authority wheresoever they are, as they are all ministers of Christ, the only universal Bishop, and the only Head of the Church. Moreover, that this holy ordinance of God may not be violated or slighted, we say that every one ought to esteem the ministers of God's Word, and the elders of the Church, very highly for their work's sake, and be at peace with them without murmuring, strife or contention, as much as possible.

32. OF THE ORDER AND DISCIPLINE OF THE CHURCH

In the meantime we believe, though it is useful and beneficial, that those, who are rulers of the Church, institute and establish certain ordinances among themselves for maintaining the body of the Church; yet they ought studiously to take care, that they do not depart from those things which Christ, our only Master, has instituted. And therefore, we reject all human inventions, and all laws, which man would introduce into the worship of God, thereby to bind and compel the conscience in any manner whatever. Therefore we admit only of that which tends to nourish and preserve concord, and unity, and to keep all men in obedience to God. For this purpose, excommunication or church discipline is requisite, with the several circumstances belonging to it, according to the Word of God.

33. OF THE SACRAMENTS

We believe, that our gracious God, on account of our weakness and infirmities has ordained the sacraments for us, thereby to seal unto us his promises, and to be pledges of the good will and grace of God toward us, and also to nourish and strengthen our faith; which he has joined to the Word of the gospel, the better to present to our senses, both that which he signifies to us by his Word, and that which he works inwardly in our hearts, thereby assuring and confirming in us the salvation which he imparts to us. For they are visible signs and seals of an inward and invisible thing, by means whereof God works in us by the power of the Holy Ghost. Therefore the signs are not in vain or insignificant, so as to deceive us. For Jesus Christ is the true object presented by them, without whom they would be of no moment. Moreover, we are satisfied with the number of sacraments which Christ our Lord has instituted, which are two only, namely, the sacrament of baptism, and the holy supper of our Lord Jesus Christ.

34. OF HOLY BAPTISM

We believe and confess that Jesus Christ, who is the end of the law, has made an end, by the shedding of his blood, of all other sheddings of blood which men could or would make as a propitiation or satisfaction for sin and that he, having abolished circumcision, which was done with blood has instituted the sacrament of baptism instead thereof; by which we are received into the Church of God, and separated from all other people and strange religions, that we may wholly belong to him, whose ensign and banner we bear: and which serves as a testimony to us, that he will forever be our gracious God and Father. Therefore he has commanded all those, who are his, to be baptized with pure water, "in the name of the Father, and of the Son, and of the Holy Ghost": thereby signifying to us, that as water washes away the filth of the body, when poured upon it, and is seen on the body of the baptized, when sprinkled upon him; so does the blood of Christ, by the power of the Holy Ghost, internally sprinkle the soul, cleanse it from its sins, and regenerate us from children of wrath, unto children of God. Not that this is effected by the external water, but by the sprinkling of the precious blood of the Son of God; who is our Red Sea, through which we must pass, to escape the tyranny of Pharaoh, that is, the devil, and to enter into the spiritual land of Canaan. Therefore the ministers, on their part, administer the sacrament, and that which is visible, but our Lord gives that which is signified by the sacrament, namely, the gifts and invisible grace; washing, cleansing and purging our souls of all filth and unrighteousness; renewing our hearts, and filling them with all comfort; giving unto us a true assurance of his fatherly goodness; putting on us the new man, and putting off the old man with all his deeds. Therefore we believe, that every man, who is earnestly studious of obtaining life eternal, ought to be but once baptized with this only baptism, without ever repeating the same: since we cannot be born twice. Neither does this baptism only avail us, at the time when the water is poured upon us, and received by us but also through the whole course of our life; therefore we detest the error of the Anabaptists, who are not content with the one only baptism they have once received, and moreover condemn the baptism of the infants of believers, whom we believe ought to be baptized and sealed with the sign of the covenant, as the children in Israel formerly were circumcised, upon the same promises which are made unto our children. And indeed Christ shed his blood no less for the washing of the children of the faithful, than for adult persons; and therefore they ought to receive the sign and sacrament of that, which Christ has done for them; as the Lord commanded in the law, that they should be made partakers of the sacrament of Christ's suffering and death, shortly after they were born, by offering for them a lamb, which was a sacrament of Jesus Christ. Moreover, what circumcision was to the Jews, that baptism is to our children. And for this reason Paul calls baptism the circumcision of Christ.

35. OF THE HOLY SUPPER OF OUR LORD JESUS CHRIST

We believe and confess, that our Saviour Jesus Christ did ordain and institute the sacrament of the holy supper, to nourish and support those whom he has already regenerated, and incorporated into his family, which is his Church. Now those, who are regenerated, have in them a twofold life, the one corporal and temporal, which they have from the first birth, and is common to all men: the other spiritual and heavenly, which is given them in their second birth, which is effected by the word of the gospel, in the communion of the body of Christ; and this life is not common, but is peculiar to God's elect. In like manner God has given us, for the support of the bodily and earthly life, earthly and common bread, which is subservient thereto, and is common to all men, even to life itself. But for the support of the spiritual and heavenly life, which believers have, he has sent us living bread, which descended from heaven, namely, Jesus Christ, who nourishes and strengthens the spiritual life of believers, when they eat him, that is to say, when they apply and receive him by faith in the spirit. Christ, that he might represent unto us this spiritual and heavenly bread, has instituted an earthly and visible bread, as a sacrament of his body, and wine as a sacrament of his blood, to testify by them unto us, that, as certainly as we receive and hold this sacrament in our hands, and eat and drink the same with our mouths, by which our life is afterwards nourished, we also do as certainly receive by faith (which is the hand and mouth of our soul) the true body and blood of Christ our only Saviour in our souls, for the support of our spiritual life. Now, as it is certain and beyond all doubt, that, that Jesus Christ has not enjoined to us the use of his sacraments in vain, so he works in us all that he represents to us by these holy signs, though the manner surpasses our understanding, and cannot be comprehended by us, as the operations of the Holy Ghost are hidden and incomprehensible. In the meantime we err not, when we say, that what is eaten and drunk by us is the proper and natural body, and the proper blood of Christ. But the manner of our partaking of the same, is not by the mouth, but by the spirit through faith. Thus then, though Christ always sits at the right hand of his Father in the heavens, yet does he not therefore cease to make us partakers of himself by faith. This feast is a spiritual table, at which Christ communicates himself with all his benefits to us, and gives us there to enjoy both himself, and the merits of his sufferings and death, nourishing, strengthening and comforting our poor comfortless souls by the eating of his flesh, quickening and refreshing them by the drinking of his blood. Further, though the sacraments are connected with the thing signified nevertheless both are not received by all men: the ungodly indeed receives the sacrament to his condemnation but he does not receive the truth of the sacrament. As Judas, and Simon the sorcerer, both indeed received the sacrament, but not Christ, who was signified by it, of whom believers only are made partakers. Lastly, we receive this holy sacrament in the assembly of the people of God with humility and reverence, keeping up amongst us the death of Christ our Saviour, with thanksgiving: making there confession of our faith, and of the Christian religion. Therefore no one ought to come to this table without having previously rightly examined himself; lest by eating of this bread and drinking of this cup, he eat and drink judgment to himself. In a word, we are excited by the use of this holy sacrament, to a fervent love towards God and our neighbour. Therefore we reject all mixtures and damnable inventions, which men have added unto, and blended with the sacraments, as profanations of them: and affirm that we ought to rest satisfied with the ordinance which Christ and his apostles have taught us, and that we must speak of them in the same manner as they have spoken.

36. OF MAGISTRATES

We believe that our gracious God, because of the depravity of mankind, has appointed kings, princes and magistrates, willing that the world should be governed by certain laws and policies; to the end that the dissoluteness of men might be restrained and all things carried on among them with good order and decency. For this purpose he has invested the magistracy with the sword, for the punishment of evildoers, and for the protection of them that do well. And their office is, not only to have regard unto, and watch for the welfare of the civil state; but also that they protect the sacred ministry; and thus may remove and prevent all idolatry and false worship; that the kingdom of antichrist may be thus destroyed and the kingdom of Christ promoted. They must therefore countenance the preaching of the Word of the gospel everywhere, that God may be honoured and worshipped by every one, as he commands in his Word. Moreover, it is the bounden duty of every one, of what state, quality, or condition soever he may be, to subject himself to the magistrates; to pay tribute, to show due honour and respect to them, and to obey them in all things which are not repugnant to the Word of God; to supplicate for them in their prayers, that God may rule and guide them in all their ways, and that we may lead a quiet and peaceable life in all godliness and honesty. Wherefore we detest the Anabaptists and other seditious people, and in general all those who reject the higher powers and magistrates, and would subvert justice, introduce community of goods, and confound that decency and good order, which God has established among men.

37. OF THE LAST JUDGMENT

Finally we believe, according to the Word of God, when the time appointed by the Lord (which is unknown to all creatures) is come, and the number of the elect complete, that our Lord Jesus Christ will come from heaven, corporally and visibly, as he ascended, with great glory and majesty to declare himself judge of the quick and the dead; burning this old world with fire and flame, to cleanse it. And then all men will personally appear before this great judge, both men and women and children, that have been from the beginning of the world to the end thereof, being summoned by the voice of the archangel, and by the sound of the trumpet of God. For all the dead shall be raised out of the earth, and their souls joined and united with their proper bodies, in which they formerly lived. As for those who shall then be living, they shall not die as the others, but be changed in the twinkling of an eye, and from corruptible, become incorruptible. Then the books (that is to say the consciences) shall be opened, and the dead judged according to what they shall have done in this world, whether it be good or evil. Nay, all men shall give an account of every idle word they have spoken, which the world only counts amusement and jest; and then the secrets and hypocrisy of men shall be disclosed and laid open before all. And therefore the consideration of this judgment, is justly terrible and dreadful to the wicked and ungodly, but most desirable and comfortable to the righteous and elect: because then their full deliverance shall be perfected, and there they shall receive the fruits of their labour and trouble which they have borne. Their innocence shall be known to all, and they shall see the terrible vengeance which God shall execute on the wicked, who most cruelly persecuted, oppressed and tormented them in this world; and who shall be convicted by the testimony of their own consciences, and being immortal, shall be tormented in that everlasting fire, which is prepared for the devil and his angels. But on the contrary, the faithful and elect shall be crowned with glory and honour; and the Son of God will confess their names before God his Father, and his elect angels; all tears shall be wiped from their eyes; and their cause which is now condemned by many judges and magistrates, as heretical and impious, will then be known to be the cause of the Son of God. And for a gracious reward, the Lord will cause them to possess such a glory, as never entered into the heart of man to conceive. Therefore we expect that great day with a most ardent desire to the end that we may fully enjoy the promises of God in Christ Jesus our Lord.

AMEN. "Even so, come, Lord Jesus." — Rev. 22:20. ▪

Canons of Dort

At the turn of the 17th century, the teachings of Jacob Arminius (which reject predestination) were gaining traction in Dutch churches. Massive disputes were erupting between the Remonstrants (Dutch Arminians, who "remonstrated," or objected to, historic Calvinism) and the Gomarists (Dutch Calvinists, supporters of Franciscus Gomarus). In 1610, in a document called the Remonstrance, forty-three followers of Jacob Arminius wrote a statement of their Arminian beliefs in five major points: (1) election based on foreseen merit, (2) universal atonement, (3) man's free will, due to only partial depravity, (4) resistible grace, and (5) the possibility of losing one's salvation.

In the hopes of settling this dispute in the Netherlands and the Church at large, from November 1618–May 1619 church leaders from across Europe and Britain met in the Synod of Dort. They had to overcome massive political opposition, and even rioting, to get there. French Protestant church leaders were not able to attend at all, having been forbidden by Louis XIII to do so.

The synod went to Scripture to examine Arminian teaching. They found it to be unscriptural, and wrote out their conclusions in the Canons of Dort. The Synod structured their Canons into five points that directly answer the five Arminian points in the Remonstrance of 1610. In recent centuries, Reformed Christians have rearranged and summarized the main points in the Canons of Dort to create the Five Points of Calvinism, or TULIP: Total depravity, Unconditional election, Limited atonement, Irresistible grace, and Perseverance of the saints.

The Canons of Dort, the Belgic Confession, and the Heidelberg Catechism together became the Three Forms of Unity, the defining confessions of the Continental Reformed Church.

FIRST HEAD OF DOCTRINE: OF DIVINE PREDESTINATION

ARTICLE 1. As all men have sinned in Adam, lie under the curse, and are deserving of eternal death, God would have done no injustice by leaving them all to perish, and delivering them over to condemnation on account of sin, according to the words of the apostle, "that every mouth may be stopped, and all the world may become guilty before God" (Rom. 3:19). And verse 23: "For all have sinned, and come short of the glory of God." And Romans 6:23: "For the wages of sin is death."

ARTICLE 2. But in this the love of God was manifested, that He sent His only begotten Son into the world, that whosoever believeth on Him should not perish, but have everlasting life. "In this was manifested the love of God toward us, because that God sent His only begotten Son into the world, that we might live through Him" (1 John 4:9). "For God so loved the world, that He gave His only begotten Son, that whosoever believeth in Him should not perish, but have everlasting life" (John 3:16).

ARTICLE 3. And that men may be brought to believe, God mercifully sends the messengers of these most joyful tidings to whom He will and at what time He pleaseth; by whose ministry men are called to repentance and faith in Christ crucified. "How then shall they call on Him in whom they have not believed? and how shall they believe in Him of whom they have not heard? and how shall they hear without a preacher? And how shall they preach, except they be sent?" (Rom. 10:14-15).

ARTICLE 4. The wrath of God abideth upon those who believe not this gospel. But such as receive it, and embrace Jesus the Savior by a true and living faith, are by Him delivered from the wrath of God and from destruction, and have the gift of eternal life conferred upon them.

ARTICLE 5. The cause or guilt of this unbelief, as well as of all other sins, is no wise in God, but in man himself; whereas faith in Jesus Christ and salvation through Him is the free gift of God, as it is written: "For by grace are ye saved through faith; and that not of yourselves: it is the gift of God" (Eph. 2:8). "For unto you it is given in the behalf of Christ, not only to believe on Him," etc. (Phil. 1:29).

ARTICLE 6. That some receive the gift of faith from God and others do not receive it proceeds from God's eternal decree, for "known unto God are all His works from the beginning of the world" (Acts 15:18). "Who worketh all things after the counsel of His own will" (Eph. 1:11). According to which decree, He graciously softens the hearts of the elect, however obstinate, and inclines them to believe, while He leaves the non-elect in His just judgment to their own wickedness and obduracy. And herein is especially displayed the profound, the merciful, and at the same time the righteous discrimination between men, equally involved in ruin; or that decree of election and reprobation revealed in the Word of God, which though men of perverse, impure and unstable minds wrest to their own destruction, yet to holy and pious souls affords unspeakable consolation.

ARTICLE 7. Election is the unchangeable purpose of God, whereby, before the foundation of the world, He hath out of mere grace, according to the sovereign good pleasure of His own will, chosen, from the whole human race, which had fallen through their own fault from their primitive state of rectitude into sin and destruction, a certain number of persons to redemption in Christ, whom He from eternity appointed the Mediator and Head of the elect, and the foundation of salvation. This elect number, though by nature neither better nor more deserving than others, but with them involved in one common misery, God hath decreed to give to Christ, to be saved by Him, and effectually to call and draw them to His communion by His Word and Spirit, to bestow upon them true faith, justification and sanctification; and having powerfully preserved them in the fellowship of His Son, finally, to glorify them for the demonstration of His mercy and for the praise of His glorious grace, as it is written: "According as He hath chosen us in Him before the foundation of the world, that we should be holy and without blame before Him in love: having predestinated us unto the adoption of children by Jesus Christ to Himself, according to the good pleasure of His will, to the praise of the glory of His grace, wherein He hath made us accepted in the beloved" (Eph. 1:4-6). And elsewhere: "Whom He did predestinate, them He also called: and whom He called, them He also justified: and whom He justified them He also glorified" (Rom. 8:30).

ARTICLE 8. There are not various decrees of election, but one and the same decree respecting all those who shall be saved, both under the Old and New Testament; since the Scripture declares the good pleasure, purpose and counsel of the divine will to be one, according to which He hath chosen us from eternity, both to grace and glory, to salvation and the way of salvation, which He hath ordained that we should walk therein.

ARTICLE 9. This election was not founded upon foreseen faith, and the obedience of faith, holiness, or any other good quality or disposition in man, as the prerequisite, cause or condition on which it depended; but men are chosen to faith and to the obedience of faith, holiness, etc.; therefore election is the fountain of every saving good, from which proceeds faith, holiness, and the other gifts of salvation, and finally eternal life itself, as its fruits and effects, according to that of the apostle: "He hath chosen us [not because we were but][1] that we should be holy, and without blame, before Him in love" (Eph. 1:4).

ARTICLE 10. The good pleasure of God is the sole cause of this gracious election, which doth not consist herein, that out of all possible qualities and actions of men God has chosen some as a condition of salvation; but that He was pleased out of the common mass of sinners to adopt some certain persons as a peculiar people to Himself, as it is written, "For the children being not yet born, neither having done any good or evil," etc., it was said (namely to Rebecca): "The elder shall serve the younger. As it is written, Jacob have I loved, but Esau have I hated" (Rom. 9:11-13). "And as many as were ordained to eternal life believed" (Acts 13:48).

ARTICLE 11. And as God Himself is most wise, unchangeable, omniscient and omnipotent, so the election made by Him can neither be interrupted nor changed, recalled or annulled; neither can the elect be cast away, nor their number diminished.

ARTICLE 12. The elect in due time, though in various degrees and in different measures, attain the assurance of this their eternal and unchangeable election, not by inquisitively prying into the secret and deep things of God, but by observing in themselves, with a spiritual joy and holy pleasure, the infallible fruits of election pointed out in the Word of God—such as a true faith in Christ, filial fear, a godly sorrow for sin, a hungering and thirsting after righteousness, etc.

ARTICLE 13. The sense and certainty of this election afford to the children of God additional matter for daily humiliation before Him, for adoring the depth of His mercies, for cleansing themselves, and rendering grateful returns of ardent love to Him, who first manifested so great love towards them. The consideration of this doctrine of election is so far from encouraging remissness in the observance of the divine commands or from sinking men in carnal security, that these, in the just

---

1 Words in brackets original.

judgment of God, are the usual effects of rash presumption or of idle and wanton trifling with the grace of election in those who refuse to walk in the ways of the elect.

ARTICLE 14. As the doctrine of divine election by the most wise counsel of God was declared by the prophets, by Christ Himself, and by the apostles, and is clearly revealed in the Scriptures, both of the Old and New Testament, so it is still to be published in due time and place in the Church of God, for which it was peculiarly designed, provided it be done with reverence, in the spirit of discretion and piety, for the glory of God's most holy Name, and for enlivening and comforting His people, without vainly attempting to investigate the secret ways of the Most High. "For I have not shunned to declare unto you all the counsel of God" (Acts 20:27); "O the depth of the riches both of the wisdom and knowledge of God! how unsearchable are His judgments, and His ways past finding out! For who hath known the mind of the Lord? or who hath been His counsellor?" (Rom. 11:33-34); "For I say, through the grace given unto me, to every man that is among you, not to think of himself more highly than he ought to think; but to think soberly, according as God hath dealt to every man the measure of faith" (Rom. 12:3); "Wherein God, willing more abundantly to shew unto the heirs of promise the immutability of His counsel, confirmed it by an oath: that by two immutable things, in which it was impossible for God to lie, we might have a strong consolation, who have fled for refuge to lay hold upon the hope set before us" (Heb. 6:17-18).

ARTICLE 15. What peculiarly tends to illustrate and recommend to us the eternal and unmerited grace of election, is the express testimony of sacred Scripture that not all, but some only are elected, while others are passed by in the eternal decree; whom God, out of His sovereign, most just, irreprehensible and unchangeable good pleasure, hath decreed to leave in the common misery into which they have willfully plunged themselves, and not to bestow upon them saving faith and the grace of conversion; but permitting them in His just judgment to follow their own ways, at last for the declaration of His justice, to condemn and perish them forever, not only on account of their unbelief, but also for all their other sins. And this is the decree of reprobation which by no means makes God the author of sin (the very thought of which is blasphemy), but declares Him to be an awful, irreprehensible, and righteous Judge and avenger thereof.

ARTICLE 16. Those who do not yet experience a lively faith in Christ, an assured confidence of soul, peace of conscience, an earnest endeavor after filial obedience, and glorying in God through Christ, efficaciously wrought in them, and do nevertheless persist in the use of the means which God hath appointed for working these graces in us, ought not to be alarmed at the mention of reprobation, nor to rank themselves among the reprobate, but diligently to persevere in the use of means, and with ardent desires devoutly and humbly to wait for a season of richer grace. Much less cause have they to be terrified by the doctrine of reprobation, who, though they seriously desire to be turned to God, to please Him only, and to be delivered from the body of death, cannot yet reach that measure of holiness and faith to which they aspire; since a merciful God has promised that He will not quench the smoking flax nor break the bruised reed. But this doctrine is justly terrible to those, who, regardless of God and of the Savior Jesus Christ, have wholly given themselves up to the cares of the world and the pleasures of the flesh, so long as they are not seriously converted to God.

ARTICLE 17. Since we are to judge of the will of God from His Word which testifies that the children of believers are holy, not by nature, but in virtue of the covenant of grace, in which they, together with the parents, are comprehended, godly parents have no reason to doubt of the election and salvation of their children whom it pleaseth God to call out of this life in their infancy.

ARTICLE 18. To those who murmur at the free grace of election and just severity of reprobation, we answer with the apostle: "Nay but, O man, who art thou that repliest against God?" (Rom. 9:20), and quote the language of our Savior: "Is it not lawful for Me to do what I will with Mine own?" (Matt. 20:15). And therefore with holy adoration of these mysteries, we exclaim in the words of the apostle: "O the depth of the riches both of the wisdom and knowledge of God! how unsearchable are His judgments, and His ways past finding out! For who hath known the mind of the Lord? or who hath been His counsellor? Or who hath first given to Him, and it shall be recompensed unto him again? For of Him, and through Him, and to Him, are all things: to whom be glory for ever. Amen" (Rom. 11:33- 36).

REJECTIONS

The true doctrine concerning election and rejection having been explained, the Synod rejects the errors of those who teach:

REJECTION 1. That the will of God to save those who would believe and would persevere in faith and in the obedience of faith, is the whole and entire decree of election unto salvation, and that nothing else concerning this decree has been revealed in God's Word.

For these deceive the simple and plainly contradict the Scriptures which declare that God will not only save those who will believe, but that He has also from eternity chosen certain particular persons to whom above others He in time will grant both faith in Christ and perseverance, as it is written: "I have manifested Thy Name unto the men which Thou gavest Me out of the world" (John 17:6). "And as many as were ordained to eternal life believed" (Acts 13:48). And: "According as He hath chosen us in Him before the foundation of the world, that we should be holy and without blame before Him in love" (Eph. 1:4).

REJECTION 2. That there are various kinds of election of God unto eternal life: the one general and indefinite, the other particular and definite; and that the latter in turn is either incomplete, revocable, non-decisive and conditional, or complete, irrevocable, decisive and absolute. Likewise: that there is one election unto faith and another unto salvation, so that election can be unto justifying faith without being a decisive election unto salvation.

For this is a fancy of men's minds, invented regardless of the Scriptures, whereby the doctrine of election is corrupted, and this golden chain of our salvation is broken: "Moreover whom He did predestinate, them He also called: and whom He called, them He also justified: and whom He justified, them He also glorified" (Rom. 8:30).

REJECTION 3. That the good pleasure and purpose of God, of which Scripture makes mention in the doctrine of election, does not consist in this, that God chose certain persons rather than others, but in this, that He chose out of all possible conditions (among which are also the works of the law), or out of the whole order of things, the act of faith which from its very nature is undeserving, as well as its incomplete obedience, as a condition of salvation, and that He would graciously consider this in itself as a complete obedience and count it worthy of the reward of eternal life.

For by this injurious error the pleasure of God and the merits of Christ are made of none effect, and men are drawn away by useless questions from the truth of gracious justification and from the simplicity of Scripture, and this declaration of the apostle is charged as untrue: "Who hath saved us, and called us with an holy calling, not according to our works, but according to His own purpose and grace, which was given us in Christ Jesus before the world began" (2 Tim. 1:9).

REJECTION 4. That in the election unto faith this condition is beforehand demanded, namely, that man should use the light of nature aright, be pious, humble, meek, and fit for eternal life, as if on these things election were in any way dependent.

For this savors of the teaching of Pelagius, and is opposed to the doctrine of the apostle, when he writes: "Among whom also we all had our conversation in times past in the lusts of our flesh, fulfilling the desires of the flesh and of the mind; and were by nature the children of wrath, even as others. But God, who is rich in mercy, for His great love wherewith He loved us, even when we were dead in sins, hath quickened us together with Christ, (by grace ye are saved); and hath raised us up together, and made us sit together in heavenly places in Christ Jesus: that in the ages to come He might show the exceeding riches of His grace in His kindness toward us through Christ Jesus. For by grace are ye saved through faith; and that not of yourselves: it is the gift of God: not of works, lest any man should boast" (Eph. 2:3-9).

REJECTION 5. That the incomplete and non-decisive election of particular persons to salvation occurred because of a foreseen faith, conversion, holiness, godliness, which either began or continued for some time; but that the complete and decisive election occurred because of foreseen perseverance unto the end in faith, conversion, holiness and godliness; and that this is the gracious and evangelical worthiness for the sake of which he who is chosen is more worthy than he who is not chosen; and that therefore faith, the obedience of faith, holiness, godliness and perseverance are not fruits of the unchangeable election unto glory, but are conditions, which, being required beforehand, were foreseen as being met by those who will be fully elected, and are causes without which the unchangeable election to glory does not occur.

This is repugnant to the entire Scripture which constantly inculcates this and similar declarations: Election is not out of works, but of Him that calleth. "That the purpose of God according to election might stand, not of works, but of Him that calleth" (Rom. 9:11). "And as many as were ordained to eternal life believed" (Acts 13:48). "He hath chosen us in Him before the foundation of the world, that we should be holy" (Eph. 1:4). "Ye have not chosen Me, but I have chosen you" (John 15:16). "But if it be of works, then is it no more grace" (Rom. 11:6). "Herein is love, not that we loved God, but that He loved us, and sent His Son" (1 John 4:10).

REJECTION 6. That not every election unto salvation is unchangeable, but that some of the elect, any decree of God notwithstanding, can yet perish and do indeed perish.

By which gross error they make God to be changeable, and destroy the comfort which the godly obtain out of the firmness of their election, and contradict the Holy Scripture which teaches that the elect cannot be led astray: "Insomuch that, if it were possible, they shall deceive the very elect" (Matt. 24:24); that Christ does not lose those whom the Father gave Him: "And this is the Father's will which hath sent Me, that of all which He hath given Me I should lose nothing" (John 6:39); and that God hath also glorified those whom He foreordained, called and justified: "Moreover whom He did predestinate, them He also called: and whom He called, them He also justified: and whom He justified, them He also glorified" (Rom. 8:30).

REJECTION 7. That there is in this life no fruit and no consciousness of the unchangeable election to glory, nor any certainty, except that which depends on a changeable and uncertain condition.

For not only is it absurd to speak of an uncertain certainty, but also contrary to the experience of the saints, who by virtue of the consciousness of their election rejoice with the apostle and praise this favor of God, Ephesians 1; who according to Christ's admonition rejoice with His disciples that their names are written in heaven, "but rather rejoice, because your names are written in heaven" (Luke 10:20); who also place the consciousness of their election over against the fiery darts of the devil, asking: "Who shall lay any thing to the charge of God's elect?" (Rom. 8:33).

REJECTION 8. That God, simply by virtue of His righteous will, did not decide either to leave anyone in the fall of Adam and in the common state of sin and condemnation, or to pass anyone by in the communication of grace which is necessary for faith and conversion.

For this is firmly decreed: "Therefore hath He mercy on whom He will have mercy, and whom He will He hardeneth" (Rom. 9:18). And also this: "It is given unto you to know the mysteries of the kingdom of heaven, but to them it is not given" (Matt. 13:11). Likewise: "I thank Thee, O Father, Lord of heaven and earth, because Thou hast hid these things from the wise and prudent, and hast revealed them unto babes. Even so, Father: for so it seemed good in Thy sight" (Matt. 11:25-26).

REJECTION 9. That the reason why God sends the gospel to one people rather than to another is not merely and solely the good pleasure of God, but rather the fact that one people is better and worthier than another to whom the gospel is not communicated.

For this Moses denies, addressing the people of Israel as follows: "Behold, the heaven and the heaven of heavens is the LORD's thy God, the earth also, with all that therein is. Only the LORD had a delight in thy fathers to love them, and He chose their seed after them, even you above all people, as it is this day" (Deut. 10:14-15). And Christ said: "Woe unto thee, Chorazin! woe unto thee, Bethsaida! for if the mighty works, which were done in you, had been done in Tyre and Sidon, they would have repented long ago in sackcloth and ashes" (Matt. 11:21).

SECOND HEAD OF DOCTRINE: OF THE DEATH OF CHRIST AND THE REDEMPTION OF MEN THEREBY

ARTICLE 1. God is not only supremely merciful, but also supremely just. And His justice requires (as He hath revealed Himself in His Word), that our sins committed against His infinite majesty should be punished, not only with temporal, but with eternal punishment, both in body and soul; which we cannot escape unless satisfaction be made to the justice of God.

ARTICLE 2. Since therefore we are unable to make that satisfaction in our own persons or to deliver ourselves from the wrath of God, He hath been pleased in

His infinite mercy to give His only begotten Son, for our surety, who was made sin, and became a curse for us and in our stead, that He might make satisfaction to divine justice on our behalf.

ARTICLE 3. The death of the Son of God is the only and most perfect sacrifice and satisfaction for sin, and is of infinite worth and value, abundantly sufficient to expiate the sins of the whole world.

ARTICLE 4. This death derives its infinite value and dignity from these considerations because the person who submitted to it was not only really man and perfectly holy, but also the only begotten Son of God, of the same eternal and infinite essence with the Father and the Holy Spirit, which qualifications were necessary to constitute Him a Savior for us; and because it was attended with a sense of the wrath and curse of God due to us for sin.

ARTICLE 5. Moreover, the promise of the gospel is, that whosoever believeth in Christ crucified, shall not perish, but have everlasting life. This promise, together with the command to repent and believe, ought to be declared and published to all nations, and to all persons promiscuously and without distinction, to whom God out of His good pleasure sends the gospel.

ARTICLE 6. And whereas many who are called by the gospel do not repent nor believe in Christ, but perish in unbelief, this is not owing to any defect or insufficiency in the sacrifice offered by Christ upon the cross, but is wholly to be imputed to themselves.

ARTICLE 7. But as many as truly believe, and are delivered and saved from sin and destruction through the death of Christ, are indebted for this benefit solely to the grace of God, given them in Christ from everlasting, and not to any merit of their own.

ARTICLE 8. For this was the sovereign counsel, and most gracious will and purpose of God the Father, that the quickening and saving efficacy of the most precious death of His Son should extend to all the elect, for bestowing upon them alone the gift of justifying faith, thereby to bring them infallibly to salvation: that is, it was the will of God, that Christ by the blood of the cross, whereby He confirmed the new covenant, should effectually redeem out of every people, tribe, nation, and language, all those, and those only, who were from eternity chosen to salvation and given to Him by the Father; that He should confer upon them faith, which together with all the other saving gifts of the Holy Spirit, He purchased for them by His death; should purge them from all sin, both original and actual, whether committed before or after believing; and having faithfully preserved them even to the end, should at last bring them free from every spot and blemish to the enjoyment of glory in His own presence forever.

ARTICLE 9. This purpose proceeding from everlasting love towards the elect has from the beginning of the world to this day been powerfully accomplished, and will henceforward still continue to be accomplished, notwithstanding all the ineffectual opposition of the gates of hell, so that the elect in due time may be gathered together into one, and that there never may be wanting a church composed of believers, the foundation of which is laid in the blood of Christ, which may steadfastly love and faithfully serve Him as their Savior, who as a bridegroom for his bride, laid down His life for them upon the cross, and which may celebrate His praises here and through all eternity.

REJECTIONS

The true doctrine (concerning redemption) having been explained, the Synod rejects the errors of those who teach:

REJECTION 1. That God the Father has ordained His Son to the death of the cross without a certain and definite decree to save any, so that the necessity, profitableness and worth of what Christ merited by His death might have existed, and might remain in all its parts complete, perfect and intact, even if the merited redemption had never in fact been applied to any person.

For this doctrine tends to the despising of the wisdom of the Father and of the merits of Jesus Christ, and is contrary to Scripture. For thus saith our Savior: "I lay down My life for the sheep, and I know them" (John 10:15, 27). And the prophet Isaiah saith concerning the Savior: "When thou shalt make His soul an offering for sin, He shall see His seed, He shall prolong his days, and the pleasure of the LORD shall prosper in his hand" (Is. 53:10). Finally, this contradicts the article of faith according to which we believe the catholic[2] Christian church.

2 The word *catholic* is an adjective from the Greek word *katholikos*, which means "universal" or "concerning the whole." It is here referring to the whole Body of Christ, the saints of God worldwide, in the past, present, and future. It does not refer to Roman Catholicism.

REJECTION 2. That it was not the purpose of the death of Christ that He should confirm the new covenant of grace through His blood, but only that He should acquire for the Father the mere right to establish with man such a covenant as He might please, whether of grace or of works.

For this is repugnant to Scripture which teaches that Christ has become the Surety and Mediator of a better, that is, the new covenant, and that a testament is of force where death has occurred. "By so much was Jesus made a surety of a better testament" (Heb. 7:22); "And for this cause He is the Mediator of the new testament, that by means of death, for the redemption of the transgressions that were under the first testament, they which are called might receive the promise of eternal inheritance"; "For a testament is of force after men are dead: otherwise it is of no strength at all while the testator liveth" (Heb. 9:15, 17).

REJECTION 3. That Christ by His satisfaction merited neither salvation itself for anyone, nor faith, whereby this satisfaction of Christ unto salvation is effectually appropriated; but that He merited for the Father only the authority or the perfect will to deal again with man, and to prescribe new conditions as He might desire, obedience to which, however, depended on the free will of man, so that it therefore might have come to pass that either none or all should fulfill these conditions.

For these adjudge too contemptuously of the death of Christ, do in no wise acknowledge the most important fruit or benefit thereby gained, and bring again out of hell the Pelagian error.

REJECTION 4. That the new covenant of grace, which God the Father, through the mediation of the death of Christ, made with man, does not herein consist that we by faith, inasmuch as it accepts the merits of Christ, are justified before God and saved, but in the fact that God having revoked the demand of perfect obedience of faith, regards faith itself and the obedience of faith, although imperfect, as the perfect obedience of the law, and does esteem it worthy of the reward of eternal life through grace.

For these contradict the Scriptures: "Being justified freely by His grace through the redemption that is in Christ Jesus: whom God hath set forth to be a propitiation through faith in His blood" (Rom. 3:24-25). And these proclaim, as did the wicked Socinus, a new and strange justification of man before God against the consensus of the whole church.

REJECTION 5. That all men have been accepted unto the state of reconciliation and unto the grace of the covenant, so that no one is worthy of condemnation on account of original sin, and that no one shall be condemned because of it, but that all are free from the guilt of original sin.

For this opinion is repugnant to Scripture which teaches that we are by nature children of wrath (Eph. 2:3).

REJECTION 6. The use of the difference between meriting and appropriating, to the end that they may instill into the minds of the imprudent and inexperienced this teaching that God, as far as He is concerned, has been minded of applying to all equally the benefits gained by the death of Christ; but that, while some obtain the pardon of sin and eternal life, and others do not, this difference depends on their own free will, which joins itself to the grace that is offered without exception, and that it is not dependent on the special gift of mercy, which powerfully works in them, that they rather than others should appropriate unto themselves this grace.

For these, while they feign that they present this distinction in a sound sense, seek to instill into the people the destructive poison of the Pelagian errors.

REJECTION 7. That Christ neither could die, needed to die, nor did die for those whom God loved in the highest degree and elected to eternal life, and did not die for these, since these do not need the death of Christ.

For they contradict the apostle, who declares: "the Son of God, who loved me, and gave Himself for me" (Gal. 2:20). Likewise: "Who shall lay any thing to the charge of God's elect? It is God that justifieth. Who is he that condemneth? It is Christ that died" (Rom. 8:33-34), namely, for them; and the Savior who says: "I lay down My life for the sheep" (John 10:15). And: "This is My commandment, That ye love one another, as I have loved you. Greater love hath no man than this, that a man lay down his life for his friends" (John 15:12-13).

THIRD AND FOURTH HEADS OF DOCTRINE: OF THE CORRUPTION OF MAN, HIS CONVERSION TO GOD, AND THE MANNER THEREOF

ARTICLE 1. Man was originally formed after the image of God. His understanding was adorned with a true and saving knowledge of his Creator and of spiritual things; his heart and will were upright; all his affections pure; and the whole man was holy; but revolting from God by the instigation of the devil, and abusing the freedom of his own will, he forfeited these excellent gifts; and on the contrary entailed on himself blindness of mind, horrible darkness, vanity and perverseness of judgment, became wicked, rebellious, and obdurate in heart and will, and impure in his affections.

ARTICLE 2. Man after the fall begat children in his own likeness. A corrupt stock produced a corrupt offspring. Hence all the posterity of Adam, Christ only excepted, have derived corruption from their original parent, not by imitation, as the Pelagians of old asserted, but by the propagation of a vicious nature.

ARTICLE 3. Therefore all men are conceived in sin, and by nature children of wrath, incapable of saving good, prone to evil, dead in sin, and in bondage thereto, and without the regenerating grace of the Holy Spirit, they are neither able nor willing to return to God, to reform the depravity of their nature, or to dispose themselves to reformation.

ARTICLE 4. There remain, however, in man since the fall, the glimmerings of natural light, whereby he retains some knowledge of God, of natural things, and of the differences between good and evil, and discovers some regard for virtue, good order in society, and for maintaining an orderly external deportment. But so far is this light of nature from being sufficient to bring him to a saving knowledge of God and to true conversion, that he is incapable of using it aright even in things natural and civil. Nay, further, this light, such as it is, man in various ways renders wholly polluted and holds it in unrighteousness, by doing which he becomes inexcusable before God.

ARTICLE 5. In the same light are we to consider the law of the decalogue, delivered by God to His peculiar people the Jews by the hands of Moses. For though it discovers the greatness of sin, and more and more convinces man thereof, yet as it neither points out a remedy nor imparts strength to extricate him from misery, and thus being weak through the flesh leaves the transgressor under the curse, man cannot by this law obtain saving grace.

ARTICLE 6. What therefore neither the light of nature, nor the law could do, that God performs by the operation of the Holy Spirit through the Word or ministry of reconciliation, which is the glad tidings concerning the Messiah, by means whereof it hath pleased God to save such as believe, as well under the Old, as under the New Testament.

ARTICLE 7. This mystery of His will God discovered to but a small number under the Old Testament; under the New (the distinction between various peoples having been removed), He reveals Himself to many without any distinction of people. The cause of this dispensation is not to be ascribed to the superior worth of one nation above another, nor to their making a better use of the light of nature, but results wholly from the sovereign good pleasure and unmerited love of God. Hence they, to whom so great and so gracious a blessing is communicated above their desert, or rather notwithstanding their demerits, are bound to acknowledge it with humble and grateful hearts, and with the apostle to adore, not curiously to pry into the severity and justice of God's judgments displayed to others, to whom this grace is not given.

ARTICLE 8. As many as are called by the gospel are unfeignedly called. For God hath most earnestly and truly declared in His Word what will be acceptable to Him; namely, that all who are called, should comply with the invitation. He, moreover, seriously promises eternal life and rest to as many as shall come to Him and believe on Him.

ARTICLE 9. It is not the fault of the gospel nor of Christ, offered therein, nor of God, who calls men by the gospel and confers upon them various gifts, that those who are called by the ministry of the Word refuse to come and be converted. The fault lies in themselves, some of whom when called, regardless of their danger, reject the word of life; others, though they receive it, suffer it not to make a lasting impression on their heart; therefore, their joy, arising only from a temporary faith, soon vanishes and they fall away; while others choke the seed of the Word by perplexing cares and the pleasures of this world, and produce no fruit. This our Savior teaches in the parable of the sower (Matt. 13).

ARTICLE 10. But that others who are called by the gospel obey the call and are converted is not to be ascribed to the proper exercise of free will, whereby one distinguishes himself above others, equally furnished with grace sufficient for faith and conversions as the proud heresy of Pelagius maintains; but it must be wholly ascribed to God, who as He has chosen His own from eternity in Christ, so He confers upon them faith and repentance, rescues them from the power of darkness, and translates them into the kingdom of His own Son, that they may show forth the praises of Him who hath called them out of darkness into His marvelous light; and may glory not in themselves, but in the Lord according to the testimony of the apostles in various places.

ARTICLE 11. But when God accomplishes His good pleasure in the elect or works in them true conversion, He not only causes the gospel to be externally preached to them and powerfully illuminates their mind by His Holy Spirit, that they may rightly understand and discern the things of the Spirit of God; but by the efficacy of the same regenerating Spirit, pervades the inmost recesses of the man; He opens the closed, and softens the hardened heart, and circumcises that which was uncircumcised, infuses new qualities into the will, which though heretofore dead, He quickens; from being evil, disobedient, and refractory, He renders it good, obedient, and pliable; actuates and strengthens it, that like a good tree, it may bring forth the fruits of good actions.

ARTICLE 12. And this is the regeneration so highly celebrated in Scripture and denominated a new creation: a resurrection from the dead, a making alive, which God works in us without our aid. But this is in no wise effected merely by the external preaching of the gospel, by moral suasion, or such a mode of operation, that after God has performed His part, it still remains in the power of man to be regenerated or not, to be converted or to continue unconverted; but it is evidently a supernatural work, most powerful, and at the same time most delightful, astonishing, mysterious, and ineffable; not inferior in efficacy to creation or the resurrection from the dead, as the Scripture inspired by the author of this work declares; so that all in whose heart God works in this marvelous manner are certainly, infallibly, and effectually regenerated, and do actually believe. Whereupon the will thus renewed is not only actuated and influenced by God, but in consequence of this influence, becomes itself active. Wherefore also, man is himself rightly said to believe and repent, by virtue of that grace received.

ARTICLE 13. The manner of this operation cannot be fully comprehended by believers in this life. Notwithstanding which, they rest satisfied with knowing and experiencing that by this grace of God they are enabled to believe with the heart, and love their Savior.

ARTICLE 14. Faith is therefore to be considered as the gift of God, not on account of its being offered by God to man, to be accepted or rejected at his pleasure; but because it is in reality conferred, breathed, and infused into him; or even because God bestows the power or ability to believe, and then expects that man should by the exercise of his own free will, consent to the terms of salvation and actually believe in Christ; but because He who works in man both to will and to do, and indeed all things in all, produces both the will to believe and the act of believing also.

ARTICLE 15. God is under no obligation to confer this grace upon any; for how can He be indebted to man, who had no previous gifts to bestow, as a foundation for such recompense? Nay, who has nothing of his own but sin and falsehood? He therefore who becomes the subject of this grace, owes eternal gratitude to God, and gives Him thanks forever. Whoever is not made partaker thereof, is either altogether regardless of these spiritual gifts and satisfied with his own condition, or is in no apprehension of danger and vainly boasts the possession of that which he has not. With respect to those who make an external profession of faith and live regular lives, we are bound, after the example of the apostle, to judge and speak of them in the most favorable manner. For the secret recesses of the heart are unknown to us. And as to others, who have not yet been called, it is our duty to pray for them to God, who calls the things that are not, as if they were. But we are in no wise to conduct ourselves towards them with haughtiness, as if we had made ourselves to differ.

ARTICLE 16. But as man by the fall did not cease to be a creature endowed with understanding and will, nor did sin which pervaded the whole race of mankind deprive him of the human nature, but brought upon him depravity and spiritual death; so also this grace of regeneration does not treat men as senseless stocks and blocks, nor takes away their will and its properties, neither does violence thereto; but spiritually quickens, heals, corrects, and at the same time sweetly and powerfully bends it; that where carnal rebellion and resistance formerly prevailed, a ready and sincere spiritual obedience begins to reign, in which the true and spiritual restoration and freedom of our will consist. Wherefore unless the admirable Author of every good work wrought in us, man could have no hope of recovering from his fall by his own free will, by the abuse of which, in a state of innocence, he plunged himself into ruin.

ARTICLE 17. As the almighty operation of God, whereby He prolongs and supports this our natural life, does not exclude, but requires the use of means, by which God of His infinite mercy and goodness hath chosen to exert His influence, so also the before-mentioned supernatural operation of God, by which we are regenerated, in no wise excludes or subverts the use of the gospel, which the most wise God has ordained to be the seed of regeneration and food of the soul. Wherefore, as the apostles, and teachers who succeeded them, piously instructed the people concerning this grace of God, to His glory, and the abasement of all pride, and in the meantime, however, neglected not to keep them by the sacred precepts of the gospel in the exercise of the Word, sacraments and discipline; so even to this day, be it far from either instructors or instructed to presume to tempt God in the church by separating what He of His good pleasure hath most intimately joined together. For grace is conferred by means of admonitions; and the more readily we perform our duty, the more eminent usually is this blessing of God working in us, and the more directly is His work advanced; to whom alone all the glory both of means, and of their saving fruit and efficacy is forever due. Amen.

REJECTIONS

The true doctrine (concerning corruption and conversion) having been explained, the Synod rejects the errors of those who teach:

REJECTION 1. That it cannot properly be said that original sin in itself suffices to condemn the whole human race or to deserve temporal and eternal punishment.

For these contradict the apostle, who declares: "Wherefore, as by one man sin entered into the world, and death by sin; and so death passed upon all men, for that all have sinned" (Rom. 5:12). And: "The judgment was by one to condemnation" (Rom. 5:16). And: "The wages of sin is death" (Rom. 6:23).

REJECTION 2. That the spiritual gifts or the good qualities and virtues, such as goodness, holiness, righteousness, could not belong to the will of man when he was first created, and that these, therefore, could not have been separated therefrom in the fall.

For such is contrary to the description of the image of God which the apostle gives in Ephesians 4:24, where he declares that it consists in righteousness and holiness, which undoubtedly belong to the will.

REJECTION 3. That in spiritual death the spiritual gifts are not separate from the will of man, since the will in itself has never been corrupted, but only hindered through the darkness of the understanding and the irregularity of the affections; and that, these hindrances having been removed, the will can then bring into operation its native powers, that is, that the will of itself is able to will and to choose, or not to will and not to choose, all manner of good which may be presented to it.

This is an innovation and an error, and tends to elevate the powers of the free will, contrary to the declaration of the prophet: "The heart is deceitful above all things, and desperately wicked" (Jer. 17:9); and of the apostle: "Among whom (sons of disobedience) also we all had our conversation in times past in the lusts of our flesh, fulfilling the desires of the flesh and of the mind" (Eph. 2:3).

REJECTION 4. That the unregenerate man is not really nor utterly dead in sin, nor destitute of all powers unto spiritual good, but that he can yet hunger and thirst after righteousness and life, and offer the sacrifice of a contrite and broken spirit, which is pleasing to God.

For these are contrary to the express testimony of Scripture. "Who were dead in trespasses and sins"; "Even when we were dead in sins" (Eph. 2:1, 5); and: "every imagination of the thoughts of his heart was only evil continually" (Gen. 6:5); "for the imagination of man's heart is evil from his youth" (Gen. 8:21). Moreover, to hunger and thirst after deliverance from misery, and after life, and to offer unto God the sacrifice of a broken spirit, is peculiar to the regenerate and those that are called blessed. "Create in me a clean heart, O God; and renew a right spirit within me"; "Then shalt Thou be pleased with the sacrifices of righteousness, with burnt offering and whole burnt offering: then shall they offer bullocks upon Thine altar" (Ps. 51:10, 19); "Blessed are they which do hunger and thirst after righteousness: for they shall be filled" (Matt. 5:6).

REJECTION 5. That the corrupt and natural man can so well use the common grace (by which they understand the light of nature), or the gifts still left him after the fall, that he can gradually gain by their good use a greater, namely, the evangelical or saving grace and salvation itself. And that in this way God on His part shows

Himself ready to reveal Christ unto all men, since He applies to all sufficiently and efficiently the means necessary to conversion.

For the experience of all ages and the Scriptures do both testify that this is untrue. "He sheweth His word unto Jacob, His statutes and His judgments unto Israel. He hath not dealt so with any nation: and as for His judgments, they have not known them" (Ps. 147:19, 20). "Who in times past suffered all nations to walk in their own ways" (Acts 14:16). And: "Now when they (Paul and his companions) had gone throughout Phrygia and the region of Galatia, and were forbidden of the Holy Ghost to preach the word in Asia, after they were come to Mysia, they assayed to go into Bithynia: but the Spirit suffered them not" (Acts 16:6, 7).

REJECTION 6. That in the true conversion of man no new qualities, powers or gifts can be infused by God into the will, and that therefore faith through which we are first converted, and because of which we are called believers, is not a quality or gift infused by God, but only an act of man, and that it cannot be said to be a gift, except in respect of the power to attain to this faith.

For thereby they contradict the Holy Scriptures which declare that God infuses new qualities of faith, of obedience, and of the consciousness of His love into our hearts: "I will put My law in their inward parts, and write it in their hearts" (Jer. 31:33). And: "I will pour water upon him that is thirsty, and floods upon the dry ground: I will pour My Spirit upon thy seed" (Is. 44:3). And: "the love of God is shed abroad in our hearts by the Holy Ghost which is given unto us" (Rom. 5:5). This is also repugnant to the continuous practice of the Church, which prays by the mouth of the prophet thus: "turn Thou me, and I shall be turned" (Jer. 31:18).

REJECTION 7. That the grace whereby we are converted to God is only a gentle advising, or (as others explain it), that this is the noblest manner of working in the conversion of man, and that this manner of working, which consists in advising, is most in harmony with man's nature; and that there is no reason why this advising grace alone should not be sufficient to make the natural man spiritual, indeed, that God does not produce the consent of the will except through this manner of advising; and that the power of the divine working, whereby it surpasses the working of Satan, consists in this, that God promises eternal, while Satan promises only temporal goods.

But this is altogether Pelagian and contrary to the whole Scripture which, besides this, teaches yet another and far more powerful and divine manner of the Holy Spirit's working in the conversion of man, as in Ezekiel: "A new heart also will I give you, and a new spirit will I put within you: and I will take away the stony heart out of your flesh, and I will give you an heart of flesh" (Ezek. 36:26).

REJECTION 8. That God in the regeneration of man does not use such powers of His omnipotence as potently and infallibly bend man's will to faith and conversion; but that all the works of grace having been accomplished, which God employs to convert man, man may yet so resist God and the Holy Spirit when God intends man's regeneration and wills to regenerate him, and indeed that man often does so resist that he prevents entirely his regeneration, and that it therefore remains in man's power to be regenerated or not.

For this is nothing less than the denial of all the efficiency of God's grace in our conversion, and the subjecting of the working of the Almighty God to the will of man, which is contrary to the apostles, who teach: "who believe, according to the working of His mighty power" (Eph. 1:19). And: "That our God would... fulfill all the good pleasure of His goodness, and the work of faith with power" (2 Thess. 1:11). And: "According as His divine power hath given unto us all things that pertain unto life and godliness" (2 Pet. 1:3).

REJECTION 9. That grace and free will are partial causes, which together work the beginning of conversion, and that grace, in order of working, does not precede the working of the will; that is, that God does not efficiently help the will of man unto conversion until the will of man moves and determines to do this.

For the ancient Church has long ago condemned this doctrine of the Pelagians according to the words of the apostle: "So then it is not of him that willeth, nor of him that runneth, but of God that sheweth mercy" (Rom. 9:16). Likewise: "For who maketh thee to differ from another? and what hast thou that thou didst not receive?" (1 Cor. 4:7). And: "For it is God which worketh in you both to will and to do of His good pleasure" (Phil. 2:13).

FIFTH HEAD OF DOCTRINE: OF THE PERSEVERANCE OF THE SAINTS

ARTICLE 1. Whom God calls, according to His purpose, to the communion of His Son, our Lord Jesus Christ, and regenerates by the Holy Spirit, He delivers also from the dominion and slavery of sin in this life; though not altogether from the body of sin and from the infirmities of the flesh, so long as they continue in this world.

ARTICLE 2. Hence spring daily sins of infirmity, and hence spots adhere to the best works of the saints, which furnish them with constant matter for humiliation before God, and flying for refuge to Christ crucified; for mortifying the flesh more and more by the spirit of prayer, and by holy exercises of piety; and for pressing forward to the goal of perfection, till being at length delivered from this body of death, they are brought to reign with the Lamb of God in heaven.

ARTICLE 3. By reason of these remains of indwelling sin, and the temptations of sin and of the world, those who are converted could not persevere in a state of grace if left to their own strength. But God is faithful, who having conferred grace, mercifully confirms and powerfully preserves them therein, even to the end.

ARTICLE 4. Although the weakness of the flesh cannot prevail against the power of God, who confirms and preserves true believers in a state of grace, yet converts are not always so influenced and actuated by the Spirit of God, as not in some particular instances sinfully to deviate from the guidance of divine grace, so as to be seduced by, and comply with the lusts of the flesh; they must, therefore, be constant in watching and prayer that they be not led into temptation. When these are neglected, they are not only liable to be drawn into great and heinous sins by Satan, the world and the flesh, but sometimes by the righteous permission of God actually fall into these evils. This the lamentable fall of David, Peter, and other saints described in Holy Scripture demonstrates.

ARTICLE 5. By such enormous sins, however, they very highly offend God, incur a deadly guilt, grieve the Holy Spirit, interrupt the exercise of faith, very grievously wound their consciences, and sometimes lose the sense of God's favor for a time, until on their returning into the right way of serious repentance, the light of God's fatherly countenance again shines upon them.

ARTICLE 6. But God, who is rich in mercy, according to His unchangeable purpose of election, does not wholly withdraw the Holy Spirit from His own people, even in their melancholy falls; nor suffers them to proceed so far as to lose the grace of adoption, and forfeit the state of justification, or to commit the sin unto death; nor does He permit them to be totally deserted, and to plunge themselves into everlasting destruction.

ARTICLE 7. For in the first place, in these falls He preserves in them the incorruptible seed of regeneration from perishing or being totally lost; and again, by His Word and Spirit, certainly and effectually renews them to repentance, to a sincere and godly sorrow for their sins, that they may seek and obtain remission in the blood of the Mediator, may again experience the favor of a reconciled God, through faith adore His mercies, and henceforward more diligently work out their own salvation with fear and trembling.

ARTICLE 8. Thus, it is not in consequence of their own merits or strength, but of God's free mercy, that they do not totally fall from faith and grace, nor continue and perish finally in their backslidings; which, with respect to themselves, is not only possible, but would undoubtedly happen; but with respect to God, it is utterly impossible, since His counsel cannot be changed nor His promise fail, neither can the call according to His purpose be revoked, nor the merit, intercession and preservation of Christ be rendered ineffectual, nor the sealing of the Holy Spirit be frustrated or obliterated.

ARTICLE 9. Of this preservation of the elect to salvation and of their perseverance in the faith, true believers for themselves may and do obtain assurance according to the measure of their faith, whereby they arrive at the certain persuasion that they ever will continue true and living members of the church; and that they experience forgiveness of sins, and will at last inherit eternal life.

ARTICLE 10. This assurance, however, is not produced by any peculiar revelation contrary to, or independent of the Word of God; but springs from faith in God's promises, which He has most abundantly revealed in His Word for our comfort; from the testimony of the Holy Spirit witnessing with our spirit that we are children and heirs of God (Rom. 8:16); and lastly, from a serious and holy desire to preserve a good conscience and to perform good works. And if the elect of God were deprived of this solid comfort that they shall finally obtain the victory and of this infallible pledge or earnest of eternal glory, they would be of all men the most miserable.

ARTICLE 11. The Scripture moreover testifies that believers in this life have to struggle with various carnal doubts and that under grievous temptations they are not always sensible of this full assurance of faith and certainty of persevering. But God, who is the Father of all consolation, does not suffer them to be tempted above that they are able, but will with the temptation also make a way to escape that they may be able to bear it (1 Cor. 10:13), and by the Holy Spirit again inspires them with the comfortable assurance of persevering.

ARTICLE 12. This certainty of perseverance, however, is so far from exciting in believers a spirit of pride or of rendering them carnally secure, that on the contrary, it is the real source of humility, filial reverence, true piety, patience in every tribulation, fervent prayers, constancy in suffering, and in confessing the truth, and of solid rejoicing in God; so that the consideration of this benefit should serve as an incentive to the serious and constant practice of gratitude and good works, as appears from the testimonies of Scripture and the examples of the saints.

ARTICLE 13. Neither does renewed confidence of persevering produce licentiousness or a disregard to piety in those who are recovering from backsliding; but it renders them much more careful and solicitous to continue in the ways of the Lord, which He hath ordained, that they who walk therein may maintain an assurance of persevering, lest by abusing His fatherly kindness, God should turn away His gracious countenance from them, to behold which is to the godly dearer than life, the withdrawing whereof is more bitter than death, and they in consequence hereof should fall into more grievous torments of conscience.

ARTICLE 14. And as it hath pleased God, by the preaching of the gospel, to begin this work of grace in us, so He preserves, continues, and perfects it by the hearing and reading of His Word, by meditation thereon, and by the exhortations, threatenings, and promises thereof, as well as by the use of the sacraments.

ARTICLE 15. The carnal mind is unable to comprehend this doctrine of the perseverance of the saints and the certainty thereof, which God hath most abundantly revealed in His Word, for the glory of His Name, and the consolation of pious souls, and which He impresses upon the hearts of the faithful. Satan abhors it; the world ridicules it; the ignorant and hypocrite abuse, and heretics oppose it;

but the spouse of Christ hath always most tenderly loved and constantly defended it as an inestimable treasure; and God, against whom neither counsel nor strength can prevail, will dispose her to continue this conduct to the end. Now, to this one God, Father, Son, and Holy Spirit, be honor and glory forever. Amen.

REJECTIONS

The true doctrine (concerning perseverance) having been explained, the Synod rejects the errors of those who teach:

REJECTION 1. That the perseverance of the true believers is not a fruit of election or a gift of God gained by the death of Christ, but a condition of the new covenant, which (as they declare) man before his decisive election and justification must fulfill through his free will.

For the Holy Scripture testifies that this follows out of election, and is given the elect in virtue of the death, the resurrection and intercession of Christ: "but the election hath obtained it, and the rest were blinded" (Rom. 11:7). Likewise: "He that spared not His own Son, but delivered Him up for us all, how shall He not with Him also freely give us all things? Who shall lay any thing to the charge of God's elect? It is God that justifieth. Who is he that condemneth? It is Christ that died, yea rather, that is risen again, who is even at the right hand of God, who also maketh intercession for us. Who shall separate us from the love of Christ?" (Rom. 8:32-35).

REJECTION 2. That God does indeed provide the believer with sufficient powers to persevere and is ever ready to preserve these in him, if he will do his duty; but that though all things which are necessary to persevere in faith and which God will use to preserve faith are made use of, it even then ever depends on the pleasure of the will whether it will persevere or not.

For this idea contains an outspoken Pelagianism, and while it would make men free, it makes them robbers of God's honor, contrary to the prevailing agreement of the evangelical doctrine, which takes from man all cause of boasting and ascribes all the praise for this favor to the grace of God alone; and contrary to the apostle, who declares that it is God "Who shall also confirm you unto the end, that ye may be blameless in the day of our Lord Jesus Christ" (1 Cor. 1:8).

REJECTION 3. That the true believers and regenerate not only can fall from justifying faith and likewise from grace and salvation wholly and to the end, but indeed often do fall from this and are lost forever.

For this conception makes powerless the grace, justification, regeneration, and continued keeping by Christ, contrary to the expressed words of the apostle Paul: "That, while we were yet sinners, Christ died for us. Much more then, being now justified by His blood, we shall be saved from wrath through Him" (Rom. 5:8, 9). And contrary to the apostle John: "Whosoever is born of God doth not commit sin; for His seed remaineth in him: and he cannot sin, because he is born of God" (1 John 3:9). And also contrary to the words of Jesus Christ: "I give unto them eternal life; and they shall never perish, neither shall any man pluck them out of My hand. My Father, which gave them Me, is greater than all; and no man is able to pluck them out of My Father's hand" (John 10:28, 29).

REJECTION 4. That true believers and regenerate can sin the sin unto death or against the Holy Spirit.

Since the same apostle John, after having spoken in the fifth chapter of his first epistle, verses 16 and 17, of those who sin unto death and having forbidden to pray for them, immediately adds to this in verse 18: "We know that whosoever is born of God sinneth not (meaning a sin of that character); but he that is begotten of God keepeth himself, and that wicked one toucheth him not" (1 John 5:18).

REJECTION 5. That without a special revelation we can have no certainty of future perseverance in this life.

For by this doctrine the sure comfort of the true believers is taken away in this life and the doubts of the papist are again introduced into the church, while the Holy Scriptures constantly deduce this assurance, not from a special and extraordinary revelation, but from the marks proper to the children of God and from the constant promises of God. So especially the apostle Paul: "Nor any other creature, shall be able to separate us from the love of God, which is in Christ Jesus our Lord" (Rom. 8:39). And John declares: "And he that keepeth His commandments dwelleth in Him, and He in him. And hereby we know that He abideth in us, by the Spirit which He hath given us" (1 John 3:24).

REJECTION 6. That the doctrine of the certainty of perseverance and of salvation from its own character and nature is a cause of indolence and is injurious to godliness, good morals, prayers and other holy exercises, but that on the contrary it is praiseworthy to doubt.

For these show that they do not know the power of divine grace and the working of the indwelling Holy Spirit. And they contradict the apostle John, who teaches the opposite with express words in his first epistle: "Beloved, now are we the sons of God, and it doth not yet appear what we shall be: but we know that, when He shall appear, we shall be like Him; for we shall see Him as He is. And every man that hath this hope in Him purifieth himself, even as He is pure" (1 John 3:2-3). Furthermore, these are contradicted by the example of the saints, both of the Old and the New Testament, who though they were assured of their perseverance and salvation, were nevertheless constant in prayers and other exercises of godliness.

REJECTION 7. That the faith of those who believe for a time does not differ from justifying and saving faith except only in duration.

For Christ Himself, in Matthew 13:20, Luke 8:13, and in other places, evidently notes, besides this duration, a threefold difference between those who believe only for a time and true believers, when He declares that the former receive the seed in stony ground, but the latter in the good ground or heart; that the former are without root, but the latter have a firm root; that the former are without fruit, but that the latter bring forth their fruit in various measure with constancy and steadfastness.

REJECTION 8. That it is not absurd that one having lost his first regeneration, is again and even often born anew.

For these deny by this doctrine the incorruptibleness of the seed of God, whereby we are born again, contrary to the testimony of the apostle Peter: "Being born again, not of corruptible seed, but of incorruptible" (1 Peter 1:23).

REJECTION 9. That Christ has in no place prayed that believers should infallibly continue in faith.

For they contradict Christ Himself, who says: "I have prayed for thee (Simon), that thy faith fail not" (Luke 22:32); and the evangelist John, who declares that Christ has not prayed for the apostles only, but also for those who through their word would believe: "Holy Father, keep through Thine own name those whom Thou hast given Me," and: "I pray not that Thou shouldest take them out of the world, but that Thou shouldest keep them from the evil"; "Neither pray I for these alone, but for them also which shall believe on Me through their word" (John 17:11, 15, 20).

CONCLUSION

And this is the perspicuous, simple, and ingenuous declaration of the orthodox doctrine respecting the five articles which have been controverted in the Belgic churches, and the rejection of the errors with which they have for some time been troubled. This doctrine the Synod judges to be drawn from the Word of God and to be agreeable to the confessions of the Reformed churches. Whence it clearly appears that some whom such conduct by no means became, have violated all truth, equity, and charity, in wishing to persuade the public:

That the doctrine of the Reformed churches concerning predestination, and the points annexed to it, by its own genius and necessary tendency, leads off the minds of men from all piety and religion; that it is an opiate administered by the flesh and the devil, and the stronghold of Satan, where he lies in wait for all; and from which he wounds multitudes, and mortally strikes through many with the darts both of despair and security; that it makes God the author of sin, unjust, tyrannical, hypocritical; that it is nothing more than interpolated Stoicism, Manichaeism, Libertinism, Turcism; that it renders men carnally secure, since they are persuaded by it that nothing can hinder the salvation of the elect, let them live as they please; and therefore, that they may safely perpetrate every species of the most atrocious crimes; and that if the reprobate should even perform truly all the works of the saints, their obedience would not in the least contribute to their salvation; that the same doctrine teaches that God, by a mere arbitrary act of His will, without the least respect or view to any sin, has predestinated the greatest part of the world to eternal damnation; and has created them for this very purpose; that in the same manner in which the election is the fountain and the cause of faith and good works, reprobation is the cause of unbelief and impiety; that many children of the faithful are torn guiltless from their mothers' breasts and tyrannically plunged into hell; so that neither baptism nor the prayers of the Church at their baptism, can at all profit by them; and many other things of the same kind which the Reformed Churches not only do not acknowledge, but even detest with their whole soul.

Wherefore, this Synod of Dort, in the name of the Lord, conjures as many as piously call upon the name of our Savior Jesus Christ, to judge of the faith of the Reformed Churches not from the calumnies, which on every side are heaped upon it; nor from the private expressions of a few among ancient and modern teachers, often dishonestly quoted or corrupted and wrested to a meaning quite foreign to their intention; but from the public confessions of the Churches themselves and from the declaration of the orthodox doctrine, confirmed by the unanimous consent of all and each of the members of the whole Synod. Moreover, the Synod warns calumniators themselves to consider the terrible judgment of God which awaits them for bearing false witness against the confessions of so many churches, for distressing the consciences of the weak, and for laboring to render suspect the society of the truly faithful. Finally, this Synod exhorts all their brethren in the gospel of Christ to conduct themselves piously and religiously in handling this doctrine, both in the universities and churches; to direct it, as well in discourse as in writing, to the glory of the divine Name, to holiness of life, and to the consolation of afflicted souls; to regulate, by the Scripture, according to the analogy of faith, not only their sentiments, but also their language; and to abstain from all those phrases which exceed the limits necessary to be observed in ascertaining the genuine sense of the holy Scriptures, and may furnish insolent sophists with a just pretext for violently assailing or even vilifying the doctrine of the Reformed churches.

May Jesus Christ, the Son of God, who, seated at the Father's right hand, gives gifts to men, sanctify us in the truth, bring to the truth those who err, shut the mouths of the calumniators of sound doctrine, and endue the faithful minister of His Word with the spirit of wisdom and discretion, that all their discourses may tend to the glory of God and the edification of those who hear them. Amen.

That this is our faith and decision we certify by subscribing our names.

Here follow the names, not only of President, Assistant President, and Secretaries of the Synod, and of the Professors of Theology in the Dutch Churches, but of all the Members who were deputed to the Synod as the Representatives of their respective Churches, that is, of the Delegates from Great Britain, the Electoral Palatinate, Hessia, Switzerland, Wetteraw, The Republic and Church of Geneva, The Republic and Church of Bremen, The Republic and Church of Emden, The Duchy of Gelderland and of Zutphen, South Holland, North Holland, Zeeland,

The Province of Utrecht, Friesland, Transylvania, The State of Groningen and Omland, Drent, The French Churches. ▪

Westminster Confession of Faith

In the 1640's, England was rather a mess. The Church had been in upheaval for over a hundred years, ever since Henry VIII broke with Rome (over personal interest, not doctrine) and made himself the head of the English Church. Then Edward VI had inherited the throne and tried to bring true Reformation to England. Then came Roman Catholic "Bloody" Mary, who had bent every nerve to erase Edward's reforming efforts. Then Elizabeth I, who had brought back the more middle-of-the-road "Anglican" form which Henry VIII had vaguely started. Elizabeth had commissioned the Act of Uniformity (which made the 1549 Book of Common Prayer the only permissible liturgy) and a confession called the Thirty-Nine Articles of Religion to unify the Church in England and resolve the troubles. It did not work.

Many Christians in England believed that the Book of Common Prayer and the doctrines that the Anglican bishops were teaching were far too Roman Catholic. But Anglicanism was now the state religion, and dissenters were ignored and dubbed "Nonconformists," or "Puritans" for their desire to purify the Church of England of its remaining Roman Catholic beliefs and practices. But those Nonconformists were no fringe minority.

In 1640, Charles I was on the throne of England and Scotland, with habits too Roman Catholic for the Reformed Christians of the land to stomach. Charles I resisted the English Puritans and Scottish Presbyterians even more aggressively than his predecessors had, and the issue was coming to a head. So, when Charles I finally summoned Parliament in 1640, the church became a major topic of discussion. Parliament called for an assembly to find a solution to the tensions; as a result, from 1643–1653, about 120 theologians and members of parliament met in Westminster Abbey to do just that.

Due to the religious bedlam of the previous century, the Church of England had not had opportunity to write a confession any more thorough than the Thirty-Nine Articles of 1563. The Westminster Assembly first tried expanding the Thirty-Nine Articles into a more thorough confession. But ten weeks in, they gave up and turned instead to the

Solemn League and Covenant, which in 1643 bound the English Parliament and the Scottish people together in support of the Reformed faith.

In 1644, Parliament asked the Westminster Assembly to write documents on Church discipline, Church government, and worship. The Assembly's writings, called the Westminster Standards, eventually included the Larger Westminster Catechism, the Shorter Westminster Catechism, the Directory for Public Worship, the Form of Church Government, and—summing up the rest—the Westminster Confession of Faith, written in 1646.

The Kirk of Scotland adopted the Westminster Confession in 1647, and so did various Presbyterians in the American colonies. Even some Congregationalists and Reformed Baptists claimed it as their confession. Parliament officially approved the confession in 1648, after some slight revisions.

But after being crowned in 1660, Charles II overthrew the Westminster Confession as the confession of the English state church, and reinstated the old form of the Anglican Church. Nonetheless, the Westminster Confession has continued to be the defining confession of other churches worldwide, even to the present day.

The version below is the original version of 1646. Throughout the accompanying Scripture references, "*Cant.*" is given as the abbreviation for *Canticle of Canticles*, an archaic title for *Song of Songs*, or *Song of Solomon*.

CHAPTER I: OF THE HOLY SCRIPTURE.

I. Although the light of nature and the works of creation and providence do so far manifest the goodness, wisdom, and power of God, as to leave men unexcusable;[(a)] yet are they not sufficient to give that knowledge of God and of His will, which is necessary unto salvation.[(b)] Therefore it pleased the Lord, at sundry times, and in divers manners, to reveal Himself, and to declare that His will unto His Church;[(c)] and afterwards, for the better preserving and propagating of the truth, and for the more sure establishment and comfort of the Church against the corruption of the flesh, and the malice of Satan and of the world, to commit the same wholly unto writing:[d] which maketh the Holy Scripture to be most necessary;[e] those former ways of God's revealing His will unto His people being now ceased.[f]

[a] *Rom. 2:14, 15; Rom. 1:19, 20; Ps. 19:1, 2, 3; Rom. 1:32, with chap. 2:1.*
[b] *I Cor. 1:21; I Cor. 2:13, 14.* [c] *Heb. 1:1.* [d] *Prov. 22:19, 20, 21; Luke 1:3, 4; Rom. 15:4; Matt. 4:4, 7, 10; Isa. 8:19, 20.*
[e] *II Tim. 3:15; II Pet. 1:19.* [f] *Heb. 1:1, 2.*

II. Under the name of Holy Scripture, or the Word of God written, are now contained all the books of the Old and New Testament, which are these:

Of the Old Testament: Genesis, Exodus, Leviticus, Numbers, Deuteronomy, Joshua, Judges, Ruth, I. Samuel, II. Samuel, I. Kings, II. Kings, I. Chronicles, II. Chronicles, Ezra, Nehemiah, Esther, Job, Psalms, Proverbs, Ecclesiastes, The Song of Songs, Isaiah, Jeremiah, Lamentations, Ezekiel, Daniel, Hosea, Joel, Amos, Obadiah, Jonah, Micah, Nahum, Habakkuk, Zephaniah, Haggai, Zechariah, Malachi.

Of the New Testament: The Gospels according to: Matthew, Mark, Luke, John; The Acts of the Apostles; Paul's Epistles: To the Romans, Corinthians I., Corinthians II., Galatians, Ephesians, Philippians, Colossians, Thessalonians I., Thessalonians II., To Timothy I., To Timothy II., To Titus, To Philemon; The Epistle to the Hebrews; The Epistle of James; The first and second Epistles of Peter; The first, second, and third Epistles of John; The Epistle of Jude; The Revelation of John.

All which are given by inspiration of God, to be the rule of faith and life.[g]

[g] *Luke 16:29, 31; Eph. 2:20; Rev. 22:18, 19; II Tim. 3:16.*

III. The books commonly called Apocrypha, not being of divine inspiration, are no part of the canon of the Scripture; and therefore are of no authority in the Church of God, nor to be any otherwise approved, or made use of, than other human writings.[h]

[h] *Luke 24:27, 44; Rom. 3:2; II Pet. 1:21.*

IV. The authority of the Holy Scripture, for which it ought to be believed and obeyed, dependeth not upon the testimony of any man, or Church; but wholly upon God (who is truth itself) the author thereof: and therefore it is to be received because it is the Word of God.[i]

[i] *II Pet. 1:19, 21; II Tim. 3:16; I John 5:9; I Thess. 2:13.*

V. We may be moved and induced by the testimony of the Church to a high and reverent esteem of the Holy Scripture.[k] And the heavenliness of the matter, the efficacy of the doctrine, the majesty of the style, the consent of all the parts, the scope of the whole (which is, to give all glory to God), the full discovery it makes of the only way of man's salvation, the many other incomparable excellencies, and the entire perfection thereof, are arguments whereby it doth abundantly evidence itself to be the Word of God: yet notwithstanding, our full persuasion and assurance of the infallible truth and divine authority thereof, is from the inward work of the Holy Spirit bearing witness by and with the Word in our hearts.[l]

[k] *I Tim. 3:15.* [l] *I John 2:20, 27; John 16:13, 14; I Cor. 2:10, 11, 12; Isa. 59:21.*

VI. The whole counsel of God concerning all things necessary for His own glory, man's salvation, faith, and life, is either expressly set down in Scripture, or by good and necessary consequence may be deduced from Scripture: unto which nothing at any time is to be added, whether by new revelations of the Spirit, or traditions of men.[m] Nevertheless we acknowledge the inward illumination of the Spirit of God to be necessary for the saving understanding of such things as are revealed in the Word:[n] and that there are some circumstances concerning the worship of God, and government of the Church, common to human actions and societies, which are to be ordered by the light of nature and Christian prudence, according to the general rules of the Word, which are always to be observed.[o]

[m] *II Tim. 3:15, 16, 17; Gal. 1:8, 9; II Thess. 2:2.* [n] *John 6:45, I Cor. 2:9 to 12.* [o] *I Cor. 11:13, 14; I Cor. 14:26, 40.*

VII. All things in Scripture are not alike plain in themselves, nor alike clear unto all:[p] yet those things which are necessary to be known, believed, and observed for salvation, are so clearly propounded and opened in some place of Scripture or other, that not only the learned, but the unlearned, in a due use of the ordinary means, may attain unto a sufficient understanding of them.[q]

[p] *II Pet. 3:16.* [q] *Psalm 119:105, 130.*

VIII. The Old Testament in Hebrew (which was the native language of the people of God of old), and the New Testament in Greek (which, at the time of the writing of it was most generally known to the nations), being immediately inspired by God, and, by His singular care and providence kept pure in all ages, are therefore authentical;[r] so as, in all controversies of religion, the Church is finally to appeal unto them.[s] But, because these original tongues are not known to all the people of God, who have right unto, and interest in the Scriptures, and are commanded, in the fear of God, to read and search them,[t] therefore they are to be translated into the vulgar language of every nation unto which they come,[u] that the Word of God dwelling plentifully in all, they may worship Him in an acceptable manner;[w] and, through patience and comfort of the Scriptures, may have hope.[x]

(r) *Matt. 5:18.* (s) *Isa. 8:20; Acts 15:15; John 5:39, 46.* (t) *John 5:39.*
(u) *I Cor. 14:6, 9, 11, 12, 24, 27, 28.* (w) *Col. 3:16.* (x) *Rom. 15:4.*

IX. The infallible rule of interpretation of Scripture is the Scripture itself: and therefore, when there is a question about the true and full sense of any Scripture (which is not manifold, but one), it must be searched and known by other places that speak more clearly.[y]

(y) *II Pet. 1:20, 21; Acts 15:15, 16.*

X. The supreme judge by which all controversies of religion are to be determined, and all decrees of councils, opinions of ancient writers, doctrines of men, and private spirits, are to be examined; and in whose sentence we are to rest; can be no other but the Holy Spirit speaking in the Scripture.[z]

(z) *Matt. 22:29, 31; Eph. 2:20 with Acts 28:25.*

CHAPTER II: OF GOD, AND OF THE HOLY TRINITY.

I. There is but one only,[a] living, and true God:[b] who is infinite in being and perfection,[c] a most pure spirit,[d] invisible,[e] without body, parts,[f] or passions,[g] immutable,[h] immense,[i] eternal,[k] incomprehensible,[l] almighty,[m] most wise,[n] most holy,[o] most free,[p] most absolute,[q] working all things according to the counsel of His own immutable and most righteous will,[r] for His own glory;[s] most loving,[t] gracious, merciful, long-suffering, abundant in goodness and truth, forgiving iniquity, transgression, and sin;[u] the rewarder of them that diligently seek Him;[w] and withal, most just and terrible in His judgments,[x] hating all sin,[y] and who will by no means clear the guilty.[z]

[a] *Deut. 6:4; I Cor. 8:4, 6.* [b] *I Thess. 1:9; Jer. 10:10.* [c] *Job 11:7, 8, 9; Job 26:14.* [d] *John 4:24.* [e] *I Tim. 1:17.* [f] *Deut. 4:15, 16; John 4:24, with Luke 24:39.* [g] *Acts 14:11, 15.* [h] *James 1:17; Mal. 3:6.* [i] *I Kings 8:27; Jer. 23:23, 24.* [k] *Ps. 90:2; I Tim. 1:17.* [l] *Ps. 145:3.* [m] *Gen. 17:1; Rev. 4:8.* [n] *Rom. 16:27.* [o] *Isa. 6:3; Rev. 4:8.* [p] *Ps. 115:3.* [q] *Exod. 3:14.* [r] *Eph. 1:11.* [s] *Prov. 16:4; Rom. 11:36.* [t] *I John 4:8, 16.* [u] *Exod. 34:6, 7.* [w] *Heb. 11:6.* [x] *Neh. 9:32, 33.* [y] *Ps. 5:5, 6.* [z] *Nah. 1:2, 3; Exod. 34:7.*

II. God hath all life,[a] glory,[b] goodness,[c] blessedness,[d] in and of Himself; and is alone in and unto Himself all-sufficient, not standing in need of any creatures which He hath made,[e] nor deriving any glory from them,[f] but only manifesting His own glory in, by, unto, and upon them: He is the alone fountain of all being, of whom, through whom, and to whom are all things;[g] and hath most sovereign dominion over them, to do by them, for them, or upon them whatsoever Himself pleaseth.[h] In His sight all things are open and manifest;[i] His knowledge is infinite, infallible, and independent upon the creature,[k] so as nothing is to Him contingent, or uncertain.[l] He is most holy in all His counsels, in all His works, and in all His commands.[m] To Him is due from angels and men, and every other creature, whatsoever worship, service, or obedience He is pleased to require of them.[n]

[a] *John 5:26.* [b] *Acts 7:2.* [c] *Ps. 119:68.* [d] *I Tim. 6:15; Rom. 9:5.* [e] *Acts 17:24, 25.* [f] *Job 22:2, 3.* [g] *Rom 11:36.* [h] *Rev. 4:11; I Tim. 6:15; Dan. 4:25, 35.* [i] *Heb. 4:13.* [k] *Rom. 11:33, 34; Ps. 147:5.* [l] *Acts 15:18; Ezek. 11:5.* [m] *Ps. 145:17; Rom. 7:12.* [n] *Rev. 5:12, 13, 14.*

III. In the unity of the Godhead there be three persons, of one substance, power, and eternity; God the Father, God the Son, and God the Holy Ghost.[o] The Father is of none, neither begotten, nor proceeding: the Son is eternally begotten of the Father:[p] the Holy Ghost eternally proceeding from the Father and the Son.[q]

[o] *I John 5:7; Matt. 3:16, 17; Matt. 28:19; II Cor. 13:14.* [p] *John 1:14, 18.* [q] *John 15:26; Gal. 4:6.*

CHAPTER III: OF GOD'S ETERNAL DECREE.

I. God from all eternity did, by the most wise and holy counsel of His own will, freely, and unchangeably ordain whatsoever comes to pass:[(a)] yet so, as thereby neither is God the author of sin,[(b)] nor is violence offered to the will of the creatures, nor is the liberty or contingency of second causes taken away, but rather established.[(c)]

[(a)] *Eph. 1:11; Rom. 11:33; Heb. 6:17; Rom. 9:15, 18.*
[(b)] *Jam. 1:13, 17; I John 1:5.* [(c)] *Acts 2:23; Matt. 17:12; Acts 4:27, 28; John 19:11; Prov. 16:33.*

II. Although God knows whatsoever may or can come to pass upon all supposed conditions,[(d)] yet hath He not decreed anything because He foresaw it as future, or as that which would come to pass upon such conditions.[(e)]

[(d)] *Acts 15:18; I Sam. 23:11, 12; Matt. 11:21, 23.* [(e)] *Rom. 9:11, 13, 16, 18.*

III. By the decree of God, for the manifestation of His glory, some men and angels[(f)] are predestinated unto everlasting life, and others fore-ordained to everlasting death.[(g)]

[(f)] *I Tim. 5:21; Matt. 25:41.* [(g)] *Rom. 9:22, 23; Eph. 1:5, 6; Prov. 16:4.*

IV. These angels and men, thus predestinated, and fore-ordained, are particularly and unchangeably designed, and their number so certain and definite, that it cannot be either increased or diminished.[(h)]

[(h)] *II Tim. 2:19; John 13:18.*

V. Those of mankind that are predestinated unto life, God, before the foundation of the world was laid, according to His eternal and immutable purpose, and the secret counsel and good pleasure of His will, hath chosen, in Christ, unto everlasting glory,[(i)] out of His mere free grace and love, without any foresight of faith or good works, or perseverance in either of them, or any other thing in the creature, as conditions, or causes moving Him thereunto:[(k)] and all to the praise of His glorious grace.[(l)]

[(i)] *Eph. 1:4, 9, 11; Rom. 8:30; II Tim. 1:9; I Thess. 5:9.*
[(k)] *Rom. 9:11, 13, 16; Eph. 1:4, 9.* [(l)] *Eph. 1:6, 12.*

VI. As God hath appointed the elect unto glory, so hath He, by the eternal and most free purpose of His will, fore-ordained all the means thereunto.[m] Wherefore they who are elected, being fallen in Adam, are redeemed by Christ,[n] are effectually called unto faith in Christ by His Spirit working in due season, are justified, adopted, sanctified,[o] and kept by His power through faith, unto salvation.[p] Neither are any other redeemed by Christ, effectually called, justified, adopted, sanctified, and saved, but the elect only.[q]

> [m] *I Pet. 1:2; Eph. 1:4, 5; Eph. 2:10; II Thess. 2:13.* [n] *I Thess. 5:9, 10; Titus 2:14.* [o] *Rom. 8:30; Eph. 1:5; II Thess. 2:13.* [p] *I Pet. 1:5.*
> [q] *John 17:9; Rom. 8:28 to the end; John 6:64, 65; John 10:26; John 8:47; I John 2:19.*

VII. The rest of mankind God was pleased, according to the unsearchable counsel of His own will, whereby He extendeth or withholdeth mercy, as He pleaseth, for the glory of His sovereign power over His creatures, to pass by; and to ordain them to dishonour and wrath, for their sin, to the praise of His glorious justice.[r]

> [r] *Matt. 11:25, 26; Rom. 9:17, 18, 21, 22; II Tim. 2:19, 20; Jude ver. 4; I Pet. 2:8.*

VIII. The doctrine of this high mystery of predestination is to be handled with special prudence and care,[s] that men attending the will of God revealed in His Word, and yielding obedience thereunto, may, from the certainty of their effectual vocation, be assured of their eternal election.[t] So shall this doctrine afford matter of praise, reverence, and admiration of God,[u] and of humility, diligence, and abundant consolation to all that sincerely obey the Gospel.[w]

> [s] *Rom. 9:20; Rom. 11:33; Deut. 29:29.* [t] *II Pet. 1:10.* [u] *Eph. 1:6; Rom. 11:33.* [w] *Rom. 11:5, 6, 20; II Pet. 1:10; Rom. 8:33; Luke 10:20.*

CHAPTER IV: OF CREATION.

I. It pleased God the Father, Son, and Holy Ghost,[a] for the manifestation of the glory of His eternal power, wisdom, and goodness,[b] in the beginning, to create, or make of nothing, the world, and all things therein whether visible or invisible, in the space of six days; and all very good.[c]

> [a] *Heb. 1:2; John 1:2, 3; Gen. 1:2; Job. 26:13; Job. 33:4.* [b] *Rom. 1:20; Jer. 10:12; Ps. 104:24; Ps. 33:5, 6.* [c] *Gen. 1 chap.; Heb. 11:3; Col. 1:16; Acts 17:24.*

II. After God had made all other creatures, He created man, male and female,[d] with reasonable and immortal souls,[e] endued with knowledge, righteousness, and true holiness, after His own image;[f] having the law of God written in their hearts,[g] and power to fulfill it:[h] and yet under a possibility of transgressing, being left to the liberty of their own will, which was subject unto change.[i] Beside this law written in their hearts, they received a command, not to eat of the tree of the knowledge of good and evil, which while they kept, they were happy in their communion with God,[k] and had dominion over the creatures.[l]

> [d] *Gen. 1:27.* [e] *Gen. 2:7 with Eccles. 12:7 & Luke 23:43 and Matt. 10:28.* [f] *Gen. 1:26; Col. 3:10; Eph. 4:24.* [g] *Rom. 2:14, 15.* [h] *Eccles. 7:29.* [i] *Gen. 3:6; Eccles. 7:29.* [k] *Gen. 2:17; Gen. 3:8, 9, 10, 11, 23.* [l] *Gen. 1:26, 28.*

CHAPTER V: OF PROVIDENCE.

I. God the great Creator of all things doth uphold,[a] direct, dispose, and govern all creatures, actions, and things,[b] from the greatest even to the least,[c] by His most wise and holy providence,[d] according to His infallible fore-knowledge,[e] and the free and immutable counsel of His own will,[f] to the praise of the glory of His wisdom, power, justice, goodness, and mercy.[g]

> [a] *Heb. 1:3.* [b] *Dan. 4:34, 35; Ps. 135:6; Acts 17:25, 26, 28; Job 38 to 41 chapters.* [c] *Matt. 10:29, 30, 31.* [d] *Prov. 15:3; Ps. 104:24; Ps. 145:17.* [e] *Acts 15:18; Ps. 94:8, 9, 10, 11.* [f] *Eph. 1:11; Ps. 33:10, 11.* [g] *Isa. 63:14; Eph. 3:10; Rom. 9:17; Gen. 45:7; Ps. 145:7.*

II. Although, in relation to the fore-knowledge and decree of God, the first Cause, all things come to pass immutably, and infallibly:[h] yet, by the same providence,

He ordereth them to fall out, according to the nature of second causes, either necessarily, freely, or contingently.[i]

[h] *Acts 2:23.* [i] *Gen. 8:22; Jer. 31:35; Exod. 21:13 with Deut. 19:5; I Kings 22:28, 34; Isa. 10:6, 7.*

III. God in His ordinary providence maketh use of means,[k] yet is free to work without,[l] above,[m] and against them at His pleasure.[n]

[k] *Acts 27:31, 44; Isa. 55:10, 11; Hos. 2:21, 22.* [l] *Hos. 1:7; Matt. 4:4; Job 34:20.* [m] *Rom. 4:19, 20, 21.* [n] *II Kings 6:6; Dan. 3:27.*

IV. The almighty power, unsearchable wisdom, and infinite goodness of God so far manifest themselves in His providence, that it extendeth itself even to the first fall, and all other sins of angels and men;[o] and that not by a bare permission,[p] but such as hath joined with it a most wise and powerful bounding,[q] and otherwise ordering and governing of them, in a manifold dispensation, to His own holy ends;[r] yet so, as the sinfulness thereof proceedeth only from the creature, and not from God, who, being most holy and righteous, neither is, nor can be, the author or approver of sin.[s]

[o] *Rom. 11:32, 33, 34; II Sam. 24:1 with I Chron. 21:1; I Kings 22:22, 23; I Chron. 10:4, 13, 14; II Sam. 16:10; Acts 2:23; Acts 4:27, 28.* [p] *Acts 14:16.* [q] *Ps. 76:10; II Kings 19:28.* [r] *Gen. 50:20; Isa. 10:6, 7, 12.* [s] *James 1:13, 14, 17; I John 2:16; Ps. 50:21.*

V. The most wise, righteous, and gracious God doth oftentimes leave for a season His own children to manifold temptations, and the corruption of their own hearts, to chastise them for their former sins, or to discover unto them the hidden strength of corruption, and deceitfulness of their hearts, that they may be humbled;[t] and, to raise them to a more close and constant dependence for their support upon Himself, and to make them more watchful against all future occasions of sin, and for sundry other just and holy ends.[u]

[t] *II Chron. 32:25, 26, 31; II Sam. 24:1.* [u] *II Cor. 12:7, 8, 9; Ps. 73 throughout; Ps. 77:1 to 12; Mark 14:66 to the end, with John 21:15, 16, 17.*

VI. As for those wicked and ungodly men whom God, as a righteous Judge, for former sins, doth blind and harden,[w] from them He not only withholdeth His grace, whereby they might have been enlightened in their understandings, and wrought upon in their hearts;[x] but sometimes also withdraweth the gifts which they had,[y] and exposeth them to such objects as their corruption makes occasions of sin;[z] and, withal, gives them over to their own lusts, the temptations of the world, and the power of Satan:[a] whereby it comes to pass that they harden themselves, even under those means which God useth for the softening of others.[b]

> [w] *Rom. 1:24, 26, 28; Rom. 11:7, 8.* [x] *Deut. 29:4.* [y] *Matt. 13:12; Matt. 25:29.* [z] *Deut. 2:30; II Kings 8:12, 13.* [a] *Ps. 81:11, 12; II Thess. 2:10, 11, 12.* [b] *Exod. 7:3 with Exod. 8:15, 32; II Cor. 2:15, 16; Isa. 8:14; I Pet. 2:7, 8; Isa. 6:9, 10 with Acts 28:26, 27.*

VII. As the providence of God doth in general reach to all creatures, so after a most special manner, it taketh care of His Church, and disposeth all things to the good thereof.[c]

> [c] *I Tim. 4:10; Amos 9:8, 9; Rom. 8:28; Isa. 43:3, 4, 5, 14.*

CHAPTER VI: OF THE FALL OF MAN, OF SIN, AND OF THE PUNISHMENT THEREOF.

I. Our first parents, being seduced by the subtlety and temptation of Satan, sinned, in eating the forbidden fruit.[a] This their sin God was pleased, according to His wise and holy counsel, to permit, having purposed to order it to His own glory.[b]

> [a] *Gen. 3:13; II Cor. 11:3.* [b] *Rom. 11:32.*

II. By this sin they fell from their original righteousness and communion, with God,[c] and so became dead in sin,[d] and wholly defiled in all the parts and faculties of soul and body.[e]

> [c] *Gen. 3:6, 7, 8; Eccles. 7:29; Rom. 3:23.* [d] *Gen. 2:17; Eph. 2:1.* [e] *Tit. 1:15; Gen. 6:5; Jer. 17:9; Rom. 3:10 to 19.*

III. They being the root of all mankind, the guilt of this sin was imputed,[f] and the same death in sin and corrupted nature conveyed, to all their posterity descending from them by ordinary generation.[g]

[f] *Gen. 1:27, 28 & Gen. 2:16, 17 and Acts 17:26 with Rom. 5:12, 15, 16, 17, 18, 19 and I Cor. 15:21, 22, 49.* [g] *Ps. 51:5; Gen. 5:3; Job 14:4, Job 15:14.*

IV. From this original corruption, whereby we are utterly indisposed, disabled, and made opposite to all good,[h] and wholly inclined to all evil,[i] do proceed all actual transgressions.[k]

[h] *Rom. 5:6; Rom. 8:7, Rom. 7:18; Col. 1:21.* [i] *Gen. 6:5; Gen. 8:21; Rom. 3:10, 11, 12.* [k] James 1:14, 15; Eph. 2:2, 3; Matt. 15:19.

V. This corruption of nature, during this life, doth remain in those that are regenerated;[l] and although it be, through Christ, pardoned and mortified, yet both itself and all the motions thereof are truly and properly sin.[m]

[l] *I John 1:8, 10; Rom. 7:14, 17, 18, 23; James 3:2; Prov. 20:9; Eccles. 7:20.* [m] *Rom. 7:5, 7, 8, 25; Gal. 5:17.*

VI. Every sin, both original and actual, being a transgression of the righteous law of God, and contrary thereunto,[n] doth, in its own nature, bring guilt upon the sinner;[o] whereby he is bound over to the wrath of God,[p] and curse of the law,[q] and so made subject to death,[r] with all miseries spiritual,[s] temporal,[t] and eternal.[u]

[n] *I John 3:4.* [o] *Rom. 2:15; Rom. 3:9, 19.* [p] *Ephes. 2:3.* [q] *Gal. 3:10.* [r] *Rom. 6:23.* [s] *Ephes. 4:18.* [t] *Rom. 8:20; Lam. 3:39.* [u] *Matt. 25:41, II Thess. 1:9.*

CHAPTER VII: OF GOD'S COVENANT WITH MAN.

I. The distance between God and the creature is so great, that although reasonable creatures do owe obedience unto Him as their Creator, yet they could never have any fruition of Him as their blessedness and reward, but by some voluntary condescension on God's part, which He hath been pleased to express by way of covenant.[a]

[a] *Isa. 40:13, 14, 15, 16, 17; Job. 9:32, 33; I Sam. 2:25; Ps. 113:5, 6; Ps. 100:2, 3; Job. 22:2, 3; Job 35:7, 8; Luke 17:10; Acts 17:24, 25.*

II. The first covenant made with man was a covenant of works,[b] wherein life was promised to Adam, and in him to his posterity,[c] upon condition of perfect and personal obedience.[d]

[b] *Gal. 3:12.* [c] *Rom. 10:5, Rom. 5:12 to 20.* [d] *Gen. 2:17; Gal. 3:10.*

III. Man by his fall having made himself incapable of life by that covenant, the Lord was pleased to make a second,[e] commonly called the covenant of grace; wherein He freely offereth unto sinners life and salvation by Jesus Christ, requiring of them faith in Him, that they may be saved,[f] and promising to give unto all those that are ordained unto life His Holy Spirit, to make them willing and able to believe.[g]

[e] *Gal. 3:21; Rom. 8:3; Rom. 3:20, 21; Gen. 3:15; Isa. 42:6.*
[f] *Mark 16:15, 16; John 3:16; Rom. 10:6, 9; Gal. 3:11.*
[g] *Ezek. 36:26, 27; John 6:44, 45.*

IV. This covenant of grace is frequently set forth in Scripture by the name of a Testament, in reference to the death of Jesus Christ the Testator, and to the everlasting inheritance, with all things belonging to it, therein bequeathed.[h]

[h] *Heb. 9:15, 16, 17; Heb. 7:22; Luke 22:20; I Cor. 11:25.*

V. This covenant was differently administered in the time of the law, and in the time of the gospel:[i] under the law, it was administered by promises, prophecies, sacrifices, circumcision, the paschal lamb, and other types and ordinances delivered to the people of the Jews, all fore-signifying Christ to come:[k] which were, for that time, sufficient and efficacious, through the operation of the Spirit, to instruct and build up the elect in faith in the promised Messiah,[l] by whom they had full remission of sins, and eternal salvation; and is called, the Old Testament.[m]

[i] *II Cor. 3:6, 7, 8, 9.* [k] *Heb. 8, 9, 10 chapters; Rom. 4:11; Col. 2:11, 12; I Cor. 5:7.* [l] *I Cor. 10:1, 2, 3, 4; Heb. 11:13; John 8:56.* [m] *Gal. 3:7, 8, 9, 14.*

VI. Under the gospel, when Christ, the substance,[(n)] was exhibited, the ordinances in which this covenant is dispensed are the preaching of the Word, and the administration of the sacraments of Baptism and the Lord's Supper:[(o)] which, though fewer in number, and administered with more simplicity, and less outward glory; yet, in them, it is held forth in more fulness, evidence, and spiritual efficacy,[(p)] to all nations, both Jews and Gentiles;[(q)] and is called the New Testament.[(r)] There are not therefore two covenants of grace, differing in substance, but one and the same, under various dispensations.[(s)]

> [(n)] *Col. 2:17.* [(o)] *Matt. 28:19, 20; I Cor. 11:23, 24, 25.* [(p)] *Heb. 12:22 to 28; Jer. 31:33, 34.* [(q)] *Matt. 28:19; Eph. 2:15, 16, 17, 18, 19.* [(r)] *Luke 22:20.* [(s)] *Gal. 3:14, 16; Rom 3:21, 22, 23, 30; Ps. 32:1 with Rom. 4:3, 6, 16, 17, 23, 24; Heb. 13:8; Acts 15:11.*

CHAPTER VIII: OF CHRIST THE MEDIATOR.

I. It pleased God, in His eternal purpose, to choose and ordain the Lord Jesus, His only begotten Son, to be the Mediator between God and man;[(a)] the Prophet,[(b)] Priest,[(c)] and King,[(d)] the Head and Saviour of His Church,[(e)] the Heir of all things,[(f)] and Judge of the world:[(g)] unto whom He did from all eternity give a people, to be His seed,[(h)] and to be by Him in time redeemed, called, justified, sanctified, and glorified.[(i)]

> [(a)] *Isa. 42:1; I Pet. 19, 20; John 3:16; I Tim. 2:5.* [(b)] *Acts 3:22.*
> [(c)] *Heb. 5:5, 6.* [(d)] *Ps. 2:6; Luke 1:33.* [(e)] *Eph. 5:23.* [(f)] *Heb. 1:2.*
> [(g)] *Acts 17:31.* [(h)] *John 17:6; Ps. 22:30, Isa. 53:10.*
> [(i)] *I Tim. 2:6; Isa. 55:4, 5; I Cor. 1:30.*

II. The Son of God, the second person in the Trinity, being very and eternal God, of one substance and equal with the Father, did, when the fulness of time was come, take upon Him man's nature,[(k)] with all the essential properties and common infirmities thereof, yet without sin:[(l)] being conceived by the power of the Holy Ghost, in the womb of the virgin Mary, of her substance.[(m)] So that two whole, perfect, and distinct natures, the Godhead and the manhood, were inseparably joined together in one person, without conversion, composition, or confusion.[(n)]

Which person is very God, and very man, yet one Christ, the only Mediator between God and man.[o]

> [k] *John 1:1, 14; I John 5:20; Phil. 2:6; Gal. 4:4.* [l] *Heb. 2:14, 16, 17; Heb. 4:15.* [m] *Luke 1:27, 31, 35; Gal. 4:4.* [n] *Luke 1:35; Col. 2:9; Rom. 9:5; I Pet. 3:18; I Tim. 3:16.* [o] *Rom. 1:3, 4; I Tim. 2:5.*

III. The Lord Jesus, in His human nature thus united to the divine, was sanctified and anointed with the Holy Spirit, above measure,[p] having in Him all the treasures of wisdom and knowledge;[q] in whom it pleased the Father that all fulness should dwell;[r] to the end that, being holy, harmless, undefiled, and full of grace and truth,[s] He might be thoroughly furnished to execute the office of a mediator and surety.[t] Which office He took not unto Himself, but was thereunto called by His Father,[u] who put all power and judgment into His hand, and gave Him commandment to execute the same.[w]

> [p] *Ps. 45:7; John 3:34.* [q] *Col. 2:3.* [r] *Col. 1:19.* [s] *Heb. 7:26; John 1:14.* [t] *Acts 10:38; Heb. 12:24; Heb. 7:22.* [u] *Heb. 5:4, 5.* [w] *John 5:22, 27; Matt. 28:18; Acts 2:36.*

IV. This office the Lord Jesus did most willingly undertake;[x] which that He might discharge, He was made under the law,[y] and did perfectly fulfill it,[z] endured most grievous torments immediately in His soul,[a] and most painful sufferings in His body;[b] was crucified, and died;[c] was buried, and remained under the power of death; yet saw no corruption.[d] On the third day He arose from the dead,[e] with the same body in which He suffered,[f] with which also he ascended into heaven, and there sitteth at the right hand of His Father,[g] making intercession,[h] and shall return to judge men and angels at the end of the world.[i]

> [x] *Ps. 40:7, 8 with Heb. 10:5 to 10; John 10:18; Phil. 2:8.* [y] *Gal. 4:4.* [z] *Matt. 3:15; Matt. 5:17.* [a] *Matt. 26:37, 38; Luke 22:44; Matt. 27:46.* [b] *Matt. 26, 27 chapters.* [c] *Phil. 2:8.* [d] *Acts. 2:23, 24, 27; Acts 13:37; Rom. 6:9.* [e] *I Cor. 15:3, 4.* [f] *John 20:25, 27.* [g] *Mark 16:19.* [h] *Rom. 8:34; Heb. 9:24; Heb. 7:25.* [i] *Rom. 14:9, 10; Acts 1:11; Acts 10:42; Matt. 13:40, 41, 42; Jude ver. 6; II Pet. 2:4.*

V. The Lord Jesus, by His perfect obedience, and sacrifice of Himself, which He, through the eternal Spirit, once offered up unto God, hath fully satisfied the justice of His Father;[k] and purchased, not only reconciliation, but an everlasting inheritance in the kingdom of heaven, for all those whom the Father hath given unto Him.[l]

[k] *Rom. 5:19; Heb. 9:14, 16; Heb. 10:14; Eph. 5:2; Rom. 3:25, 26.*
[l] *Dan. 9:24, 26; Col. 1:19, 20; Eph. 1:11, 14; John 17:2; Heb. 9:12, 15.*

VI. Although the work of redemption was not actually wrought by Christ till after His incarnation, yet the virtue, efficacy, and benefits thereof were communicated unto the elect in all ages successively from the beginning of the world, in and by those promises, types, and sacrifices, wherein He was revealed, and signified to be the seed of the woman which should bruise the serpent's head; and the Lamb slain from the beginning of the world: being yesterday and to-day the same, and forever.[m]

[m] *Gal. 4:4, 5; Gen. 3:15; Rev. 13:8; Heb. 13:8.*

VII. Christ, in the work of mediation, acteth according to both natures, by each nature doing that which is proper to itself:[n] yet, by reason of the unity of the person, that which is proper to one nature, is sometimes in Scripture attributed to the person denominated by the other nature.[o]

[n] *Heb. 9:14; I Pet. 3:18.* [o] *Acts 20:28; John 3:13; I John 3:16.*

VIII. To all those for whom Christ hath purchased redemption, He doth certainly and effectually apply and communicate the same,[p] making intercession for them,[q] and revealing unto them, in and by the Word, the mysteries of salvation,[r] effectually persuading them by His Spirit to believe and obey, and governing their hearts by His Word and Spirit;[s] overcoming all their enemies by His almighty power and wisdom, in such manner, and ways, as are most consonant to His wonderful and unsearchable dispensation.[t]

[p] *John 6:37, 39; John 10:15, 16.* [q] *I John 2:1, 2; Rom. 8:34.*
[r] *John 15:13, 15; Eph. 1:7, 8, 9; John 17:6.* [s] *John 14:26; Heb. 12:2; II Cor. 4:13; Rom. 8:9, 14; Rom. 15:18, 19; John 17:17.*
[t] *Ps. 110:1; I Cor. 15:25, 26; Mal. 4:2, 3; Col. 2:15.*

CHAPTER IX: OF FREE WILL.

I. God hath endued the will of man with that natural liberty, that is neither forced, nor by any absolute necessity of nature determined to good or evil.[a]

[a] *Matt. 17:12; James 1:14; Deut. 30:19.*

II. Man, in his state of innocency, had freedom and power to will and to do that which was good, and well pleasing to God;[b] but yet, mutably, so that he might fall from it.[c]

[b] *Eccles. 7:29; Gen. 1:26.* [c] *Gen. 2:16, 17; Gen. 3:6.*

III. Man, by his fall into a state of sin, hath wholly lost all ability of will to any spiritual good accompanying salvation:[d] so as, a natural man, being altogether averse from that good,[e] and dead in sin,[f] is not able, by his own strength, to convert himself, or to prepare himself thereunto.[g]

[d] *Rom. 5:6; Rom 8:7; John 15:5.* [e] *Rom. 3:10, 12.* [f] *Eph. 2:1, 5; Col. 2:13.* [g] *John 6:44, 65; Eph. 2:2, 3, 4, 5; I Cor. 2:14; Titus 3:3, 4, 5.*

IV. When God converts a sinner, and translates him into the state of grace, He freeth him from his natural bondage under sin;[h] and, by His grace alone, enables him freely to will and to do that which is spiritually good;[i] yet so, as that by reason of his remaining corruption, he doth not perfectly, nor only, will that which is good, but doth also will that which is evil.[k]

[h] *Col. 1:13; John 8:34, 36.* [i] *Phil. 2:13; Rom. 6:18, 22.*
[k] *Gal. 5:17; Rom. 7:15, 18, 19, 21, 23.*

V. The will of man is made perfectly and immutably free to do good alone, in the state of glory only.[l]

[l] *Eph. 4:13; Heb. 12:23; I John 3:2; Jude ver. 24.*

CHAPTER X: OF EFFECTUAL CALLING.

I. All those whom God hath predestinated unto life, and those only, He is pleased in His appointed and accepted time effectually to call,[a] by His Word and Spirit,[b] out of that state of sin and death, in which they are by nature, to grace and salvation by Jesus Christ;[c] enlightening their minds spiritually and savingly to understand the things of God,[d] taking away their heart of stone, and giving unto them a heart of flesh;[e] renewing their wills, and, by His almighty power determining them to that which is good,[f] and effectually drawing them to Jesus Christ:[g] yet so, as they come most freely, being made willing by His grace.[h]

[a] *Rom. 8:30; Rom. 11:7; Eph. 1:10, 11.* [b] *II Thess. 2:13, 14; II Cor. 3:3, 6.* [c] *Rom. 8:2; Eph. 2:1, 2, 3, 4, 5; II Tim. 1:9, 10.* [d] *Acts 26:18; I Cor. 2:10, 12; Eph. 1:17, 18.* [e] *Ezek. 36:26.* [f] *Ezek. 11:19; Phil. 2:13; Deut. 30:6; Ezek. 36:27.* [g] *Eph. 1:19; John 6:44, 45.* [h] *Cant. 1:4; Ps. 110:3; John 6:37; Rom. 6:16, 17, 18.*

II. This effectual call is of God's free and special grace alone, not from anything at all foreseen in man,[i] who is altogether passive therein, until being quickened and renewed by the Holy Spirit,[k] he is thereby enabled to answer this call, and to embrace the grace offered and conveyed in it.[l]

[i] *II Tim. 1:9; Tit. 3:4, 5; Eph. 2:4, 5, 8, 9; Rom. 9:11.* [k] *I Cor. 2:14; Rom. 8:7; Eph. 2:5.* [l] *John 6:37; Ezek. 36:27; John 5:25.*

III. Elect infants, dying in infancy, are regenerated, and saved by Christ through the Spirit,[m] who worketh when, and where, and how He pleaseth:[n] so also, are all other elect persons who are uncapable of being outwardly called by the ministry of the Word.[o]

[m] *Luke 18:15, 16, and Acts 2:38, 39 and John 3:3, 5 and I John 5:12 & Rom. 8:9 compared.* [n] *John 3:8.* [o] *I John 5:12; Acts 4:12.*

IV. Others, not elected, although they may be called by the ministry of the Word,[p] and may have some common operations of the Spirit,[q] yet they never truly come unto Christ, and therefore cannot be saved:[r] much less can men, not professing the Christian religion, be saved in any other way whatsoever, be they never so diligent to frame their lives according to the light of nature, and the law of that religion they do profess.[s] And to assert and maintain that they may, is very pernicious, and to be detested.[t]

[p] *Matt. 22:14.* [q] *Matt. 7:22; Matt. 13:20, 21; Heb. 6:4, 5.* [r] *John 6:64, 65, 66; John 8:24.* [s] *Acts 4:12; John 14:6; Eph. 2:12; John 4:22; John 17:3.* [t] *II John ver. 9, 10, 11; I Cor. 16:22; Gal. 1:6, 7, 8.*

CHAPTER XI: OF JUSTIFICATION.

I. Those whom God effectually calleth, He also freely justifieth;[(a)] not by infusing righteousness into them, but by pardoning their sins, and by accounting and accepting their persons as righteous, not for anything wrought in them, or done by them, but for Christ's sake alone; nor by imputing faith itself, the act of believing, or any other evangelical obedience to them, as their righteousness, but by imputing the obedience and satisfaction of Christ unto them,[(b)] they receiving and resting on Him and His righteousness by faith; which faith they have not of themselves, it is the gift of God.[(c)]

> [(a)] *Rom. 8:30; Rom. 3:24.* [(b)] *Rom. 4:5, 6, 7, 8; II Cor. 5:19, 21; Rom. 3:22, 24, 25, 27, 28; Tit. 3:5, 7; Eph. 1:7; Jer. 23:6; I Cor. 1:30, 31; Rom. 5:17, 18, 19.* [(c)] *Acts 10:43; Gal. 2:16; Phil. 3:19; Acts 13:38, 39; Eph. 2:7, 8.*

II. Faith, thus receiving and resting on Christ and His righteousness, is the alone instrument of justification;[(d)] yet is it not alone in the person justified, but is ever accompanied with all other saving graces, and is no dead faith, but worketh by love.[(e)]

> [(d)] *John 1:12; Rom. 3:28; Rom. 5:1.* [(e)] *Jam. 2:17, 22, 26; Gal. 5:6.*

III. Christ, by His obedience and death, did fully discharge the debt of all those that are thus justified, and did make a proper, real, and full satisfaction to His Father's justice in their behalf.[(f)] Yet, inasmuch as He was given by the Father for them;[(g)] and His obedience and satisfaction accepted in their stead;[(h)] and both freely, not for anything in them; their justification is only of free grace;[(i)] that both the exact justice, and rich grace of God, might be glorified in the justification of sinners.[(k)]

> [(f)] *Rom. 5:8, 9, 10, 19; I Tim. 2:5, 6; Heb. 10:10, 14; Dan. 9:24, 26; Isa. 53:4, 5, 6, 10, 11, 12.* [(g)] *Rom. 8:32.* [(h)] *II Cor. 5:21; Matt. 3:17; Eph. 5:2.* [(i)] *Rom. 3:24; Eph. 1:7.* [(k)] *Rom. 3:26; Eph. 2:7.*

IV. God did, from all eternity, decree to justify all the elect,[(l)] and Christ did, in the fulness of time, die for their sins, and rise again for their justification:[(m)] nevertheless, they are not justified, until the Holy Spirit doth, in due time, actually apply Christ unto them.[n]

[l] *Gal. 3:8; I Pet. 1:2, 19, 20; Rom. 8:30.* [m] *Gal. 4:4; I Tim. 2:6; Rom. 4:25.* [n] *Col. 1:21, 22; Gal. 2:16; Tit. 3:3, 4, 5, 6, 7.*

V. God doth continue to forgive the sins of those that are justified:[o] and although they can never fall from the state of justification;[p] yet they may, by their sins, fall under God's fatherly displeasure, and not have the light of His countenance restored unto them, until they humble themselves, confess their sins, beg pardon, and renew their faith and repentance.[q]

[o] *Matt. 6:12; I John 1:7, 9; I John 2:1, 2.* [p] *Luke 22:32; John 10:28; Heb. 10:14.* [q] *Ps. 89:31, 32, 33; Ps. 51:7, 8, 9, 10, 11, 12; Ps. 32:5; Matt. 26:75; I Cor. 11:30, 32; Luke 1:20.*

VI. The justification of believers under the Old Testament was, in all these respects, one and the same with the justification of believers under the New Testament.[r]

[r] *Gal. 3:9, 13, 14; Rom. 4:22, 23, 24; Heb. 13:8.*

CHAPTER XII: OF ADOPTION.

All those that are justified, God vouchsafeth, in and for His only Son Jesus Christ, to make partakers of the grace of adoption:[a] by which they are taken into the number, and enjoy the liberties and privileges of the children of God,[b] have His name put upon them,[c] receive the spirit of adoption,[d] have access to the throne of grace with boldness,[e] are enabled to cry, Abba, Father,[f] are pitied,[g] protected,[h] provided for,[i] and chastened by Him as by a Father;[k] yet never cast off,[l] but sealed to the day of redemption,[m] and inherit the promises,[n] as heirs of everlasting salvation.[o]

[a] *Eph. 1:5.* [b] *Gal. 4:4, 5; Rom. 8:17; John 1:12.* [c] *Jer. 14:9; II Cor. 6:18; Rev. 3:12.* [d] *Rom. 8:15.* [e] *Eph. 3:12; Rom. 5:2.* [f] *Gal. 4:6.* [g] *Ps. 103:13.* [h] *Prov. 14:26.* [i] *Matt. 6:30, 32; I Pet. 5:7.* [k] *Heb. 12:6.* [l] *Lam. 3:31.* [m] *Eph. 4:30.* [n] *Heb. 6:12.* [o] *I Pet. 1:3, 4; Heb. 1:14.*

CHAPTER XIII: OF SANCTIFICATION.

I. They who are once effectually called and regenerated, having a new heart and a new spirit created in them, are further sanctified, really and personally, through the virtue of Christ's death and resurrection,[a] by His Word and Spirit dwelling in them:[b] the dominion of the whole body of sin is destroyed,[c] and the several lusts thereof are more and more weakened and mortified;[d] and they more and more quickened and strengthened in all saving graces,[e] to the practice of true holiness, without which no man shall see the Lord.[f]

> [a] *I Cor. 6:11; Acts 20:32; Phil. 3:10; Rom. 6:5, 6.* [b] *John 17:17; Eph. 5:26; II Thess. 2:13.* [c] *Rom. 6:6, 14.* [d] *Gal. 5:24; Rom. 8:13.* [e] *Col. 1:11; Eph. 3:16, 17, 18, 19.* [f] *II Cor. 7:1; Heb. 12:14.*

II. This sanctification is throughout, in the whole man;[g] yet imperfect in this life, there abiding still some remnants of corruption in every part:[h] whence ariseth a continual and irreconcilable war; the flesh lusting against the Spirit, and the Spirit against the flesh.[i]

> [g] *I Thess. 5:23.* [h] *I John 1:10; Rom. 7:18, 23; Phil. 3:12.* [i] *Gal. 5:17; I Pet. 2:11.*

III. In which war, although the remaining corruption, for a time, may much prevail;[k] yet through the continual supply of strength from the sanctifying Spirit of Christ, the regenerate part doth overcome;[l] and so, the saints grow in grace,[m] perfecting holiness in the fear of God.[n]

> [k] *Rom. 7:23.* [l] *Rom. 6:14; I John 5:4; Eph. 4:15, 16.* [m] *II Pet. 3:18; II Cor. 3:18.* [n] *II Cor. 7:1.*

CHAPTER XIV: OF SAVING FAITH.

I. The grace of faith, whereby the elect are enabled to believe to the saving of their souls,[a] is the work of the Spirit of Christ in their hearts;[b] and is ordinarily wrought by the ministry of the Word:[c] by which also, and by the administration of the sacraments, and prayer, it is increased and strengthened.[d]

> [a] *Heb. 10:39.* [b] *II Cor. 4:13; Eph. 1:17, 18, 19; Eph. 2:8.* [c] *Rom. 10:14, 17.* [d] *I Pet. 2:2; Acts 20:32; Rom. 4:11; Luke 17:5; Rom. 1:16, 17.*

II. By this faith, a Christian believeth to be true whatsoever is revealed in the Word, for the authority of God Himself speaking therein;[e] and acteth differently upon that which each particular passage thereof containeth; yielding obedience to the commands,[f] trembling at the threatenings,[g] and embracing the promises of God for this life, and that which is to come.[h] But the principal acts of saving faith are accepting, receiving, and resting upon Christ alone for justification, sanctification, and eternal life, by virtue of the covenant of grace.[i]

(e) *John 4:42; I Thess. 2:13; I John 5:10; Acts 24:14.* (f) *Rom. 16:26.* (g) *Isa. 66:2.* (h) *Heb. 11:13; I Tim. 4:8.* (i) *John 1:12; Acts 16:31; Gal. 2:20; Acts 15:11.*

III. This faith is different in degrees, weak or strong;[k] may be often and many ways assailed, and weakened, but gets the victory;[l] growing up in many to the attainment of a full assurance through Christ,[m] who is both the author and finisher of our faith.[n]

(k) *Heb. 5:13, 14; Rom. 4:19, 20; Matt. 6:30; Matt. 8:10.*
(l) *Luke 22:31, 32; Eph. 6:16; I John 5:4, 5.*
(m) *Heb. 6:11, 12; Heb. 10:22; Col. 2:2.* (n) *Heb. 12:2.*

CHAPTER XV: OF REPENTANCE UNTO LIFE.

I. Repentance unto life is an evangelical grace,[a] the doctrine whereof is to be preached by every minister of the Gospel, as well as that of faith in Christ.[b]

(a) *Zech. 12:10; Acts 11:18.* (b) *Luke 24:47; Mark 1:15; Acts 20:21.*

II. By it, a sinner, out of the sight and sense not only of the danger, but also of the filthiness and odiousness of his sins, as contrary to the holy nature and righteous law of God; and upon the apprehension of his mercy in Christ to such as are penitent, so grieves for, and hates his sins, as to turn from them all unto God,[c] purposing and endeavouring to walk with Him in all the ways of His commandments.[d]

(c) *Ezek. 18:30, 31; Ezek. 36:31; Isa. 30:22; Ps. 51:4; Jer. 31:18, 19; Joel 2:12, 13; Amos 5:15; Ps. 119:128; II Cor. 7:11.* (d) *Ps. 119:6, 59, 106; Luke 1:6; II Kings 23:25.*

III. Although repentance be not to be rested in, as any satisfaction for sin, or any cause of the pardon thereof,[e] which is the act of God's free grace in Christ;[f] yet is it of such necessity to all sinners, that none may expect pardon without it.[g]

[e] *Ezek. 36:31, 32; Ezek. 16:61, 62, 63.* [f] *Hosea 14:2, 4; Rom. 3:24; Eph. 1:7.* [g] *Luke 13:3, 5; Acts 17:30, 31.*

IV. As there is no sin so small, but it deserves damnation,[h] so there is no sin so great, that it can bring damnation upon those who truly repent.[i]

[h] *Rom. 6:23; Rom. 5:12; Matt. 12:36.* [i] *Isa. 55:7; Rom. 8:1; Isa. 1:16, 18.*

V. Men ought not to content themselves with a general repentance, but it is every man's duty to endeavour to repent of his particular sins, particularly.[k]

[k] *Ps. 19:13; Luke 19:8; I Tim. 1:13, 15.*

VI. As every man is bound to make private confession of his sins to God, praying for the pardon thereof;[l] upon which, and the forsaking of them, he shall find mercy:[m] so, he that scandalizeth his brother, or the Church of Christ, ought to be willing, by a private or public confession, and sorrow for his sin, to declare his repentance to those that are offended,[n] who are thereupon to be reconciled to him, and in love to receive him.[o]

[l] *Ps. 51:4, 5, 7, 9, 14; Ps. 32:5, 6.* [m] *Prov. 28:13; I John 1:9.*
[n] *James 5:16; Luke 17:3, 4; Joshua 7:19; Ps. 51 throughout.* [o] *II Cor. 2:8.*

CHAPTER XVI: OF GOOD WORKS.

I. Good works are only such as God hath commanded in His holy Word,[a] and not such as, without the warrant thereof, are devised by men, out of blind zeal, or upon any pretence of good intention.[b]

[a] *Micah 6:8; Rom. 12:2; Heb. 13:21.* [b] *Matt. 15:9; Isa. 29:13; I Pet. 1:18; Rom. 10:2; John 16:2; I Sam. 15:21, 22, 23.*

II. These good works, done in obedience to God's commandments, are the fruits and evidences of a true and lively faith:[c] and by them believers manifest their thankfulness,[d] strengthen their assurance,[e] edify their brethren,[f] adorn the profession of the Gospel,[g] stop the mouths of the adversaries,[h] and glorify God,[i] whose workmanship they are, created in Christ Jesus thereunto;[k] that, having their fruit unto holiness, they may have the end, eternal life.[l]

[c] *James 2:18, 22.* [d] *Ps. 116:12, 13; I Pet. 2:9.* [e] *I John 2:3, 5; II Pet. 1:5, 6, 7, 8, 9, 10.* [f] *II Cor. 9:2; Matt. 5:16.* [g] *Tit. 2:5, 9, 10, 11, 12; I Tim. 6:1.* [h] *I Pet. 2:15.* [i] *I Pet. 2:12; Phil. 1:11; John 15:8.* [k] *Eph. 2:10.* [l] *Rom. 6:22.*

III. Their ability to do good works is not at all of themselves, but wholly from the Spirit of Christ.[m] And that they may be enabled thereunto, besides the graces they have already received, there is required an actual influence of the same Holy Spirit, to work in them to will and to do of His good pleasure:[n] yet are they not hereupon to grow negligent, as if they were not bound to perform any duty, unless upon a special motion of the Spirit; but they ought to be diligent in stirring up the grace of God that is in them.[o]

[m] *John 15:4, 5; Ezek. 36:26, 27.* [n] *Phil. 2:13; Phil. 4:13; II Cor. 3:5.* [o] *Phil. 2:12; Heb. 6:11, 12; II Pet. 1:3, 5, 10, 11; Isa. 64:7; II Tim. 1:6; Acts 26:6, 7; Jude ver. 20, 21.*

IV. They, who in their obedience attain to the greatest height which is possible in this life, are so far from being able to supererogate, and to do more than God requires, as that they fall short of much which in duty they are bound to do.[p]

[p] *Luke 17:10; Neh. 13:22; Job 9:2, 3; Gal. 5:17.*

V. We cannot, by our best works, merit pardon of sin, or eternal life at the hand of God, by reason of the great disproportion that is between them and the glory to come; and the infinite distance that is between us and God, whom, by them, we can neither profit, nor satisfy for the debt of our former sins,[q] but when we have done all we can, we have done but our duty, and are unprofitable servants;[r] and because, as they are good, they proceed from His Spirit;[s] and as they are wrought by us, they are defiled, and mixed with so much weakness and imperfection, that they cannot endure the severity of God's judgment.[t]

[q] *Rom. 3:20; Rom. 4:2, 4, 6; Eph. 2:8, 9; Tit. 3:5, 6, 7; Rom. 8:18; Ps. 16:2; Job 22:2, 3; Job 35:7, 8.* [r] *Luke 17:10.* [s] *Gal. 5:22, 23.* [t] *Isa. 64:6; Gal. 5:17; Rom. 7:15, 18; Ps. 143:2; Ps. 130:3.*

VI. Yet notwithstanding, the persons of believers being accepted through Christ, their good works also are accepted in Him,[u] not as though they were in this life wholly unblamable and unreproveable in God's sight;[w] but that He, looking upon them in His Son, is pleased to accept and reward that which is sincere, although accompanied with many weaknesses and imperfections.[x]

[u] *Eph. 1:6; I Pet. 2:5; Exod. 28:38; Gen. 4:4 with Heb. 11:4.* [w] *Job. 9:20; Ps. 143:2.* [x] *Heb. 13:20, 21; II Cor. 8:12; Heb. 6:10; Matt. 25:21, 23.*

VII. Works done by unregenerate men, although, for the matter of them, they may be things which God commands, and of good use both to themselves and others:[y] yet, because they proceed not from a heart purified by faith;[z] nor are done in a right manner according to the Word;[a] nor to a right end, the glory of God;[b] they are therefore sinful, and cannot please God, or make a man meet to receive grace from God.[c] And yet, their neglect of them is more sinful, and displeasing unto God.[d]

[y] *II Kings 10:30, 31; I Kings 21:27, 29; Phil. 1:15, 16, 18.* [z] *Gen. 4:5 with Heb. 11:4; Heb. 11:6.* [a] *I Cor. 13:3; Isa. 1:12.* [b] *Matt. 6:2, 5, 16.* [c] *Hag. 2:14; Tit. 1:15; Amos 5:22, 23; Hosea 1:4; Rom. 9:16; Titus 3:5.* [d] *Ps. 14:4; Ps. 36:3; Job 21:14, 15; Matt. 25:41, 42, 43, 45; Matt. 23:23.*

CHAPTER XVII: OF THE PERSEVERANCE OF THE SAINTS.

I. They, whom God hath accepted in His Beloved, effectually called, and sanctified by His Spirit, can neither totally, nor finally, fall away from the state of grace: but shall certainly persevere therein to the end, and be eternally saved.[a]

[a] *Phil. 1:6; II Pet. 1:10; John 10:28, 29; I John 3:9; I Pet. 1:5, 9.*

II. This perseverance of the saints depends not upon their own free will, but upon the immutability of the decree of election, flowing from the free and unchangeable love of God the Father;[b] upon the efficacy of the merit and intercession of Jesus Christ;[c] the abiding of the Spirit, and of the seed of God within them;[d] and the nature of the covenant of grace:[(e)] from all which ariseth also the certainty and infallibility thereof.[(f)]

[(b)] *II Tim. 2:18, 19; Jer. 31:3.* [(c)] *Heb. 10:10, 14; Heb. 13:20, 21; Heb. 9:12, 13, 14, 15; Rom. 8:33 to the end; John 17:11, 24; Luke 22:32; Heb. 7:25.* [(d)] *John 14:16, 17; I John 2:27; I John 3:9.* [(e)] *Jer. 32:40.* [(f)] *John 10:28; II Thess. 3:3; I John 2:19.*

III. Nevertheless, they may, through the temptations of Satan and of the world, the prevalency of corruption remaining in them, and the neglect of the means of their preservation, fall into grievous sins;[(g)] and, for a time, continue therein:[(h)] whereby they incur God's displeasure,[(i)] and grieve His Holy Spirit,[(k)] come to be deprived of some measure of their graces and comforts,[(l)] have their hearts hardened,[(m)] and their consciences wounded,[(n)] hurt and scandalize others,[(o)] and bring temporal judgments upon themselves.[(p)]

[(g)] *Matt. 26:70, 72, 74.* [(h)] *Ps. 51 title and ver. 14.* [(i)] *Isa. 64:5, 7, 9; II Sam. 11:27.* [(k)] *Eph. 4:30.* [(l)] *Ps. 51:8, 10, 12; Rev. 2:4; Cant. 5:2, 3, 4, 6.* [(m)] *Isa. 63:17; Mark 6:52; Mark 16:14.* [(n)] *Ps. 32:3, 4; Ps. 51:8.* [(o)] *II Sam. 12:14.* [(p)] *Ps. 89:31, 32; I Cor. 11:32.*

CHAPTER XVIII: OF THE ASSURANCE OF GRACE AND SALVATION.

I. Although hypocrites and other unregenerate men may vainly deceive themselves with false hopes, and carnal presumptions of being in the favour of God, and estate of salvation;[(a)] which hope of theirs shall perish:[(b)] yet such as truly believe in the Lord Jesus, and love Him in sincerity, endeavouring to walk in all good conscience before Him, may, in this life, be certainly assured that they are in the state of grace,[(c)] and may rejoice in the hope of the glory of God, which hope shall never make them ashamed.[(d)]

[(a)] *Job 8:13, 14; Mic. 3:11; Deut. 29:19; John 8:41.* [(b)] *Matt. 7:22, 23.* [(c)] *I John 2:3; I John 3:14, 18, 19, 21, 24; I John 5:13.* [(d)] *Rom. 5:2, 5.*

II. This certainty is not a bare conjectural and probable persuasion, grounded upon a fallible hope;[(e)] but an infallible assurance of faith, founded upon the divine truth of the promises of salvation,[f] the inward evidence of those graces unto which these promises are made,[g] the testimony of the Spirit of adoption witnessing with our spirits that we are the children of God:[h] which Spirit is the earnest of our inheritance, whereby we are sealed to the day of redemption.[i]

> [e] *Heb. 6:11, 19.* [f] *Heb. 6:17, 18.* [g] *II Pet. 1:4, 5, 10, 11; I John 2:3; I John 3:14; II Cor. 1:12.* [h] *Rom. 8:15, 16.* [i] *Eph. 1:13, 14; Eph. 4:30; II Cor. 1:21, 22.*

III. This infallible assurance doth not so belong to the essence of faith, but that a true believer may wait long, and conflict with many difficulties before he be partaker of it:[k] yet, being enabled by the Spirit to know the things which are freely given him of God, he may without extraordinary revelation, in the right use of ordinary means, attain thereunto.[l] And therefore it is the duty of everyone to give all diligence to make his calling and election sure;[m] that thereby his heart may be enlarged in peace and joy in the Holy Ghost, in love and thankfulness to God, and in strength and cheerfulness in the duties of obedience, the proper fruits of this assurance:[n] so far is it from inclining men to looseness.[o]

> [k] *I John 5:13; Isa. 50:10; Mark 9:24; Ps. 88 throughout; Ps. 77 to ver. 12.* [l] *I Cor. 2:12; I John 4:13; Heb. 6:11, 12; Eph. 3:17, 18, 19.* [m] *II Pet. 1:10.* [n] *Rom. 5:1, 2, 5; Rom. 14:17; Rom. 15:13; Eph. 1:3, 4; Ps. 4:6, 7; Ps. 119:32.* [o] *I John 2:1, 2; Rom. 6:1, 2; Tit. 2:11, 12, 14; II Cor. 7:1; Rom. 8:1, 12; I John 3:2, 3; Ps. 130:4; I John 1:6, 7.*

IV. True believers may have the assurance of their salvation divers ways shaken, diminished, and intermitted; as, by negligence in preserving of it, by falling into some special sin, which woundeth the conscience and grieveth the Spirit; by some sudden or vehement temptation, by God's withdrawing the light of His countenance, and suffering even such as fear Him to walk in darkness and to have no light:[p] yet are they never so utterly destitute of that seed of God, and life of faith, that love of Christ and the brethren, that sincerity of heart, and conscience of duty, out of which, by the operation of the Spirit, this assurance may, in due time, be revived;[q] and by the which, in the mean time, they are supported from utter despair.[r]

[p] *Cant. 5:2, 3, 6; Ps. 51:8, 12, 14; Eph. 4:30, 31; Ps. 77:1 to 10; Matt. 26:69, 70, 71, 72; Ps. 31:22; Ps. 88 throughout; Isa. 50:10.*

[q] *I John 3:9; Luke 22:32; Job 13:15; Ps. 73:15; Ps. 51:8, 12; Isa. 50:10.*

[r] *Mic. 7:7, 8, 9; Jer. 32:40; Isa. 54:7, 8, 9, 10; Ps. 22:1; Ps. 88 throughout.*

CHAPTER XIX: OF THE LAW OF GOD.

I. God gave to Adam a law, as a covenant of works, by which He bound him and all his posterity to personal, entire, exact, and perpetual obedience; promised life upon the fulfilling, and threatened death upon the breach of it: and endued him with power and ability to keep it.[a]

[a] *Gen. 1:26, 27 with Gen. 2:17; Rom. 2:14, 15; Rom. 10:5; Rom. 5:12, 19; Gal. 3:10, 12; Eccles. 7:29; Job 28:28.*

II. This law, after his fall, continued to be a perfect rule of righteousness, and, as such, was delivered by God upon Mount Sinai, in ten commandments, and written in two tables:[b] the four first commandments containing our duty towards God; and the other six our duty to man.[c]

[b] *James 1:25; James 2:8, 10, 11, 12; Rom. 13:8, 9; Deut. 5:32; Deut. 10:4; Ex. 34:1.* [c] *Matt. 22:37, 38, 39, 40.*

III. Beside this law, commonly called moral, God was pleased to give to the people of Israel, as a church under age, ceremonial laws, containing several typical ordinances, partly of worship, prefiguring Christ, His graces, actions, sufferings, and benefits;[d] and partly holding forth divers instructions of moral duties.[e] All which ceremonial laws are now abrogated, under the New Testament.[f]

[d] *Heb. 9 chap.; Heb. 10:1; Gal. 4:1, 2, 3; Col. 2:17.* [e] *I Cor. 5:7; II Cor. 6:17; Jude ver. 23.* [f] *Col. 2:14, 16, 17; Dan. 9:27; Eph. 2:15, 16.*

IV. To them also, as a body politic, He gave sundry judicial laws, which expired together with the State of that people; not obliging any other now, further than the general equity thereof may require.(g)

(g) *Ex. 21 chap.; Ex. 22:1 to 29; Gen. 49:10 with I Pet. 2:13, 14; Matt. 5:17, with ver. 38, 39; I Cor. 9:8, 9, 10.*

V. The moral law doth for ever bind all, as well justified persons as others, to the obedience thereof;(h) and that, not only in regard of the matter contained in it, but also in respect of the authority of God the Creator, who gave it:(i) neither doth Christ, in the Gospel, any way dissolve, but much strengthen this obligation.(k)

(h) *Rom. 13:8, 9, 10; Eph. 6:2; I John 2:3, 4, 7, 8.* (i) *James 2:10, 11.*
(k) *Matt. 5:17, 18, 19; James 2:8; Rom. 3:31.*

VI. Although true believers be not under the law, as a covenant of works, to be thereby justified, or condemned;(l) yet is it of great use to them, as well as to others; in that, as a rule of life informing them of the will of God, and their duty, it directs, and binds them to walk accordingly;(m) discovering also the sinful pollutions of their nature, hearts, and lives;(n) so as, examining themselves thereby, they may come to further conviction of, humiliation for, and hatred against sin;(o) together with a clearer sight of the need they have of Christ, and the perfection of His obedience.(p) It is likewise of use to the regenerate, to restrain their corruptions, in that it forbids sin:(q) and the threatenings of it serve to show what even their sins deserve; and what afflictions, in this life, they may expect for them, although freed from the curse thereof threatened in the law.(r) The promises of it, in like manner, show them God's approbation of obedience, and what blessings they may expect upon the performance thereof;(s) although not as due to them by the law, as a covenant of works.(t) So as, a man's doing good, and refraining from evil, because the law encourageth to the one and deterreth from the other, is no evidence of his being under the law; and not under grace.(u)

(l) *Rom. 6:14; Gal. 2:16; Gal. 3:13; Gal. 4:4, 5; Acts 13:39; Rom. 8:1.* (m) *Rom. 7:12, 22, 25; Ps. 119:4, 5, 6; I Cor. 7:19; Gal. 5:14, 16, 18, 19, 20, 21, 22, 23.* (n) *Rom. 7:7; Rom. 3:20.* (o) *James 1:23, 24, 25; Rom. 7:9, 14, 24.* (p) *Gal. 3:24; Rom. 7:24, 25; Rom. 8:3, 4.* (q) *Jam. 2:11; Ps. 119:101, 104, 128.* (r) *Ezra 9:13, 14; Ps. 89:30, 31, 32, 33, 34.* (s) *Lev. 26:1 to 14 with II Cor. 6:16; Eph. 6:2, 3; Ps. 37:11 with Matt. 5:5; Ps. 19:11.* (t) *Gal. 2:16; Luke 17:10.* (u) *Rom. 6:12, 14; I Pet. 3:8, 9, 10, 11, 12, with Ps. 34:12, 13, 14, 15, 16; Heb. 12:28, 29.*

VII. Neither are the forementioned uses of the law contrary to the grace of the Gospel, but do sweetly comply with it;(w) the Spirit of Christ subduing and enabling the will of man to do that, freely and cheerfully, which the will of God, revealed in the law, requireth to be done.(x)

(w) *Gal. 3:21.* (x) *Ezek. 36:27; Heb. 8:10 with Jer. 31:33.*

CHAPTER XX: OF CHRISTIAN LIBERTY, AND LIBERTY OF CONSCIENCE.

I. The liberty which Christ hath purchased for believers under the Gospel consists in their freedom from the guilt of sin, and condemning wrath of God, the curse of the moral law;(a) and, in their being delivered from this present evil world, bondage to Satan, and dominion of sin;(b) from the evil of afflictions, the sting of death, the victory of the grave, and everlasting damnation;(c) as also, in their free access to God,(d) and their yielding obedience unto Him, not out of slavish fear, but a child-like love and willing mind.(e) All which were common also to believers under the law.(f) But, under the New Testament, the liberty of Christians is further enlarged, in their freedom from the yoke of the ceremonial law, to which the Jewish Church was subjected;(g) and in greater boldness of access to the throne of grace,(h) and in fuller communications of the free Spirit of God, than believers under the law did ordinarily partake of.[i]

[a] *Tit. 2:14; I Thess. 1:10; Gal. 3:13.* [b] *Gal. 1:4; Col. 1:13; Acts 26:18; Rom. 6:14.* [c] *Rom. 8:28; Ps. 119:71; I Cor. 15:54, 55, 56, 57; Rom. 8:1.* [d] *Rom. 5:1, 2.* [e] *Rom. 8:14, 15; I John 4:18.* [f] *Gal. 3:9, 14.* [g] *Gal. 4:1, 2, 3, 6, 7; Gal. 5:1; Acts 15:10, 11.* [h] *Heb. 4:14, 16; Heb. 10:19, 20, 21, 22.* [i] *John 7:38, 39; II Cor. 3:13, 17, 18.*

II. God alone is Lord of the conscience,[k] and hath left it free from the doctrines and commandments of men, which are in any thing contrary to His Word; or beside it, if matters of faith or worship.[l] So that, to believe such doctrines, or to obey such commands, out of conscience,[m] is to betray true liberty of conscience: and the requiring of an implicit faith, and an absolute and blind obedience is to destroy liberty of conscience, and reason also.[n]

[k] *Jam. 4:12; Rom. 14:4.* [l] *Acts 4:19; Acts 5:29; I Cor. 7:23; Matt. 23:8, 9, 10; II Cor. 1:24; Matt. 15:9.* [m] *Col. 2:20, 22, 23; Gal. 1:10; Gal. 2:4, 5; Gal. 5:1.* [n] *Rom. 10:17; Rom. 14:23; Isa. 8:20; Acts 17:11; John 4:22; Hos. 5:11; Rev. 13:12, 16, 17; Jer. 8:9.*

III. They who, upon pretence of Christian liberty, do practice any sin, or cherish any lust, do thereby destroy the end of Christian liberty, which is, that being delivered out of the hands of our enemies, we might serve the Lord, without fear, in holiness and righteousness before Him, all the days of our life.[o]

[o] *Gal. 5:13; I Pet. 2:16; II Pet. 2:19; John 8:34; Luke 1:74, 75.*

IV. And because the powers which God hath ordained, and the liberty which Christ hath purchased, are not intended by God to destroy, but mutually to uphold and preserve one another; they who, upon pretence of Christian liberty, shall oppose any lawful power, or the lawful exercise of it, whether it be civil or ecclesiastical, resist the ordinance of God.[p] And, for their publishing of such opinions, or maintaining of such practices, as are contrary to the light of nature, or to the known principles of Christianity, whether concerning faith, worship, or conversation; or, to the power of godliness; or, such erroneous opinions or practices, as either in their own nature, or in the manner of publishing or maintaining them, are destructive to the external peace and order which Christ hath established in the Church, they may lawfully be called to account, and proceeded against by the censures of the Church,[q] and by the power of the civil magistrate.[r]

[p] *Matt. 12:25; I Pet. 2:13, 14, 16; Rom. 13:1 to 8; Heb. 13:17.*

[q] *Rom. 1:32 with I Cor. 5:1, 5, 11, 13; II John ver. 10, 11, and II Thess. 3:14, and I Tim. 6:3, 4, 5, and Tit. 1:10, 11, 13, and Tit. 3:10 with Matt. 18:15, 16, 17; I Tim. 1:19, 20; Rev. 2:2, 14, 15, 20; Rev. 3:9.*

[r] *Deut. 13:6 to 12; Rom. 13:3, 4 with II John ver. 10, 11; Ezra 7:23, 25, 26, 27, 28; Rev. 17:12, 16, 17; Neh. 13:15, 17, 21, 22, 25, 30; II Kings 23:5, 6, 9, 20, 21; II Chron. 34:33; II Chron. 15:12, 13, 16; Dan. 3:29; I Tim. 2:2; Isa. 49:23; Zech. 13:2, 3.*

CHAPTER XXI: OF RELIGIOUS WORSHIP AND THE SABBATH-DAY.

I. The light of nature showeth that there is a God, who hath lordship and sovereignty over all, is good, and doth good unto all, and is therefore to be feared, loved, praised, called upon, trusted in, and served, with all the heart, and with all the soul, and with all the might.[a] But the acceptable way of worshipping the true God is instituted by Himself, and so limited by His own revealed will, that He may not be worshipped according to the imaginations and devices of men, or the suggestions of Satan, under any visible representation, or any other way not prescribed in the holy Scripture.[b]

[a] *Rom. 1:20; Acts 17:24; Ps. 119:68; Jer. 10:7; Ps. 31:23; Ps. 18:3; Rom. 10:12; Ps. 62:8; Josh. 24:14; Mark 12:33.* [b] *Deut. 12:32; Matt. 15:9; Acts 17:25; Matt. 4:9, 10; Deut. 4:15 to 20; Exod. 20:4, 5, 6; Col. 2:23.*

II. Religious worship is to be given to God, the Father, Son, and Holy Ghost; and to Him alone;[c] not to angels, saints, or any other creature:[d] and since the fall, not without a Mediator; nor in the mediation of any other but of Christ alone.[e]

[c] *Matt. 4:10 with John 5:23 and II Cor. 13:14.* [d] *Col. 2:18, Rev. 19:10; Rom. 1:25.* [e] *John 14:6; I Tim. 2:5; Eph. 2:18; Col. 3:17.*

III. Prayer, with thanksgiving, being one special part of religious worship,[f] is by God required of all men:[g] and that it may be accepted, it is to be made in the name of the Son,[h] by the help of His Spirit,[i] according to His will,[k] with understanding, reverence, humility, fervency, faith, love, and perseverance;[l] and, if vocal, in a known tongue.[m]

> [f] *Phil. 4:6.* [g] *Ps. 65:2.* [h] *John 14:13, 14; I Pet. 2:5.* [i] *Rom. 8:26.* [k] *I John 5:14.* [l] *Ps. 47:7; Eccles. 5:1, 2; Heb. 12:28; Gen. 18:27; James 5:16; James 1:6, 7; Mark 11:24; Matt. 6:12, 14, 15; Col. 4:2; Eph. 6:18.* [m] *I Cor. 14:14.*

IV. Prayer is to be made for things lawful;[n] and for all sorts of men living, or that shall live hereafter:[o] but not for the dead,[p] nor for those of whom it may be known that they have sinned the sin unto death.[q]

> [n] *I John 5:14.* [o] *I Tim. 2:1, 2; John 17:20; II Sam. 7:29; Ruth 4:12.* [p] *II Sam. 12:21, 22, 23 with Luke 16:25, 26; Rev. 14:13.* [q] *I John 5:16.*

V. The reading of the Scriptures with godly fear,[r] the sound preaching[s] and conscionable hearing of the Word, in obedience unto God, with understanding, faith and reverence;[t] singing of psalms with grace in the heart;[u] as also, the due administration and worthy receiving of the sacraments instituted by Christ; are all parts of the ordinary religious worship of God:[w] beside religious oaths,[x] vows,[y] solemn fastings,[z] and thanksgivings, upon special occasions,[a] which are, in their several times and seasons, to be used in a holy and religious manner.[b]

> [r] *Acts 15:21; Rev. 1:3.* [s] *II Tim. 4:2.* [t] *James 1:22; Acts 10:33; Matt. 13:19; Heb. 4:2; Isa. 66:2.* [u] *Col. 3:16; Eph. 5:19; James 5:13.* [w] *Matt. 28:19; I Cor. 11:23 to 29; Acts 2:42.* [x] *Deut. 6:13 with Neh. 10:29.* [y] *Isa. 19:21 with Eccles. 5:4, 5.* [z] *Joel 2:12; Esther 4:16; Matt. 9:15; I Cor. 7:5.* [a] *Ps. 107 throughout; Esther 9:22.* [b] *Heb. 12:28.*

VI. Neither prayer, nor any other part of religious worship, is now under the Gospel either tied unto, or made more acceptable by any place in which it is performed, or towards which it is directed:[c] but God is to be worshipped everywhere,[d] in spirit and truth;[e] as in private families[f] daily,[g] and in secret each one by himself;[h] so, more solemnly, in the public assemblies, which are not carelessly or willfully to be neglected, or forsaken, when God, by His Word or providence, calls thereunto.[i]

[c] *John 4:21.* [d] *Mal. 1:11; I Tim. 2:8.* [e] *John 4:23, 24.* [f] *Jer. 10:25; Deut. 6:6, 7; Job 1:5; II Sam. 6:18, 20; I Pet. 3:7; Acts 10:2.* [g] *Matt. 6:11.* [h] *Matt. 6:6; Eph. 6:18.* [i] *Isa. 56:6, 7; Heb. 10:25; Prov. 1:20, 21, 24; Prov. 8:34; Acts 13:42; Luke 4:16; Acts 2:42.*

VII. As it is the law of nature, that, in general, a due proportion of time be set apart for the worship of God; so, in His Word, by a positive, moral, and perpetual commandment, binding all men, in all ages, He hath particularly appointed one day in seven, for a Sabbath, to be kept holy unto Him:[k] which, from the beginning of the world to the resurrection of Christ, was the last day of the week; and, from the resurrection of Christ, was changed into the first day of the week,[l] which, in Scripture, is called the Lord's Day,[m] and is to be continued to the end of the world, as the Christian Sabbath.[n]

[k] *Exod. 20:8, 10, 11; Isa. 56:2, 4, 6, 7.* [l] *Gen. 2:2, 3; I Cor. 16:1, 2; Acts 20:7.* [m] *Rev. 1:10.* [n] *Exod. 20:8, 10, with Matt. 5:17, 18.*

VIII. This Sabbath is then kept holy unto the Lord, when men, after a due preparing of their hearts, and ordering of their common affairs beforehand, do not only observe an holy rest, all the day, from their own works, words, and thoughts about their worldly employments and recreations,[o] but also are taken up the whole time in the public and private exercises of His worship, and in the duties of necessity and mercy.[p]

[o] *Exod. 20:8; Exod. 16:23, 25, 26, 29, 30; Exod. 31:15, 16, 17; Isa. 58:13; Neh. 13:15, 16, 17, 18, 19, 21, 22.*
[p] *Isa. 58:13; Matt. 12:1 to 13.*

CHAPTER XXII: OF LAWFUL OATHS AND VOWS.

I. A lawful oath is a part of religious worship,[a] wherein, upon just occasion, the person swearing solemnly calleth God to witness what he asserteth, or promiseth, and to judge him according to the truth or falsehood of what he sweareth.[b]

[a] *Deut. 10:20.* [b] *Exod. 20:7; Lev. 19:12; II Cor. 1:23, II Chron. 6:22, 23.*

II. The name of God only is that by which men ought to swear; and therein it is to be used with all holy fear and reverence.[c] Therefore, to swear vainly or rashly, by that glorious and dreadful Name; or, to swear at all by any other thing, is sinful, and to be abhorred.[d] Yet, as in matters of weight and moment, an oath is warranted by the Word of God, under the New Testament, as well as under the Old;[e] so a lawful oath, being imposed by lawful authority, in such matters ought to be taken.[f]

(c) *Deut. 6:13.* (d) *Exod. 20:7; Jer. 5:7; Matt. 5:34, 37; James 5:12.* (e) *Heb. 6:16; II Cor. 1:23; Isa. 65:16.* (f) *I Kings 8:31; Neh. 13:25; Ezra 10:5.*

III. Whosoever taketh an oath ought duly to consider the weightiness of so solemn an act; and therein to avouch nothing, but what he is fully persuaded is the truth.[g] Neither may any man bind himself by oath to anything but what is good and just, and what he believeth so to be, and what he is able and resolved to perform.[h] Yet is it a sin to refuse an oath touching anything that is good and just, being imposed by lawful authority.[i]

(g) *Exod. 20:7; Jer. 4:2.* (h) *Gen. 24:2, 3, 5, 6, 8, 9.* (i) *Num. 5:19, 21; Neh. 5:12; Exod. 22:7, 8, 9, 10, 11.*

IV. An oath is to be taken in the plain and common sense of the words, without equivocation, or mental reservation.[k] It cannot oblige to sin: but in anything not sinful, being taken, it binds to performance, although to a man's own hurt.[l] Not is it to be violated, although made to heretics, or infidels.[m]

(k) *Jer. 4:2; Ps. 24:4.* (l) *I Sam. 25:22, 32, 33, 34; Ps. 15:4.* (m) *Ezek. 17:16, 18, 19; Josh. 9:18, 19 with II Sam. 21:1.*

IV. A vow is of the like nature with a promissory oath, and ought to be made with the like religious care, and to be performed with the like faithfulness.[n]

(n) *Isa. 19:21; Eccles. 5:4, 5, 6; Ps. 61:8; Ps. 66:13, 14.*

VI. It is not to be made to any creature, but to God alone:[o] and that it may be accepted, it is to be made voluntarily, out of faith, and conscience of duty, in way of thankfulness for mercy received, or for the obtaining of what we want; whereby we more strictly bind ourselves to necessary duties; or to other things, so far and so long as they may fitly conduce thereunto.[p]

[o] *Ps. 76:11; Jer. 44:25, 26.* [p] *Deut. 23:21, 22, 23; Ps. 50:14; Gen. 28:20, 21, 22; I Sam. 1:11; Ps. 66:13, 14; Ps. 132:2, 3, 4, 5.*

VII. No man may vow to do anything forbidden in the Word of God, or what would hinder any duty therein commanded, or which is not in his own power, and for the performance whereof he hath no promise of ability from God.[q] In which respects, Popish monastical vows of perpetual single life, professed poverty, and regular obedience, are so far from being degrees of higher perfection, that they are superstitious and sinful snares, in which no Christian may entangle himself.[r]

[q] *Acts 23:12, 14; Mark 6:26; Numb. 30:5, 8, 12, 13.*

[r] *Matt. 19:11, 12; I Cor. 7:2, 9; Eph. 4:28; I Peter 4:2; I Cor. 7:23.*

CHAPTER XXIII: OF THE CIVIL MAGISTRATE.

I. God, the supreme Lord and King of all the world, hath ordained civil magistrates, to be, under Him, over the people, for His own glory, and the public good: and, to this end, hath armed them with the power of the sword, for the defence and encouragement of them that are good, and for the punishment of evil doers.[a]

[a] *Rom. 13:1, 2, 3, 4; I Pet. 2:13, 14.*

II. It is lawful for Christians to accept and execute the office of a magistrate, when called thereunto;[b] in the managing whereof, as they ought especially to maintain piety, justice, and peace, according to the wholesome laws of each commonwealth;[c] so for that end, they may lawfully now, under the New Testament, wage war, upon just and necessary occasion.[d]

[b] *Prov. 8:15, 16; Rom. 13:1, 2, 4.* [c] *Ps. 2:10, 11, 12; I Tim. 2:2; Ps. 82:3, 4; II Sam. 23:3; I Pet. 2:13.* [d] *Luke 3:14; Rom. 13:4; Matt. 8:9, 10; Acts 10:1, 2; Rev. 17:14, 16.*

III. The civil magistrate may not assume to himself the administration of the Word and sacraments, or the power of the keys of the kingdom of heaven:[e] yet he hath authority, and it is his duty, to take order, that unity and peace be preserved in the Church, that the truth of God be kept pure and entire; that all blasphemies and heresies be suppressed; all corruptions and abuses in worship and discipline prevented or reformed; and all the ordinances of God duly settled, administrated, and observed.[f] For the better effecting whereof, he hath power to call synods, to be present at them, and to provide that whatsoever is transacted in them be according to the mind of God.[g]

> [e] *II Chron. 26:18 with Matt. 18:17 and Matt. 16:19; I Cor. 12:28, 29; Eph. 4:11, 12; I Cor. 4:1, 2; Rom. 10:15; Heb. 5:4.* [f] *Isa. 49:23; Ps. 122:9; Ezra 7:23, 25, 26, 27, 28; Lev. 24:16; Deut. 13:5, 6, 12; I Kings 18:4; I Chron. 13:1 to 9; II Kings 23:1 to 26; II Chron. 34:33; II Chron. 15:12, 13.* [g] *II Chron. 19:8, 9, 10, 11; II Chron. 29 and 30; Matt. 2:4, 5.*

IV. It is the duty of people to pray for magistrates,[h] to honour their persons,[i] to pay them tribute or other dues,[k] to obey their lawful commands, and to be subject to their authority, for conscience' sake.[l] Infidelity, or difference in religion, doth not make void the magistrates' just and legal authority, nor free the people from their due obedience to them:[m] from which ecclesiastical persons are not exempted,[n] much less hath the Pope any power and jurisdiction over them in their dominions, or over any of their people; and, least of all, to deprive them of their dominions, or lives, if he shall judge them to be heretics, or upon any other pretence whatsoever.[o]

> [h] *I Tim. 2:1, 2.* [i] *I Pet. 2:17.* [k] *Rom. 13:6, 7.* [l] *Rom. 13:5; Tit. 3:1.* [m] *I Pet. 2:13, 14, 16.* [n] *Rom. 13:1; I Kings 2:35; Acts 25:9, 10, 11; II Pet. 2:1, 10, 11; Jude ver. 8, 9, 10, 11.* [o] *II Thess. 2:4; Rev. 13:15, 16, 17.*

CHAPTER XXIV: OF MARRIAGE AND DIVORCE.

I. Marriage is to be between one man and one woman: neither is it lawful for any man to have more than one wife, nor for any woman to have more than one husband; at the same time.[a]

> [a] *Gen. 2:24; Matt. 19:5, 6; Prov. 2:17.*

II. Marriage was ordained for the mutual help of husband and wife,[b] for the increase of mankind with a legitimate issue, and of the Church with an holy seed;[c] and for preventing of uncleanness.[d]

[b] *Gen. 2:18.* [c] *Mal. 2:15.* [d] *I Cor. 7:2, 9.*

III. It is lawful for all sorts of people to marry, who are able with judgment to give their consent.[e] Yet is it the duty of Christians to marry only in the Lord:[f] and therefore such as profess the true reformed religion should not marry with infidels, papists, or other idolaters: neither should such as are godly be unequally yoked, by marrying with such as are notoriously wicked in their life, or maintain damnable heresies.[g]

[e] *Heb. 13:4; I Tim. 4:3; I Cor. 7:36, 37, 38; Gen. 24:57, 58.*
[f] *I Cor. 7:39.* [g] *Gen. 34:14; Exod. 34:16; Deut. 7:3, 4; I Kings 11:4; Neh. 13:25, 26, 27; Mal. 2:11, 12; II Cor. 6:14.*

IV. Marriage ought not to be within the degrees of consanguinity or affinity forbidden by the Word;[h] nor can such incestuous marriages ever be made lawful by any law of man or consent of parties, so as those persons may live together as man and wife.[i] The man may not marry any of his wife's kindred nearer in blood than he may of his own; nor the woman of her husband's kindred nearer in blood than of her own.[k]

[h] *Lev. 18 ch.; I Cor. 5:1; Amos 2:7.*
[i] *Mark 6:18; Lev. 18:24, 25, 26, 27, 28.* [k] *Lev. 20:19, 20, 21.*

V. Adultery or fornication committed after a contract, being detected before marriage, giveth just occasion to the innocent party to dissolve that contract.[l] In the case of adultery after marriage, it is lawful for the innocent party to sue out a divorce:[m] and, after the divorce, to marry another, as if the offending party were dead.[n]

[l] *Matt. 1:18, 19, 20.* [m] *Matt. 5:31, 32.* [n] *Matt. 19:9; Rom. 7:2, 3.*

VI. Although the corruption of man be such as is apt to study arguments unduly to put asunder those whom God hath joined together in marriage: yet nothing but adultery, or such willful desertion as can no way be remedied by the Church or civil magistrate, is cause sufficient of dissolving the bond of marriage:[o] wherein, a public and orderly course of proceeding is to be observed; and the persons concerned in it not left to their own wills and discretion, in their own case.(p)

(o) *Matt. 19:8, 9; I Cor. 7:15; Matt. 19:6.* (p) *Deut. 24:1, 2, 3, 4.*

CHAPTER XXV: OF THE CHURCH.

I. The catholic or universal Church which is invisible, consists of the whole number of the elect, that have been, are, or shall be gathered into one, under Christ the Head thereof; and is the spouse, the body, the fulness of Him that filleth all in all.(a)

(a) *Eph. 1:10, 22, 23; Eph. 5:23, 27, 32; Col. 1:18.*

II. The visible Church, which is also catholic or universal under the Gospel (not confined to one nation as before under the law), consists of all those throughout the world that profess the true religion;(b) and of their children:(c) and is the kingdom of the Lord Jesus Christ,(d) the house and family of God,(e) out of which there is no ordinary possibility of salvation.(f)

(b) *I Cor. 1:2; I Cor. 12:12, 13; Ps. 2:8; Rev. 7:9; Rom. 15:9, 10, 11, 12.*
(c) *I Cor. 7:14; Acts 2:39; Ezek. 16:20, 21; Rom. 11:16; Gen. 3:15; Gen. 17:7.* (d) *Matt. 13:47; Isa. 9:7.* (e) *Eph. 2:19; Eph. 3:15.* (f) *Acts 2:47.*

III. Unto this catholic visible Church Christ hath given the ministry, oracles, and ordinances of God, for the gathering and perfecting of the saints, in this life, to the end of the world: and doth by His own presence and Spirit, according to His promise, make them effectual thereunto.(g)

(g) *I Cor. 12:28; Eph. 4:11, 12, 13; Matt. 28:19, 20; Isa. 59:21.*

IV. This catholic Church hath been sometimes more, sometimes less visible.(h) And particular Churches, which are members thereof, are more or less pure, according as the doctrine of the Gospel is taught and embraced, ordinances administered, and public worship performed more or less purely in them.(i)

(h) *Rom. 11:3, 4; Rev. 12:6, 14.* (i) *Rev. 2 and 3; I Cor. 5:6, 7.*

V. The purest Churches under heaven are subject both to mixture and error:(k) and some have so degenerated, as to become no Churches of Christ, but synagogues of Satan.[l] Nevertheless, there shall be always a Church on earth, to worship God according to His will.[m]

[k] *I Cor. 13:12; Rev. 2 and 3; Matt. 13:24, 25, 26, 27, 28, 29, 30, 47.*
[l] *Rev. 18:2; Rom. 11:18, 19, 20, 21, 22.* [m] *Matt. 16:18; Ps. 72:17; Ps. 102:28; Matt. 28:19, 20.*

VI. There is no other head of the Church, but the Lord Jesus Christ;[n] nor can the Pope of Rome, in any sense, be head thereof; but is that Antichrist, that man of sin, and son of perdition, that exalteth himself, in the Church, against Christ and all that is called God.[o]

[n] *Col. 1:18; Eph. 1:22.*
[o] *Matt. 23:8, 9, 10; II Thess. 2:3, 4, 8, 9; Rev. 13:6.*

CHAPTER XXVI: OF THE COMMUNION OF THE SAINTS.

I. All saints, that are united to Jesus Christ their Head by His Spirit and by faith, have fellowship with Him in His grace, sufferings, death, resurrection, and glory:[a] and, being united to one another in love, they have communion in each other's gifts and graces,[b] and are obliged to the performance of such duties, public and private, as do conduce to their mutual good, both in the inward and outward man.[c]

[a] *John 1:3; Eph. 3:16, 17, 18, 19; John 1:16; Eph. 2:5, 6; Phil. 3:10; Rom. 6:5, 6; II Tim. 2:12.* [b] *Eph. 4:15, 16; I Cor. 12:7; I Cor. 3:21, 22, 23; Col. 2:19.* [c] *I Thess. 5:11, 14; Rom. 1:11, 12, 14; I John 3:16, 17, 18; Gal. 6:10.*

II. Saints by profession are bound to maintain a holy fellowship and communion in the worship of God; and in performing such other spiritual services as tend to their mutual edification;[d] as also in relieving each other in outward things, according to their several abilities, and necessities. Which communion, as God offereth opportunity, is to be extended unto all those who, in every place, call upon the name of the Lord Jesus.[e]

[d] *Heb. 10:24, 25; Acts 2:42, 46; Isa. 2:3; I Cor. 11:20.*
[e] *Acts 2:44, 45; I John 3:17; II Cor. 8 and 9 chapters; Acts 11:29, 30.*

III. This communion which the saints have with Christ, doth not make them, in any wise, partakers of the substance of His Godhead; or to be equal with Christ, in any respect: either of which to affirm is impious and blasphemous.[f] Nor doth their communion one with another, as saints, take away, or infringe the title or propriety which each man hath in his goods and possessions.[g]

[f] *Col. 1:18, 19; I Cor. 8:6; Isa. 42:8; I Tim. 6:15, 16; Ps. 45:7, with Heb. 1:8, 9.* [g] *Exod. 20:15; Eph. 4:28; Acts 5:4.*

CHAPTER XXVII: OF THE SACRAMENTS.

I. Sacraments are holy signs and seals of the covenant of grace,[a] immediately instituted by God,[b] to represent Christ and His benefits; and to confirm our interest in Him;[c] as also, to put a visible difference between those that belong unto the Church, and the rest of the world;[d] and solemnly to engage them to the service of God in Christ, according to His Word.[e]

[a] *Rom. 4:11; Gen. 17:7, 10.* [b] *Matt. 28:19; I Cor. 11:23.*

[c] *I Cor. 10:16; I Cor. 11:25, 26; Gal. 3:17.*

[d] *Rom. 15:8; Exod. 12:48; Gen. 34:14.*

[e] *Rom. 6:3, 4; I Cor. 10:16, 21.*

II. There is in every sacrament a spiritual relation, or sacramental union, between the sign and the thing signified: whence it comes to pass, that the names and effects of the one are attributed to the other.[f]

[f] *Gen. 17:10; Matt. 26:27, 28; Tit. 3:5.*

III. The grace which is exhibited in or by the sacraments rightly used, is not conferred by any power in them; neither doth the efficacy of a sacrament depend upon the piety or intention of him that doth administer it:[g] but upon the work of the Spirit,[h] and the word of institution, which contains, together with a precept authorizing the use thereof, a promise of benefit to worthy receivers.[i]

[g] *Rom. 2:28, 29; I Pet. 3:21.* [h] *Matt. 3:11; I Cor. 12:13.*

[i] *Matt. 26:27, 28; Matt. 28:19, 20.*

IV. There are only two sacraments ordained by Christ our Lord in the Gospel; that is to say, Baptism and the Supper of the Lord: neither of which may be dispensed by any but by a minister of the Word lawfully ordained.[k]

[k] *Matt. 28:19; I Cor. 11:20, 23, I Cor. 4:1; Heb. 5:4.*

V. The sacraments of the Old Testament, in regard to the spiritual things thereby signified and exhibited, were, for substance, the same with those of the New.[l]

[l] *I Cor. 10:1, 2, 3, 4.*

CHAPTER XXVIII: OF BAPTISM.

I. Baptism is a sacrament of the New Testament, ordained by Jesus Christ,[a] not only for the solemn admission of the party baptized into the visible Church;[b] but also, to be unto him a sign and seal of the covenant of grace,[c] of his ingrafting into Christ,[d] of regeneration,[e] of remission of sins,[f] and of his giving up unto God through Jesus Christ, to walk in the newness of life.[g] Which sacrament is, by Christ's own appointment, to be continued in His Church until the end of the world.[h]

[a] *Matt. 28:19.* [b] *I Cor. 12:13.* [c] *Rom. 4:11 with Col. 2:11, 12.*
[d] *Gal. 3:27; Rom. 6:5.* [e] *Tit. 3:5.* [f] *Mark 1:4.* [g] *Rom. 6:3, 4.*
[h] *Matt. 28:19, 20.*

II. The outward element to be used in this sacrament is water, wherewith the party is to be baptized, in the name of the Father, and of the Son, and of the Holy Ghost, by a minister of the Gospel, lawfully called thereunto.[i]

[i] *Matt. 3:11; John 1:33; Matt. 28:19, 20.*

III. Dipping of the person into the water is not necessary; but Baptism is rightly administered by pouring or sprinkling water upon the person.[k]

[k] *Heb. 9:10, 19, 20, 21, 22; Acts 2:41; Acts 16:33; Mark 7:4.*

IV. Not only those that do actually profess faith in and obedience unto Christ,[l] but also the infants of one or both believing parents, are to be baptized.[m]

[l] *Mark 16:15, 16; Acts 8:37, 38.* [m] *Gen. 17:7, 9, 10 with Gal. 3:9, 14 and Col. 2:11, 12 & Acts 2:38, 39 & Rom. 4:11, 12; I Cor. 7:14; Matt. 28:19; Mark 10:13, 14, 15, 16; Luke 18:15.*

V. Although it be a great sin to contemn or neglect this ordinance,[n] yet grace and salvation are not so inseparably annexed unto it, as that no person can be regenerated or saved without it;[o] or, that all that are baptized are undoubtedly regenerated.[p]

[n] *Luke 7:30 with Exod. 4:24, 25, 26.*

[o] *Rom. 4:11; Acts 10:2, 4, 22, 31, 45, 47.* [p] *Acts 8:13, 23.*

VI. The efficacy of Baptism is not tied to that moment of time wherein it is administered;[q] yet notwithstanding, by the right use of this ordinance, the grace promised is not only offered, but really exhibited and conferred, by the Holy Ghost, to such (whether of age or infants) as that grace belongeth unto, according to the counsel of God's own will, in His appointed time.[r]

[q] *John 3:5, 8.* [r] *Gal. 3:27; Titus 3:5; Eph. 5:25, 26; Acts 2:38, 41.*

VII. The sacrament of Baptism is but once to be administered unto any person.[s]

[s] *Titus 3:5.*

CHAPTER XXIX: OF THE LORD'S SUPPER.

I. Our Lord Jesus, in the night wherein He was betrayed, instituted the sacrament of His body and blood, called the Lord's Supper, to be observed in His Church, unto the end of the world, for the perpetual remembrance of the sacrifice of Himself in His death; the sealing all benefits thereof unto true believers, their spiritual nourishment and growth in Him, their further engagement in and to all duties which they owe unto Him; and to be a bond and pledge of their communion with Him, and with each other, as members of His mystical body.[a]

[a] *I Cor. 11:23, 24, 25, 26; I Cor. 10:16, 17, 21; I Cor. 12:13.*

II. In this sacrament, Christ is not offered up to His Father; nor any real sacrifice made at all for remission of sins of the quick or dead;[b] but only a commemoration of that one offering up of Himself, by Himself, upon the cross, once for all: and a spiritual oblation of all possible praise unto God for the same:[c] so that the Popish sacrifice of the mass (as they call it) is most abominably injurious to Christ's one, only sacrifice, the alone propitiation for all the sins of His elect.[d]

[b] *Heb. 9:22, 25, 26, 28.* [c] *I Cor. 11:24, 25, 26; Matt. 26:26, 27.*
[d] *Heb. 7:23, 24, 27; Heb. 10:11, 12, 14, 18.*

III. The Lord Jesus hath, in this ordinance, appointed His ministers to declare His word of institution to the people; to pray, and bless the elements of bread and wine, and thereby to set them apart from a common to a holy use; and to take and break the bread, to take the cup, and (they communicating also themselves) to give both to the communicants;[e] but to none who are not then present in the congregation.[f]

[e] *Matt. 26:26, 27, 28 & Mark 14:22, 23, 24 and Luke 22:19, 20 with I Cor. 11:23, 24, 25, 26.* [f] *Acts. 20:7; I Cor. 11:20.*

IV. Private masses, or receiving this sacrament by a priest or any other alone;[g] as likewise, the denial of the cup to the people,[h] worshipping the elements, the lifting them up or carrying them about for adoration, and the reserving them for any pretended religious use; are all contrary to the nature of this sacrament, and to the institution of Christ.[i]

[g] *I Cor. 10:16.* [h] *Mark 14:23; I Cor. 11:25, 26, 27, 28, 29.* [i] *Matt. 15:9.*

V. The outward elements in this sacrament, duly set apart to the uses ordained by Christ, have such relation to Him crucified, as that, truly, yet sacramentally only, they are sometimes called by the name of the things they represent, to wit, the body and blood of Christ;[k] albeit in substance and nature they still remain truly and only bread and wine, as they were before.[l]

[k] *Matt. 26:26, 27, 28.* [l] *I Cor. 11:26, 27, 28; Matt. 26:29.*

VI. That doctrine which maintains a change of the substance of bread and wine into the substance of Christ's body and blood (commonly called transubstantiation) by consecration of a priest, or by any other way, is repugnant, not to Scripture alone, but even to common sense and reason; overthroweth the nature of the sacrament, and hath been, and is the cause of manifold superstitions; yea, of gross idolatries.[m]

[m] *Acts 3:21 with I Cor. 11:24, 25, 26; Luke 24:6, 39.*

VII. Worthy receivers outwardly partaking of the visible elements in this sacrament,[n] do then also, inwardly by faith, really and indeed, yet not carnally and corporally, but spiritually, receive and feed upon Christ crucified, and all benefits of His death: the body and blood of Christ being then, not corporally or carnally, in, with, or under the bread and wine; yet, as really, but spiritually, present to the faith of believers in that ordinance, as the elements themselves are to their outward senses.[o]

[n] *I Cor. 11:28.* [o] *I Cor. 10:16.*

VIII. Although ignorant and wicked men receive the outward elements in this sacrament: yet they receive not the thing signified thereby, but by their unworthy coming thereunto are guilty of the body and blood of the Lord to their own damnation. Wherefore, all ignorant and ungodly persons, as they are unfit to enjoy communion with Him, so are they unworthy of the Lord's table; and cannot, without great sin against Christ while they remain such, partake of these holy mysteries,[p] or be admitted thereunto.[q]

[p] *I Cor. 11:27, 28, 29; II Cor. 6:14, 15, 16.*

[q] *I Cor. 5:6, 7, 13; II Thess. 3:6, 14, 15; Matt. 7:6.*

CHAPTER XXX: OF CHURCH CENSURES.

I. The Lord Jesus, as King and Head of His Church, hath therein appointed a government, in the hand of Church officers, distinct from the civil magistrate.[a]

[a] *Isa. 9:6, 7; I Tim. 5:17; I Thess. 5:12; Acts 20:17, 28; Heb. 13:7, 17, 24; I Cor. 12:28; Matt. 28:18, 19, 20.*

II. To these officers the keys of the kingdom of heaven are committed: by virtue whereof, they have power respectively to retain, and remit sins; to shut that kingdom against the impenitent, both by the Word and censures; and to open it unto penitent sinners, by the ministry of the Gospel, and by absolution from censures, as occasion shall require.[b]

[b] *Matt. 16:19; Matt. 18:17, 18; John 20:21, 22, 23; II Cor. 2:6, 7, 8.*

III. Church censures are necessary, for the reclaiming and gaining of offending brethren, for deterring of others from the like offenses, for purging out of that leaven which might infect the whole lump, for vindicating the honour of Christ, and the holy profession of the Gospel, and for preventing the wrath of God, which might justly fall upon the Church, if they should suffer His covenant and the seals thereof to be profaned by notorious and obstinate offenders.[c]

[c] *I Cor. 5 chap.; I Tim. 5:20; Matt. 7:6; I Tim. 1:20; I Cor. 11:27 to the end, with Jude ver. 23.*

IV. For the better attaining of these ends, the officers of the Church are to proceed by admonition; suspension from the sacrament of the Lord's Supper for a season; and by excommunication from the Church; according to the nature of the crime, and demerit of the person.[d]

[d] *I Thess. 5:12; II Thess. 3:6, 14, 15; I Cor. 5:4, 5, 13; Matt. 18:17; Tit. 3:10.*

CHAPTER XXXI: OF SYNODS AND COUNCILS.

I. For the better government, and further edification of the Church, there ought to be such assemblies as are commonly called synods or councils.[a]

[a] *Acts 15:2, 4, 6.*

II. As magistrates may lawfully call a synod of ministers, and other fit persons, to consult and advise with, about matters of religion;[b] so, if magistrates be open enemies to the Church, the ministers of Christ of themselves, by virtue of their office, or they, with other fit persons upon delegation from their Churches, may meet together in such assemblies.[c]

[b] *Isa. 49:23; I Tim. 2:1, 2; II Chron. 19:8, 9, 10, 11; II Chron. 29, 30 chaps.; Matt. 2:4, 5; Prov. 11:14.* [c] *Acts 15:2, 4, 22, 23, 25.*

III. It belongs to synods and councils, ministerially to determine controversies of faith and cases of conscience; to set down rules and directions for the better ordering of the public worship of God, and government of his Church; to receive complaints in cases of maladministration, and authoritatively to determine the same: which decrees and determinations, if consonant to the Word of God, are to be received with reverence and submission; not only for their agreement with the Word, but also for the power whereby they are made, as being an ordinance of God appointed thereunto in His Word.[(d)]

(d) *Acts 15:15, 19, 24, 27, 28, 29, 30, 31; Acts 16:4; Matt. 18:17, 18, 19, 20.*

III. All synods or councils, since the Apostles' times, whether general or particular, may err; and many have erred. Therefore they are not to be made the rule of faith, or practice; but to be used as a help in both.[(e)]

(e) *Eph. 2:20; Acts 17:11; I Cor. 2:5; II Cor. 1:24.*

IV. Synods and councils are to handle, or conclude, nothing, but that which is ecclesiastical: and are not to intermeddle with civil affairs which concern the commonwealth; unless by way of humble petition, in cases extraordinary; or by way of advice, for satisfaction of conscience, if they be thereunto required by the civil magistrate.[(f)]

(f) *Luke 12:13, 14; John 18:36.*

CHAPTER XXXII: OF THE STATE OF MAN AFTER DEATH, AND OF THE RESURRECTION OF THE DEAD.

I. The bodies of men, after death, return to dust and see corruption:[(a)] but their souls (which neither die nor sleep) having an immortal subsistence, immediately return to God who gave them:[(b)] the souls of the righteous, being then made perfect in holiness, are received into the highest heavens, where they behold the face of God, in light and glory, waiting for the full redemption of their bodies.[(c)] And the souls of the wicked are cast into hell, where they remain in torments and utter darkness, reserved to the judgment of the great day.[(d)] Beside these two places, for souls separated from their bodies, the Scripture acknowledgeth none.

(a) *Gen. 3:19; Acts 13:36.* (b) *Luke 23:43; Eccles. 12:7.*

(c) *Heb. 12:23; II Cor. 5:1, 6, 8; Phil. 1:23, with Acts 3:21 & Eph. 4:10.*

(d) *Luke 16:23, 24; Acts 1:25; Jude ver. 6, 7; I Pet. 3:19.*

II. At the last day, such as are found alive shall not die, but be changed:[(e)] and all the dead shall be raised up, with the selfsame bodies, and none other, although with different qualities, which shall be united again to their souls for ever.[(f)]

[(e)] *I Thess. 4:17; I Cor. 15:51, 52.* [(f)] *Job 19:26, 27; I Cor. 15:42, 43, 44.*

III. The bodies of the unjust shall, by the power of Christ, be raised to dishonour: the bodies of the just, by His Spirit, unto honour; and be made conformable to His own glorious body.[(g)]

[(g)] *Acts 24:15; John 5:28, 29; I Cor. 15:43; Phil. 3:21.*

CHAPTER XXXIII: OF THE LAST JUDGMENT.

I. God hath appointed a day, wherein He will judge the world in righteousness, by Jesus Christ,[(a)] to whom all power and judgment is given of the Father.[(b)] In which day, not only the apostate angels shall be judged,[(c)] but likewise all persons that have lived upon earth shall appear before the tribunal of Christ, to give an account of their thoughts, words, and deeds; and to receive according to what they have done in the body, whether good or evil.[(d)]

[(a)] *Acts 17:31.* [(b)] *John 5:22, 27.* [(c)] *I Cor. 6:3; Jude ver. 6; II Pet. 2:4.*
[(d)] *II Cor. 5:10; Eccles. 12:14; Rom. 2:16; Rom. 14:10, 12; Matt. 12:36, 37.*

II. The end of God's appointing this day is for the manifestation of the glory of His mercy, in the eternal salvation of the elect; and of His justice, in the damnation of the reprobate who are wicked and disobedient. For then shall the righteous go into everlasting life, and receive that fulness of joy and refreshing, which shall come from the presence of the Lord: but the wicked who know not God, and obey not the Gospel of Jesus Christ, shall be cast into eternal torments, and be punished with everlasting destruction from the presence of the Lord, and from the glory of His power.[(e)]

[(e)] *Matt. 25:31 to the end; Rom. 2:5, 6; Rom. 9:22, 23; Matt. 25:21; Acts 3:19; II Thess. 1:7, 8, 9, 10.*

III. As Christ would have us to be certainly persuaded that there shall be a day of judgment, both to deter all men from sin, and for the greater consolation of the godly in their adversity;[(f)] so will He have that day unknown to men, that they may shake off all carnal security, and be always watchful, because they know not at what hour the Lord will come; and may be ever prepared to say, Come, Lord Jesus, come quickly, Amen.[g]

> [f] *II Pet. 3:11, 14; II Cor. 5:10, 11; II Thess. 1:5, 6, 7; Luke 21:27, 28; Rom. 8:23, 24, 25.* [g] *Matt. 24:36, 42, 43, 44; Mark 13:35, 36, 37; Luke 12:35, 36; Rev. 22:20.* ▪

Savoy Declaration

Feeling the need to distinguish themselves from Arminian Baptists and Anabaptists, leaders from seven Calvinist Baptist congregations had gathered to write the First London Baptist Confession of 1644, "for the vindication of the truth and information of the ignorant." It was "corrected and enlarged" and republished in 1646.

But after the mostly-Presbyterian Westminster Assembly wrote the Westminster Confession of Faith in 1646, many Calvinist Baptist accepted that as their confession—but they tacked on the Savoy Declaration, an extra chapter written by John Owen in 1658.

CHAPTER XX: OF THE GOSPEL, AND OF THE EXTENT OF THE GRACE THEREOF

I. The covenant of works being broken by sin, and made unprofitable unto life, God was pleased to give unto the elect the promise of Christ, the seed of the woman, as the means of calling them, and begetting in them faith and repentance: in this promise the gospel, as to the substance of it, was revealed, and was therein effectual for the conversion and salvation of sinners.

II. This promise of Christ, and salvation by him, is revealed only in and by the Word of God; neither do the works of creation or providence, with the light of nature, make discovery of Christ, or of grace by him, so much as in a general or obscure way; much less that men destitute of the revelation of him by the promise or gospel, should be enabled thereby to attain saving faith or repentance.

III. The revelation of the gospel unto sinners, made in divers times, and by sundry parts, with the addition of promises and precepts for the obedience required therein, as to the nations and persons to whom it is granted, is merely of the sovereign will and good pleasure of God, not being annexed by virtue of any promise to the due improvement of men's natural abilities, by virtue of common light received without it, which none ever did make or can so do. And therefore in all ages the preaching of the gospel hath been granted unto persons and nations, as to the extent or straitening of it, in great variety, according to the counsel of the will of God.

IV. Although the gospel be the only outward means of revealing Christ and saving grace, and is as such abundantly sufficient thereunto; yet that men who are dead in trespasses, may be born again, quickened or regenerated, there is moreover necessary an effectual, irresistible work of the Holy Ghost upon the whole soul, for the producing in them a new spiritual life, without which no other means are sufficient for their conversion unto God. ▪

Second London Baptist Confession of 1689

During the tumult of the 16th and 17th centuries, Baptists and Congregationalists in Britain suffered the same persecutions as the Presbyterians. To distinguish their distinct beliefs, several Baptist congregations had written the First London Baptist Confession in 1644, and then largely subscribed to the 1646 Westminster Confession also (with slight alterations, e.g., the Savoy Declaration)

Though they differed from their paedobaptist brethren on certain points, the Reformed Baptists recognized that, in the essential doctrines, they agreed with the Presbyterians who had subscribed to the Westminster Confession of Faith. Wanting to make this general unity plain, Baptists across Britain anonymously published the Second London Baptist Confession in 1677. It was intentionally modeled after the Westminster Confession and the Savoy Declaration, with many passages adopted word for word. The main difference was the framers' convictions about baptism.

Then, in 1688, the "Glorious Revolution" under William and Mary brought the repressive persecution under Charles I and Charles II to a halt. To cement this happy revolution, Parliament passed the Toleration Act in 1689, which extended religious freedom to Nonconformists (such as Baptists), who had long protested the state-established Church of England. The Act of Toleration made it safe for Nonconformists to gather in large numbers again. In 1689, they did just that. Reformed Baptists from over 100 different English and Welsh congregations met in London to revise and openly republish the Second London Baptist Confession. Ever after, it has been familiarly known as "The 1689."

Throughout the accompanying Scripture references, "*Cant.*" is given as the abbreviation for *Canticle of Canticles*, an archaic title for *Song of Songs*, or *Song of Solomon*.

CHAPTER 1: OF THE HOLY SCRIPTURES

PARAGRAPH 1. The Holy Scripture is the only sufficient, certain, and infallible rule of all saving knowledge, faith, and obedience,(1) although the light of nature, and the works of creation and providence do so far manifest the goodness, wisdom, and power of God, as to leave men inexcusable; yet they are not sufficient to give that knowledge of God and His will which is necessary unto salvation.(2) Therefore it pleased the Lord at sundry times and in diversified manners to reveal Himself, and to declare (that) His will unto His church;(3) and afterward for the better preserving and propagating of the truth, and for the more sure establishment and comfort of the church against the corruption of the flesh, and the malice of Satan, and of the world, to commit the same wholly unto writing; which makes the Holy Scriptures to be most necessary, those former ways of God's revealing His will unto His people being now completed.(4)

(1) *2 Tim. 3:15-17; Isa. 8:20; Luke 16:29, 31; Eph. 2:20.*

(2) *Rom. 1:19-21, 2:14, 15; Psalm 19:1-3.* (3) *Heb. 1:1.*

(4) *Prov. 22:19-21; Rom. 15:4; 2 Pet. 1:19, 20.*

PARAGRAPH 2. Under the name of Holy Scripture, or the Word of God written, are now contained all the books of the Old and New Testaments, which are these:

Of the Old Testament: Genesis, Exodus, Leviticus, Numbers, Deuteronomy, Joshua, Judges, Ruth, 1 Samuel, 2 Samuel, 1 Kings, 2 Kings, 1 Chronicles, 2 Chronicles, Ezra, Nehemiah, Esther, Job, Psalms, Proverbs, Ecclesiastes, The Song of Solomon, Isaiah, Jeremiah, Lamentations, Ezekiel, Daniel, Hosea, Joel, Amos, Obadiah, Jonah, Micah, Nahum, Habakkuk, Zephaniah, Haggai, Zechariah, Malachi.

Of the New Testament: Matthew, Mark, Luke, John, Acts, Romans 1 Corinthians, 2 Corinthians, Galatians, Ephesians, Philippians, Colossians, 1 Thessalonians, 2 Thessalonians, 1 Timothy, 2 Timothy, Titus, Philemon, Hebrews, James, 1 Peter, 2 Peter, 1 John, 2 John, 3 John, Jude, Revelation.

All of which are given by the inspiration of God, to be the rule of faith and life.(5)

(5) *2 Tim. 3:16.*

PARAGRAPH 3. The books commonly called Apocrypha, not being of divine inspiration, are no part of the canon or rule of the Scripture, and, therefore, are of no authority to the church of God, nor to be any otherwise approved or made use of than other human writings.[6]

[6] *Luke 24:27, 44; Rom. 3:2.*

PARAGRAPH 4. The authority of the Holy Scripture, for which it ought to be believed, depends not upon the testimony of any man or church, but wholly upon God (who is truth itself), the author thereof; therefore it is to be received because it is the Word of God.[7]

[7] *2 Pet. 1:19-21; 2 Tim. 3:16; 2 Thess. 2:13; 1 John 5:9.*

PARAGRAPH 5. We may be moved and induced by the testimony of the church of God to a high and reverent esteem of the Holy Scriptures; and the heavenliness of the matter, the efficacy of the doctrine, and the majesty of the style, the consent of all the parts, the scope of the whole (which is to give all glory to God), the full discovery it makes of the only way of man's salvation, and many other incomparable excellencies, and entire perfections thereof, are arguments whereby it does abundantly evidence itself to be the Word of God; yet notwithstanding, our full persuasion and assurance of the infallible truth, and divine authority thereof, is from the inward work of the Holy Spirit bearing witness by and with the Word in our hearts.[8]

[8] *John 16:13, 14; 1 Cor. 2:10-12; 1 John 2:20, 27.*

PARAGRAPH 6. The whole counsel of God concerning all things necessary for His own glory, man's salvation, faith and life, is either expressly set down or necessarily contained in the Holy Scripture: unto which nothing at any time is to be added, whether by new revelation of the Spirit, or traditions of men.[9] Nevertheless, we acknowledge the inward illumination of the Spirit of God to be necessary for the saving understanding of such things as are revealed in the Word,[10] and that there are some circumstances concerning the worship of God, and government of the church, common to human actions and societies, which are to be ordered by the light of nature and Christian prudence, according to the general rules of the Word, which are always to be observed.[11]

[9] *2 Tim. 3:15-17; Gal. 1:8,9.* [10] *John 6:45; 1 Cor. 2:9-12.*

[11] *1 Cor. 11:13, 14; 1 Cor. 14:26, 40.*

PARAGRAPH 7. All things in Scripture are not alike plain in themselves, nor alike clear unto all;[12] yet those things which are necessary to be known, believed and observed for salvation, are so clearly propounded and opened in some place of Scripture or other, that not only the learned, but the unlearned, in a due use of ordinary means, may attain to a sufficient understanding of them.[13]

(12) *2 Pet. 3:16.* (13) *Ps. 19:7; Psalm 119:130.*

PARAGRAPH 8. The Old Testament in Hebrew (which was the native language of the people of God of old),[14] and the New Testament in Greek (which at the time of the writing of it was most generally known to the nations), being immediately inspired by God, and by His singular care and providence kept pure in all ages, are therefore authentic; so as in all controversies of religion, the church is finally to appeal to them.[15] But because these original tongues are not known to all the people of God, who have a right unto, and interest in the Scriptures, and are commanded in the fear of God to read,[16] and search them,[17] therefore they are to be translated into the vulgar language of every nation unto which they come,[18] that the Word of God dwelling plentifully in all, they may worship Him in an acceptable manner, and through patience and comfort of the Scriptures may have hope.[19]

(14) *Rom. 3:2.* (15) *Isa. 8:20.* (16) *Acts 15:15.* (17) *John 5:39.*
(18) *1 Cor. 14:6, 9, 11, 12, 24, 28.* (19) *Col. 3:16.*

PARAGRAPH 9. The infallible rule of interpretation of Scripture is the Scripture itself; and therefore when there is a question about the true and full sense of any Scripture (which are not many, but one), it must be searched by other places that speak more clearly.[20]

(20) *2 Pet. 1:20, 21; Acts 15:15, 16.*

PARAGRAPH 10. The supreme judge, by which all controversies of religion are to be determined, and all decrees of councils, opinions of ancient writers, doctrines of men, and private spirits, are to be examined, and in whose sentence we are to rest, can be no other but the Holy Scripture delivered by the Spirit, into which Scripture so delivered, our faith is finally resolved.[21]

(21) *Matt. 22:29, 31, 32; Eph. 2:20; Acts 28:23.*

CHAPTER 2: OF GOD AND OF THE HOLY TRINITY

PARAGRAPH 1. The Lord our God is but one only living and true God;[1] whose subsistence is in and of Himself,[2] infinite in being and perfection; whose essence cannot be comprehended by any but Himself;[3] a most pure spirit,[4] invisible, without body, parts, or passions, who only hath immortality, dwelling in the light which no man can approach unto;[5] who is immutable,[6] immense,[7] eternal,[8] incomprehensible, almighty,[9] every way infinite, most holy,[10] most wise, most free, most absolute; working all things according to the counsel of His own immutable and most righteous will,[11] for His own glory;[12] most loving, gracious, merciful, long-suffering, abundant in goodness and truth, forgiving iniquity, transgression, and sin; the rewarder of them that diligently seek Him,[13] and withal most just and terrible in His judgments,[14] hating all sin,[15] and who will by no means clear the guilty.[16]

> [1] *1 Cor. 8:4, 6; Deut. 6:4.* [2] *Jer. 10:10; Isa. 48:12.* [3] *Exod. 3:14.* [4] *John 4:24.* [5] *1 Tim. 1:17; Deut. 4:15, 16.* [6] *Mal. 3:6.* [7] *1 Kings 8:27; Jer. 23:23.* [8] *Ps. 90:2.* [9] *Gen. 17:1.* [10] *Isa. 6:3.* [11] *Ps. 115:3; Isa. 46:10.* [12] *Prov. 16:4; Rom. 11:36.* [13] *Exod. 34:6, 7; Heb. 11:6.* [14] *Neh. 9:32, 33.* [15] *Ps. 5:5, 6.* [16] *Exod. 34:7; Nahum 1:2, 3.*

PARAGRAPH 2. God, having all life,[17] glory,[18] goodness,[19] blessedness, in and of Himself, is alone in and unto Himself all-sufficient, not standing in need of any creature which He hath made, nor deriving any glory from them,[20] but only manifesting His own glory in, by, unto, and upon them; He is the alone fountain of all being, of whom, through whom, and to whom are all things,[21] and He hath most sovereign dominion over all creatures, to do by them, for them, or upon them, whatsoever Himself pleases;[22] in His sight all things are open and manifest,[23] His knowledge is infinite, infallible, and independent upon the creature, so as nothing is to Him contingent or uncertain;[24] He is most holy in all His counsels, in all His works,[25] and in all His commands; to Him is due from angels and men, whatsoever worship,[26] service, or obedience, as creatures they owe unto the Creator, and whatever He is further pleased to require of them.

[17] *John 5:26.* [18] *Ps. 148:13.* [19] *Ps. 119:68.* [20] *Job 22:2, 3.* [21] *Rom. 11:34-36.* [22] *Dan. 4:25, 34, 35.* [23] *Heb. 4:13.* [24] *Ezek. 11:5; Acts 15:18.* [25] *Ps. 145:17.* [26] *Rev. 5:12-14.*

PARAGRAPH 3. In this divine and infinite Being there are three subsistences, the Father, the Word or Son, and Holy Spirit,[27] of one substance, power, and eternity, each having the whole divine essence, yet the essence undivided:[28] the Father is of none, neither begotten nor proceeding; the Son is eternally begotten of the Father;[29] the Holy Spirit proceeding from the Father and the Son;[30] all infinite, without beginning, therefore but one God, who is not to be divided in nature and being, but distinguished by several peculiar relative properties and personal relations; which doctrine of the Trinity is the foundation of all our communion with God, and comfortable dependence on Him.

[27] *1 John 5:7; Matt. 28:19; 2 Cor. 13:14.* [28] *Exod. 3:14; John 14:11; I Cor. 8:6.* [29] *John 1:14, 18.* [30] *John 15:26; Gal. 4:6.*

CHAPTER 3: OF GOD'S DECREE

PARAGRAPH 1. God hath decreed in himself, from all eternity, by the most wise and holy counsel of His own will, freely and unchangeably, all things, whatsoever comes to pass;[1] yet so as thereby is God neither the author of sin nor hath fellowship with any therein;[2] nor is violence offered to the will of the creature, nor yet is the liberty or contingency of second causes taken away, but rather established;[3] in which appears His wisdom in disposing all things, and power and faithfulness in accomplishing His decree.[4]

[1] *Isa. 46:10; Eph. 1:11; Heb. 6:17; Rom. 9:15, 18.* [2] *James 1:13; 1 John 1:5.* [3] *Acts 4:27, 28; John 19:11.* [4] *Num. 23:19; Eph. 1:3-5.*

PARAGRAPH 2. Although God knoweth whatsoever may or can come to pass, upon all supposed conditions,[5] yet hath He not decreed anything, because He foresaw it as future, or as that which would come to pass upon such conditions.[6]

[5] *Acts 15:18.* [6] *Rom. 9:11, 13, 16, 18.*

PARAGRAPH 3. By the decree of God, for the manifestation of His glory, some men and angels are predestinated, or foreordained to eternal life through Jesus Christ,(7) to the praise of His glorious grace;(8) others being left to act in their sin to their just condemnation, to the praise of His glorious justice.(9)

(7) *I Tim. 5:21; Matt. 25:34.* (8) *Eph. 1:5,6.* (9) *Rom. 9:22, 23; Jude 4.*

PARAGRAPH 4. These angels and men thus predestinated and foreordained, are particularly and unchangeably designed, and their number so certain and definite, that it cannot be either increased or diminished.(10)

(10) *2 Tim. 2:19; John 13:18.*

PARAGRAPH 5. Those of mankind that are predestinated to life, God, before the foundation of the world was laid, according to His eternal and immutable purpose, and the secret counsel and good pleasure of His will, hath chosen in Christ unto everlasting glory, out of His mere free grace and love,(11) without any other thing in the creature as a condition or cause moving Him thereunto.(12)

(11) *Eph. 1:4, 9, 11; Rom. 8:30; 2 Tim. 1:9; I Thess. 5:9.*

(12) *Rom. 9:13, 16; Eph. 2:5, 12.*

PARAGRAPH 6. As God hath appointed the elect unto glory, so He hath, by the eternal and most free purpose of His will, foreordained all the means thereunto;(13) wherefore they who are elected, being fallen in Adam, are redeemed by Christ,(14) are effectually called unto faith in Christ, by His Spirit working in due season, are justified, adopted, sanctified,(15) and kept by His power through faith unto salvation;(16) neither are any other redeemed by Christ, or effectually called, justified, adopted, sanctified, and saved, but the elect only.(17)

(13) *1 Pet. 1:2; 2; Thess. 2:13.* (14) *1 Thess. 5:9, 10.*

(15) *Rom. 8:30; 2 Thess. 2:13.* (16) *1 Pet. 1:5.* (17) *John 10:26, 17:9, 6:64.*

PARAGRAPH 7. The doctrine of the high mystery of predestination is to be handled with special prudence and care, that men attending the will of God revealed in His Word, and yielding obedience thereunto, may, from the certainty of their effectual vocation, be assured of their eternal election;(18) so shall this doctrine afford matter of praise,[19] reverence, and admiration of God, and of humility,[20] diligence, and abundant consolation to all that sincerely obey the gospel.[21]

[18] *1 Thess. 1:4,5; 2 Pet. 1:10.* [19] *Eph. 1:6; Rom. 11:33.*
[20] *Rom. 11:5, 6, 20.* [21] *Luke 10:20.*

CHAPTER 4: OF CREATION

PARAGRAPH 1. In the beginning it pleased God the Father, Son, and Holy Spirit,[1] for the manifestation of the glory of His eternal power,[2] wisdom, and goodness, to create or make the world, and all things therein, whether visible or invisible, in the space of six days, and all very good.[3]

[1] *John 1:2,3; Heb. 1:2; Job 26:13.* [2] *Rom. 1:20.* [3] *Col. 1:16; Gen. 1:31.*

PARAGRAPH 2. After God had made all other creatures, He created man, male and female,[4] with reasonable and immortal souls,[5] rendering them fit unto that life to God for which they were created; being made after the image of God, in knowledge, righteousness, and true holiness;[6] having the law of God written in their hearts,[7] and power to fulfill it, and yet under a possibility of transgressing, being left to the liberty of their own will, which was subject to change.[8]

[4] *Gen. 1:27.* [5] *Gen. 2:7.* [6] *Eccles. 7:29; Gen. 1:26.*
[7] *Rom. 2:14, 15.* [8] *Gen. 3:6.*

PARAGRAPH 3. Besides the law written in their hearts, they received a command not to eat of the tree of knowledge of good and evil,[9] which while they kept, they were happy in their communion with God, and had dominion over the creatures.[10]

[9] *Gen. 2:17.* [10] *Gen. 1:26, 28.*

CHAPTER 5: OF DIVINE PROVIDENCE

PARAGRAPH 1. God the good Creator of all things, in His infinite power and wisdom does uphold, direct, dispose, and govern all creatures and things,[1] from the greatest even to the least,[2] by His most wise and holy providence, to the end for the which they were created, according unto His infallible foreknowledge, and the free and immutable counsel of His own will; to the praise of the glory of His wisdom, power, justice, infinite goodness, and mercy.[3]

(1) *Heb. 1:3; Job 38:11; Isa. 46:10, 11; Ps. 135:6.*
(2) *Matt. 10:29-31.* (3) *Eph. 1:11.*

PARAGRAPH 2. Although in relation to the foreknowledge and decree of God, the first cause, all things come to pass immutably and infallibly;[4] so that there is not anything befalls any by chance, or without His providence;[5] yet by the same providence He ordered them to fall out according to the nature of second causes, either necessarily, freely, or contingently.[6]

(4) *Acts 2:23.* (5) *Prov. 16:33.* (6) *Gen. 8:22.*

PARAGRAPH 3. God, in his ordinary providence makes use of means,[7] yet is free to work without,[8] above,[9] and against them[10] at His pleasure.

(7) *Acts 27:31, 44; Isa. 55:10, 11.* (8) *Hosea 1:7.* (9) *Rom. 4:19-21.*
(10) *Dan. 3:27.*

PARAGRAPH 4. The almighty power, unsearchable wisdom, and infinite goodness of God, so far manifest themselves in His providence, that His determinate counsel extends itself even to the first fall, and all other sinful actions both of angels and men;[11] and that not by a bare permission, which also He most wisely and powerfully binds, and otherwise orders and governs,[12] in a manifold dispensation to His most holy ends;[13] yet so, as the sinfulness of their acts proceeds only from the creatures, and not from God, who, being most holy and righteous, neither is nor can be the author or approver of sin.[14]

(11) *Rom. 11:32-34; 2 Sam. 24:1; 1 Chron. 21:1.* (12) *2 Kings 19:28; Ps. 76:10.* (13) *Gen. 1:20; Isa. 10:6, 7, 12.* (14) *Ps. 1;21; 1 John 2:16.*

PARAGRAPH 5. The most wise, righteous, and gracious God does often times leave for a season His own children to manifold temptations and the corruptions of their own hearts, to chastise them for their former sins, or to discover unto them the hidden strength of corruption and deceitfulness of their hearts, that they may be humbled; and to raise them to a more close and constant dependence for their support upon Himself; and to make them more watchful against all future occasions of sin, and for other just and holy ends.[15] So that whatsoever befalls any of His elect is by His appointment, for His glory, and their good.[16]

(15) *2 Chron. 32:25, 26, 31; 2 Cor. 12:7-9.* (16) *Rom. 8:28.*

PARAGRAPH 6. As for those wicked and ungodly men whom God, as the righteous judge, for former sin does blind and harden;[17] from them He not only withholds His grace, whereby they might have been enlightened in their understanding, and wrought upon their hearts;[18] but sometimes also withdraws the gifts which they had,[19] and exposes them to such objects as their corruption makes occasion of sin;[20] and withal, gives them over to their own lusts, the temptations of the world, and the power of Satan,[21] whereby it comes to pass that they harden themselves, under those means which God uses for the softening of others.[22]

(17) *Rom. 1:24-26, 28, 11:7, 8.* (18) *Deut. 29:4.* (19) *Matt. 13:12.*
(20) *Deut. 2:30; 2 Kings 8:12, 13.* (21) *Ps. 81:11,12; 2 Thess. 2:10-12.*
(22) *Exod. 8:15, 32; Isa. 6:9, 10; 1 Pet. 2:7, 8.*

PARAGRAPH 7. As the providence of God does in general reach to all creatures, so after a more special manner it takes care of His church, and disposes of all things to the good thereof.[23]

(23) *1 Tim. 4:10; Amos 9:8, 9; Isa. 43:3-5.*

CHAPTER 6: OF THE FALL OF MAN, OF SIN, AND OF THE PUNISHMENT THEREOF

PARAGRAPH 1. Although God created man upright and perfect, and gave him a righteous law, which had been unto life had he kept it, and threatened death upon the breach thereof,[1] yet he did not long abide in this honor; Satan using the subtlety of the serpent to subdue Eve, then by her seducing Adam, who, without any compulsion, did willfully transgress the law of their creation, and the command given to them, in eating the forbidden fruit,[2] which God was pleased, according to His wise and holy counsel to permit, having purposed to order it to His own glory.

(1) *Gen. 2:16, 17.* (2) *Gen. 3:12, 13; 2 Cor. 11:3.*

PARAGRAPH 2. Our first parents, by this sin, fell from their original righteousness and communion with God, and we in them whereby death came upon all:[3] all becoming dead in sin,[4] and wholly defiled in all the faculties and parts of soul and body.[5]

[3] *Rom. 3:23.* [4] *Rom 5:12, etc.*

[5] *Titus 1:15; Gen. 6:5; Jer. 17:9; Rom. 3:10-19.*

PARAGRAPH 3. They being the root, and by God's appointment, standing in the room and stead of all mankind, the guilt of the sin was imputed, and corrupted nature conveyed, to all their posterity descending from them by ordinary generation,[6] being now conceived in sin,[7] and by nature children of wrath,[8] the servants of sin, the subjects of death,[9] and all other miseries, spiritual, temporal, and eternal, unless the Lord Jesus set them free.[10]

[6] *Rom. 5:12-19; 1 Cor. 15:21, 22, 45, 49.* [7] *Ps. 51:5; Job 14:4.*

[8] *Eph. 2:3.* [9] *Rom. 6:20, 5:12.* [10] *Heb. 2:14, 15; 1 Thess. 1:10.*

PARAGRAPH 4. From this original corruption, whereby we are utterly indisposed, disabled, and made opposite to all good, and wholly inclined to all evil,[11] do proceed all actual transgressions.[12]

[11] *Rom. 8:7; Col. 1:21.* [12] *James 1:14, 15; Matt. 15:19.*

PARAGRAPH 5. The corruption of nature, during this life, does remain in those that are regenerated;[13] and although it be through Christ pardoned and mortified, yet both itself, and the first motions thereof, are truly and properly sin.[14]

[13] *Rom. 7:18, 23; Eccles. 7:20; 1 John 1:8.* [14] *Rom. 7:23-25; Gal. 5:17.*

CHAPTER 7: OF GOD'S COVENANT

PARAGRAPH 1. The distance between God and the creature is so great, that although reasonable creatures do owe obedience to Him as their creator, yet they could never have attained the reward of life but by some voluntary condescension on God's part, which He hath been pleased to express by way of covenant.[1]

[1] *Luke 17:10; Job 35:7, 8.*

PARAGRAPH 2. Moreover, man having brought himself under the curse of the law by his fall, it pleased the Lord to make a covenant of grace,[2] wherein He freely offers unto sinners life and salvation by Jesus Christ, requiring of them faith in Him, that they may be saved;[3] and promising to give unto all those that are ordained unto eternal life, His Holy Spirit, to make them willing and able to believe.[4]

(2) *Gen. 2:17; Gal. 3:10; Rom. 3:20, 21.* (3) *Rom. 8:3; Mark 16:15, 16; John 3:16.* (4) *Ezek. 36:26, 27; John 6:44, 45; Ps. 110:3.*

PARAGRAPH 3. This covenant is revealed in the gospel; first of all to Adam in the promise of salvation by the seed of the woman,[5] and afterwards by farther steps, until the full discovery thereof was completed in the New Testament;[6] and it is founded in that eternal covenant transaction that was between the Father and the Son about the redemption of the elect;[7] and it is alone by the grace of this covenant that all the posterity of fallen Adam that ever were saved did obtain life and blessed immortality, man being now utterly incapable of acceptance with God upon those terms on which Adam stood in his state of innocency.[8]

(5) *Gen. 3:15.* (6) *Heb. 1:1.* (7) *2 Tim. 1:9; Titus 1:2.*
(8) *Heb. 11:6, 13; Rom. 4:1, 2, etc; Acts 4:12; John 8:56.*

CHAPTER 8: OF CHRIST THE MEDIATOR

PARAGRAPH 1. It pleased God, in His eternal purpose, to choose and ordain the Lord Jesus, His only begotten Son, according to the covenant made between them both, to be the mediator between God and man;[1] the prophet,[2] priest,[3] and king;[4] head and savior of the church,[5] the heir of all things,[6] and judge of the world;[7] unto whom He did from all eternity give a people to be His seed and to be by Him in time redeemed, called, justified, sanctified, and glorified.[8]

(1) *Isa. 42:1; 1 Pet. 1:19, 20.* (2) *Acts 3:22.* (3) *Heb. 5:5, 6.*
(4) *Ps. 2:6; Luke 1:33.* (5) *Eph. 1:22, 23.* (6) *Heb. 1:2.* (7) *Acts 17:31.*
(8) *Isa. 53:10; John 17:6; Rom. 8:30.*

PARAGRAPH 2. The Son of God, the second person in the Holy Trinity, being very and eternal God, the brightness of the Father's glory, of one substance and equal with Him who made the world, who upholds and governs all things He has made, did, when the fullness of time was complete, take upon Him man's nature, with all the essential properties and common infirmities of it,[9] yet without sin;[10] being conceived by the Holy Spirit in the womb of the Virgin Mary, the Holy Spirit coming down upon her: and the power of the Most High overshadowing her; and so was made of a woman of the tribe of Judah, of the seed of Abraham and David according to the Scriptures;[11] so that two whole, perfect, and distinct natures were inseparably joined together in one person, without conversion, composition, or confusion; which person is very God and very man, yet one Christ, the only mediator between God and man.[12]

[9] *John 1:14; Gal. 4:4.* [10] *Rom. 8:3; Heb. 2:14, 16, 17, 4:15.*
[11] *Matt. 1:22, 23.* [12] *Luke 1:27, 31, 35; Rom. 9:5; 1 Tim. 2:5.*

PARAGRAPH 3. The Lord Jesus, in His human nature thus united to the divine, in the person of the Son, was sanctified and anointed with the Holy Spirit above measure,[13] having in Him all the treasures of wisdom and knowledge;[14] in whom it pleased the Father that all fullness should dwell,[15] to the end that being holy, harmless, undefiled,[16] and full of grace and truth,[17] He might be throughly furnished to execute the office of mediator and surety;[18] which office He took not upon himself, but was thereunto called by His Father;[19] who also put all power and judgement in His hand, and gave Him commandment to execute the same.[20]

[13] *Ps. 45:7; Acts 10:38; John 3:34.* [14] *Col. 2:3.* [15] *Col. 1:19.*
[16] *Heb. 7:26.* [17] *John 1:14.* [18] *Heb. 7:22.* [19] *Heb. 5:5.*
[20] *John 5:22, 27; Matt. 28:18; Acts 2:36.*

PARAGRAPH 4. This office the Lord Jesus did most willingly undertake,[21] which that He might discharge He was made under the law,[22] and did perfectly fulfill it, and underwent the punishment due to us, which we should have born and suffered,[23] being made sin and a curse for us;[24] enduring most grievous sorrows in His soul, and most painful sufferings in His body;[25] was crucified, and died, and remained in the state of the dead, yet saw no corruption:[26] on the third day He arose from the dead[27] with the same body in which He suffered,[28] with which He also ascended into heaven,[29] and there sits at the right hand of His Father making intercession,[30] and shall return to judge men and angels at the end of the world.[31]

(21) *Ps. 40:7, 8; Heb. 10:5-10; John 10:18.* (22) *Gal 4:4; Matt. 3:15.*
(23) *Gal. 3:13; Isa. 53:6; 1 Pet. 3:18.* (24) *2 Cor. 5:21.* (25) *Matt. 26:37, 38; Luke 22:44; Matt. 27:46.* (26) *Acts 13:37.* (27) *1 Cor. 15:3, 4.*
(28) *John 20:25, 27.* (29) *Mark 16:19; Acts 1:9-11.* (30) *Rom. 8:34; Heb. 9:24.* (31) *Acts 10:42; Rom. 14:9,10; Acts 1:11; 2 Pet. 2:4.*

PARAGRAPH 5. The Lord Jesus, by His perfect obedience and sacrifice of Himself, which He through the eternal Spirit once offered up to God, has fully satisfied the justice of God,[32] procured reconciliation, and purchased an everlasting inheritance in the kingdom of heaven, for all those whom the Father has given unto Him.[33]

(32) *Heb. 9:14, 10:14; Rom. 3:25, 26.* (33) *John 17:2; Heb. 9:15.*

PARAGRAPH 6. Although the price of redemption was not actually paid by Christ until after His incarnation, yet the virtue, efficacy, and benefit thereof were communicated to the elect in all ages, successively from the beginning of the world, in and by those promises, types, and sacrifices wherein He was revealed, and signified to be the seed which should bruise the serpent's head;[34] and the Lamb slain from the foundation of the world,[35] being the same yesterday, and today and for ever.[36]

(34) *1 Cor. 4:10; Heb. 4:2; 1 Pet. 1:10, 11.* (35) *Rev. 13:8.* (36) *Heb. 13:8.*

PARAGRAPH 7. Christ, in the work of mediation, acts according to both natures, by each nature doing that which is proper to itself; yet by reason of the unity of the person, that which is proper to one nature is sometimes in Scripture, attributed to the person denominated by the other nature.[37]

(37) *John 3:13; Acts 20:28.*

PARAGRAPH 8. To all those for whom Christ has obtained eternal redemption, He does certainly and effectually apply and communicate the same, making intercession for them;[38] uniting them to Himself by His Spirit, revealing to them, in and by His Word, the mystery of salvation, persuading them to believe and obey,[39] governing their hearts by His Word and Spirit,[40] and overcoming all their enemies by His almighty power and wisdom,[41] in such manner and ways as are most consonant to His wonderful and unsearchable dispensation; and all of free and absolute grace, without any condition foreseen in them to procure it.(42)

(38) *John 6:37, 10:15, 16, 17:9; Rom. 5:10.*

(39) *John 17:6; Eph. 1:9; 1 John 5:20.* (40) *Rom. 8:9, 14.*

(41) *Ps. 110:1; 1 Cor. 15:25, 26.* (42) *John 3:8; Eph. 1:8.*

PARAGRAPH 9. This office of mediator between God and man is proper only to Christ, who is the prophet, priest, and king of the church of God; and may not be either in whole, or any part thereof, transferred from Him to any other.(43)

(43) *Tim. 2:5.*

PARAGRAPH 10. This number and order of offices is necessary; for in respect of our ignorance, we stand in need of His prophetical office;(44) and in respect of our alienation from God, and imperfection of the best of our services, we need His priestly office to reconcile us and present us acceptable unto God;(45) and in respect to our averseness and utter inability to return to God, and for our rescue and security from our spiritual adversaries, we need His kingly office to convince, subdue, draw, uphold, deliver, and preserve us to His heavenly kingdom.(46)

(44) *John 1:18.* (45) *Col. 1:21; Gal. 5:17.*

(46) *John 16:8; Ps. 110:3; Luke 1:74, 75.*

CHAPTER 9: OF FREE WILL

PARAGRAPH 1. God has endued the will of man with that natural liberty and power of acting upon choice, that it is neither forced, nor by any necessity of nature determined to do good or evil.(1)

(1) *Matt. 17:12; James 1:14; Deut. 30:19.*

PARAGRAPH 2. Man, in his state of innocency, had freedom and power to will and to do that which was good and well-pleasing to God,(2) but yet was unstable, so that he might fall from it.(3)

(2) *Eccles. 7:29.* (3) *Gen. 3:6.*

PARAGRAPH 3. Man, by his fall into a state of sin, has wholly lost all ability of will to any spiritual good accompanying salvation;(4) so as a natural man, being altogether averse from that good, and dead in sin,[5] is not able by his own strength to convert himself, or to prepare himself thereunto.[6]

[4] *Rom. 5:6, 8:7.* [5] *Eph. 2:1, 5.* [6] *Titus 3:3-5; John 6:44.*

PARAGRAPH 4. When God converts a sinner, and translates him into the state of grace, He frees him from his natural bondage under sin,[7] and by His grace alone enables him freely to will and to do that which is spiritually good;[8] yet so as that by reason of his remaining corruptions, he does not perfectly, nor only will, that which is good, but does also will that which is evil.[9]

[7] *Col. 1:13; John 8:36.* [8] *Phil. 2:13.* [9] *Rom. 7:15, 18, 19, 21, 23.*

PARAGRAPH 5. This will of man is made perfectly and immutably free to good alone in the state of glory only.[10]

[10] *Eph. 4:13.*

CHAPTER 10: OF EFFECTUAL CALLING

PARAGRAPH 1. Those whom God hath predestinated unto life, He is pleased in His appointed, and accepted time, effectually to call,[1] by His Word and Spirit, out of that state of sin and death in which they are by nature, to grace and salvation by Jesus Christ;[2] enlightening their minds spiritually and savingly to understand the things of God;[3] taking away their heart of stone, and giving to them a heart of flesh;[4] renewing their wills, and by His almighty power determining them to that which is good, and effectually drawing them to Jesus Christ;[5] yet so as they come most freely, being made willing by His grace.[6]

[1] *Rom. 8:30, 11:7; Eph. 1:10, 11; 2 Thess. 2:13, 14.*
[2] *Eph. 2:1-6.* [3] *Acts 26:18; Eph. 1:17, 18.* [4] *Ezek. 36:26.*
[5] *Deut. 30:6; Ezek. 36:27; Eph. 1:19.* [6] *Ps. 110:3; Cant. 1:4.*

PARAGRAPH 2. This effectual call is of God's free and special grace alone, not from anything at all foreseen in man, nor from any power or agency in the creature,[7] being wholly passive therein, being dead in sins and trespasses, until being quickened and renewed by the Holy Spirit;[8] he is thereby enabled to answer this call, and to embrace the grace offered and conveyed in it, and that by no less power than that which raised up Christ from the dead.[9]

[7] *2 Tim. 1:9; Eph. 2:8.* [8] *1 Cor. 2:14; Eph. 2:5; John 5:25.*
[9] *Eph. 1:19, 20.*

PARAGRAPH 3. Elect infants dying in infancy are regenerated and saved by Christ through the Spirit;[10] who works when, and where, and how He pleases;[11] so also are all elect persons, who are incapable of being outwardly called by the ministry of the Word.

[10] *John 3:3, 5, 6.* [11] *John 3:8.*

PARAGRAPH 4. Others not elected, although they may be called by the ministry of the Word, and may have some common operations of the Spirit,[12] yet not being effectually drawn by the Father, they neither will nor can truly come to Christ, and therefore cannot be saved:[13] much less can men that do not receive the Christian religion be saved; be they never so diligent to frame their lives according to the light of nature and the law of that religion they do profess.[14]

[12] *Matt. 22:14, 13:20, 21; Heb 6:4, 5.*
[13] *John 6:44, 45, 65; 1 John 2:24, 25.* [14] *Acts 4:12; John 4:22, 17:3.*

CHAPTER 11: OF JUSTIFICATION

PARAGRAPH 1. Those whom God effectually calls, he also freely justifies,[1] not by infusing righteousness into them, but by pardoning their sins, and by accounting and accepting their persons as righteous;[2] not for anything wrought in them, or done by them, but for Christ's sake alone;[3] not by imputing faith itself, the act of believing, or any other evangelical obedience to them, as their righteousness; but by imputing Christ's active obedience unto the whole law, and passive obedience in his death for their whole and sole righteousness by faith,[4] which faith they have not of themselves; it is the gift of God.[5]

[1] *Rom. 3:24, 8:30.* [2] *Rom. 4:5-8; Eph. 1:7.* [3] *1 Cor. 1:30, 31; Rom. 5:17-19.* [4] *Phil. 3:8, 9; Eph. 2:8-10.* [5] *John 1:12; Rom. 5:17.*

PARAGRAPH 2. Faith thus receiving and resting on Christ and his righteousness, is the alone instrument of justification;[6] yet is not alone in the person justified, but is ever accompanied with all other saving graces, and is no dead faith, but works by love.[(7)]

[(6)] *Rom. 3:28.* [(7)] *Gal.5:6; James 2:17, 22, 26.*

PARAGRAPH 3. Christ, by his obedience and death, did fully discharge the debt of all those who are justified; and did, by the sacrifice of himself in the blood of his cross, undergoing in their stead the penalty due to them, make a proper, real, and full satisfaction to God's justice in their behalf;[(8)] yet, in as much as he was given by the Father for them, and his obedience and satisfaction accepted in their stead, and both freely, not for anything in them,[(9)] their justification is only of free grace, that both the exact justice and rich grace of God might be glorified in the justification of sinners.[(10)]

[(8)] *Heb. 10:14; 1 Pet. 1:18, 19; Isa. 53:5, 6.* [(9)] *Rom. 8:32; 2 Cor. 5:21.*
[(10)] *Rom. 3:26; Eph. 1:6, 7, 2:7.*

PARAGRAPH 4. God did from all eternity decree to justify all the elect,[(11)] and Christ did in the fullness of time die for their sins, and rise again for their justification;[(12)] nevertheless, they are not justified personally, until the Holy Spirit in time does actually apply Christ to them.[(13)]

[(11)] *Gal. 3:8, 1 Pet. 1:2, 1 Tim. 2:6.* [(12)] *Rom. 4:25.*
[(13)] *Col. 1:21,22, Titus 3:4-7.*

PARAGRAPH 5. God continues to forgive the sins of those that are justified,[(14)] and although they can never fall from the state of justification,[(15)] yet they may, by their sins, fall under God's fatherly displeasure;[(16)] and in that condition they usually do not have the light of his countenance restored to them, until they humble themselves, beg pardon, and renew their faith and repentance.[(17)]

[(14)] *Matt. 6:12; 1 John 1:7, 9.* [(15)] *John 10:28.* [(16)] *Ps. 89:31-33.*
[(17)] *Ps. 32:5, Ps. 51; Matt. 26:75.*

PARAGRAPH 6. The justification of believers under the Old Testament was, in all these respects, one and the same with the justification of believers under the New Testament.[(18)]

[(18)] *Gal. 3:9; Rom. 4:22-24.*

CHAPTER 12: OF ADOPTION

PARAGRAPH 1. All those that are justified, God conferred, in and for the sake of his only Son Jesus Christ, to make partakers of the grace of adoption,(1) by which they are taken into the number, and enjoy the liberties and privileges of the children of God,(2) have his name put on them,(3) receive the spirit of adoption,(4) have access to the throne of grace with boldness, are enabled to cry Abba, Father,(5) are pitied,(6) protected,(7) provided for,(8) and chastened by him as by a Father,(9) yet never cast off,(10) but sealed to the day of redemption,(11) and inherit the promises as heirs of everlasting salvation.(12)

(1) *Eph. 1:5; Gal. 4:4, 5.* (2) *John 1:12; Rom. 8:17.* (3) *2 Cor. 6:18; Rev. 3:12.* (4) *Rom. 8:15.* (5) *Gal. 4:6; Eph. 2:18.* (6) *Ps. 103:13.* (7) *Prov. 14:26; 1 Pet. 5:7.* (8) *Heb. 12:6.* (9) *Isa. 54:8, 9.* (10) *Lam. 3:31.* (11) *Eph. 4:30.* (12) *Heb. 1:14, 6:12.*

CHAPTER 13: OF SANCTIFICATION

PARAGRAPH 1. They who are united to Christ, effectually called, and regenerated, having a new heart and a new spirit created in them through the virtue of Christ's death and resurrection, are also farther sanctified, really and personally,(1) through the same virtue, by his Word and Spirit dwelling in them;(2) the dominion of the whole body of sin is destroyed,(3) and the several lusts of it are more and more weakened and mortified,(4) and they more and more quickened and strengthened in all saving graces,(5) to the practice of all true holiness, without which no man shall see the Lord.(6)

(1) *Acts 20:32; Rom. 6:5, 6.* (2) *John 17:17; Eph. 3:16-19; 1 Thess. 5:21-23.* (3) *Rom. 6:14.* (4) *Gal. 5:24.* (5) *Col. 1:11.* (6) *2 Cor. 7:1; Heb. 12:14.*

PARAGRAPH 2. This sanctification is throughout the whole man,(7) yet imperfect in this life; there abides still some remnants of corruption in every part,(8) wherefrom arises a continual and irreconcilable war; the flesh lusting against the Spirit, and the Spirit against the flesh.(9)

(7) *1 Thess. 5:23.* (8) *Rom. 7:18, 23.* (9) *Gal. 5:17; 1 Pet. 2:11.*

PARAGRAPH 3. In which war, although the remaining corruption for a time may much prevail,[(10)] yet, through the continual supply of strength from the sanctifying Spirit of Christ, the regenerate part does overcome;[(11)] and so the saints grow in grace, perfecting holiness in the fear of God, pressing after an heavenly life, in evangelical obedience to all the commands which Christ as Head and King, in his Word has prescribed to them.[(12)]

[(10)] *Rom. 7:23.* [(11)] *Rom. 6:14.* [(12)] *Eph. 4:15, 16; 2 Cor. 3:18, 7:1.*

CHAPTER 14: OF SAVING FAITH

PARAGRAPH 1. The grace of faith, whereby the elect are enabled to believe to the saving of their souls, is the work of the Spirit of Christ in their hearts,[(1)] and is ordinarily wrought by the ministry of the Word;[(2)] by which also, and by the administration of baptism and the Lord's supper, prayer, and other means appointed of God, it is increased and strengthened.[(3)]

[(1)] *2 Cor. 4:13; Eph. 2:8.* [(2)] *Rom. 10:14, 17.*

[(3)] *Luke 17:5; 1 Pet. 2:2; Acts 20:32.*

PARAGRAPH 2. By this faith a Christian believes to be true whatsoever is revealed in the Word for the authority of God himself,[(4)] and also apprehends an excellency therein above all other writings and all things in the world,[(5)] as it bears forth the glory of God in his attributes, the excellency of Christ in his nature and offices, and the power and fullness of the Holy Spirit in his workings and operations: and so is enabled to cast his soul upon the truth consequently believed;[(6)] and also acts differently upon that which each particular passage thereof contains; yielding obedience to the commands,[(7)] trembling at the threatenings,[(8)] and embracing the promises of God for this life and that which is to come;[(9)] but the principle acts of saving faith have immediate relation to Christ, accepting, receiving, and resting upon him alone for justification, sanctification, and eternal life, by virtue of the covenant of grace.[(10)]

[(4)] *Acts 24:14.* [(5)] *Ps. 19:7-10, 69:72.* [(6)] *2 Tim. 1:12.* [(7)] *John 15:14.*

[(8)] *Isa. 116:2.* [(9)] *Heb. 11:13.* [(10)] *John 1:12; Acts 16:31; Gal 2:20; Acts 15:11.*

PARAGRAPH 3. This faith, although it be in different stages, and may be weak or strong,[11] yet it is in the least degree of it different in the kind or nature of it, as is all other saving grace, from the faith and common grace of temporary believers;[12] and therefore, though it may be many times assailed and weakened, yet it gets the victory,[13] growing up in many to the attainment of a full assurance through Christ,[14] who is both the author and finisher of our faith.[15]

(11) *Heb. 5:13, 14; Matt. 6:30; Rom. 4:19, 20.* (12) *2 Pet. 1:1.*

(13) *Eph. 6:16; 1 John 5:4, 5.* (14) *Heb. 6:11, 12; Col. 2:2.* (15) *Heb. 12:2.*

CHAPTER 15: OF REPENTANCE UNTO LIFE AND SALVATION

PARAGRAPH 1. Such of the elect that are converted at riper years, having sometime lived in the state of nature, and therein served divers pleasures, God in their effectual calling gives them repentance to life.[1]

(1) *Titus 3:2-5.*

PARAGRAPH 2. Whereas there is none that does good and does not sin,[2] and the best of men may, through the power and deceitfulness of their corruption dwelling in them, with the prevalency of temptation, fall in to great sins and provocations; God has, in the covenant of grace, mercifully provided that believers so sinning and falling be renewed through repentance unto salvation.[3]

(2) *Eccles. 7:20.* (3) *Luke 22:31, 32.*

PARAGRAPH 3. This saving repentance is an evangelical grace,[4] whereby a person, being by the Holy Spirit made sensible of the manifold evils of his sin, does, by faith in Christ, humble himself for it with godly sorrow, detestation of it, and self-abhorrancy,[5] praying for pardon and strength of grace, with a purpose and endeavor, by supplies of the Spirit, to walk before God unto all well-pleasing in all things.[6]

(4) *Zech. 12:10; Acts 11:18.* (5) *Ezek. 36:31; 2 Cor. 7:11.* (6) *Ps. 119:6, 128.*

PARAGRAPH 4. As repentance is to be continued through the whole course of our lives, upon the account of the body of death, and the motions thereof, so it is every man's duty to repent of his particular known sins particularly.[(7)]

(7) *Luke 19:8; 1 Tim. 1:13, 15.*

PARAGRAPH 5. Such is the provision which God has made through Christ in the covenant of grace for the preservation of believers unto salvation, that although there is no sin so small but it deserves damnation,[(8)] yet there is no sin so great that it shall bring damnation to them that repent,[(9)] which makes the constant preaching of repentance necessary.

(8) *Rom. 6:23.* (9) *Isa. 1:16-18, 55:7.*

CHAPTER 16: OF GOOD WORKS

PARAGRAPH 1. Good works are only such as God has commanded in his Holy Word,[(1)] and not such as without the warrant thereof are devised by men out of blind zeal, or upon any pretense of good intentions.[(2)]

(1) *Mic. 6:8; Heb. 13:21.* (2) *Matt. 15:9; Isa. 29:13.*

PARAGRAPH 2. These good works, done in obedience to God's commandments, are the fruits and evidences of a true and lively faith;[(3)] and by them believers manifest their thankfulness,[(4)] strengthen their assurance,[(5)] edify their brethren, adorn the profession of the gospel,[(6)] stop the mouths of the adversaries, and glory God,[(7)] whose workmanship they are, created in Christ Jesus thereunto,[(8)] that having their fruit unto holiness they may have the end eternal life.[(9)]

(3) *James 2:18, 22.* (4) *Ps. 116:12, 13.* (5) *1 John 2:3, 5; 2 Pet. 1:5-11.*
(6) *Matt. 5:16.* (7) *1 Tim. 6:1; 1 Pet. 2:15; Phil. 1:11.* (8) *Eph. 2:10.*
(9) *Rom 6:22.*

PARAGRAPH 3. Their ability to do good works is not all of themselves, but wholly from the Spirit of Christ;[(10)] and that they may be enabled thereunto, besides the graces they have already received, there is necessary an actual influence of the same Holy Spirit, to work in them and to will and to do of his good pleasure;[(11)] yet they are not bound to perform any duty, unless upon a special motion of the Spirit, but they ought to be diligent in stirring up the grace of God that is in them.[(12)]

[(10)] *John 15:4, 5.* [(11)] *2 Cor. 3:5; Phil. 2:13.*

[(12)] *Phil. 2:12; Heb. 6:11, 12; Isa. 64:7.*

PARAGRAPH 4. They who in their obedience attain to the greatest height which is possible in this life, are so far from being able to supererogate, and to do more than God requires, as that they fall short of much which in duty they are bound to do.[(13)]

[(13)] *Job 9:2, 3; Gal. 5:17; Luke 17:10.*

PARAGRAPH 5. We cannot by our best works merit pardon of sin or eternal life at the hand of God, by reason of the great disproportion that is between them and the glory to come, and the infinite distance that is between us and God, whom by them we can neither profit nor satisfy for the debt of our former sins;[(14)] but when we have done all we can, we have done but our duty, and are unprofitable servants; and because they are good they proceed from his Spirit,[(15)] and as they are wrought by us they are defiled and mixed with so much weakness and imperfection, that they cannot endure the severity of God's punishment.[(16)]

[(14)] *Rom. 3:20; Eph. 2:8, 9; Rom. 4:6.* [(15)] *Gal. 5:22, 23.*

[(16)] *Isa. 64:6; Ps. 43:2.*

PARAGRAPH 6. Yet notwithstanding the persons of believers being accepted through Christ, their good works also are accepted in him;[(17)] not as thought they were in this life wholly unblamable and unreprovable in God's sight, but that he, looking upon them in his Son, is pleased to accept and reward that which is sincere, although accompanied with many weaknesses and imperfection.[(18)]

[(17)] *Eph. 1:5; 1 Pet. 1:5.* [(18)] *Matt. 25:21, 23; Heb. 6:10.*

PARAGRAPH 7. Works done by unregenerate men, although for the matter of them they may be things which God commands, and of good use both to themselves and to others;[(19)] yet because they proceed not from a heart purified by faith,[(20)] nor are done in a right manner according to the Word,[(21)] nor to a right end, the glory of God,[(22)] they are therefore sinful, and cannot please God, nor make a man meet to receive the grace from God,[23] and yet their neglect for them is more sinful and displeasing to God.[24]

> [19] *2 Kings 10:30; 1 Kings 21:27, 29.* [20] *Gen. 4:5; Heb. 11:4, 6.*
> [21] *1 Cor. 13:1.* [22] *Matt. 6:2, 5.* [23] *Amos 5:21,22; Rom. 9:16; Titus 3:5.*
> [24] *Job 21:14,15; Matt. 25:41-43.*

CHAPTER 17: OF THE PERSEVERANCE OF THE SAINTS

PARAGRAPH 1. Those whom God has accepted in the beloved, effectually called and sanctified by his Spirit, and given the precious faith of his elect unto, can neither totally nor finally fall from the state of grace, but shall certainly persevere therein to the end, and be eternally saved, seeing the gifts and callings of God are without repentance, from which source he still begets and nourishes in them faith, repentance, love, joy, hope, and all the graces of the Spirit unto immortality;[1] and though many storms and floods arise and beat against them, yet they shall never be able to take them off that foundation and rock which by faith they are fastened upon; notwithstanding, through unbelief and the temptations of Satan, the sensible sight of the light and love of God may for a time be clouded and obscured from them,[2] yet he is still the same, and they shall be sure to be kept by the power of God unto salvation, where they shall enjoy their purchased possession, they being engraved upon the palm of his hands, and their names having been written in the book of life from all eternity.[3]

> [1] *John 10:28, 29; Phil. 1:6; 2 Tim. 2:19; 1 John 2:19.*
> [2] *Ps. 89:31, 32; 1 Cor. 11:32.* [3] *Mal. 3:6.*

PARAGRAPH 2. This perseverance of the saints depends not upon their own free will, but upon the immutability of the decree of election,[4] flowing from the free and unchangeable love of God the Father, upon the efficacy of the merit and intercession of Jesus Christ and union with him,[5] the oath of God,[6] the abiding of his Spirit, and the seed of God within them,[7] and the nature of the covenant of grace;[8] from all which ariseth also the certainty and infallibility thereof.

> [4] *Rom. 8:30, 9:11, 16.* [5] *Rom. 5:9, 10; John 14:19.*
> [6] *Heb. 6:17, 18.* [7] *1 John 3:9.* [8] *Jer. 32:40.*

PARAGRAPH 3. And though they may, through the temptation of Satan and of the world, the prevalency of corruption remaining in them, and the neglect of means of their preservation, fall into grievous sins, and for a time continue therein,(9) whereby they incur God's displeasure and grieve his Holy Spirit,(10) come to have their graces and comforts impaired,(11) have their hearts hardened, and their consciences wounded,(12) hurt and scandalize others, and bring temporal judgments upon themselves,(13) yet shall they renew their repentance and be preserved through faith in Christ Jesus to the end.(14)

(9) *Matt. 26:70, 72, 74.* (10) *Isa. 64:5, 9; Eph. 4:30.* (11) *Ps. 51:10, 12.*
(12) *Ps. 32:3, 4.* (13) *2 Sam. 12:14.* (14) *Luke 22:32, 61, 62.*

CHAPTER 18: OF THE ASSURANCE OF GRACE AND SALVATION

PARAGRAPH 1. Although temporary believers and other unregenerate men, may vainly deceive themselves with false hopes and carnal presumptions of being in the favor of God and in a state of salvation, which hope of theirs shall perish;(1) yet such as truly believe in the Lord Jesus, and love him in sincerity, endeavouring to walk in all good conscience before him, may in this life be certainly assured that they are in the state of grace, and may rejoice in the hope of the glory of God,(2) which hope shall never make them ashamed.(3)

(1) *Job 8:13, 14; Matt. 7:22, 23.*
(2) *1 John 2:3, 3:14, 18, 19, 21, 24, 5:13.* (3) *Rom. 5:2, 5.*

PARAGRAPH 2. This certainty is not a bare conjectural and probable persuasion grounded upon a fallible hope, but an infallible assurance of faith,(4) founded on the blood and righteousness of Christ revealed in the Gospel;(5) and also upon the inward evidence of those graces of the Spirit unto which promises are made,(6) and on the testimony of the Spirit of adoption, witnessing with our spirits that we are the children of God;(7) and, as a fruit thereof, keeping the heart both humble and holy.(8)

(4) *Heb. 6:11, 19.* (5) *Heb. 6:17, 18.* (6) *2 Pet. 1:4,5, 10, 11.*
(7) *Rom. 8:15, 16.* (8) *1 John 3:1-3*

PARAGRAPH 3. This infallible assurance does not so belong to the essence of faith, but that a true believer may wait long, and struggle with many difficulties before he be partaker of it;[9] yet being enabled by the Spirit to know the things which are freely given him of God, he may, without extraordinary revelation, in the right use of means, attain thereunto:[10] and therefore it is the duty of every one to give all diligence to make his calling and election sure, that thereby his heart may be enlarged in peace and joy in the Holy Spirit, in love and thankfulness to God, and in strength and cheerfulness in the duties of obedience, the proper fruits of this assurance;[11]—so far is it from inclining men to looseness.[12]

(9) *Isa. 50:10; Ps. 88; Ps. 77:1-12.* (10) *1 John 4:13; Heb. 6:11, 12.*
(11) *Rom. 5:1, 2, 5, 14:17; Ps. 119:32.* (12) *Rom. 6:1, 2; Titus 2:11, 12, 14.*

PARAGRAPH 4. True believers may have the assurance of their salvation divers ways shaken, diminished, and intermitted; as by negligence in preserving of it,[13] by falling into some special sin which wounds the conscience and grieves the Spirit;[14] by some sudden or vehement temptation,[15] by God's withdrawing the light of his countenance, and suffering even such as fear him to walk in darkness and to have no light,[16] yet are they never destitute of the seed of God[17] and life of faith,[18] that love of Christ and the brethren, that sincerity of heart and conscience of duty out of which, by the operation of the Spirit, this assurance may in due time be revived,[19] and by the which, in the meantime, they are preserved from utter despair.[20]

(13) *Cant. 5:2, 3, 6.* (14) *Ps. 51:8, 12, 14.* (15) *Ps. 116:11; 77:7, 8, 31:22.*
(16) *Ps. 30:7.* (17) *1 John 3:9.* (18) *Luke 22:32.* (19) *Ps. 42:5, 11.*
(20) *Lam. 3:26-31.*

CHAPTER 19: OF THE LAW OF GOD

PARAGRAPH 1. God gave to Adam a law of universal obedience written in his heart, and a particular precept of not eating the fruit of the tree of knowledge of good and evil;[1] by which he bound him and all his posterity to personal, entire, exact, and perpetual obedience;[2] promised life upon the fulfilling, and threatened death upon the breach of it, and endued him with power and ability to keep it.[3]

(1) *Gen. 1:27; Eccles. 7:29.* (2) *Rom. 10:5.* (3) *Gal. 3:10, 12.*

PARAGRAPH 2. The same law that was first written in the heart of man continued to be a perfect rule of righteousness after the fall,[4] and was delivered by God upon Mount Sinai, in ten commandments, and written in two tables, the four first containing our duty towards God, and the other six, our duty to man.[5]

[4] *Rom. 2:14,15.* [5] *Deut. 10:4.*

PARAGRAPH 3. Besides this law, commonly called moral, God was pleased to give to the people of Israel ceremonial laws, containing several typical ordinances, partly of worship, prefiguring Christ, his graces, actions, sufferings, and benefits;[6] and partly holding forth divers instructions of moral duties,[7] all which ceremonial laws being appointed only to the time of reformation, are, by Jesus Christ the true Messiah and only law-giver, who was furnished with power from the Father for that end abrogated and taken away.[8]

[6] *Heb. 10:1; Col. 2:17.* [7] *1 Cor. 5:7.* [8] *Col. 2:14, 16, 17; Eph. 2:14, 16.*

PARAGRAPH 4. To them also he gave sundry judicial laws, which expired together with the state of that people, not obliging any now by virtue of that institution; their general equity only being of modern use.[9]

[9] *1 Cor. 9:8-10.*

PARAGRAPH 5. The moral law does for ever bind all, as well justified persons as others, to the obedience thereof,[10] and that not only in regard of the matter contained in it, but also in respect of the authority of God the Creator, who gave it;[11] neither does Christ in the Gospel any way dissolve, but much strengthen this obligation.[12]

[10] *Rom. 13:8-10; James 2:8, 10-12.* [11] *James 2:10, 11.*
[12] *Matt. 5:17-19; Rom. 3:31.*

PARAGRAPH 6. Although true believers are not under the law as a covenant of works, to be thereby justified or condemned,[13] yet it is of great use to them as well as to others, in that as a rule of life, informing them of the will of God and their duty, it directs and binds them to walk accordingly; discovering also the sinful pollutions of their natures, hearts, and lives, so as examining themselves thereby, they may come to further conviction of, humiliation for, and hatred against, sin;[14] together with a clearer sight of the need they have of Christ and the perfection of his obedience; it is likewise of use to the regenerate to restrain their corruptions, in that it forbids sin; and the threatenings of it serve to show what even their sins deserve, and what afflictions in this life they may expect for them, although freed from the curse and unallayed rigour thereof. The promises of it likewise show them God's approbation of obedience, and what blessings they may expect upon the performance thereof, though not as due to them by the law as a covenant of works; so as man's doing good and refraining from evil, because the law encourages to the one and deters from the other, is no evidence of his being under the law and not under grace.(15)

(13) *Rom. 6:14; Gal. 2:16; Rom. 8:1, 10:4.* (14) *Rom. 3:20, 7:7, etc.*
(15) *Rom. 6:12-14; 1 Pet. 3:8-13.*

PARAGRAPH 7. Neither are the aforementioned uses of the law contrary to the grace of the Gospel, but do sweetly comply with it,(16) the Spirit of Christ subduing and enabling the will of man to do that freely and cheerfully which the will of God, revealed in the law, requires to be done.(17)

(16) *Gal. 3:21.* (17) *Ezek. 36:27.*

CHAPTER 20: OF THE GOSPEL AND OF THE EXTENT OF THE GRACE THEREOF

PARAGRAPH 1. The covenant of works being broken by sin, and made unprofitable unto life, God was pleased to give forth the promise of Christ, the seed of the woman, as the means of calling the elect, and begetting in them faith and repentance;(1) in this promise the gospel, as to the substance of it, was revealed, and [is] therein effectual for the conversion and salvation of sinners.(2)

(1) *Gen. 3:15.* (2) *Rev. 13:8.*

PARAGRAPH 2. This promise of Christ, and salvation by him, is revealed only by the Word of God;(3) neither do the works of creation or providence, with the light of nature, make discovery of Christ, or of grace by him, so much as in a general or obscure way;(4) much less that men destitute of the revelation of Him by the promise or gospel, should be enabled thereby to attain saving faith or repentance.(5)

(3) *Rom. 1:17.* (4) *Rom. 10:14, 15, 17.* (5) *Prov. 29:18; Isa. 25:7; 60:2, 3.*

PARAGRAPH 3. The revelation of the gospel to sinners, made in divers times and by sundry parts, with the addition of promises and precepts for the obedience required therein, as to the nations and persons to whom it is granted, is merely of the sovereign will and good pleasure of God;[6] not being annexed by virtue of any promise to the due improvement of men's natural abilities, by virtue of common light received without it, which none ever made, or can do so;[7] and therefore in all ages, the preaching of the gospel has been granted unto persons and nations, as to the extent or straitening of it, in great variety, according to the counsel of the will of God.

(6) *Ps. 147:20; Acts 16:7.* (7) *Rom. 1:18-32.*

PARAGRAPH 4. Although the gospel be the only outward means of revealing Christ and saving grace, and is, as such, abundantly sufficient thereunto; yet that men who are dead in trespasses may be born again, quickened or regenerated, there is moreover necessary an effectual insuperable work of the Holy Spirit upon the whole soul, for the producing in them a new spiritual life;[8] without which no other means will effect their conversion unto God.[9]

(8) *Ps. 110:3; 1 Cor. 2:14; Eph. 1:19, 20.* (9) *John 6:44; 2 Cor. 4:4, 6.*

CHAPTER 21: OF CHRISTIAN LIBERTY AND LIBERTY OF CONSCIENCE

PARAGRAPH 1. The liberty which Christ has purchased for believers under the gospel, consists in their freedom from the guilt of sin, the condemning wrath of God, the severity and curse of the law,[1] and in their being delivered from this present evil world,[2] bondage to Satan,[3] and dominion of sin,[4] from the evil of afflictions,[5] the fear and sting of death, the victory of the grave,[6] and everlasting damnation:[7] as also in their free access to God, and their yielding obedience unto Him, not out of slavish fear,[8] but a child-like love and willing mind.[9] All which were common also to believers under the law for the substance of them;[10] but under the New Testament the liberty of Christians is further enlarged, in their freedom from the yoke of a ceremonial law, to which the Jewish church was subjected, and in greater boldness of access to the throne of grace, and in fuller communications of the free Spirit of God, than believers under the law did ordinarily partake of.[11]

> [1] *Gal. 3:13.* [2] *Gal. 1:4.* [3] *Acts 26:18.* [4] *Rom. 8:3.* [5] *Rom. 8:28.* [6] *1 Cor. 15:54-57.* [7] *2 Thess. 1:10.* [8] *Rom. 8:15.* [9] *Luke 1:73-75; 1 John 4:18.* [10] *Gal. 3;9, 14.* [11] *John 7:38, 39; Heb. 10:19-21.*

PARAGRAPH 2. God alone is Lord of the conscience,[12] and has left it free from the doctrines and commandments of men which are in any thing contrary to his word, or not contained in it.[13] So that to believe such doctrines, or obey such commands out of conscience, is to betray true liberty of conscience;[14] and the requiring of an implicit faith, an absolute and blind obedience, is to destroy liberty of conscience and reason also.[15]

> [12] *James 4:12; Rom. 14:4.* [13] *Acts 4:19, 29; 1 Cor. 7:23; Matt. 15:9.* [14] *Col. 2:20, 22, 23.* [15] *1 Cor. 3:5; 2 Cor. 1:24.*

PARAGRAPH 3. They who upon pretence of Christian liberty do practice any sin, or cherish any sinful lust, as they do thereby pervert the main design of the grace of the gospel to their own destruction,[16] so they wholly destroy the end of Christian liberty, which is, that being delivered out of the hands of all our enemies, we might serve the Lord without fear, in holiness and righteousness before Him, all the days of our lives.[17]

> [16] *Rom. 6:1, 2.* [17] *Gal. 5:13; 2 Pet. 2:18, 21.*

CHAPTER 22: OF RELIGIOUS WORSHIP AND THE SABBATH DAY

PARAGRAPH 1. The light of nature shows that there is a God, who has lordship and sovereignty over all; is just, good and does good to all; and is therefore to be feared, loved, praised, called upon, trusted in, and served, with all the heart and all the soul, and with all the might.[1] But the acceptable way of worshipping the true God, is instituted by himself,[2] and so limited by his own revealed will, that he may not be worshipped according to the imagination and devices of men, nor the suggestions of Satan, under any visible representations, or any other way not prescribed in the Holy Scriptures.[(3)]

[(1)] *Jer. 10:7; Mark 12:33.* [(2)] *Deut. 12:32.* [(3)] *Exod. 20:4-6.*

PARAGRAPH 2. Religious worship is to be given to God the Father, Son, and Holy Spirit, and to him alone;[(4)] not to angels, saints, or any other creatures;[(5)] and since the fall, not without a mediator,[(6)] nor in the mediation of any other but Christ alone.[(7)]

[(4)] *Matt. 4:9,10; John 6:23; Matt. 28:19.*
[(5)] *Rom. 1:25; Col. 2:18; Rev. 19:10.* [(6)] *John 14:6.* [(7)] *1 Tim. 2:5.*

PARAGRAPH 3. Prayer, with thanksgiving, being one part of natural worship, is by God required of all men.[(8)] But that it may be accepted, it is to be made in the name of the Son,[(9)] by the help of the Spirit,[(10)] according to his will;[(11)] with understanding, reverence, humility, fervency, faith, love, and perseverance; and when with others, in a known tongue.[(12)]

[(8)] *Ps. 95:1-7, 65:2.* [(9)] *John 14:13, 14.* [(10)] *Rom. 8:26.*
[(11)] *1 John 5:14.* [(12)] *1 Cor. 14:16, 17.*

PARAGRAPH 4. Prayer is to be made for things lawful, and for all sorts of men living, or that shall live hereafter;[(13)] but not for the dead,[(14)] nor for those of whom it may be known that they have sinned the sin unto death.[(15)]

[(13)] *1 Tim. 2:1,2; 2 Sam. 7:29.* [(14)] *2 Sam. 12:21-23.* [(15)] *1 John 5:16.*

PARAGRAPH 5. The reading of the Scriptures,[(16)] preaching, and hearing the Word of God,[(17)] teaching and admonishing one another in psalms, hymns, and spiritual songs, singing with grace in our hearts to the Lord;[(18)] as also the administration of baptism,[(19)] and the Lord's supper,[(20)] are all parts of religious worship of God, to be performed in obedience to him, with understanding, faith, reverence, and godly fear; moreover, solemn humiliation, with fastings,[(21)] and thanksgivings, upon special occasions, ought to be used in an holy and religious manner.[(22)]

[(16)] *1 Tim. 4:13.* [(17)] *2 Tim. 4:2; Luke 8:18.* [(18)] *Col. 3:16; Eph. 5:19.*
[(19)] *Matt. 28:19, 20.* [(20)] *1 Cor. 11:26.* [(21)] *Esther 4:16; Joel 2:12.*
[(22)] *Exod. 15:1-19, Ps. 107.*

PARAGRAPH 6. Neither prayer nor any other part of religious worship, is now under the gospel, tied unto, or made more acceptable by any place in which it is performed, or towards which it is directed; but God is to be worshipped everywhere in spirit and in truth;[23] as in private families[24] daily,[25] and in secret each one by himself;[26] so more solemnly in the public assemblies, which are not carelessly nor willfully to be neglected or forsaken, when God by his word or providence calls thereunto.[27]

[23] *John 4:21; Mal. 1:11; 1 Tim. 2:8.* [24] *Acts 10:2.*
[25] *Matt. 6:11; Ps. 55:17.* [26] *Matt. 6:6.* [27] *Heb. 10:25; Acts 2:42.*

PARAGRAPH 7. As it is the law of nature, that in general a proportion of time, by God's appointment, be set apart for the worship of God, so by his Word, in a positive moral, and perpetual commandment, binding all men, in all ages, he has particularly appointed one day in seven for a sabbath to be kept holy unto him,[28] which from the beginning of the world to the resurrection of Christ was the last day of the week, and from the resurrection of Christ was changed into the first day of the week, which is called the Lord's Day:[29] and is to be continued to the end of the world as the Christian Sabbath, the observation of the last day of the week being abolished.

[28] *Exod. 20:8.* [29] *1 Cor. 16:1, 2; Acts 20:7; Rev. 1:10.*

PARAGRAPH 8. The sabbath is then kept holy unto the Lord, when men, after a due preparing of their hearts, and ordering their common affairs aforehand, do not only observe a holy rest all day, from their own works, words and thoughts, about their worldly employment and recreations,[30] but are also taken up the whole time in the public and private exercises of his worship, and in the duties of necessity and mercy.[31]

[30] *Isa. 58:13; Neh. 13:15-22.* [31] *Matt. 12:1-13.*

CHAPTER 23: OF LAWFUL OATHS AND VOWS

PARAGRAPH 1. A lawful oath is a part of religious worship, wherein the person swearing in truth, righteousness, and judgment, solemnly calls God to witness what he swears,[1] and to judge him according to the truth or falseness thereof.[2]

[1] *Exod. 20:7; Deut. 10:20; Jer. 4:2.* [2] *2 Chron. 6:22, 23.*

PARAGRAPH 2. The name of God only is that by which men ought to swear; and therein it is to be used, with all holy fear and reverence; therefore to swear vainly or rashly by that glorious and dreadful name, or to swear at all by any other thing, is sinful, and to be abhorred;[(3)] yet as in matter of weight and moment, for confirmation of truth, and ending all strife, an oath is warranted by the word of God;[(4)] so a lawful oath being imposed by lawful authority in such matters, ought to be taken.[(5)]

(3) *Matt. 5:34,37; James 5:12.* (4) *Heb. 6:16; 2 Cor. 1:23.* (5) *Neh. 13:25.*

PARAGRAPH 3. Whosoever takes an oath warranted by the word of God, ought duly to consider the weightiness of so solemn an act, and therein to avouch nothing but what he knows to be truth; for that by rash, false, and vain oaths, the Lord is provoked, and for them this land mourns.[(6)]

(6) *Lev. 19:12; Jer. 23:10.*

PARAGRAPH 4. An oath is to be taken in the plain and common sense of the words, without equivocation or mental reservation.[(7)]

(7) *Ps. 24:4.*

PARAGRAPH 5. A vow, which is not to be made to any creature, but to God alone, is to be made and performed with all religious care and faithfulness;[(8)] but popish monastical vows of perpetual single life,[(9)] professed poverty,[(10)] and regular obedience, are so far from being degrees of higher perfection, that they are superstitious and sinful snares, in which no Christian may entangle himself.[(11)]

(8) *Ps. 76:11; Gen. 28:20-22.* (9) *1 Cor. 7:2, 9.* (10) *Eph. 4:28.* (11) *Matt. 19:1.*

CHAPTER 24: OF THE CIVIL MAGISTRATE

PARAGRAPH 1. God, the supreme Lord and King of all the world, has ordained civil magistrates to be under him, over the people, for his own glory and the public good; and to this end has armed them with the power of the sword, for defence and encouragement of them that do good, and for the punishment of evil doers.[(1)]

(1) *Rom. 13:1-4.*

PARAGRAPH 2. It is lawful for Christians to accept and execute the office of a magistrate when called thereunto; in the management whereof, as they ought especially to maintain justice and peace,[2] according to the wholesome laws of each kingdom and commonwealth, so for that end they may lawfully now, under the New Testament, wage war upon just and necessary occasions.[3]

(2) *2 Sam. 23:3; Ps. 82:3, 4.* (3) *Luke 3:14.*

PARAGRAPH 3. Civil magistrates being set up by God for the ends aforesaid; subjection, in all lawful things commanded by them, ought to be yielded by us in the Lord, not only for wrath, but for conscience' sake;[4] and we ought to make supplications and prayers for kings and all that are in authority, that under them we may live a quiet and peaceable life, in all godliness and honesty.[5]

(4) *Rom. 13:5-7; 1 Pet. 2:17.* (5) *1 Tim. 2:1, 2.*

CHAPTER 25: OF MARRIAGE

PARAGRAPH 1. Marriage is to be between one man and one woman; neither is it lawful for any man to have more than one wife, nor for any woman to have more than one husband at the same time.[1]

(1) *Gen. 2:24; Mal. 2:15; Matt. 19:5, 6.*

PARAGRAPH 2. Marriage was ordained for the mutual help of husband and wife,[2] for the increase of mankind with a legitimate issue,[3] and the preventing of uncleanness.[4]

(2) *Gen. 2:18.* (3) *Gen. 1:28.* (4) *1 Cor. 7:2, 9.*

PARAGRAPH 3. It is lawful for all sorts of people to marry, who are able with judgment to give their consent;[5] yet it is the duty of Christians to marry in the Lord;[6] and therefore such as profess the true religion, should not marry with infidels, or idolaters; neither should such as are godly, be unequally yoked, by marrying with such as are wicked in their life, or maintain damnable heresy.[7]

(5) *Heb. 13:4; 1 Tim. 4:3.* (6) *1 Cor. 7:39.* (7) *Neh. 13:25-27.*

PARAGRAPH 4. Marriage ought not to be within the degrees of consanguinity or affinity, forbidden in the Word;[8] nor can such incestuous marriages ever be made lawful, by any law of man or consent of parties, so as those persons may live together as man and wife.[9]

(8) *Lev. 18.* (9) *Mark 6:18; 1 Cor. 5:1.*

CHAPTER 26: OF THE CHURCH

PARAGRAPH 1. The catholic or universal church, which (with respect to the internal work of the Spirit and truth of grace) may be called invisible, consists of the whole number of the elect, that have been, are, or shall be gathered into one, under Christ, the head thereof; and is the spouse, the body, the fulness of him that fills all in all.[1]

[1] *Heb. 12:23; Col. 1:18; Eph. 1:10, 22, 23, 5:23, 27, 32.*

PARAGRAPH 2. All persons throughout the world, professing the faith of the gospel, and obedience unto God by Christ according unto it, not destroying their own profession by any errors everting the foundation, or unholiness of conversation, are and may be called visible saints;[2] and of such ought all particular congregations to be constituted.[3]

[2] *1 Cor. 1:2; Acts 11:26.* [3] *Rom. 1:7; Eph. 1:20-22.*

PARAGRAPH 3. The purest churches under heaven are subject to mixture and error;[4] and some have so degenerated as to become no churches of Christ, but synagogues of Satan;[5] nevertheless Christ always has had, and ever shall have a kingdom in this world, to the end thereof, of such as believe in him, and make profession of his name.[6]

[4] *1 Cor. 5; Rev. 2, 3.* [5] *Rev. 18:2; 2 Thess. 2:11, 12.*
[6] *Matt. 16:18; Ps. 72:17, 102:28; Rev. 12:17.*

PARAGRAPH 4. The Lord Jesus Christ is the Head of the church, in whom, by the appointment of the Father, all power for the calling, institution, order or government of the church, is invested in a supreme and sovereign manner;[7] neither can the Pope of Rome in any sense be head thereof, but is that antichrist, that man of sin, and son of perdition, that exalts himself in the church against Christ, and all that is called God; whom the Lord shall destroy with the brightness of his coming.[8]

[7] *Col. 1:18; Matt. 28:18-20; Eph. 4:11, 12.* [8] *2 Thess. 2:2-9.*

PARAGRAPH 5. In the execution of this power wherewith he is so intrusted, the Lord Jesus calls out of the world unto himself, through the ministry of his word, by his Spirit, those that are given unto him by his Father,[9] that they may walk before him in all the ways of obedience, which he prescribes to them in his word.[10] Those thus called, he commands to walk together in particular societies, or churches, for their mutual edification, and the due performance of that public worship, which he requires of them in the world.[11]

[9] *John 10:16; John 12:32.* [10] *Matt. 28:20.* [11] *Matt. 18:15-20.*

PARAGRAPH 6. The members of these churches are saints by calling, visibly manifesting and evidencing (in and by their profession and walking) their obedience unto that call of Christ;[12] and do willingly consent to walk together, according to the appointment of Christ; giving up themselves to the Lord, and one to another, by the will of God, in professed subjection to the ordinances of the Gospel.[13]

[12] *Rom. 1:7; 1 Cor. 1:2.* [13] *Acts 2:41, 42, 5:13, 14; 2 Cor. 9:13.*

PARAGRAPH 7. To each of these churches therefore gathered, according to his mind declared in his word, he has given all that power and authority, which is in any way needful for their carrying on that order in worship and discipline, which he has instituted for them to observe; with commands and rules for the due and right exerting, and executing of that power.[14]

[14] *Matt. 18:17, 18; 1 Cor. 5:4, 5, 5:13, 2 Cor. 2:6-8.*

PARAGRAPH 8. A particular church, gathered and completely organized according to the mind of Christ, consists of officers and members; and the officers appointed by Christ to be chosen and set apart by the church (so called and gathered), for the peculiar administration of ordinances, and execution of power or duty, which he intrusts them with, or calls them to, to be continued to the end of the world, are bishops or elders, and deacons.[15]

[15] *Acts 20:17, 28; Phil. 1:1.*

PARAGRAPH 9. The way appointed by Christ for the calling of any person, fitted and gifted by the Holy Spirit, unto the office of bishop or elder in a church, is, that he be chosen thereunto by the common suffrage of the church itself;[16] and solemnly set apart by fasting and prayer, with imposition of hands of the eldership of the church, if there be any before constituted therein;[17] and of a deacon that he be chosen by the like suffrage, and set apart by prayer, and the like imposition of hands.[18]

[16] *Acts 14:23.* [17] *1 Tim. 4:14.* [18] *Acts 6:3, 5, 6.*

PARAGRAPH 10. The work of pastors being constantly to attend the service of Christ, in his churches, in the ministry of the word and prayer, with watching for their souls, as they that must give an account to Him;[19] it is incumbent on the churches to whom they minister, not only to give them all due respect, but also to communicate to them of all their good things according to their ability,[20] so as they may have a comfortable supply, without being themselves entangled in secular affairs;[21] and may also be capable of exercising hospitality towards others;[22] and this is required by the law of nature, and by the express order of our Lord Jesus, who has ordained that they that preach the Gospel should live of the Gospel.[23]

(19) *Acts 6:4; Heb. 13:17.* (20) *1 Tim. 5:17,18; Gal. 6:6, 7.*
(21) *2 Tim. 2:4.* (22) *1 Tim. 3:2.* (23) *1 Cor. 9:6-14*

PARAGRAPH 11. Although it be incumbent on the bishops or pastors of the churches, to be instant in preaching the word, by way of office, yet the work of preaching the word is not so peculiarly confined to them but that others also gifted and fitted by the Holy Spirit for it, and approved and called by the church, may and ought to perform it.[24]

(24) *Acts 11:19-21; 1 Pet. 4:10, 11.*

PARAGRAPH 12. As all believers are bound to join themselves to particular churches, when and where they have opportunity so to do; so all that are admitted unto the privileges of a church, are also under the censures and government thereof, according to the rule of Christ.[25]

(25) *1 Thess. 5:14; 2 Thess. 3:6, 14, 15.*

PARAGRAPH 13. No church members, upon any offence taken by them, having performed their duty required of them towards the person they are offended at, ought to disturb any church-order, or absent themselves from the assemblies of the church, or administration of any ordinances, upon the account of such offence at any of their fellow members, but to wait upon Christ, in the further proceeding of the church.[26]

(26) *Matt. 18:15-17; Eph. 4:2,* 3.

PARAGRAPH 14. As each church, and all the members of it, are bound to pray continually for the good and prosperity of all the churches of Christ,[27] in all places, and upon all occasions to further every one within the bounds of their places and callings, in the exercise of their gifts and graces, so the churches, when planted by the providence of God, so as they may enjoy opportunity and advantage for it, ought to hold communion among themselves, for their peace, increase of love, and mutual edification.(28)

(27) *Eph. 6:18; Ps. 122:6.* (28) *Rom. 16:1, 2; 3 John 8-10.*

PARAGRAPH 15. In cases of difficulties or differences, either in point of doctrine or administration, wherein either the churches in general are concerned, or any one church, in their peace, union, and edification; or any member or members of any church are injured, in or by any proceedings in censures not agreeable to truth and order: it is according to the mind of Christ, that many churches holding communion together, do, by their messengers, meet to consider, and give their advice in or about that matter in difference, to be reported to all the churches concerned;(29) howbeit these messengers assembled, are not intrusted with any church-power properly so called; or with any jurisdiction over the churches themselves, to exercise any censures either over any churches or persons; or to impose their determination on the churches or officers.(30)

(29) *Acts 15:2, 4, 6, 22, 23, 25.* (30) *2 Cor. 1:24; 1 John 4:1.*

CHAPTER 27: OF THE COMMUNION OF THE SAINTS

PARAGRAPH 1. All saints that are united to Jesus Christ, their head, by his Spirit, and faith, although they are not made thereby one person with him, have fellowship in his graces, sufferings, death, resurrection, and glory;(1) and, being united to one another in love, they have communion in each others gifts and graces,(2) and are obliged to the performance of such duties, public and private, in an orderly way, as do conduce to their mutual good, both in the inward and outward man.(3)

(1) *1 John 1:3; John 1:16; Phil. 3:10; Rom. 6:5, 6.*

(2) *Eph. 4:15, 16; 1 Cor. 12:7; 3:21-23.*

(3) *1 Thess. 5:11, 14; Rom. 1:12; 1 John 3:17, 18; Gal. 6:10.*

PARAGRAPH 2. Saints by profession are bound to maintain a holy fellowship and communion in the worship of God, and in performing such other spiritual services as tend to their mutual edification;[4] as also in relieving each other in outward things according to their several abilities, and necessities;[5] which communion, according to the rule of the gospel, though especially to be exercised by them, in the relation wherein they stand, whether in families,[6] or churches,[7] yet, as God offers opportunity, is to be extended to all the household of faith, even all those who in every place call upon the name of the Lord Jesus; nevertheless their communion one with another as saints, does not take away or infringe the title or propriety which each man has in his goods and possessions.[8]

(4) *Heb. 10:24, 25, 3:12, 13.* (5) *Acts 11:29, 30.* (6) *Eph. 6:4.*
(7) *1 Cor. 12:14-27.* (8) *Acts 5:4; Eph. 4:28.*

CHAPTER 28: OF BAPTISM AND THE LORD'S SUPPER

PARAGRAPH 1. Baptism and the Lord's Supper are ordinances of positive and sovereign institution, appointed by the Lord Jesus, the only lawgiver, to be continued in his church to the end of the world.[1]

(1) *Matt. 28:19, 20; 1 Cor. 11:26.*

PARAGRAPH 2. These holy appointments are to be administered by those only who are qualified and thereunto called, according to the commission of Christ.[2]

(2) *Matt. 28:19; 1 Cor. 4:1.*

CHAPTER 29: OF BAPTISM

PARAGRAPH 1. Baptism is an ordinance of the New Testament, ordained by Jesus Christ, to be unto the party baptized, a sign of his fellowship with him, in his death and resurrection; of his being engrafted into him;[3] of remission of sins;[4] and of giving up into God, through Jesus Christ, to live and walk in newness of life.[5]

(3) *Rom. 6:3-5; Col. 2:12; Gal. 3:27.* (4) *Mark 1:4; Acts 22:16.*
(5) *Rom. 6:4.*

PARAGRAPH 2. Those who do actually profess repentance towards God, faith in, and obedience to, our Lord Jesus Christ, are the only proper subjects of this ordinance.[6]

(6) *Mark 16:16; Acts 8:36, 37, 2:41, 8:12, 18:8.*

PARAGRAPH 3. The outward element to be used in this ordinance is water, wherein the party is to be baptized, in the name of the Father, and of the Son, and of the Holy Spirit.(7)

(7) *Matt. 28:19, 20; Acts 8:38.*

PARAGRAPH 4. Immersion, or dipping of the person in water, is necessary to the due administration of this ordinance.(8)

(8) *Matt. 3:16; John 3:23*

CHAPTER 30: OF THE LORD'S SUPPER

PARAGRAPH 1. The supper of the Lord Jesus was instituted by him the same night wherein he was betrayed, to be observed in his churches, unto the end of the world, for the perpetual remembrance, and showing to all the world the sacrifice of himself in his death,(1) confirmation of the faith of believers in all the benefits thereof, their spiritual nourishment, and growth in him, their further engagement in, and to all duties which they owe to him; and to be a bond and pledge of their communion with him, and with each other.(2)

(1) *1 Cor. 11:23-26.* (2) *1 Cor. 10:16, 17, 21.*

PARAGRAPH 2. In this ordinance Christ is not offered up to his Father, nor any real sacrifice made at all for remission of sin of the quick or dead, but only a memorial of that one offering up of himself by himself upon the cross, once for all;(3) and a spiritual oblation of all possible praise unto God for the same.(4) So that the popish sacrifice of the mass, as they call it, is most abominable, injurious to Christ's own sacrifice the alone propitiation for all the sins of the elect.

(3) *Heb. 9:25, 26, 28.* (4) *1 Cor. 11:24; Matt. 26:26, 27.*

PARAGRAPH 3. The Lord Jesus hath, in this ordinance, appointed his ministers to pray, and bless the elements of bread and wine, and thereby to set them apart from a common to a holy use, and to take and break the bread; to take the cup, and, they communicating also themselves, to give both to the communicants.(5)

(5) *1 Cor. 11:23-26, etc.*

PARAGRAPH 4. The denial of the cup to the people, worshipping the elements, the lifting them up, or carrying them about for adoration, and reserving them for any pretended religious use, are all contrary to the nature of this ordinance, and to the institution of Christ.(6)

(6) *Matt. 26:26-28, 15:9; Exod. 20:4, 5.*

PARAGRAPH 5. The outward elements in this ordinance, duly set apart to the use ordained by Christ, have such relation to him crucified, as that truly, although in terms used figuratively, they are sometimes called by the names of the things they represent, in other words, the body and blood of Christ,(7) albeit, in substance and nature, they still remain truly and only bread and wine, as they were before.(8)

(7) *1 Cor. 11:27.* (8) *1 Cor. 11:26-28.*

PARAGRAPH 6. That doctrine which maintains a change of the substance of bread and wine, into the substance of Christ's body and blood, commonly called transubstantiation, by consecration of a priest, or by any other way, is repugnant not to Scripture alone,(9) but even to common sense and reason, overthrows the nature of the ordinance, and has been, and is, the cause of manifold superstitions, yea, of gross idolatries.(10)

(9) *Acts 3:21; Luke 14:6, 39.* (10) *1 Cor. 11:24, 25.*

PARAGRAPH 7. Worthy receivers, outwardly partaking of the visible elements in this ordinance, do then also inwardly by faith, really and indeed, yet not carnally and corporally, but spiritually receive, and feed upon Christ crucified, and all the benefits of his death; the body and blood of Christ being then not corporally or carnally, but spiritually present to the faith of believers in that ordinance, as the elements themselves are to their outward senses.(11)

(11) *1 Cor. 10:16, 11:23-26.*

PARAGRAPH 8. All ignorant and ungodly persons, as they are unfit to enjoy communion with Christ, so are they unworthy of the Lord's table, and cannot, without great sin against him, while they remain such, partake of these holy mysteries, or be admitted thereunto;(12) yea, whosoever shall receive unworthily, are guilty of the body and blood of the Lord, eating and drinking judgment to themselves.(13)

(12) *2 Cor. 6:14, 15.* (13) *1 Cor. 11:29; Matt. 7:6.*

CHAPTER 31: OF THE STATE OF MAN AFTER DEATH, AND OF THE RESURRECTION OF THE DEAD

PARAGRAPH 1. The bodies of men after death return to dust, and see corruption;[(1)] but their souls, which neither die nor sleep, having an immortal subsistence, immediately return to God who gave them.[(2)] The souls of the righteous being then made perfect in holiness, are received into paradise, where they are with Christ, and behold the face of God in light and glory, waiting for the full redemption of their bodies;[(3)] and the souls of the wicked are cast into hell; where they remain in torment and utter darkness, reserved to the judgment of the great day;[(4)] besides these two places, for souls separated from their bodies, the Scripture acknowledgeth none.

(1) *Gen. 3:19; Acts 13:36.* (2) *Eccles. 12:7.* (3) *Luke 23:43; 2 Cor. 5:1,6,8; Phil. 1:23; Heb. 12:23.* (4) *Jude 6, 7; 1 Peter 3:19; Luke 16:23, 24.*

PARAGRAPH 2. At the last day, such of the saints as are found alive, shall not sleep, but be changed;[(5)] and all the dead shall be raised up with the selfsame bodies, and none other;[(6)] although with different qualities, which shall be united again to their souls forever.[(7)]

(5) *1 Cor. 15:51, 52; 1 Thess. 4:17.* (6) *Job 19:26, 27.* (7) *1 Cor. 15:42, 43.*

PARAGRAPH 3. The bodies of the unjust shall, by the power of Christ, be raised to dishonour; the bodies of the just, by his Spirit, unto honour, and be made conformable to his own glorious body.[(8)]

(8) *Acts 24:15; John 5:28,29; Phil. 3:21*

CHAPTER 32: OF THE LAST JUDGEMENT

PARAGRAPH 1. God has appointed a day wherein he will judge the world in righteousness, by Jesus Christ;[(1)] to whom all power and judgment is given of the Father; in which day, not only the apostate angels shall be judged,[(2)] but likewise all persons that have lived upon the earth shall appear before the tribunal of Christ, to give an account of their thoughts, words, and deeds, and to receive according to what they have done in the body, whether good or evil.[(3)]

(1) *Acts 17:31; John 5:22, 27.* (2) *1 Cor. 6:3; Jude 6.* (3) *2 Cor. 5:10; Eccles. 12:14; Matt. 12:36; Rom. 14:10, 12; Matt. 25:32-46.*

PARAGRAPH 2. The end of God's appointing this day, is for the manifestation of the glory of his mercy, in the eternal salvation of the elect; and of his justice, in the eternal damnation of the reprobate, who are wicked and disobedient;[(4)] for then shall the righteous go into everlasting life, and receive that fulness of joy and glory with everlasting rewards, in the presence of the Lord; but the wicked, who do not know God, and do not obey the gospel of Jesus Christ, shall be cast aside into everlasting torments,[(5)] and punished with everlasting destruction, from the presence of the Lord, and from the glory of his power.[(6)]

(4) *Rom. 9:22, 23.* (5) *Matt. 25:21, 34; 2 Tim. 4:8.*
(6) *Matt. 25:46; Mark 9:48; 2 Thess. 1:7-10.*

PARAGRAPH 3. As Christ would have us to be certainly persuaded that there shall be a day of judgment, both to deter all men from sin,[(7)] and for the greater consolation of the godly in their adversity,[(8)] so will he have the day unknown to men, that they may shake off all carnal security, and be always watchful, because they know not at what hour the Lord will come,[(9)] and may ever be prepared to say, Come Lord Jesus; come quickly.[(10)] Amen.

(7) *2 Cor. 5:10, 11.* (8) *2 Thess. 1:5-7.*
(9) *Mark 13:35-37; Luke 12:35-40.* (10) *Rev. 22:20.*

ENDING STATEMENT AND SIGNATORIES

We the Ministers, and Messengers of, and concerned for upwards of, one hundred Baptized Churches, in England and Wales (denying Arminianism), being met together in London, from the third of the seventh month to the eleventh of the same, 1689, to consider of some things that might be for the glory of God, and the good of these congregations, have thought meet (for the satisfaction of all other Christians that differ from us in the point of Baptism) to recommend to their perusal the confession of our faith, which confession we own, as containing the doctrine of our faith and practice, and do desire that the members of our churches respectively do furnish themselves therewith.

Hansard Knollys, Pastor, Broken Wharf, London
William Kiffin, Pastor, Devonshire-square, London
John Harris, Pastor, Joiner's Hall, London
William Collins, Pastor, Petty France, London
Hurcules Collins, Pastor, Wapping, London
Robert Steed, Pastor, Broken Wharf, London
Leonard Harrison, Pastor, Limehouse, London
George Barret, Pastor, Mile End Green, London
Isaac Lamb, Pastor, Pennington-street, London
Richard Adams, Minister, Shad Thames, Southwark
Benjamin Keach, Pastor, Horse-lie-down, Southwark
Andrew Gifford, Pastor, Bristol, Fryars, Som. & Glouc.
Thomas Vaux, Pastor, Broadmead, Som. & Glouc.
Thomas Winnel, Pastor, Taunton, Som. & Glouc.
James Hitt, Preacher, Dalwood, Dorset
Richard Tidmarsh, Minister, Oxford City, Oxon
William Facey, Pastor, Reading, Berks
Samuel Buttall, Minister, Plymouth, Devon
Christopher Price, Minister, Abergayenny, Monmouth
Daniel Finch, Minister, Kingsworth, Herts
John Ball, Minister, Tiverton, Devon
Edmond White, Pastor, Evershall, Bedford
William Prichard, Pastor, Blaenau, Monmouth
Paul Fruin, Minister, Warwick, Warwick
Richard Ring, Pastor, Southhampton, Hants
John Tomkins, Minister, Abingdon, Berks
Toby Willes, Pastor, Bridgewater, Somerset
John Carter, Pastor, Steventon, Bedford
James Webb, Pastor, Devizes, Wilts
Richard Sutton, Pastor, Tring, Herts
Robert Knight, Pastor, Stukeley, Bucks
Edward Price, Pastor, Hereford City, Hereford
William Phipps, Pastor, Exon, Devon

William Hawkins, Pastor, Dimmock, Gloucester
Samuel Ewer, Pastor, Hemstead, Herts
Edward Man, Pastor, Houndsditch, London
Charles Archer, Pastor, Hock-Norton, Oxon

In the name of and on the behalf of the whole assembly. ▪

CATECHISMS

ONCE LIKE-MINDED Christians had determined precisely what they believed, they turned their attention to training the next generation to carry on faithful Christianity. The word *catechism* comes from the Greek *katécheó,* which means "to instruct orally." In order to carry out the parental mandate to "teach them diligently" (Deuteronomy 6:7), pastors and fathers wrote catechisms designed to systematically disciple their children in biblical doctrine. Once a child has memorized a catechism, he or she has an arsenal of biblically informed answers to give when they battle doubt or are questioned about their faith. A catechized child is a child who is "prepared to make a defense" (1 Peter 3:15).

In some Christians' minds, the concept of catechizing is connected with Roman Catholicism, but there is nothing papal about training children using questions and answers. Catechisms have been used by generations of Christians in many denominations, but there is a particularly rich history of catechizing children within the Reformed Church.

After creeds and confessions have asked the question, "Christians, what do we believe?" catechisms turn and say, "Children, this is what we believe. Be ready—it's your turn." ▪

Luther's Small Catechism

In 1529, Martin Luther visited several Protestant congregations and came away appalled at the state of family religion in Germany. "They all maintain that they are Christians," wrote Luther, "that they have been baptized, and that they have received the Lord's Supper. Yet they cannot recite the Lord's Prayer, the Creed, or the Ten Commandments; they live as if they were irrational creatures, and now that the gospel has come to them, they grossly abuse their Christian liberty."

Luther looked to fathers to remedy the problem. To help Christian fathers be intentional and thorough in training their children in the knowledge of God, Luther wrote a catechism. He prepared two versions of it, a smaller and a larger, and published them both in 1529. The Small Catechism was intended for families and children, and the Larger Catechism for adults, clergy, and children who had completed the more rudimentary one.

The following is taken from Joseph Stump's 1907 translation.

PART I

THE TEN COMMANDMENTS

In the plain form in which they are to be taught by the head of a family.

THE FIRST COMMANDMENT

I am the Lord thy God. Thou shalt have no other gods before Me.

What is meant by this Commandment?

We should fear, love, and trust in God above all things.

THE SECOND COMMANDMENT

Thou shalt not take the Name of the Lord thy God in vain; for the Lord will not hold him guiltless that taketh His Name in vain.

What is meant by this Commandment?

We should so fear and love God as not to curse, swear, conjure, lie, or deceive, by His Name, but call upon Him in every time of need, and worship Him with prayer, praise, and thanksgiving.

THE THIRD COMMANDMENT

Remember the Sabbath-day, to keep it holy.

What is meant by this Commandment?

We should so fear and love God as not to despise His Word and the preaching of the Gospel, but deem it holy, and willing to hear and learn it.

THE FOURTH COMMANDMENT

Honor thy father and thy mother, that thy days may be long upon the land which the Lord thy God giveth thee.

What is meant by this Commandment?

We should so fear and love God as not to despise nor displease our parents and superiors, but honor, serve, obey, love, and esteem them.

THE FIFTH COMMANDMENT

Thou shalt not kill.

What is meant by this Commandment?

We should so fear and love God as not to do our neighbor any bodily harm or injury, but rather assist and comfort him in danger and want.

THE SIXTH COMMANDMENT

Thou shalt not commit adultery.

What is meant by this Commandment?

We should so fear and love God as to be chaste and pure in our words and deeds, each one also loving and honoring his wife or her husband.

THE SEVENTH COMMANDMENT

Thou shalt not steal.

What is meant by this Commandment?

We should so fear and love God as not to rob our neighbor of his money or property, nor bring it into our possession by unfair dealing or fraudulent means, but rather assist him to improve and protect it.

THE EIGHT COMMANDMENT

Thou shalt not bear false witness against thy neighbor.

What is meant by this Commandment?

We should so fear and love God as not deceitfully to belie, betray, slander, nor raise injurious reports against our neighbor, but apologize for him, speak well of him, and put the most charitable construction on all his actions.

THE NINTH COMMANDMENT

Thou shalt not covet thy neighbor's house.

What is meant by this Commandment?

We should so fear and love God as not to desire by craftiness to gain possession of our neighbor's inheritance or home, or to obtain it under the pretext of a legal right, but be ready to assist and serve him in the preservation of his own.

THE TENTH COMMANDMENT

Thou shalt not covet thy neighbor's wife, nor his manservant, nor his maid-servant, nor his ox, nor his ass, nor anything that is thy neighbor's.

What is meant by this Commandment?

We should so fear and love God as not to alienate our neighbor's wife from him, entice away his servants, nor let loose his cattle, but use our endeavors that they may remain and discharge their duty to him.

What does God declare concerning all these Commandments?

He says: I the Lord thy God am a jealous God, visiting the iniquity of the fathers upon the children unto the third and fourth generation of them that hate Me; and showing mercy unto thousands of them that love Me and keep my commandments.

What is meant by this declaration?

God threatens to punish all those who transgress these commandments. We should, therefore, dread His displeasure, and not act contrarily to these commandments. But He promises grace and every blessing to all who keep them. We should, therefore, love and trust in Him, and cheerfully do what He has commanded us.

PART II

THE CREED[1]

In the plain form in which it is to be taught by the head of a family.

FIRST ARTICLE – OF CREATION

I believe in God the Father Almighty, Maker of heaven and earth.

What is meant by this Article?

I believe that God has created me and all that exists; that He has given and still preserves to me my body and soul with all my limbs and senses, my reason and all the faculties of my mind, together with my raiment, food, home, and family, and all my property; that He daily provides me abundantly with all the necessaries of life, protects me from all danger, and preserves me and guards me against all evil; all which He does out of pure, paternal, and divine goodness and mercy, without any merit or worthiness in me; for all which I am in duty bound to thank, praise, serve, and obey Him. This is most certainly true.

SECOND ARTICLE – OF REDEMPTION

And in Jesus Christ His only Son, our Lord; who was conceived by the Holy Ghost, born of the Virgin Mary; suffered under Pontius Pilate, was crucified, dead, and buried; He descended into hell; the third day He rose again from

1 The Apostles' Creed (see page 12).

the dead; He ascended into heaven, and sitteth on the right hand of God the Father Almighty; from thence He shall come to judge the quick and the dead.

What is meant by this Article?

I believe that Jesus Christ, true God, begotten of the Father from eternity, and also true man, born of the Virgin Mary, is my Lord; who has redeemed me, a lost and condemned creature, secured and delivered me from all sins, from death, and from the power of the devil, not with silver and gold, but with His holy and precious blood, and with His innocent sufferings and death; in order that I might be His, live under Him in His kingdom, and serve Him in everlasting righteousness, innocence, and blessedness; even as He is risen from the dead, and lives and reigns to all eternity. This is most certainly true.

THIRD ARTICLE – OF SANCTIFICATION

I believe in the Holy Ghost; the holy Christian Church, the Communion of Saints; the Forgiveness of sins; the Resurrection of the body; and the Life everlasting. Amen.

What is meant by this Article?

I believe that I cannot by my own reason or strength believe in Jesus Christ my Lord, or come to Him; but the Holy Ghost has called me through the Gospel, enlightened me by His gifts, and sanctified and preserved me in the true faith; in like manner as He calls, gathers, enlightens, and sanctifies the whole Christian Church on earth, and preserves it in union with Jesus Christ in the true faith; in which Christian Church He daily forgives abundantly all my sins, and the sins of all believers, and will raise up me and all the dead at the last day, and will grant everlasting life to me and to all who believe in Christ. This is most certainly true.

PART III

THE LORD'S PRAYER

In the plain form in which it is to be taught by the head of a family.

INTRODUCTION

Our Father Who art in heaven.

What is meant by this Introduction?

God would thereby affectionately encourage us to believe that He is truly our Father, and that we are His children indeed, so that we may call upon Him with all cheerfulness and confidence, even as beloved children entreat their affectionate parent.

FIRST PETITION

Hallowed be Thy Name.

What is meant by this Petition?

The Name of God is indeed holy in itself; but we pray in this petition that it may be hallowed also by us.

How is this effected?

When the Word of God is taught in its truth and purity, and we, as the children of God, lead holy lives, in accordance with it; to this may our blessed Father in heaven help us! But whoever teaches and lives otherwise than as God's Word prescribes, profanes the Name of God among us; from this preserve us, Heavenly Father!

SECOND PETITION

Thy kingdom come.

What is meant by this Petition?

The kingdom of God comes indeed of itself, without our prayer; but we pray in this petition that it may come unto us also.

When is this effected?

When our Heavenly Father gives us His Holy Spirit, so that by His grace we believe His holy Word, and live a godly life here on earth, and in heaven for ever.

THIRD PETITION

Thy will be done on earth, as it is in heaven.

What is meant by this Petition?

The good and gracious will of God is done indeed without our prayer; but we pray in this petition that it may be done by us also.

When is this effected?

When God frustrates and brings to naught every evil counsel and purpose, which would hinder us from hallowing the Name of God, and prevent His kingdom from coming to us, such as the will of the devil, of the world, and of our own flesh; and when He strengthens us, and keeps us steadfast in His Word, and in the faith, even unto our end. This is His gracious and good will.

FOURTH PETITION

Give us this day our daily bread.

What is meant by this Petition?

God gives indeed without our prayer even to the wicked also their daily bread; but we pray in this petition that He would make us sensible of His benefits, and enable us to receive our daily bread with thanksgiving.

What is implied in the words: "Our daily bread"?

All things that pertain to the wants and the support of this present life; such as food, raiment, money, goods, house and land, and other property; a believing spouse and good children; trustworthy servants and faithful magistrates; favorable seasons, peace and health; education and honor; true friends, good neighbors, and the like.

FIFTH PETITION

And forgive us our trespasses, as we forgive those who trespass against us.

What is meant by this Petition?

We pray in this petition, that our Heavenly Father would not regard our sins, nor deny us our requests on account of them; for we are not worthy of anything for which we pray, and have not merited it; but that He would grant us all things through grace, although we daily commit much sin, and deserve chastisement alone. We will therefore, on our part, both heartily forgive, and also readily do good to those who may injure or offend us.

SIXTH PETITION

And lead us not into temptation.

What is meant by this Petition?

God indeed tempts no one to sin; but we pray in this petition that God would so guard and preserve us, that the devil, the world, and our own flesh, may not deceive us, nor lead us into error and unbelief, despair, and other great and shameful sins; and that, though we may be thus tempted, we may, nevertheless, finally prevail and gain the victory.

SEVENTH PETITION

But deliver us from evil.

What is meant by this Petition?

We pray in this petition, as in a summary, that our Heavenly Father would deliver us from all manner of evil, whether it affect the body or soul, property or character, and, at last, when the hour of death shall arrive, grant us a happy end, and graciously take as from this world of sorrow to Himself in heaven.

CONCLUSION

For Thine is the kingdom, and the power, and the glory, for ever and ever. Amen.

What is meant by the word "Amen"?

That I should be assured that such petitions are acceptable to our Heavenly Father, and are heard by Him; for He Himself has commanded us to pray in this manner, and has promised that He will hear us. Amen, Amen, that is, Yea, yea, it shall be so.

PART IV

THE SACRAMENT OF HOLY BAPTISM

In the plain form in which it is to be taught by the head of a family.

What is Baptism?

Baptism is not simply water, but it is the water comprehended in God's command, and connected with God's Word.

What is that Word of God?

It is that which our Lord Jesus Christ spoke, as it is recorded in the last chapter of Matthew, verse 19: "Go ye, and teach all nations, baptizing them in the Name of the Father, and of the Son, and of the Holy Ghost."

What gifts or benefits does Baptism confer?

It works forgiveness of sins, delivers from death and the devil, and confers everlasting salvation on all who believe, as the Word and promise of God declare.

What are such words and promises of God?

Those which our Lord Jesus Christ spoke, as they are recorded in the last chapter of Mark, verse 16: "He that believeth and is baptized, shall be saved; but he that believeth not, shall be damned."

How can water produce such great effects?

It is not the water indeed that produces these effects, but the Word of God which accompanies and is connected with the water, and our faith, which relies on the Word of God connected with the water. For the water, without the Word of God, is simply water and no baptism. But when connected with the Word of God, it is a baptism, that is, a gracious water of life, and a "washing of regeneration" in the Holy Ghost; as St. Paul says to Titus, in the third chapter, verses 5-8: "According to His mercy He saved us, by the washing of regeneration, and renewing of the Holy Ghost; which He shed on us abundantly through Jesus Christ our Saviour; that being justified by His grace, we should be made heirs according to the hope of eternal life. This is a faithful saying."

What does such baptizing with water signify?

It signifies that the old Adam in us is to be drowned, and destroyed by daily sorrow and repentance, together with all sins and evil lusts; and that again, the new man should daily come forth and rise, that shall live in the presence of God in righteousness and purity forever.

Where is it so written?

St. Paul, in the Epistle to the Romans, chapter 6, verse 4, says: "We are buried with Christ by Baptism into death; that like as He was raised up from the dead by the glory of the Father, even so we also should walk in newness of life."

OF CONFESSION

What is Confession?

Confession consists of two parts: the one is, that we confess our sins; the other, that we receive absolution or forgiveness through the pastor as of God himself, in no wise doubting, but firmly believing that our sins are thus forgiven before God in heaven.

What sins ought we to confess?

In the presence of God we should acknowledge ourselves guilty of all manner of sins, even of those which we do not ourselves perceive; as we do in the Lord's

Prayer. But in the presence of the pastor we should confess those sins alone of which we have knowledge, and which we feel in our hearts.

Which are these?

Here reflect on your condition, according to the Ten Commandments, namely: Whether you are a father or mother, a son or daughter, a master or mistress, a manservant or maidservant—whether you have been disobedient, unfaithful, slothful—whether you have injured any one by words or actions-whether you have stolen, neglected, or wasted aught, or done other evil.

PART V

THE SACRAMENT OF THE ALTAR, OR, THE LORD'S SUPPER

In the plain form in which it is to be taught by the head of a family.

What is the Sacrament of the Altar?

It is the true Body and Blood of our Lord Jesus Christ, under the bread and wine, given unto us Christians to eat and to drink, as it was instituted by Christ Himself.

Where is it so written?

The Holy Evangelists, Matthew, Mark, and Luke, together with St. Paul, write thus: "Our Lord Jesus Christ, the same night in which He was betrayed, took bread: and when He had given thanks, He brake it, and gave it to His disciples, and said, Take, eat; this is my Body, which is given for you: this do, in remembrance of Me. After the same manner also He took the cup, when He had supped, gave thanks, and gave it to them, saying, Drink ye all of it: this cup is the new testament in my Blood, which is shed for you, for the remission of sins: this do, as oft as ye drink it, in remembrance of Me."

What benefits are derived from such eating and drinking?

They are pointed out in these words; "given and shed for you, for the remission of sins." Namely, through these words, the remission of sins, life and salvation are granted unto us in the Sacrament. For where there is remission of sins, there are also life and salvation.

How can the bodily eating and drinking produce such great effects?

The eating and the drinking, indeed, do not produce them, but the words which stand here, namely: "given, and shed for you, for the remission of sins." These words are, besides the bodily eating and drinking, the chief things in the Sacrament; and he who believes these words, has that which they declare and set forth, namely, the remission of sins.

Who is it, then, that receives this Sacrament worthily?

Fasting and bodily preparation are indeed a good external discipline; but he is truly worthy and well prepared who believes these words, "given and shed for you, for the remission of sins." But he who does not believe these words, or who doubts, is unworthy and unfit: for the words: "FOR YOU," require truly believing hearts.

MORNING AND EVENING PRAYER

In the plain form in which it is to be taught by the head of a family.

MORNING

In the Morning, when thou risest, thou shalt say:

In the Name of the Father, and of the Son, and of the Holy Ghost, Amen.

Then, kneeling or standing, thou shalt say the Apostles' Creed and the Lord's Prayer. Then mayest then say this Prayer:

I give thanks unto Thee, Heavenly Father, through Jesus Christ Thy dear Son, that Thou hast protected me through the night from all danger and harm; and I beseech Thee to preserve and keep me this day also, from all sin and evil; that in all my thoughts, words, and deeds, I may serve and please Thee. Into Thy hands I commend my body and soul, and all that is mine. Let Thy holy angel have charge concerning me, that the wicked one may have no power over me. Amen.

And then shouldst thou go with joy to thy work, after a Hymn, or the Ten Commandments, or whatever thy devotion may suggest.

EVENING

In the Evening, when thou goest to bed, thou shalt say:

In the Name of the Father, and of the Son, and of the Holy Ghost. Amen.

Then, kneeling or standing, thou shalt say the Apostles' Creed and the Lord's Prayer. Then mayest thou say this Prayer:

I give thanks unto Thee, Heavenly Father, through Jesus Christ Thy dear Son, that Thou hast this day so graciously protected me, and I beseech Thee to forgive me all my sins, and the wrong which I have done, and by Thy great mercy defend me from all the perils and dangers of this night. Into thy hands I commend my body and soul, and all that is mine. Let Thy holy angel have charge concerning me, that the wicked one may have no power over me. Amen.

And then lie down, in peace, and sleep.

BLESSING AND THANKSGIVING AT TABLE

In the plain form in which they are to be taught by the head of a family.

BEFORE MEAT

Before meat, the members of the family surrounding the table reverently and with folded hands, there shall be said:

The eyes of all wait upon Thee, O Lord: and Thou givest them their meat in due season. Thou openest Thine hand, and satisfiest the desire of every living thing.

Then shall be said the Lord's Prayer, and after that this Prayer:

O Lord God, Heavenly Father, bless unto us these Thy gifts, which of Thy tender kindness Thou hast bestowed upon us, through Jesus Christ our Lord. Amen.

After meat, reverently and with folded hands, there shall be said:

O give thanks unto the Lord, for He is good: for His mercy endureth for ever. He giveth food to all flesh; He giveth to the beast his food, and to the young ravens which cry. The Lord taketh pleasure in them that tear Him; in those that hope in His mercy,

Then shall be said the Lord's Prayer, and after that this Prayer:

We give thanks, to Thee, O God. Our Father, for all Thy benefits, through Jesus Christ our Lord, Who with Thee liveth and reigneth, for ever and ever. Amen.

TABLE OF DUTIES[2]

Or, certain passages of the Scriptures, selected for various orders and conditions of men, wherein their respective duties are set forth.

BISHOPS, PASTORS, AND PREACHERS

"Therefore an overseer must be above reproach, the husband of one wife, sober-minded, self-controlled, respectable, hospitable, able to teach, not a drunkard, not violent but gentle, not quarrelsome, not a lover of money. He must manage his own household well, with all dignity keeping his children submissive, for if someone does not know how to manage his own household, how will he care for God's church? He must not be a recent convert, or he may become puffed up with conceit and fall into the condemnation of the devil." — **1 TIMOTHY 3:2-6 (ESV)**

"He must hold firm to the trustworthy word as taught, so that he may be able to give instruction in sound doctrine and also to rebuke those who contradict it." — **TITUS 1:9 (ESV)**

WHAT DUTIES HEARERS OWE THEIR BISHOPS

"In the same way, the Lord commanded that those who proclaim the gospel should get their living by the gospel." — **1 CORINTHIANS 9:14 (ESV)**

"Let the one who is taught the word share all good things with the one who teaches." — **GALATIANS 6:6 (ESV)**

---

2 Publisher's note: because this part of Luther's catechism is simply a listing of Scriptures, we have taken the liberty of changing the verses into the ESV to make it easier for modern ears to understand.

"Let the elders who rule well be considered worthy of double honor, especially those who labor in preaching and teaching. For the Scripture says, 'You shall not muzzle an ox when it treads out the grain,' and, 'The laborer deserves his wages.'" — **1 TIMOTHY 5:17-18 (ESV)**

"Obey your leaders and submit to them, for they are keeping watch over your souls, as those who will have to give an account. Let them do this with joy and not with groaning, for that would be of no advantage to you." — **HEBREWS 13:17 (ESV)**

MAGISTRATES

"Let every person be subject to the governing authorities. For there is no authority except from God, and those that exist have been instituted by God. Therefore whoever resists the authorities resists what God has appointed, and those who resist will incur judgment. For rulers are not a terror to good conduct, but to bad. Would you have no fear of the one who is in authority? Then do what is good, and you will receive his approval, for he is God's servant for your good. But if you do wrong, be afraid, for he does not bear the sword in vain. For he is the servant of God, an avenger who carries out God's wrath on the wrongdoer." — **ROMANS 13:1-4 (ESV)**

WHAT DUTIES SUBJECTS OWE MAGISTRATES

"Therefore render to Caesar the things that are Caesar's, and to God the things that are God's." — **MATTHEW 22:21 (ESV)**

"Let every person be subject to the governing authorities. For there is no authority except from God, and those that exist have been instituted by God.... Therefore one must be in subjection, not only to avoid God's wrath but also for the sake of conscience. For because of this you also pay taxes, for the authorities are ministers of God, attending to this very thing. Pay to all what is owed to them: taxes to whom taxes are owed, revenue to whom revenue is owed, respect to whom respect is owed, honor to whom honor is owed." — **ROMANS 13:1, 5-7 (ESV)**

"First of all, then, I urge that supplications, prayers, intercessions, and thanksgivings be made for all people, for kings and all who are in high positions, that we may lead a peaceful and quiet life, godly and dignified in every way." — 1 TIMOTHY 2:1-2 (ESV)

"Remind them to be submissive to rulers and authorities, to be obedient, to be ready for every good work," — TITUS 3:1 (ESV)

"Be subject for the Lord's sake to every human institution, whether it be to the emperor as supreme, or to governors as sent by him to punish those who do evil and to praise those who do good." — 1 PETER 2:13-14 (ESV)

HUSBANDS

"Likewise, husbands, live with your wives in an understanding way, showing honor to the woman as the weaker vessel, since they are heirs with you of the grace of life, so that your prayers may not be hindered." — 1 PETER 3:7 (ESV)

"Husbands, love your wives, and do not be harsh with them." — COLOSSIANS 3:19 (ESV)

WIVES

"Wives, submit to your own husbands, as to the Lord." — EPHESIANS 5:22 (ESV)

"For this is how the holy women who hoped in God used to adorn themselves, by submitting to their own husbands, as Sarah obeyed Abraham, calling him lord. And you are her children, if you do good and do not fear anything that is frightening." — 1 PETER 3:6 (ESV)

PARENTS

"Fathers, do not provoke your children to anger, but bring them up in the discipline and instruction of the Lord." — EPHESIANS 6:4 (ESV)

CHILDREN

"Children, obey your parents in the Lord, for this is right. 'Honor your father and mother' (this is the first commandment with a promise), 'that it may go well with you and that you may live long in the land.'" — **EPHESIANS 6:1-3 (ESV)**

MALE AND FEMALE SERVANTS AND LABORERS

"Bondservants, obey your earthly masters with fear and trembling, with a sincere heart, as you would Christ, not by the way of eye-service, as people-pleasers, but as bondservants of Christ, doing the will of God from the heart, rendering service with a good will as to the Lord and not to man, knowing that whatever good anyone does, this he will receive back from the Lord, whether he is a bondservant or is free." — **EPHESIANS 6:5-8 (ESV)**

MASTERS AND MISTRESSES

"Masters, do the same to them, and stop your threatening, knowing that he who is both their Master and yours is in heaven, and that there is no partiality with him." — **EPHESIANS 6:9 (ESV)**

YOUNG PERSONS IN GENERAL

"Likewise, you who are younger, be subject to the elders. Clothe yourselves, all of you, with humility toward one another, for 'God opposes the proud but gives grace to the humble.' Humble yourselves, therefore, under the mighty hand of God so that at the proper time he may exalt you," — **1 PETER 5:5-6 (ESV)**

WIDOWS

"She who is truly a widow, left all alone, has set her hope on God and continues in supplications and prayers night and day, but she who is self-indulgent is dead even while she lives." — **1 TIMOTHY 5:5-6 (ESV)**

CHRISTIANS IN GENERAL

"For the commandments, 'You shall not commit adultery, You shall not murder, You shall not steal, You shall not covet,' and any other commandment, are summed up in this word: 'You shall love your neighbor as yourself.' Love does no wrong to a neighbor; therefore love is the fulfilling of the law." — **ROMANS 13:9-10 (ESV)**

"First of all, then, I urge that supplications, prayers, intercessions, and thanksgivings be made for all people, for kings and all who are in high positions, that we may lead a peaceful and quiet life, godly and dignified in every way." — **1 TIMOTHY 2:1-2 (ESV)**

CHRISTIAN QUESTIONS AND ANSWERS

After confession and instruction in the Ten Commandments, the Creed, the Lord's Prayer, and the Sacraments of Baptism and the Lord's Supper, the pastor may ask, or Christians may ask themselves these questions:

Do you believe that you are a sinner?

Yes, I believe it. I am a sinner.

How do you know this?

From the Ten Commandments, which I have not kept.

Are you sorry for your sins?

Yes, I am sorry that I have sinned against God.

What have you deserved from God because of your sins?

His wrath and displeasure, temporal death, and eternal damnation. See Romans 6:21-23.

Do you hope to be saved?

Yes, that is my hope.

In whom then do you trust?

In my dear Lord Jesus Christ.

Who is Christ?

The Son of God, true God and man.

How many Gods are there?

Only one, but there are three persons: Father, Son, and Holy Spirit.

What has Christ done for you that you trust in Him?

He died for me and shed His blood for me on the cross for the forgiveness of sins.

Did the Father also die for you?

He did not. The Father is God only, as is the Holy Spirit; but the Son is both true God and true man. He died for me and shed his blood for me.

How do you know this?

From the holy Gospel, from the words instituting the Sacrament, and by His body and blood given me as a pledge in the Sacrament.

What are the Words of Institution?

Our Lord Jesus Christ, on the night when He was betrayed, took bread and when He had given thanks, He broke it and gave it to the disciples and said: "Take eat; this is My body, which is given for you. This do in remembrance of Me." In the same way also He took the cup after supper, and when He had given thanks, He gave it to them, saying: "Drink of it, all of you; this cup is the new testament in My blood, which is shed for you for the forgiveness of sins. This do, as often as you drink it, in remembrance of Me."

Do you believe, then, that the true body and blood of Christ are in the Sacrament?

Yes, I believe it.

What convinces you to believe this?

The word of Christ: Take, eat, this is My body; drink of it, all of you, this is My blood.

What should we do when we eat His body and drink His blood, and in this way receive His pledge?

We should remember and proclaim His death and the shedding of His blood, as He taught us: This do, as often as you drink it, in remembrance of Me.

Why should we remember and proclaim His death?

First, so that we may learn to believe that no creature could make satisfaction for our sins. Only Christ, true God and man, could do that. Second, so we may learn to be horrified by our sins, and to regard them as very serious. Third, so we may find joy and comfort in Christ alone, and through faith in Him be saved.

What motivated Christ to die and make full payment for your sins?

His great love for His Father and for me and other sinners, as it is written in John 14; Romans 5; Galatians 2; and Ephesians 5.

Finally, why do you wish to go to the Sacrament?

That I may learn to believe that Christ, out of great love, died for my sin, and also learn from Him to love God and my neighbor.

What should admonish and encourage a Christian to receive the Sacrament frequently?

First, both the command and the promise of Christ the Lord. Second, his own pressing need, because of which the command, encouragement, and promise are given.

But what should you do if you are not aware of this need and have no hunger and thirst for the Sacrament?

To such a person no better advice can be given than this: first, he should touch his body to see if he still has flesh and blood. Then he should believe what the Scriptures say of it in Galatians 5 and Romans 7. Second, he should look around to see whether he is still in the world, and remember that there will be no lack of sin and trouble, as the Scriptures say in John 15-16 and in 1 John 2 and 5. Third, he will certainly have the devil also around him, who with his lying and murdering day and night will let him have no peace, within or without, as the Scriptures picture him in John 8 and 16; 1 Peter 5; Ephesians 6; and 2 Timothy 2.

NOTE: *These questions and answers are no child's play, but are drawn up with great earnestness of purpose by the venerable and devout Dr. Luther for both young and old. Let each one pay attention and consider it a serious matter; for St. Paul writes to the Galatians in chapter six: "Do not be deceived: God cannot be mocked."* ▪

Geneva Catechism

A few years after writing his epic Institutes of the Christian Religion, *and after becoming pastor of the church in Geneva, John Calvin wrote a children's catechism. But he soon realized that his catechism was too difficult for children, so he revised it and republished it as the Geneva Catechism. In 1560 Calvin revised his catechism yet again and published it in the form given here. The Geneva Catechism was mainly used in Geneva and Scotland. It fell out of popularity after the Heidelberg and Westminster Catechisms were written, but both drew significantly from Calvin's Geneva Catechism.*

The catechism reads like a conversation—a probing discussion between a master and a student. Hence, the Geneva Catechism not only offers a thorough course in theology, but also practical training in logic and apologetics.

---

1. **What is the chief end of human life?**
To know God.

2. **Why do you say that?**
Because He created us and placed us in this world to be glorified in us. And it is indeed right that our life, of which He Himself is the beginning, should be devoted to His glory.

3. **What is the sovereign good of man?**
The same thing.

4. **Why do you hold that to be the sovereign good?**
Because without it our condition is more miserable than that of brute-beasts.

5. **Hence, then, we see that nothing worse can happen to a man than to live without God.**
It is so.

6. **What is the true and right knowledge of God?**
When we know Him in order that we may honour Him.

7. **How do we honour Him aright?**
We put our reliance on Him, by serving Him in obedience to His will, by calling upon Him in all our need, seeking salvation and every good thing in Him, and acknowledging with heart and mouth that all our good proceeds from Him.

8. **To consider these things in order, and explain them more fully—what is the first point?**
To rely upon God.

9. **How can we do that?**
First by knowing Him as almighty and perfectly good.

10. **Is this enough?**
No.

11. **Why?**
Because we are unworthy that He should show His power in helping us, or employ His goodness toward us.

12. **What more, then, is required?**
That we be certain that He loves us, and desires to be our Father, and Saviour.

13. **How do we know that?**
By His Word, in which He declares His mercy to us in Christ, and assures us of His love toward us.

14. **Then the foundation for true reliance upon God is to know Him in Jesus Christ? (John 17:3)**
That is true.

15. **What then briefly is the substance of this knowledge?**
It is contained in the Confession of Faith used by all Christians. It is commonly called the Apostles' Creed, because it is a summary of the true faith which

has always been held in Christ's Church, and was derived from the pure doctrine of the Apostles.

16. **Recite it.**

[*See page 12.*]

17. **In order to expound this confession in detail, into how many parts do we divide it?**

Into four principal parts.

18. **What are they?**

The first is about God the Father; the second about His Son Jesus Christ, which also includes the whole history of our redemption; the third is about the Holy Spirit; the fourth is about the Church, and the gracious gifts of God conferred on her.

19. **Since there is but one God, why do you mention the Father, Son, and Holy Spirit, who are three?**

Because in the one essence of God, we have to look on the Father as the beginning and origin, and the first cause of all things; then the Son, who is Eternal Wisdom; and the Holy Spirit who is His virtue and power shed abroad over all creatures, but still perpetually resident in Himself.

20. **You mean then that there is no objection to our understanding that these three persons are distinctly in one Godhead, that God is not therefore divided?**

Just so.

21. **Now repeat the first part.**

"I believe in God the Father Almighty, Maker of heaven and earth."

22. **Why do you call Him Father?**

It is with reference to Christ who is His eternal Word, begotten of Him before time, and being sent into this world was demonstrated and declared to be His Son. But since God is the Father of Jesus Christ, it follows that He is our Father also.

23. **In what sense do you mean that He is Almighty?**
That does not mean that He has a power which He does not exercise, but that He disposes all things by His Providence, governs the world by His will, ruling all as it seems good to Him.

24. **You mean that the power of God is not idle, but consider rather that His hand is always engaged in working, so that nothing is done except through Him, with His permission and His decree.**
It is so.

25. **Why do you add that He is Creator of heaven and earth?**
Because He has manifested Himself to us by works (Psalm 104; Romans 1:20) we ought to seek Him in them. Our mind cannot comprehend His essence. But the world is for us like a mirror in which we may contemplate Him in so far as it is expedient for us to know Him.

26. **Do you not understand by "heaven and earth" all other creatures?**
Yes indeed; under these two words all are included, because they are all heavenly and earthly.

27. **But why do you call God a Creator only, seeing that it is much more to uphold and preserve creatures in their state, than to have once created them?**
This term does not signify that God brought His works into being at a single stroke, and then left them without a care for them. We ought rather to understand, that as the world was made by God in the beginning, so now it is preserved by Him in its estate, so that the heavens, the earth and all creatures do no continue in their being apart from this power. Besides, seeing that He holds all things in His hand, it follows that the government and lordship over them belongs to Him. Therefore, in that He is Creator of heaven and earth, it is His to rule the whole order of nature by His goodness and power and wisdom. It is He who sends rain and drought, hail, tempest and fair weather, fruitfulness and barrenness, health and sickness. In short, all things are under His command, to serve Him as it seems good to Him.

28. **But what about wicked men and devils? Are they also subject to Him?**
Although He does not guide them by His Holy Spirit, nevertheless He curbs them by His power, so that they cannot budge unless He permits them. He even constrains them to execute His will, although it is against their own intention and purpose.

29. **What good do you derive from the knowledge of this fact?**
Very much. It would go ill with us if devils and wicked men had power to do anything in spite of the will of God. Moreover we could never be at rest in our minds if we were exposed to them in danger, but when we know that they are curbed by the will of God, so that they can do nothing without His permission, then we may rest and breathe again, for God has promised to protect and defend us.

30. **Let us now come to the second part.**
"And in Jesus Christ His only Son our Lord," etc.

31. **What, briefly, does it comprehend?**
That we acknowledge the Son of God as our Saviour, and the means by which He has redeemed us from death, and acquired salvation.

32. **What is the meaning of the name, Jesus, which you give to Him?**
It means Saviour, and was given to Him by the angel at the command of God. (Matthew 1:21)

33. **Is this of more importance than if men had given it?**
Oh, yes. For since God wills that He be called so, He must be so in truth.

34. **What, next, is meant by the name of Christ?**
By this title His office is still better expressed—for it signifies that He was appointed by the Father to be ordained King, Priest, and Prophet.

35. **How do you know that?**
Because according to the Scripture, anointing is used for these three things. Also, because they are attributed to Him many times.

36. **But with what kind of oil was He anointed?**
Not with visible oil as was used for ancient kings, priests, and prophets, but this anointing was by the grace of the Holy Spirit, who is the reality signified by that outward anointing made in time past. (Isaiah 61:1; Psalm 45:7)

37. **But what is this Kingdom of which you speak?**
It is spiritual, and consists in the Word and Spirit of God, and includes righteousness and life.

38. **What of the priesthood?**
It is the office and prerogative of presenting Himself before God to obtain grace and favour, and appease His wrath in offering a sacrifice which is acceptable to Him.

39. **In what sense do you call Christ a Prophet?**
Because on coming down into the world (Isaiah 7:14) He was the sovereign messenger and ambassador of God His Father, to give full exposition of God's will toward the world and so put an end to all prophecies and revelations. (Hebrews 1:2)

40. **But do you derive any benefit from this?**
All this is for our good. For Jesus Christ has received all these gifts in order that He may communicate them to us, and that all of us may receive out of His fullness.

41. **Expound this to me more fully.**
He received the Holy Spirit in full perfection with all His graces, that He may lavish them upon us and distribute them, each according to the measure and portion which the Father knows to be expedient. (Ephesians 4:7) Thus we may draw from Him as from a fountain all the spiritual blessings we possess.

42. **What does His Kingdom minister to us?**
By it, we are set at liberty in our conscience and are filled with His spiritual riches in order to live in righteousness and holiness, and we are also armed with power to overcome the devil, the flesh, and the world—the enemies of our souls.

43. **What about His priesthood?**
First, by means of it He is the Mediator who reconciles us to God His Father; and secondly, through Him we have access to present ourselves to God, and offer Him ourselves in sacrifice with all that belongs to us. And in this way we are companions of His priesthood.

44. **There remains His Prophetic office.**
Since this office was given to the Lord Jesus to be the Master and Teacher of His own, its end is to bring us the true knowledge of the Father and of His Truth, so that we may be scholars in the household of God.

45. **You would conclude, then, that the title of Christ includes three offices which God has given His Son, in order to communicate virtue and fruit to His faithful people?**
That is so.

46. **Why do you call Him the only Son of God, seeing that God calls us all His children?**
We are children of God not by nature, but only by adoption and by grace, in that God wills to regard us as such. (Ephesians 1:5) But the Lord Jesus who was begotten of the substance of His Father, and is of one essence with Him, is rightly called the only Son of God (John 1:14; Hebrews 1:2) for there is no other who is God's Son by nature.

47. **You mean to say, then, that this honour is proper to Him alone, and belongs to Him by nature, but is communicated to us through a gracious gift, in that we are His numbers.**
That is so. Hence in regard to this communication He is called elsewhere "the first-born among many brethren." (Romans 8:29; Colossians 1:15)

48. **How is He "our Lord"?**
Because He is appointed by the Father to have us under His government, to administer the Kingdom and the Lordship of God in heaven and on earth, and to be the Head of men and believers. (Ephesians 5:23; Colossians 1:18)

49. **What is meant by what follows?**
It declares how the Son of God was anointed by the Father to be our Saviour. That is to say, He assumed human flesh, and accomplished all things necessary to our salvation, as enunciated here.

50. **What do you mean by the two clauses, "Conceived of the Holy Ghost, born of the Virgin Mary"?**
That He was formed in womb of the Virgin Mary, of her proper substance, to be the seed of David, as had been foretold (Psalm 132:11), and yet that this was wrought by the miraculous operation of the Holy Spirit, without the cooperation of a man. (Matthew 1:18; Luke 1:35)

51. **Was it then required that He should put on our very flesh?**
Yes, because it was necessary that the disobedience committed by man against God should be redressed in human nature. And moreover He could not otherwise be our Mediator to reconcile us to God His Father. (1 Timothy 2:5; Hebrews 4:15)

52. **You say that Christ had to become man, to fulfill the office of Saviour, as in our very person.**
Yes, indeed. For we must recover in Him all that we lack in ourselves, and this cannot be done in any other way.

53. **But why was that effected by the Holy Spirit, and not by the work of man according to the order of nature?**
As the seed of man is in itself corrupt, it was necessary that the power of the Holy Spirit should intervene in this conception, in order to preserve our Lord from all corruption, and to fill Him with holiness.

54. **Thus we are shown that He who is to sanctify others was free from every stain, and from His mother's womb He was consecrated to God in purity from the very beginning, in order that He may not be subject to the universal corruption of the human race.**
So I understand it.

55. **Why do you go immediately from His birth to His death, passing over the whole history of His life?**
Because nothing is said here about what belongs properly to the substance of our redemption.

56. **Why is it not said simply and in a word that He died, while Pontius Pilate is spoken of, under whom He suffered?**
That is not only to make us certain of the history, but is also meant to signify that His death involved condemnation.

57. **How is that?**
He died to suffer the punishment due to us, and thus to deliver us from it. However, because we were guilty before the judgment of God as evil-doers, in order to represent us in person He was pleased to appear before the tribunal of an earthly judge, and to be condemned by his mouth, that we might be acquitted before the throne of the celestial Judge.

58. **But Pilate pronounced Him innocent, and therefore did not condemn Him as if He were worthy of death. (Matthew 27:24; Luke 23:14)**
Both were involved. He was justified by the testimony of the judge, to show that He did not suffer for His own unworthiness but for ours and yet He was solemnly condemned by the sentence of the same judge, to show that He is truly our surety, receiving condemnation for us in order to acquit us from it.

59. **That is well said, for if He had been a sinner He could not have suffered death for others; and yet in order that His condemnation might be our deliverance, He had to be reckoned among transgressors. (Isaiah 53:12)**
I understand so.

60. **Is there greater importance in His having been crucified than if He had been put death in another way?**
Yes, as Paul also shows us when he says that He hanged on a tree to take our curse upon Himself and acquit us of it. (Galatians 3:13) For that kind of death was accursed of God. (Deuteronomy 21:23)

61. **What? Is it not to dishonour the Lord Jesus, to say He was subjected to the curse, and that before God?**
By no means, for in taking it upon Himself He abolished it, by His power, yet in such a way that He did not cease to be blessed throughout in order that He might fill us with His blessing.

62. **Explain the rest.**
Since death was the curse on man as a result of sin, Jesus Christ has endured it, and in enduring it overcame it. And to show that He underwent a real death, He chose to be placed in the tomb like other men.

63. **But nothing seems to redound to us from this victory, since we do not cease to die.**
That is no obstacle. The death of believers is nothing else than a way of entering into a better life.

64. **Hence it follows that we ought no longer to dread death as if it were a fearful thing, but we should willingly follow Jesus Christ our Head and Captain, who precedes us, not in order to let us perish, but in order to save us.**
That is so.

65. **What is the meaning of the additional clause: "He descended into hell"?**
That He not only suffered natural death, which is the separation of the body from the soul, but also that His soul was pierced with amazing anguish, which St. Peter calls the pains of death. (Acts 2:24)

66. **Why and how did that happen to Him?**
Because He presented Himself to God in order to make satisfaction in the name of sinners, it was necessary that He should suffer fearful distress of conscience, as if He had been forsaken by God, and even as if God had become hostile to Him. It was in this extremity that He cried, "My God, my God, why hast thou forsaken me?" (Matthew 27:46; Mark 15:34)

67. **Was His Father then opposed to Him?**
No. But He had to be afflicted in this way in fulfillment of what had been foretold by Isaiah, that "he was smitten by the hand of God for our sins and wounded for our transgressions." (Isaiah 53:5; 1 Peter 2:24)

68. **But since He is God Himself, how could He be in such dread, as if He were forsaken by God?**
We must hold that it was according to His human nature that He was in that extremity: and that in order to allow this, His Deity held itself back a little, as if concealed, that is, did not show its power.

69. **How is it possible that Jesus Christ, who is the salvation of the world, should have been under such damnation?**
He was not to remain under it. For though He experienced the horror we have spoken of, He was by no means oppressed by it. On the contrary, He battled with the power of hell, to break and destroy it.

70. **Thus we see the difference between the torment which He suffered and that which sinners experience when God punishes them in His wrath. For what He suffered for a time in Himself is perpetual in the others, and what was only a needle to sting Him is to them a sword to deliver a mortal wound.**
It is so, for Jesus Christ, even in the midst of such distress, did not cease to hope in God. But sinners whom God condemns rush into despair, defy, and even blaspheme Him.

71. **May we not gather from this what fruit we receive from the death of Jesus Christ?**
Yes, indeed. And, first, we see that it is a sacrifice by which He has made satisfaction for us before the judgment of God, and so has appeased the wrath of God and reconciled us to Him. Secondly, that His blood is the laver by which our souls are cleansed from all stains. Finally, that by this death our sins are effaced, so as never to be remembered before God, and thus the debt which was against us is abolished.

72. **Do we not have any other benefit from it?**
Yes, we do. If we are true members of Christ, our old man is crucified, our flesh is mortified, so that evil desires no longer reign in us.

73. **Expound the next article.**
This is it: "On the third day He rose again from the dead." By this He declared Himself the conqueror of death and sin, for by His resurrection He swallowed up death, broke the fetters of the devil, and destroyed all his powers. (1 Peter 3:22)

74. **In how many ways does this resurrection benefit us?**
First, by it righteousness was fully acquired for us. Secondly, it is also a sure pledge to us that we shall rise again one day in immortal glory. (1 Corinthians 15:20-23) Thirdly, if we truly participate in His resurrection, even now we are raised in newness of life, to serve God and to live a holy life according to His pleasure. (Romans 6:4)

75. **Continue.**
"He ascended into heaven."

76. **Did He ascend in such a way that He is no longer on earth?**
Yes. For after He had performed all that He was enjoined by the Father, and was required for our salvation, there was no need for Him to remain on earth.

77. **What benefit do we obtain from this ascension?**
The benefit is twofold. For inasmuch as Jesus Christ entered heaven in our name, as He had descended for our sake, He has given us an entry, and assured us that the door, previously shut because of sin, is now open for us. (Romans 6:8-11) Secondly, He appears before the face of the Father as our Intercessor and Advocate. (Hebrews 7:25)

78. **But did Christ in going to heaven withdraw from us, in such a way that He has now ceased to be with us?**
No. On the contrary, He has promised that He will be with us to the end. (Matthew 28:20)

79. **Is it in bodily presence that He remains with us?**
No, for it is one thing to speak of His body which was taken up into heaven, and another to speak of His power, which is spread abroad everywhere. (Luke 24:51; Acts 2:33)

80. **How do you understand that He "sitteth on the right hand of the Father"?**
It means that He has received the dominion of heaven and earth, so that He reigns and rules over all. (Matthew 28:18)

81. **But what is meant by "right hand," and by "sitteth"?**
It is a similitude taken from earthly princes, who are wont to place on their right hand those whom they make their lieutenants to govern in their name.

82. **You do not mean anything more then than Paul when he says that Christ had been appointed Head of the Church, and raised above all principality, has secured a Name which is above every name. (Ephesians 1:22, 4:15; Philippians 2:9)**
That is so.

83. **Continue.**
"From thence He will come to judge the quick and the dead." That is to say, He will appear again from heaven in judgment, as He was seen to ascend. (Acts 1:11)

84. **As the judgment is not to be before the end of the world, how do you say that some men will then be alive, and thus will be dead, seeing it is appointed to al men once to die? (Hebrews 9:27-28)**
Paul answers this question when he says, that those who then survive will suddenly be changed so that their corruption will be abolished, and their bodies will put on incorruption. (1 Corinthians 15:52; 1 Thessalonians 4:17)

85. **You understand then that this change will be for them like a death, for it will abolish their first nature, and raise them up in a new state.**
That is it.

86. **Does the fact that Christ is to come gain to judge the world bring us any consolation?**
Yes, indeed. For we are certain that He will appear only for our salvation.

87. **We should not then fear the last judgment, and have a horror of it?**
No, since we are not to come before any other judge than He who is our Advocate, and who has taken our cause in hand to defend us.

88. **Let us come now to the third part.**
This is faith in the Holy Spirit.

89. **What do we gain by it?**
The knowledge that as God has redeemed and saved us by Jesus Christ, He will also make us partakers of this redemption and salvation, through His Holy Spirit.

90. **How?**
As the blood of Christ is our cleansing, the Holy Spirit must sprinkle our consciences with it that they may be cleansed. (1 Peter 1:19)

91. **This requires a clearer explanation.**
I mean that the Holy Spirit, while He dwells in our hearts, makes us feel the virtue of our Lord Jesus. (Romans 5:5) For He enlightens us to know His benefits; He seals and imprints them in our souls, and makes room for them in us. (Ephesians 1:13) He regenerates us and makes us new creatures, so that through Him we receive all the blessings and gifts which are offered to us in Jesus Christ.

92. **What follows?**
The fourth part, where it is said that we believe in the Catholic Church.

93. **What is the Catholic Church?**
The community of the faithful which God has ordained and elected to eternal life.

94. **Is it necessary to believe this article?**
Yes, indeed, unless we want to make the death of Christ of none effect, and all that has already been said. The fruit that proceeds from it is the Church.

95. **You mean then that up to this point we have spoken of the cause and foundation of salvation, how God has received us in love through the mediation of Jesus, and has confirmed this grace in us through His Holy Spirit. But now the effect and fulfillment of all this is explained in order to give us greater certainty.**
It is so.

96. **In what sense do you call the Church holy?**
All whom God has chosen He justifies, and reforms to holiness and innocence, that His glory may be reflected in them. (Romans 8:30) And so Jesus Christ sanctified the Church which He redeemed, that it might be glorious and without blemish. (Ephesians 5:25-27)

97. **What is meant by the word Catholic, or Universal?**
It is meant to signify, that there is only one Head of the faithful, so they must all be united in one body, so that there are not several churches but one only, which is extended throughout the whole world. (Ephesians 4:15; 1 Corinthians 12:12,27)

98. **And what is the meaning of what follows concerning the communion of saints?**
That is added to express more clearly the unity which exists among the members of the Church. Moreover by this we are given to understand, that all the benefits that the Lord gives to the Church, are for the good and salvation of every Church, because they all have communion together.

99. **But is this holiness which you attribute to the Church already perfect?**
Not as long as she battles in this world, for elements of imperfection always remain and will never be entirely removed, until she is united completely to Jesus Christ her Head, by whom she is sanctified.

100. **Can this Church be known in any other way than by believing in her?**
There is indeed the visible Church of God, for the recognition of which He has certain signs, but here we speak properly of the fellowship of those whom He has elected to salvation which cannot be seen plainly by the eye.

101. **What comes next?**
I believe in "the forgiveness of sins."

102. **What do you understand by this word "forgiveness"?**
That God by His pure goodness forgives and pardons the sins of believers, so that they are not brought to account before His judgment, in order to be punished.

103. **Hence it follows that it is not at all through our own satisfaction that we desire to have God's pardon?**
That is true; for the Lord Jesus has made payment and born the punishment. We on our part could not make any recompense to God, but may only receive pardon for all our misdeeds through the pure generosity of God.

104. **Why do you insert this article after the Church?**
Because no man obtains pardon for his sins without being previously incorporated into the people of God, persevering in unity and communion with the Body of Christ in such a way as to be a true member of the Church.

105. **And so outside the Church there is nothing but damnation and death?**
Certainly, for all those who separate themselves from the community of the faithful to form a sect on its own, have no hope of salvation so long as they are in schism.

106. **What follows?**
I believe in "the resurrection of the flesh and the life everlasting."

107. **Why is this article inserted?**
To show us that our happiness is not situated on the earth. This serves a two-fold end. We are to learn to pass through this world as though it were a foreign country, treating lightly all earthly things and declining to set our

hearts on them. Secondly, we are not to lose courage, no matter how much we fail to perceive as yet the fruit of the grace which the Lord has wrought for us in Jesus Christ, but wait patiently until the time of revelation.

108. **How will this resurrection take place?**

Those who were formerly dead will resume their bodies, but with another quality; that is, they will no longer be subject to death or corruption, even although their substance will remain the same. Those who will survive God will miraculously raise up through a sudden change, as it is said. (1 Corinthians 15:52)

109. **Will this resurrection not be common to the evil and the good?**

Yes indeed, but not in the same way. Some will rise to salvation and joy, others to condemnation and death. (John 5:29; Matthew 25:46)

110. **Why then is eternal life only spoken of here, and hell not at all?**

Because nothing is set down in this summary that does not tend to the consolation of faithful consciences. It relates to us only the benefits which God performs for His servants. Accordingly no mention is made of the wicked, who are excluded from His Kingdom.

111. **Since we have the foundation on which faith is laid, we should be quite able to gather from it what true faith is.**

Yes, indeed, It is a sure and steadfast knowledge of the love of God toward us, according as He declares in His gospel that He is our Father and Saviour (through the mediation of Jesus Christ).

112. **Can we have this by ourselves, or does it come from God?**

Scripture teaches that it is the singular gift of the Holy Spirit, and experience also demonstrates it.

113. **How so?**

Our mind is too weak to comprehend the spiritual wisdom of God which is revealed to us by faith, and our hearts are too prone either to defiance or to a perverse confidence in ourselves or creaturely things. But the Holy Spirit enlightens us to make us capable of understanding what would otherwise be incomprehensible to us, and fortifies us in certitude, sealing and imprinting the promises of salvation on our hearts.

114. **What good comes to us from this faith, when we have it?**
It justifies us before God, and makes us obtain eternal life.

115. **How so? Is not man justified by good works in a holy life and in conformity to God?**
If any one be found so perfect, he might well be deemed righteous, but since we are all poor sinners, we must look elsewhere for a worthiness in which to make answer before the judgment of God.

116. **But are all our works so reprobate that they cannot merit grace before God?**
First, all that we do of ourselves, by our own nature, is vicious, and therefore cannot please God. He condemns them all.

117. **You say then that before God has received us in His grace, we can nothing but sin, just as a bad tree cannot but produce bad fruit? (Matthew 7:17)**
It is so. For even if our works appear beautiful outwardly, yet they are evil, since the heart, to which God looks, is perverted.

118. **Hence you conclude, that we cannot by our merits anticipate God, and so induce Him to be kind to us, but on the contrary that we do nothing but provoke Him to be against us?**
Yes. And therefore I say: merely through His goodness, without any regard to our works, He is pleased to accept us freely in Jesus Christ, imputing His righteousness to us, and does not impute our sins to us. (Titus 3:5-7)

119. **What do you mean then by saying that a man is justified by faith?**
That in believing the promises of the gospel and in receiving them in true affiance of the heart, we enter into this righteousness.

120. **You mean then that as God offers righteousness to us by the gospel, so it is by faith that we receive it?**
Yes.

121. **But after God has once received us, are the works which we do by His grace, not pleasing to Him?**
Yes, they are, in that He generously accepts them, not however in virtue of their own worthiness.

122. **How is that? Are they not accepted as worthy, seeing that they proceed from the Holy Spirit?**
No. For there is always some weakness in them, the weakness of our flesh, through which they are defiled.

123. **By what means, then, are they made acceptable?**
It is by faith. That is to say, that a person is assured in his conscience that God will not examine him harshly, but covering his defects and impurities by the purity of Jesus Christ, He will regard him as perfect.

124. **But can we say from this that a Christian man is justified by works after God has called him, or that through them he merits the love of God, and so obtains eternal life?**
No. On the contrary, it is said that no man living will be justified in His sight. (Psalm 143:2) Therefore we have to pray that He will not enter into judgment with us, nor call us to account.

125. **You do not mean therefore that the good works of believers are useless?**
No. For God promises to reward them fully, both in this world and in Paradise. But this comes from His gratuitous love toward us: moreover He buries all our faults, so as never to remember them.

126. **But can we believe that we are justified, without doing good works?**
That is impossible. For to believe in Jesus Christ is to receive Him as He has given Himself to us. He promises not only to deliver us from death and restore us to favour with God His Father, through the merit of His innocence, but also to regenerate us by His Spirit, that we may be enabled to live in holiness.

127. **Faith, then, not only does not make us careless of good works, but is the root from which they are produced.**

It is so, and for this reason, the doctrine of the Gospel is comprehended in these two points, faith and repentance.

128. **What is repentance?**

Dissatisfaction with and a hatred of evil and a love good proceeding from the fear of God, and inducing us to mortify our flesh, so that we may be governed and led by the Holy Spirit, in the service of God.

129. **But this second point we have mentioned concerning the Christian life.**

Yes, and we said that the true and legitimate service of God is to obey His will.

130. **Why?**

Because He will not be served according to our own imagination, but in the way that pleases Him.

131. **What rule has He given us by which we may direct our life?**

His law.

132. **What does it contain?**

It is divided into two parts: the first contains four commandments, the other six. Thus there are ten in all.

133. **Who made this division?**

God Himself, who delivered it to Moses written on two table, and declared that it was reduced into ten words. (Exodus 32:15, 34:29; Deuteronomy 4:13, 10:1)

134. **What is the content of the first table?**

The way of the true worship of God.

135. **And the second?**

How we are to live with our neighbours, and what we owe them.

136. **Repeat the first commandment.**
Hear, O Israel, I am the Lord thy God, who brought thee out of the land of Egypt, out of the house of bondage: thou shalt have no other gods before Me. (Exodus 20:2-3; Deuteronomy 5:6-7)

137. **Explain the meaning.**
At first He makes a kind of preface for the whole law. For in calling Himself the Eternal and the Creator of the world, He claims authority to command. Then He declares that He is our God, in order that we may esteem His doctrine. For if He is our Saviour, that is good reason why we should be an obedient people to Him.

138. **But is not that which He says after the deliverance from the land of Egypt, addressed particularly to the people of Israel?**
Yes, it does refer to the physical deliverance of Israel, but it also applies to us all in a general way, in that He has delivered our souls from the spiritual captivity of sin, and the tyranny of the devil.

139. **Why does He mention this at the beginning of His law?**
To remind us how much we are bound to obey His good pleasure, and what gratitude it should be on our part if we do the contrary.

140. **And what does He require briefly in this first commandment?**
That we reserve for Him alone the honour that belongs to Him, and do not transfer it elsewhere.

141. **What is the honour due Him?**
To adore Him alone, to call upon Him, to have our affiance in Him, and all similar things due to His majesty.

142. **Why is it said "Before my face"?**
Since He who sees and knows all is the judge of the secret thoughts of men, it means that He wants to be worshiped as God, not only by outward confession, but also in pure trust and affection of heart.

143. **Turn to the second commandment.**
Thou shalt not make unto thee a graven image, nor any form that is in heaven above, or on the earth beneath, or in the water under the earth. Thou shalt not do honour to them.

144. **Does He entirely forbid us to make any image?**
No, but He forbids us to make any image with which to represent God, or to worship Him.

145. **Why is it unlawful to represent God visibly?**
Because there is no resemblance between Him who is eternal Spirit and incomprehensible, and corporal, dead, corruptible and visible matter. (Deuteronomy 4:15; Isaiah 40:7; Romans 1:23; Acts 17:24-25)

146. **You think then that it does dishonour to His majesty to represent Him in this way?**
Yes.

147. **What kind of worship is here condemned?**
When we come before an image intending to pray, or bow our knee before it; or to make any other sign of reverence, as if God were there showing Himself to us.

148. **This does not mean that all sculpture or painting is universally forbidden, but only all images used in the service of God, or in worshiping Him in visible things, or indeed for any abuse of them in idolatry of any kind whatsoever.**
That is so.

149. **Now to what end shall we refer this commandment?**
With the first commandment, God declared that He alone, and no one beside Him, should be worshiped: so now He shows us the correct form of worship, in order that He may draw us away from all superstitions, and carnal ceremonies.

150. **Let us proceed.**
He adds a warning that He is the Eternal, our God, strong and jealous, visiting the iniquity of the fathers upon the children of them who hate Him, to the third and fourth generation.

151. **Why does He make mention of His might?**
To indicate that He has power to maintain His glory.

152. **What is meant by jealousy?**
That He cannot allow an associate. For as He has given Himself to us out of His infinite goodness, so He would have us to be entirely His. And this is the chastity of our souls, to be consecrated and dedicated to Him. On the other hand it is a spiritual whoredom for us to turn away from Him to any superstition.

153. **How is this to be understood, that He punishes the sin of the fathers on their children?**
To give us a greater fear of Him. He says not only that He will inflict punishment on those who offend Him, but that their offspring also will be cursed after them.

154. **But is it not contrary to the justice of God to punish someone for others?**
If we consider the condition of the human race, the question is answered. For by nature we are all cursed, and we cannot complain of God when He leaves us in this condition. Moreover as He manifests His grace and love toward His servants in blessing their children, so this is a testimony to His punishment of the wicked, when He leaves their seed accursed.

155. **What more does He say?**
To incite us by gentleness, He says that He will have mercy on all who love Him and observe His commandments, to a thousand generations.

156. **Does He mean that the obedience of a faithful man will save the whole of his race, even if they are still wicked?**
No, but that He will extend His goodness toward the faithful to such an extent, that in love for them He will make Himself known to their children,

not only to prosper them according to the flesh, but to sanctify them by His Spirit, that He might make them obedient to His will.

157. **But this is not always so.**
No. For as the Lord reserves for Himself the freedom to show mercy to the children of the ungodly, so on the other hand He retains the power to elect or reject in the generation of the faithful as it seems good to Him. (Romans 9:15-22) However, He does this in such a way that men may acknowledge that this promise is not vain or fallacious. (Romans 2:6-10)

158. **Why does He mention here a thousand generations, and in regard to punishment, mention only three or four?**
To signify that it is His nature to exercise kindness and gentleness much more than strictness or severity, as He testifies, when He says that He is ready to show mercy, but slow to anger. (Exodus 34:6-7; Psalm 103:8)

159. **Let us come to the third commandment.**
Thou shalt not take the name of the Lord thy God in vain.

160. **What does this mean?**
He forbids us to abuse the name of God, not only in perjury, but also in superfluous and idle swearing.

161. **Can the name of God we used lawfully in oaths?**
Yes, when they are necessary, i.e., in order to uphold the truth, when it requires it, and in maintaining love and concord among us.

162. **Does He reprove no other oaths, then those which are a dishonour to God?**
In this one case He gives us a general instruction never to utter the name of God except with fear and humility in order to glorify it. For since it is holy and honourable, we ought to guard against taking the Name of God in such a way that we appear to hold it in contempt, or give others occasion to vilify it.

163. **How is this to be done?**
By never thinking or speaking of God and His works without honour and reverence.

164. **What follows?**
A warning, that He will not hold him guiltless, who takes His name in vain.

165. **Since elsewhere He gives a general warning that He will punish all transgressors, what is the advantage of this warning?**
He wants to declare how highly He regards the glory of His name, explicitly mentioning that He will not suffer anyone to despise it, so that we may be all the more careful to hold it in reverence.

166. **Let us come to the fourth commandment.**
Remember the Sabbath day, to keep it holy. Sis days shalt thou labour, and do all thy work: But the seventh is the Sabbath of the Lord thy God: in it thou shalt not do any work, thou, nor thy son, nor thy daughter, thy man-servant, nor thy maid-servant, nor thy cattle, nor thy stranger that is within thy gates: For in six days the Lord made heaven and earth, the sea, and all that in them is, and rested the seventh day, and hallowed it.

167. **Does He order us to labour six days a week that we may rest on the seventh?**
Not precisely, but in allowing us to labour for six days, He excepts the seventh, on which it is not right to be engaged in work.

168. **Does He thus forbid us all work one day a week?**
This commandment has a particular reason, for the observance of rest is part of the ceremonies of the ancient Law, which was abolished at the coming of Jesus Christ.

169. **Do you mean that this commandment properly belongs to the Jews, and that it was given for the time of the Old Testament?**
I do, in so far as it is ceremonial.

170. **How is that? Is there anything else in it besides the ceremony?**
It was given for three reasons.

171. **What are they?**
To represent spiritual rest, in aid of ecclesiastical polity, and for the relief of servants.

172. **What is this spiritual rest?**
It is to cease from our own works, that the Lord may work in us.

173. **How is that done?**
By mortifying our flesh, that is, renouncing our own nature, so that God may govern us by His Spirit.

174. **Is this to be done only one day a week?**
This is to be done continually. After we have once begun, we must continue all our life.

175. **Why, then, is a certain day appointed to represent this?**
It is not required that the representation should be altogether identical with the truth, but it is sufficient that there should be some resemblance.

176. **But why is the seventh day appointed rather than any other day?**
The number seven implies perfection in Scripture. Thus it is suited to denote perpetuity. It reminds us also that our spiritual rest is only begun in this life, and will not be perfect until we depart from this world.

177. **But what is meant when our Lord asserts that we must rest as He did?**
After having created all His works in six days, He dedicated the seventh to the contemplation of His works. And in order better to induce us to do this, He set before us His own example. For nothing is so desirable as to be conformed to Him.

178. **Must we meditate continually on the works of God, or is it sufficient on one day out of seven?**
We must do it every hour, but because of our weakness, one day is specially appointed. And this is the polity of which I spoke.

179. **What order, then, is to be observed on that day?**
That the people meet to hear the doctrine of God, to engage in common prayer, and bear witness to their faith and religion.

180. **What do you mean by saying that this commandment is also given to provide for the relief of servants?**
To give some relaxation to those who are under the power of others. And likewise, this tends to maintain a common polity. For everyone accustoms himself to labour for the rest of the time, when there is one day for rest.

181. **Let us now see how this commandment addresses itself to us.**
As for the ceremony, it was abolished, for we have the accomplishment of it in Christ Jesus.

182. **How?**
Our old man is crucified, through the power of His death, and through His resurrection we are raised up to newness of life. (Romans 6:6)

183. **What else is there here for us?**
That we observe the order constituted in the Church, to hear the Word of God, to engage in public prayers and in the Sacraments, and that we do not contravene the spiritual order among the faithful.

184. **And does the figure give us any further benefit?**
Yes, indeed. It should lead us to the truth, namely, that being true members of Christ, we should cease from our own works, and put ourselves under His government.

185. **Let us come to the second table.**
It begins, "Honour thy father and thy mother."

186. **What do you mean by "honour"?**
That children be humble and obedient toward their parents, doing them honour and reverence, helping them and being at their command, as they are bound.

187. **Proceed further.**
God adds a promise to the commandment, "That thy days may be prolonged on the land which the Lord thy God will give thee."

188. **What does that mean?**
That God will give long life to those who honour their father and mother as they ought.

189. **Seeing this life is full of misery, why does God promise man as a favour that he will live long?**
However miserable it may be, life on earth is a blessing from God to the faithful, if only for this reason, that in it God testifies to His fatherly love in supporting them in it.

190. **Does it follow conversely, that the man who dies prematurely is cursed of God?**
By no means. Rather does it sometimes happen that the Lord withdraws from this world more quickly those whom He loves most.

191. **In so doing, how does He fulfill His promise?**
All that God promises us in earthly blessings, we must receive under this condition, viz. that it is expedient for our spiritual salvation. For it would be poor indeed if that did not take precedence.

192. **What of those who are rebellious against their father and mother?**
Not only will God punish them at the last judgment, but here also God will exercise judgment on their bodies, it may be by letting them die before their time, or ignominiously, or in some other way.

193. **Does He not speak expressly of the land of Canaan in this promise?**
Yes, so far as the children of Israel are concerned, but the term ought to have a more general meaning for us. For seeing that the earth is the Lord's, whatever be the country we inhabit, He assigns it to us for our habitation. (Psalm 24:1, 89:12, 115:16)

194. **Is that all there is to the commandment?**

Though father and mother only are mentioned, nevertheless all superiors are intended, as the reason is the same.

195. **What is the reason?**

That God has given them pre-eminence; for there is no authority whether of parents, or princes, or of any others who are over us, but what God has ordained. (Romans 13:1)

196. **Repeat the sixth commandment.**

Thou shalt not kill.

197. **Does it forbid nothing but murder?**

Yes, indeed. For seeing it is God who speaks, He gives us law not only for outward deeds, but primarily for the affections of our heart.

198. **You mean then that there is some kind of inward murder which God forbids to us?**

I do: hatred and rancour, and desire to do evil to our neighbor.

199. **Is it sufficient for us not to hate or to bear ill will?**

No, for in condemning hatred God signifies that He requires us to love our neighbours and seek their salvation, and all this with true affection and without simulation.

200. **State the seventh commandment.**

Thou shalt not commit adultery.

201. **What is the essence of this?**

That all fornication is cursed by God, and therefore we must abstain from it if we do not want to provoke His anger against us.

202. **Does it not require anything else?**

We must always regard the nature of the Lawgiver, who does not halt at the outward act, but requires the affection of the heart.

203. **What more then does it mean?**
Since our bodies and our souls are temples of the Holy Spirit (1 Corinthians 3:16, 6:15; 2 Corinthians 6:16), we must preserve them in uprightness. And so we must be chaste not only in deed, but also in desire, word and gesture. Accordingly no part of us is to be polluted with unchastity.

204. **Let us come to the eighth commandment.**
Thou shalt not steal.

205. **Is it only meant to prohibit the thefts which are punished by justice, or does it extend further?**
It refers to all civil traffic and unscrupulous means of acquiring our neighbour's goods, whether by violence, or fraud, or in any other kind of way that God has not allowed.

206. **Is it enough to abstain from evil deeds, or is covetousness also included here?**
We must ever return to this, that the Lawgiver is spiritual, that He does not speak simply of outward thefts, but all schemes, wishes and plans to enrich ourselves at the expense of our neighbour.

207. **What are we to do then?**
We must do our duty in preserving for every man his own.

208. **What is the ninth commandment?**
Thou shalt not bear false witness against thy neighbour.

209. **Does it forbid perjury in court, or any kind of lying against our neighbour?**
In mentioning this one case it gives a general instruction, that we are not to speak evil of our neighbour falsely, nor by our slanders and lies are we do him harm in his possessions, or in his reputations.

210. **But why does He expressly mention public perjury?**
That He may give us a greater abhorrence of this vice of evil speaking and slander, telling us that if a man accustom himself to slandering and defaming his neighbour, he will soon descend to perjury in court.

211. **Does He only forbid evil speaking, or does He also include evil thinking?**
Both of them, for the reason already stated. For whatever it is wrong to do before men, it is wrong to wish before God.

212. **Then summarize its meaning.**
He enjoins us not to be inclined to misjudge and defame our neighbours, but rather to esteem them highly, as far as the truth will permit, and to preserve their good reputation in our speech.

213. **Let us come to the last commandment.**
Thou shalt not covet thy neighbour's house, thou shalt not covet thy neighbour's wife, nor his man-servant, nor his maid-servant, nor his ox, nor his ass, nor any thing that is thy neighbour's.

214. **Seeing that the whole law is spiritual, as you have so often said before, and the other commandments are not only to order outward acts, but also the affections of the heart, what more is added here?**
The Lord wished by the other commandments to rule our affections and will, but here He imposes a law also on our thoughts, which, though charged with covetousness and desire, yet stop short of an active intention.

215. **Do you mean that the least temptation that enters into the thought of a believer is sin, even though he resists it and does not consent to it?**
It is certain that all evil thoughts proceed from the infirmity of our flesh, even though we do not consent to them. But I say that this commandment speaks of concupiscence which tickles and pierces the heart of man, without bringing him to a deliberate purpose.

216. **You say then that the evil affections which involve a definite act of will or resolution are already condemned, but now the Lord requires of us such integrity, that no wicked desire may enter our hearts, to solicit and incite them to evil.**
That is right.

217. **Can we now give a short summary of the whole law?**

We can, reducing it to two articles—the first of which is that we are to love God with all our heart, and with all our soul, and with all our strength; the second that we love our neighbours as ourselves.

218. **What is meant by the love of God?**

To love Him as God is to have and hold Him as Lord, Saviour and Father, and this requires reverence, honour, faith, and obedience along with love.

219. **What does "with all our heart" signify, and "with all our soul, and with all our strength"?**

Such a zeal and such a vehemence, that there is in us no desire, no will, no intention and no thought, contrary to this love.

220. **What is the meaning of the second article?**

As we are by nature prone to love ourselves, that this affection overcomes all others, so love to our neighbour should be so predominant in our hearts as to direct and govern us and be the rule of all our thoughts and actions.

221. **What do you understand by "our neighbours"?**

Not only our parents and friends, or those acquainted with us, but also those who are unknown to us, and even our enemies.

222. **But what connection do they have with us?**

That which God has placed among all men on earth, and is so inviolable, that it cannot be abolished by the malice of any man.

223. **You say, then, that if any man hate us, the blame is his own, and yet according to the order of God, he does not cease to be our neighbour, and we are to regard him as such?**

It is so.

224. **Seeing that the law of God comprises the form of worshiping Him aright, should not the Christian man live according to its command?**

Yes indeed. But there is some infirmity in us, so that no man acquits himself perfectly in it.

225. **Why then does the Lord require a perfection which is beyond our ability?**
He requires nothing which we are not bound to perform. Nevertheless, provided we take care to conform our life to what we are told here, although we are very far from reaching perfection, the Lord does not impute our faults to us.

226. **Do you speak of all men in general, or of believers only?**
He who is not yet regenerated by the Spirit of God cannot begin to do the least of the commandments. Moreover, even if a person could be found who had fulfilled some part of the law, he would not acquit himself before God, for our Lord pronounces that all those who have not fulfilled all the things contained in it, will be accursed. (Deuteronomy 27:26; Galatians 3:10)

227. **Hence we must conclude that the law has a two-fold office, in accordance with the fact that there are two classes of men.**
Yes, in regard to unbelievers it seems but to convict and make them inexcusable before God. (Romans 3:3) And this is what Paul says, that it is the ministry of death, and condemnation. (2 Corinthians 3:6,9) In regard to believers, it has a very different use.

228. **What?**
First, in that it shows them that they cannot justify themselves by their works, it humbles them and disposes them to seek their salvation in Jesus Christ. (Romans 3:3) Secondly, inasmuch as it requires of them much more than they are able to perform, it admonishes them to pray unto the Lord, that He may give them strength and power (Galatians 4:6), and at the same time reminds them of their perpetual quilt, that they may not presume to be proud. Thirdly it is a kind of bridle, by which they are kept in the fear of God.

229. **We say then that although during this mortal life we will never fulfill the Law, such perfection is not required of us in vain, for it shows us the mark at which we ought to aim, that each of us, according to the grace God has bestowed on him, may strive continually to press toward it, and to advance day by day.**
That is as I understand it.

230. **Do we not have perfect rule of goodness in the Law?**
Yes, and therefore God demands nothing from us, but to follow it; and, on the other hand, repudiates and rejects all that a man undertakes to do beyond what it contains. The only sacrifice He requires is obedience. (1 Samuel 15:22; Jeremiah 7:21-23)

231. **What is the purpose then of all the admonitions, reproofs, commandments, and exhortations made both by Prophets and Apostles?**
They are nothing else than declarations of the Law, leading us into obedience to it rather than turning us away from it.

232. **But nothing is said about particular vocations?**
When it is said that we are to render to every one his due, we may well infer what the duty of each is in his own vocation. Moreover as we have already said, this is expounded for us in the whole of Scripture, for what the Lord has set down in this summary, He treats of there, and with much fuller teaching.

233. **Since we have spoken sufficiently of the service of God, which is the second part of His worship, let us now speak of the third part.**
We said it was the invocation of God in all our needs.

234. **Do you think that He alone is to be invoked?**
Yes, for He requires this as the worship proper to His Deity.

235. **If it is so, in what way is it legitimate for us to ask the aid of men?**
There is a great difference between these two things. For we call upon God to protest that we expect no good but from Him, and that we have no refuge elsewhere, and yet we ask the assistance of men, as far as He permits, and has given them the power and means of helping us.

236. **You mean that when we seek the succour of men, there is nothing to prevent our calling upon God alone, seeing that we do not put our reliance on them, and do not seek their aid except in so far as God has ordained**

them to be ministers and dispensers of His blessings, in order to assist us.

That is true. And indeed, every benefit that comes to us we should take as coming from God Himself, as in truth it is He who sends it to us by their hands.

237. **Nevertheless, should we not give thanks to men for the kindness which they do to us?**

Certainly, if only for the reason that God honours them by communicating His blessings to us through their hands, for in this way He lays us under obligation to Him, and wishes us to be mindful of them.

238. **Can we not conclude from this that it is wrong to invoke angels, and saints who have departed from this world?**

Yes, indeed; for God has not assigned to saints this office of aiding and assisting us. And in regard to angels, though He employs their ministry for our salvation, nevertheless He does not wish us to invoke them, nor to address ourselves to them.

239. **You say, then, that all that conflicts with the order instituted by the Lord, contravenes His will?**

Yes, for it is a sure sign of infidelity if we are not contented with what the Lord gives to us. Moreover, if instead of having a refuge in God alone, in obedience to His command, we have recourse to them, putting something of our reliance on them, we fall into idolatry, seeing we transfer to them that which God has reserved for Himself.

240. **Let us now speak of the way of prayer to God. Is it sufficient to pray with the tongue, or does prayer require also the spirit and the heart?**

The tongue is not always necessary, but there must be understanding and affection.

241. **How will you prove that?**

Since God is Spirit, He always requires the heart, and especially in prayer, in which we enter into communication with Him, wherefore He promises to be near to those only who call upon Him in truth. (Psalm 145:18) On the other hand, He curses all who pray to Him in hypocrisy, and without affection. (Isaiah 29:13-14)

242. **All prayers, then, made only with the mouth are vain?**
Not only vain, but also displeasing to God.

243. **What kind of affection should we have in prayer?**
First, that we feel our misery and poverty, and that this feeling should beget sorrow and anguish in us. Secondly, that we have an earnest desire to obtain grace from God. This desire will also kindle our hearts, and engender in us an ardent longing to pray.

244. **Does this derive from our nature, or from the grace of God?**
Here God must come to our aid, for we are too dull, but the Spirit of God helps us with groanings that cannot be uttered, and forms in our hearts the affection and zeal that God requires, as Paul says. (Romans 8:26; Galatians 4:6)

245. **Does this mean that we have not to incite and urge ourselves to pray?**
By no means. On the contrary, when we do not feel such a disposition within us we should beseech the Lord to put it into us, so as to make us capable and fit to pray as we ought.

246. **You do not, however, mean that the tongue is quite useless in prayer?**
Not at all, for sometimes it helps the mind, sustaining and keeping it from being drawn away from God so easily. Besides, since more than all the other members it was formed to the glory of God, it is very reasonable that it should be employed by all means for this purpose. Moreover, the zeal of the heart by its own ardour and vehemence often constrains the tongue to speak quite spontaneously.

247. **If so, what about prayer in an unknown tongue?**
It is a mockery of God, and a perverse hypocrisy. (1 Corinthians 14:14)

248. **But when we pray to God, is it a venture in which we do not know whether we will succeed or not? Or ought we to be certain that our praying will be heard?**
The ground of our prayers should always be, that they will received by God, and that we shall obtain what we request as far is it is expedient for us. And therefore St. Paul says that true prayer comes from faith. (Romans 10:14) For if we have no reliance upon the goodness of God, it will be impossible for us to call upon Him in truth.

249. **And what of those who doubt, not knowing if God hears or not?**
Their prayers are utterly void, since they have no promise, for He says that whatever we ask, believing, we shall receive. (Matthew 21:22; Mark 11:24)

250. **It remains to learn how and in whose name we can have the boldness to present ourselves before God, seeing that we are so unworthy in ourselves.**
First we have promises on which we must rest, without considering our worthiness. (Psalm 50:15, 91:3, 145:18; Isaiah 30:15, 65:24; Jeremiah 29:12; Joel 3:5) Secondly, if we are children of God, He induces and urges us by His Holy Spirit to betake ourselves to Him familiarly, as to our Father. (Matthew 9:2, 22; etc.) And lest we, who are poor worms of the earth, and miserable sinners, should be afraid to appear before His glorious majesty, He gives us our Lord Jesus Christ as a Mediator (1 Timothy 2:5; Hebrews 4:16; 1 John 2:1), that through Him we may have access and have no doubt of finding grace.

251. **Do you understand that we are to call upon God only, in the Name of Jesus Christ?**
I understand so, for we have an express commandment about this. And in it we are promised that by His intercession our requests will be heard. (John 14:13)

252. **It is not, then, temerity or foolish presumption on our part, if we presume to address God personally, seeing that we have Jesus Christ for our**

Advocate, and if we set Him before us, that God may for His sake be gracious to us and accept us?
No, for we pray as it were by His mouth, since He gives us entrance and audience, and intercedes for us. (Romans 8:34)

253. **Let us now speak of the substance of our prayers. Can we ask for all that comes into our mind, or is there a certain rule to be observed about it?**
If we followed our fantasy, our prayers would be very badly ordered. We are so ignorant that we cannot judge what it is good to ask: Moreover, all our desires are so intemperate that it is necessary that we should not give them a loose rein.

254. **What is to be done, then?**
That God Himself should instruct us, according to what He knows to be expedient; that we do nothing but follow Him, as if He were leading us by the hand.

255. **What instructions has He given?**
He has given us ample instructions throughout Scripture; but that we may address ourselves the better to a definite end, He has given us a form in which He has briefly comprehended everything that is legitimate and expedient for us to pray for.

256. **Repeat it.**
Our Lord Jesus Christ, being asked by His Disciples to teach them how to pray, answered that they should pray thus (Matthew 6:9-13; Luke 11:1-4): "Our Father, which art in heaven, hallowed by thy name. Thy kingdom come. Thy will be done, as it is in heaven. Give us this day our daily bread. And forgive us our debts, as we forgive our debtors. And lead us not into temptation; but deliver us from evil: For thine is the kingdom, and the power, and the glory, for ever. Amen."

257. **To make it easier to understand, tell me how many sentences it contains.**
Six, of which the first three concern the glory of God alone, without any reference to ourselves; the other three are for us, and concern our blessing and profit.

258. **Are we then to ask God for anything from which no benefit redounds to us?**
It is true that God, by His infinite goodness, so arranges and orders things, that nothing tends to the glory of His Name without being also salutary to us. Therefore, when His name is sanctified, He turns it to our sanctification; when His Kingdom comes, we are, in a way, sharers in it. But in desiring and asking all these things, we ought to have regard only for His glory, without thinking of ourselves, or seeking our own profit.

259. **According to what you say, the first three of these requests are expedient for us, and yet they ought not to be made with any other intention that of desiring that God may be glorified.**
It is so. And similarly, although the last three requests are appointed as prayers for what is expedient to us, yet even in them we ought to seek the glory of God, so that it may be the end of all our desires.

260. **Let us come to the exposition. And before we go any further, why is God called our Father, rather than by some other name?**
Since it is essential that our consciences have a steadfast assurance, when we pray, our God gives Himself a name which suggests only gentleness and kindness, in order to take away from us all doubt and anxiety, and to give us boldness in coming to Him personally.

261. **Shall we then dare to go to God familiarly, as a child to his father?**
Yes, in fact with greater assurance of obtaining what we ask. For if we, being evil, cannot refuse our children bread and meat when they ask, how much less will our heavenly Father, who is not only good, but sovereign goodness itself. (Matthew 7:11)

262. **Can we not prove from this very Name, what has been said, viz. that prayer should be grounded on the intercession of Jesus Christ?**
Yes, certainly. For God does not acknowledge us as His children, except in so far as we are members of His Son.

263. **Why do you not call God your God, but call Him our Father together?**
Each believer may indeed call Him his own Father, but in this formula Jesus Christ instructs us to pray together, to remind us that in our prayers we are to exercise charity towards our neighbours, and not only to care for ourselves.

264. **What is meant by the clause "who art in heaven"?**
It is just the same as if I were to call Him exalted, mighty, incomprehensible.

265. **To what end, and for what reason?**
That when we call upon Him, we may learn to lift our thoughts on high, and not to have any carnal or earthly thoughts of Him, not to measure Him by our apprehension, nor to subject Him to our will, but to adore His glorious Majesty in humility. It teaches us also to have more reliance on Him, since He is Governor and Master of all.

266. **Now expound the first petition.**
The Name of God is His renown, with which He is celebrated among men. We pray then that His glory may be exalted above all, and in all things.

267. **Do you think that His glory can increase or decrease?**
Not in itself. But this means that it may be manifested, as it ought to be, that all the works which God performs may appear glorious, as indeed they are, so that He Himself may be glorified in every way.

268. **What do you understand by the Kingdom of God in the second petition?**
It consists principally of two things: that He leads His own, and governs them by His Spirit, and on the other hand casts down and confounds the reprobate who refuse to subject themselves to His rule, and so makes it clear that there is no power which can resist His power.

269. **In what sense do you pray that this Kingdom may come?**
That day by day the Lord may increase the numbers of the faithful, that day by day He may increasingly bestow His graces upon them, until He has filled them completely; moreover, that He cause His truth to shine more and more and manifest His justice, so that Satan and the powers of darkness may be put to confusion, and all iniquity be destroyed and abolished.

270. **Is that not taking place today?**
Yes indeed—in part, but we pray that it may continually increase and advance, until at last it comes to its perfection in the day of judgment, in which God alone will be exalted, and ever creature will be humbled before His Majesty, and He will be all in all. (1 Corinthians 15:28)

271. **What do you mean by asking that the will of God may be done?**
That all creatures may be brought under obedience to Him, and so that everything may be done according to His good will.

272. **Do you mean that nothing can be done contrary to His will?**
We ask not only that He may bring all things to pass, as He has determined in His counsel, but also that, putting down all rebellion, He may bring all wills to conform to His own.

273. **In so doing, do we not renounce our own wills?**
We do, not only that He may overthrow our desires, which are at variance with His own good will, bringing them all to nought, but also that He may create in us new spirits and new hearts, so that we may will nothing of ourselves, but rather that His Spirit may will in us, and bring us into full agreement with Him.

274. **Why do you add "on earth as it is in heaven"?**
Since His heavenly creatures or His angels have it as their own object to obey Him, promptly without opposition, we desire that the same thing may be done on earth, that is, that all men may yield themselves in voluntary obedience.

275. Let us come to the second part. What mean you by "the daily bread" you ask for?

In general, everything that we need for our body, not only food and clothing, but all that God knows to be expedient for us, that we may be able to eat our bread in peace.

276. But why do you ask God to give you your food, when He orders us to win it, by working with our hands?

Though He commands us to work for our living, nevertheless it is not our labour, industry, and diligence, that provide us with food, but the blessing of God alone, which makes the labour of our hands to prosper. Moreover we ought to understand that it is not meat that nourishes us, although we have it owing to His command, but the power of the Lord alone who uses it as His instrument. (Deuteronomy 8:3,17)

277. Why do you call it yours, when you ask God to give it to you?

Because of the kindness of God it becomes ours, though it is by no means due to us. We are also reminded by this not to desire the bread of others, but only that which we acquire by legitimate means, according to the ordinance of God.

278. Why do you say "daily" and "this day"?

That we may learn to be content, and not to covet more than our need requires.

279. Since this prayer is common to all, how can the rich, who have an abundance of good things to provide for a long time, ask for bread each day?

The rich, as well as the poor, should understand that none of these things profit them, unless the Lord grant them the use of them, and by His grace make it profitable to them. Thus in having we have nothing, unless He gives it to us.

280. What does the fifth petition contain?

That it pleases God to pardon our sins.

281. **Is any man living so righteous, that He does not need to make this petition?**
No, for the Lord Jesus gave this form of prayer to His Apostles for His Church. Wherefore he who would exempt himself from this, must renounce the community of Christians. And indeed Scripture testifies to us that even the most perfect man seeking to justify himself before God in a single matter, will be found guilty in a thousand. (Job 9:3) Thus the only refuge we may have is in His mercy.

282. **How do you think that such remission is granted to us?**
As the words of Jesus Christ used declare: because our sins are debts, making us liable to eternal death, we pray that God will pardon us out of His sheer kindness.

283. **You mean, them, that it is by the gratuitous goodness of God that we obtain remission of sins?**
Yes, for we can offer no satisfaction for the smallest sin we commit, if God does no exercise His sheer kindness toward us in forgiving us them all.

284. **What gain and profit do we receive, when God pardons our sins?**
We are acceptable to Him, just as if we were righteous and innocent, and our consciences are assured of His paternal love, from which comes salvation and life.

285. **When you pray that He may forgive us as we forgive our debtors, do you mean that in pardoning men we merit pardon from God?**
By no means, for then pardon would not be by grace, and would not be founded, as it ought to be, on the satisfaction which Jesus Christ made for us in His death. But since by forgetting the injuries done to ourselves, we follow His gentleness and clemency, and so demonstrate that we are His children, God has given us this as a sign in confirmation that we are His children. On the other hand, He indicates to us that we cannot expect anything at His judgment but utter severity and extreme rigour, if we are not ready to pardon and show mercy to others who are guilty toward us.

286. **Do you think, then, God refuses to have as His children those who cannot forget the offenses committed against them, so that they cannot hope to be partakers of His grace?**

Yes. And He intends that all men may know that with what measure they mete to their neighbours, it shall be measured to them.

287. **What follows?**

"Lead us not into temptation, but deliver us from evil."

288. **Do you treat this as one petition?**

Yes, for the second part is an explanation of the first part.

289. **What is the substance of it?**

That God does not allow us to fall to evil, or permit us to be overcome by the devil, and the lustful desires of our flesh, which strive against us (Romans 7:23), but He gives us strength to resist, sustains us by His hand, takes us into His safe keeping, to defend and lead us.

290. **How is this done?**

When He governs us by His Spirit, to make us love the good, and hate the evil, follow justice, and flee from sin. By the power of His Spirit, we may overcome the devil, sin and the flesh.

291. **Do we stand in need of this?**

Yes, for the devil continually watches for us, like a roaring lion ready to devour us. (1 Peter 5:8) We are so feeble and frail that he would immediately overcome us, if God did not fortify us, that we might be victorious over him.

292. **What does the word "temptation" signify?**

The wiles and assaults of the devil, which he uses to attack us, seeing that our natural judgment is prone to be deceived and to deceive us, and our will is always ready to addict itself to evil rather than to good.

293. **But why do you pray God not to lead you into evil, when this is the proper office of Satan the devil?**

As God by His mercy preserves the faithful, and does not permit the devil to seduce them, or sin to overcome them, so those whom He means to punish He not only abandons, and deprives of His grace, but also yields to the devil to be subjected to his tyranny, blinds them and delivers them over to a reprobate mind.

294. **What is intended by the addition, "For thine is the kingdom, and the power, and the glory, for ever"?**

To remind us again that our prayers are altogether grounded on the power and goodness of God, and not on ourselves, for we are not worthy to open our mouth in prayer; and also that we may learn to close our prayers in His praise.

295. **Is it lawful to ask anything else, not mentioned here?**

Although we are free to use other words, and another form and manner, yet not prayer will ever please God which does not correspond to this as the only rule of right prayer.

296. **It is time to come to the fourth part of worship we are to render to God.**

We said that this consists in acknowledging with the heart and confirming with the mouth that God is the author of all good, that thereby we may glorify Him.

297. **Has He given us any rule for this?**

All the praises and thanksgivings contained in Scripture ought to be our rule and guide.

298. **Is there nothing regarding this in the Lord's Prayer?**

Yes there is, for when we pray that His name may be hallowed, we pray that He may be glorified in all His works, as indeed He is—that He may be praised for His justice when He punishes, for His mercy when He pardons, and for His faithfulness when He fulfills His promises; in short, that there is nothing in which His glory does not shine forth. This is to ascribe to Him the praise for all blessing.

299. **What shall we infer from all that we have said?**
What truth itself tells us, and was stated at the outset, viz. that this is eternal life: to know one true God the Father, and Jesus Christ whom He has sent (John 17:3)—to know Him, I say, in order that we may worship Him aright, that He may be not only our Master, but also our Father and Saviour, and we be in turn His children and servants, and a people dedicated to His glory.

300. **How can we attain to such a blessedness?**
For this end God has left us His holy Word, which is, as it were, an entry into His heavenly Kingdom.

301. **Where do you find this Word?**
It is comprised for us in the Holy Scriptures.

302. **How are we to use it in order to profit by it?**
By receiving it with the full consent of our conscience, as truth come down from heaven, submitting ourselves to it in right obedience, loving it with a true affection by having it imprinted in our hearts, we may follow it entirely and conform ourselves to it.

303. **Is all this within our own power?**
None of it; but God works them in us in this way by His Holy Spirit.

304. **But are we not to take trouble and be diligent, and zealously strive by hearing and reading its teaching, as it is declared to us?**
Yes, indeed: first, each one of us in particular ought to study it: and above all, we are frequently to attend the sermons in which this Word is expounded in the assembly of the Christians.

305. **Do you mean that it is not enough for people to read it privately at home, without altogether hearing its teaching in common?**
That is just what I mean, while God provides the way for it.

306. **Why do you say that?**
Because Jesus Christ has established this order in His Church (Ephesians 4:11), and He has declared this to be the only means of edifying and preserving it. Thus we must keep ourselves to it and not be wiser than our Master.

307. **Is it necessary, then, that there should be pastors?**
Yes; and that we should hear them, receiving the teaching of the Lord in humility by their mouth. Therefore whoever despises them and refuses to hear them, rejects Jesus Christ, and separates himself from the fellowship of the faithful. (Matthew 10:40; Luke 10:16)

308. **But is it enough to have been instructed by them once, or ought he to continue to do this?**
It is little to have begun, unless you go on to persevere. We must continue to be disciples of Christ right to the end. But He has ordained the ministers of the Church to teach in His Name.

309. **Is there no other means than the Word by which God communicates Himself to us?**
To the preaching of His Word He has conjoined the Sacraments.

310. **What is a Sacrament?**
An outward attestation of the grace of God which, by a visible sign, represents spiritual things to imprint the promises of God more firmly in our hearts, and to make us more sure of them.

311. **What? Does a visible and natural sign have this power to assure the conscience?**
No, not of itself, but in so far as it is ordained of God for this end.

312. **Seeing it is the proper office of the Holy Spirit to seal the promises of God in our hearts, how do you attribute this to the Sacraments?**
There is a great difference between the one and the other. The Spirit of God in very truth is the only One who can touch and move our hearts, enlighten our minds, and assure our consciences; so that all this ought to be judged as His own work, that praise may be ascribed to Him alone. Nevertheless, the

Lord Himself makes use of the Sacraments as inferior instruments according as it seems good to Him, without in any way detracting from the power of the Holy Spirit.

313. **You think, then, that the efficacy of the Sacraments does not consist in the outward element, but proceeds entirely from the Spirit of God?**
Yes; for the Lord is pleased to work by these instruments which He has instituted: without detracting from His own power.

314. **And what moves God to do that?**
For the alleviation of our weaknesses. If we were spiritual by nature, like the angels, we could behold God and His graces. But as we are bound up with our bodies, it is needful for us that God should make use of figures to represent to us spiritual and heavenly things, for otherwise we could not comprehend them. At the same time, it is expedient for us to have all our senses exercised in His Holy promises, in order to confirm us in them.

315. **Since God has introduced the Sacraments to meet our need, it would be arrogance and presumption to think that we could dispense with them.**
Certainly: hence he who voluntarily abstains from using them thinks that he has no need of them, condemns Jesus Christ, rejects His grace, and quenches His Holy Spirit.

316. **But what assurance of grace can the Sacraments give, seeing that good and bad both receive them?**
Although the unbelievers and the wicked make of non-effect the grace offered them through the Sacraments, yet it does not follow that the proper nature of the Sacraments is also made of non-effect.

317. **How, then, and when do the Sacraments produce this effect?**
When we receive them in faith, seeking Jesus Christ alone and His grace in them.

318. **Why do you say that we must seek Jesus Christ in them?**
I mean that we are not to be taken up with the earthly sign so as to seek our salvation in it, nor are we to imagine that it has a peculiar power enclosed

within it. On the contrary, we are to employ the sign as a help, to lead us directly to the Lord Jesus, that we may find in Him our salvation and all our well-being.

319. **Seeing that faith is required, why do you say that they are given to confirm us in faith, to assure us of the promises of God?**
It is not sufficient for faith once to be generated in us. It must be nourished and sustained, that it may grow day by day and be increased within us. To nourish, strengthen, and increase it, God gives us the Sacraments. This is what Paul indicates when he says that they are used to seal the promises of God in our hearts. (Romans 4:11)

320. **But is it not a sign of unbelief when the promises of God are not firm enough for us, without support?**
It is a sign of the smallness and weakness of faith, and such is indeed the faith of the children of God, who do not, however, cease to be faithful, although their faith is still imperfect. As long as we live in this world some elements of unfaithfulness remain in our flesh, and therefore we must always advance and grow in faith.

321. **How many Sacraments are there in the Christian Church?**
There are only two Sacraments common to all which the Lord Jesus has instituted for the whole company of the faithful.

322. **What are they?**
Baptism and the Holy Supper.

323. **What likeness and difference is there between them?**
Baptism is for us a kind of entrance into the Church of God, for it testifies that instead of our being strangers to Him, God receives us as members of His family. The Supper testifies that God as a good Father carefully feeds and refreshes the members of His household.

324. **That the meaning may be more clear to us, let us treat of them separately. First, what is the meaning of Baptism?**

It consists of two parts. The Lord represents to us in it, first, the forgiveness of our sins (Ephesians 5:26-27) and, secondly, our regeneration or spiritual renewal. (Romans 6:4)

325. **What resemblance has water with these things in order to represent them?**

The forgiveness of sins is a kind of washing, by which our souls are cleansed from their defilements, just as the stains of the body are washed away by water.

326. **What about the other part?**

The beginning of our regeneration and its end is our becoming new creatures, through the Spirit of God. Therefore the water is poured on the head as a sign of death, but in such a way that our resurrection is also represented, for instead of being drowned in water, what happens to us is only for a moment.

327. **You do not mean that the water is a washing of the soul.**

By no means, for that pertains to the blood of Christ alone, which was shed in order to wipe away all our stains and render us pure and unpolluted before God. (1 John 1:7; 1 Peter 1:19) This is fulfilled in us when our consciences are sprinkled by the Holy Spirit. But by the Sacrament that is sealed to us.

328. **Do you think that the water is only a figure to us?**

It is such a figure that the reality is conjoined with it, for God does not promise us anything in vain. Accordingly it is certain that in Baptism the forgiveness of sins is offered to us and we receive it.

329. **Is this grace fulfilled indiscriminately in all?**

No, for some make it of no effect by their perversity. Nevertheless, the Sacrament loses nothing of its nature, although none but believers feel its efficacy.

330. **From what does regeneration get its power?**

From the death and resurrection of Christ. His death has had this effect, that through it our old Adam is crucified, and our evil nature is, as it were, buried, so that it no longer has the strength to rule over us. And the renewal of our life, in obedience to the righteousness of God, derives from the resurrection of Christ.

331. **How is this grace applied to us in Baptism?**
In it we are clothed with Jesus Christ, and receive His Spirit, provided that we do not make ourselves unworthy of the promises given to us in it.

332. **What is the proper use of Baptism on our part?**
It consists in faith and in repentance. That is, assurance that we have our spiritual purity in Christ, and in feeling within us, and declaring to our neighbours by our works, that His Spirit dwells in us to mortify our natural desires and bring us to follow the Will of God.

333. **If this is required, how is it that we baptize infants?**
It is not said that faith and repentance should always precede the reception of the Sacrament, but they are only required from those who are capable of them. It is sufficient, then, if infants produce and manifest the fruit of their Baptism after they come to the age of discretion.

334. **Can you show that there is nothing inconsistent in this?**
Circumcision was also a Sacrament of repentance, as Moses and the prophets declare (Deuteronomy 10:16, 30:6; Jeremiah 4:4); and was a Sacrament of faith, as St. Paul says (Romans 4:11-12). And yet God has not excluded little children from it.

335. **But can you show that they are now admitted to Baptism for the same reason as in the case of circumcision?**
Yes, for the promises which God anciently gave to His people of Israel are now extended to the whole world.

336. **But does it follow from this that we are to use the sign also?**
That becomes evident when everything is considered. Jesus Christ has not made us partakers of His grace, which formerly had been bestowed on the people of Israel, in order to diminish it in us, or make it more obscure, but rather to manifest it and to bestow it upon us in increased abundance.

337. **Do you reckon that if we denied Baptism to little infants, the grace of God would then be diminished by the coming of Christ?**
Yes; for the sign of the bounty and mercy of God toward our children, which they had in ancient times, would be wanting in our case, the very sign which ministers so greatly to our consolation, and to confirm the promise already given in the Command.

338. **You mean then that since God in ancient times declared Himself to be the Saviour of little infants, and wanted to have this promise sealed on their bodies by an external Sacrament, it is right that confirmation of it should not be less after the advent of Christ, since the same promise remains and indeed is more clearly attested by the Word and ratified in action.**
Yes. And besides, since it is quite evident that the power and the substance of Baptism pertain to little children, to deny them the sign, which is inferior to the substance, would be to do them injury.

339. **On what conditions should we baptize little children?**
As a sign and testimony that they are heirs of God's blessing promised to the seed of the faithful, that when they come of age they are to acknowledge the truth of their Baptism, in order to derive benefit from it.

340. **Let us speak of the Supper. And, first, what is its signification?**
Our Lord instituted it to assure us that by the communication of His body and blood, our souls are nourished, in the hope of eternal life.

341. **But why does the Lord represent His body by the bread and His blood by the wine?**
To signify that as it is the particular virtue of bread to nourish our bodies, to refresh and sustain us in this mortal life, so it pertains to His body to act toward our souls, i.e., in nourishing and quickening them spiritually, so His blood is our joy, our refreshing and our spiritual strength.

342. **Do you mean that we must truly communicate in the body and blood of the Lord?**

I understand so. But since the whole affiance of our salvation rests in the obedience which He has rendered to God, His Father, in order that it may be imputed to us as if it were ours, we must possess Him: for His blessings are not ours, unless He gives Himself to us first.

343. **But did He not give Himself to us when He exposed Himself to death, to reconcile us to God His Father, and deliver us from damnation?**

That is true; but it is not enough for us unless we receive Him, in order that we may feel in ourselves the fruit and the efficacy of His death and passion.

344. **Is not the way to receive Him by faith?**

Yes. Not only in believing that He died and rose again, in order to deliver us from eternal death, and acquire life for us, but also that He dwells in us, and conjoined with us in a union as the Head with the members, that by virtue of this conjunction He may make us partakers of all His grace.

345. **Does this communion take place apart from the Supper alone?**

Yes, indeed, we have it through the Gospel, as St. Paul declares (1 Corinthians 1:9): in that the Lord Jesus Christ promises us in it, that we are flesh of His flesh and bone of His bone (Ephesians 5:30), that He is that living bread which came down from heaven to nourish our souls (John 6:51), and that we are one with Him, as He is one with the Father. (John 17:21)

346. **What is the blessing that we have in the Sacrament, and what more does it minister to us?**

This communion is more abundantly confirmed in us, ratified as it were, for although Jesus Christ is truly communicated to us both by Baptism and by the Gospel, nevertheless this only in part, and not fully.

347. **What then fully do we have through the sign of the bread?**

That the body of the Lord Jesus which was once offered to reconcile us to God, is now given to us, to certify to us that we have part in this reconciliation.

348. **What do we have in the sign of the wine?**
That the Lord Jesus, who once shed His blood in payment and satisfaction for our offences, gives it to us to drink, that we may have no doubt at all of receiving its fruit.

349. **According to your replies, the Supper takes us back to the death and passion of Jesus Christ, that we may communicate in its virtue?**
Yes, for then the unique and perpetual sacrifice was offered for our redemption. Therefore there remains for us nought but to enjoy it.

350. **The Supper, then, was not instituted in order to offer up the body of Jesus the Son to the Father?**
No, for this office pertains to none but Him alone, since He is the eternal Priest. (Hebrews 5:5) But He commands us only to receive His body, not to offer it. (Matthew 26:26)

351. **Why is there a double sign?**
Our Lord has appointed it for the sake of our weakness, in order to teach us that He is not only food to our souls, but drink also, so that we may seek our nourishment wholly and entirely in Him, and not elsewhere.

352. **Should all men equally use the second sign, that is, the chalice?**
Yes, this is according to the commandment of Jesus Christ, against which nothing is to be attempted.

353. **Do we have in the Supper simply the testimony of the things already mentioned, or are they truly given to us in it?**
See that Jesus Christ is the Truth, there can be no doubt that the promises which He made at the Supper, are actually fulfilled in it, and that what He figures in it is made true. Thus in accordance with what He promises and represents in the Sacrament, I do not doubt that He makes us partakers of His very substance, in order to unite us with Himself in one life.

354. **But how can this be, when the body of Jesus Christ is in heaven, and we are pilgrims on this earth?**
By the incomprehensible power of His Spirit, who conjoins things separated by distance.

355. **You do not think, then, either that the body is enclosed in the bread, or the blood in the chalice?**
No. On the contrary, in order to have the reality of the Sacraments, we must lift up our hearts on high to heaven, where Jesus Christ is in the glory of His Father, from whence we expect Him in our redemption, and do not seek Him in these corruptible elements.

356. **You understand, then, that there are two things in this Sacrament, material bread and wine, which we see by the eye, handle by the hands, and perceive by the taste, and Jesus Christ by whom our souls are inwardly nourished?**
Yes, but in such a way that we have in it also a testimony and a kind of pledge for the resurrection of our bodies, in that they are made partakers in the sign of life.

357. **What is the right use of this Sacrament?**
That which St. Paul declares, namely that a man examine himself before he approach to it. (1 Corinthians 11:28)

358. **In what is he to examine himself?**
Whether he is a true member of Jesus Christ.

359. **By what sign can he know this?**
If he has a true faith and repentance, if he loves his neighbour in true charity, and is not tainted by hatred or rancour or discord.

360. **But is it necessary to have perfect faith and charity?**
Both should be entire and unfeigned, but to have such a perfection, from which nothing is wanting, will not be found among men. Moreover the Supper would have been instituted in vain if no one could receive it unless he were entirely perfect.

361. **Imperfection, then, does not prevent us from approaching it.**
On the contrary, the Supper would be of no use to us, if we were not imperfect. It is an aid and support for our weakness.

362. **Do these two Sacraments not serve another end?**
Yes, they do. They are also signs and marks of our profession. That is to say, by them we declare that we are of the people of God, and make confession of our Christianity.

363. **How ought we to judge a man who never wishes to use it?**
He could not be regarded as a Christian, for in so doing he refuses to confess himself as such, and tacitly, as it were, disavows Jesus Christ.

364. **Is it sufficient to receive each once?**
Baptism is only ordered to be received once, and may not lawfully be repeated. But this is not so with the Supper.

365. **What is the reason for that?**
By Baptism God introduces and receives us into His Church. After He has received us, He signifies by the Supper that He wishes continually to nourish us.

366. **To whom does it belong truly to baptize and administer the Supper?**
To those who are publicly charged to teach in the Church. For the preaching of the Word and the distribution of the Sacraments are things conjoined.

367. **Is there any certain proof for this?**
Yes, indeed. Our Lord specially charged His Apostles to baptize as well as to preach. (Matthew 28:19) In regard to the Supper He ordered all to follow His example. Moreover He performed the office of a minister in order to give it to others.

368. **But ought pastors, who are appointed to dispense the Sacraments, to admit without discretion all who present themselves there?**
In regard to Baptism, as it is administered today only to infants, there is no need for discrimination; but in the Supper the minister ought to take heed not to give it to a man whom he recognizes to be entirely unworthy.

369. **Why so?**
Because it would pollute and dishonour the Sacrament.

370. **But our Lord admitted Judas to the Supper, impious though he was?**
His iniquity was still hidden, and although our Lord knew it, yet it was not evident to all.

371. **What then is to be done with hypocrites?**
The minister cannot exclude them as unworthy, but must wait until God has revealed their iniquity.

372. **But what if he knows or has been warned that someone is unworthy?**
That would not be sufficient to exclude him, unless there were a legitimate investigation and decision of the Church.

373. **Then there ought to be some order and polity regarding this.**
Yes, if the Church is to be well ordered. Some persons must be appointed to watch out for the offences that may be committed. And they, with the authority of the Church, should refuse communion to those who are quite unfit, and to whom communion cannot be given without dishonouring God and scandalizing the faithful. ▪

Heidelberg Catechism

In the mid-16th century, Elector Frederick III was in control of the most powerful electorate (province) in the German Empire, called the Palatinate. By the grace of God, Frederick was also a faithful Reformed Christian. In 1562 he commissioned Heidelberg University to write a catechism that would systematically train Christian youth and give pastors and teachers a structure from which to teach. Traditionally it is believed that Zacharius Ursinus, a professor at Heidelberg, and Caspar Olevianus, Frederick's court preacher, did most of the writing, but the catechism was rightly credited as being a collective effort of the theology faculty at Heidelberg University.

The framers had the first edition ready by the end of 1562. Its preface was written by Elector Frederick III himself. In early 1563 the Heidelberg Catechism was approved by a Synod in Heidelberg and published in German. From the very beginning the catechism included Scripture references to show that it was founded on Scripture alone. The first edition of the catechism consisted of 128 questions, but at the Elector's request new sentences were added to the second and third editions, and eventually a new eightieth question was added which condemned the Roman Catholic mass. In its first year, the Heidelberg Catechism went through four editions and was translated into Latin. The Latin edition divided the questions among the fifty-two Lord's Days in a year, so that ministers could use the catechism to teach their congregations week by week. Some ministers began using the Heidelberg Catechism as the basis of their Sunday afternoon sermons.

The Heidelberg Catechism, the Canons of Dort, and the Belgic Confession together became known as the Three Forms of Unity, the defining confessions of the Continental Reformed Church.

LORD'S DAY 1

1. **What is your only comfort in life and death?**

That I am not my own, (1) but belong with body and soul, both in life and in death, (2) to my faithful Saviour Jesus Christ. (3) He has fully paid for all my sins with His precious blood, (4) and has set me free from all the power of the devil. (5) He also preserves me in such a way (6) that without the will of my heavenly Father not a hair can fall from my head; (7) indeed, all things must work together for my salvation. (8) Therefore, by His Holy Spirit He also assures me of eternal life (9) and makes me heartily willing and ready from now on to live for Him. (10)

(1) *I Cor. 6:19, 20* (2) *Rom. 14:7-9.* (3) *I Cor. 3:23; Tit. 2:14.* (4) *I Pet. 1:18, 19; I John 1:7; 2:2.* (5) *John 8:34-36; Heb. 2:14, 15; I John 3:8.* (6) *John 6:39, 40; 10:27-30; II Thess. 3:3; I Pet. 1:5.* (7) *Matt. 10:29-31; Luke 21:16-18.* (8) *Rom. 8:28.* (9) *Rom. 8:15, 16; II Cor. 1:21, 22; 5:5; Eph. 1:13, 14.* (10) *Rom. 8:14.*

2. **What do you need to know in order to live and die in the joy of this comfort?**

First, how great my sins and misery are; (1) second, how I am delivered from all my sins and misery; (2) third, how I am to be thankful to God for such deliverance. (3)

(1) *Rom. 3:9, 10; I John 1:10.* (2) *John 17:3; Acts 4:12; 10:43.* (3) *Matt. 5:16; Rom. 6:13; Eph. 5:8-10; I Pet. 2:9, 10.*

PART I: HUMAN MISERY

LORD'S DAY 2

3. **From where do you know your sins and misery?**

From the law of God. (1)

(1) *Rom. 3:20.*

4. **What does God's law require of us?**

Christ teaches us this in a summary in Matthew 22: You shall love the LORD your God with all your heart, and with all your soul, and with all your mind.[1] This is the great and first commandment. And a second is like it, You shall love your neighbour as yourself. On these two commandments depend all the law and the prophets.[2]

[1] *Deut. 6:5.* [2] *Lev. 19:18.*

5. **Can you keep all this perfectly?**

No,[1] I am inclined by nature to hate God and my neighbour.[2]

[1] *Rom. 3:10, 23; I John 1:8, 10.* [2] *Gen. 6:5; 8:21; Jer. 17:9; Rom. 7:23; 8:7; Eph. 2:3; Tit. 3:3.*

LORD'S DAY 3

6. **Did God, then, create man so wicked and perverse?**

No, on the contrary, God created man good[1] and in His image,[2] that is, in true righteousness and holiness,[3] so that he might rightly know God His Creator,[4] heartily love Him, and live with Him in eternal blessedness to praise and glorify Him.[5]

[1] *Gen. 1:31.* [2] *Gen. 1:26, 27.* [3] *Eph. 4:24.* [4] *Col. 3:10.* [5] *Ps. 8.*

7. **From where, then, did man's depraved nature come?**

From the fall and disobedience of our first parents, Adam and Eve, in Paradise,[1] for there our nature became so corrupt[2] that we are all conceived and born in sin.[3]

[1] *Gen. 3.* [2] *Rom. 5:12, 18, 19.* [3] *Ps. 51:5.*

8. **But are we so corrupt that we are totally unable to do any good and inclined to all evil?**

Yes,[1] unless we are regenerated by the Spirit of God.[2]

[1] *Gen. 6:5; 8:21; Job 14:4; Is. 53:6.* [2] *John 3:3-5.*

LORD'S DAY 4

9. **Is God, then, not unjust by requiring in His law what man cannot do?**
No, for God so created man that he was able to do it. [(1)] But man, at the instigation of the devil, [(2)] in deliberate disobedience [(3)] robbed himself and all his descendants of these gifts. [(4)]

[(1)] *Gen. 1:31.* [(2)] *Gen. 3:13; John 8:44; I Tim. 2:13, 14.* [(3)] *Gen. 3:6.* [(4)] *Rom. 5:12, 18, 19.*

10. **Will God allow such disobedience and apostasy to go unpunished?**
Certainly not. He is terribly displeased with our original sin as well as our actual sins. Therefore He will punish them by a just judgment both now and eternally, [(1)] as He has declared: [(2)] Cursed be every one who does not abide by all things written in the book of the law, and do them (Galatians 3:10).

[(1)] *Ex. 34:7; Ps. 5:4-6; 7:10; Nah. 1:2; Rom. 1:18; 5:12; Eph. 5:6; Heb. 9:27.* [(2)] *Deut. 27:26.*

11. **But is God not also merciful?**
God is indeed merciful, [(1)] but He is also just. [(2)] His justice requires that sin committed against the most high majesty of God also be punished with the most severe, that is, with everlasting, punishment of body and soul. [(3)]

[(1)] *Ex. 20:6; 34:6, 7; Ps. 103:8, 9.* [(2)] *Ex. 20:5; 34:7; Deut. 7:9-11; Ps. 5:4-6; Heb. 10:30, 31.* [(3)] *Matt. 25:45,46.*

PART II: DELIVERANCE

LORD'S DAY 5

12. **Since, according to God's righteous judgment we deserve temporal and eternal punishment, how can we escape this punishment and be again received into favour?**
God demands that His justice be satisfied. [(1)] Therefore full payment must be made either by ourselves or by another. [(2)]

[(1)] *Ex. 20:5; 23:7; Rom. 2:1-11.* [(2)] *Is. 53:11; Rom. 8:3, 4.*

13. Can we ourselves make this payment?

Certainly not. On the contrary, we daily increase our debt. (1)

(1) *Ps. 130:3; Matt. 6:12; Rom. 2:4, 5.*

14. Can any mere creature pay for us?

No. In the first place, God will not punish another creature for the sin which man has committed. (1) Furthermore, no mere creature can sustain the burden of God's eternal wrath against sin and deliver others from it. (2)

(1) *Ezek. 18:4, 20; Heb. 2:14-18.* (2) *Ps. 130:3; Nah. 1:6.*

15. What kind of mediator and deliverer must we seek?

One who is a true (1) and righteous (2) man, and yet more powerful than all creatures; that is, one who is at the same time true God. (3)

(1) *I Cor. 15:21; Heb. 2:17.* (2) *Is. 53:9; II Cor. 5:21; Heb. 7:26.*

(3) *Is. 7:14; 9:6; Jer. 23:6; John 1:1; Rom. 8:3, 4.*

LORD'S DAY 6

16. Why must He be a true and righteous man?

He must be a true man because the justice of God requires that the same human nature which has sinned should pay for sin. (1) He must be a righteous man because one who himself is a sinner cannot pay for others. (2)

(1) *Rom: 5:12, 15; I Cor. 15:21; Heb. 2:14-16.*

(2) *Heb. 7:26, 27; I Pet. 3:18.*

17. Why must He at the same time be true God?

He must be true God so that by the power of His divine nature (1) He might bear in His human nature the burden of God's wrath, (2) and might obtain for us and restore to us righteousness and life. (3)

(1) *Is. 9:5.* (2) *Deut. 4:24; Nah. 1:6; Ps. 130:3.*

(3) *Is. 53:5, 11; John 3:16; II Cor. 5:21.*

18. **But who is that Mediator who at the same time is true God and a true and righteous man?**
Our Lord Jesus Christ, (1) whom God made our wisdom, our righteousness and sanctification and redemption (I Corinthians 1:30).
(1) *Matt. 1:21-23; Luke 2:11; I Tim. 2:5; 3:16.*

19. **From where do you know this?**
From the holy gospel, which God Himself first revealed in Paradise. (1) Later, He had it proclaimed by the patriarchs (2) and prophets, (3) and foreshadowed by the sacrifices and other ceremonies of the law. (4) Finally, He had it fulfilled through His only Son. (5)
(1) *Gen. 3:15.* (2) *Gen. 12:3; 22:18; 49:10.* (3) *Is. 53; Jer. 23:5, 6; Mic. 7:18-20; Acts 10:43; Heb. 1:1.* (4) *Lev. 1:7; John 5:46; Heb. 10:1-10.* (5) *Rom. 10:4; Gal. 4:4, 5; Col. 2:17.*

LORD'S DAY 7

20. **Are all men, then, saved by Christ just as they perished through Adam?**
No. Only those are saved who by a true faith are grafted into Christ and accept all His benefits. (1)
(1) *Matt. 7:14; John 1:12; 3:16, 18, 36; Rom. 11:16-21.*

21. **What is true faith?**
True faith is a sure knowledge whereby I accept as true all that God has revealed to us in His Word. (1) At the same time it is a firm confidence (2) that not only to others, but also to me, (3) God has granted forgiveness of sins, everlasting righteousness, and salvation, (4) out of mere grace, only for the sake of Christ's merits. (5) This faith the Holy Spirit works in my heart by the gospel. (6)
(1) *John 17:3, 17; Heb. 11:1-3; James 2:19.*
(2) *Rom. 4:18-21; 5:1; 10:10; Heb. 4:16.* (3) *Gal. 2:20.*
(4) *Rom. 1:17; Heb. 10:10.* (5) *Rom.3:20-26; Gal. 2:16; Eph. 2:8-10.*
(6) *Acts 16:14; Rom. 1:16; 10:17; I Cor. 1:21.*

22. What, then, must a Christian believe?

All that is promised us in the gospel, (1) which the articles of our catholic and undoubted Christian faith teach us in a summary.

(1) *Matt. 28:19; John 20:30, 31.*

23. What are these articles?

I believe in God the Father almighty, Creator of heaven and earth. I believe in Jesus Christ, His only begotten Son, our Lord; He was conceived by the Holy Spirit, born of the virgin Mary; suffered under Pontius Pilate, was crucified, dead, and buried; He descended into hell; On the third day He arose from the dead; He ascended into heaven, and sits at the right hand of God the Father almighty; from there He will come to judge the living and the dead. I believe in the Holy Spirit; I believe a holy catholic Christian church, the communion of saints; the forgiveness of sins; the resurrection of the body; and the life everlasting.[1]

LORD'S DAY 24

24. How are these articles divided?

Into three parts: the first is about God the Father and our creation; the second about God the Son and our redemption; the third about God the Holy Spirit and our sanctification.

25. Since there is only one God, (1) why do you speak of three persons, Father, Son, and Holy Spirit?

Because God has so revealed Himself in His Word (2) that these three distinct persons are the one, true, eternal God.

(1) *Deut. 6:4; Is. 44:6; 45:5; I Cor. 8:4, 6.* (2) *Gen. 1:2, 3; Is. 61:1; 63:8-10; Matt. 3:16, 17; 28:18, 19; Luke 4:18; John 14:26; 15:26; II Cor. 13:14; Gal. 4:6; Tit. 3:5, 6.*

---

1 Essentially the Apostles' Creed (see page 12).

LORD'S DAY 9

26. **What do you believe when you say: I believe in God the Father almighty, Creator of heaven and earth?**
That the eternal Father of our Lord Jesus Christ, who out of nothing created heaven and earth and all that is in them, (1) and who still upholds and governs them by His eternal counsel and providence, (2) is, for the sake of Christ His Son, my God and my Father. (3) In Him I trust so completely as to have no doubt that He will provide me with all things necessary for body and soul, (4) and will also turn to my good whatever adversity He sends me in this life of sorrow. (5) He is able to do so as almighty God, (6) and willing also as a faithful Father. (7)

(1) *Gen. 1 and 2; Ex. 20:11; Job 38 and 39; Ps. 33:6; Is. 44:24; Acts 4:24; 14:15.* (2) *Ps. 104:27-30; Matt. 6:30; 10:29; Eph. 1:11.* (3) *John 1:12, 13; Rom. 8:15, 16; Gal. 4:4-7; Eph. 1:5.* (4) *Ps. 55:22; Matt. 6:25, 26; Luke 12:22-31.* (5) *Rom. 8:28.* (6) *Gen. 18:14; Rom. 8:31-39.* (7) *Matt. 6:32, 33; 7:9-11.*

LORD'S DAY 10

27. **What do you understand by the providence of God?**
God's providence is His almighty and ever present power, (1) whereby, as with His hand, He still upholds heaven and earth and all creatures, (2) and so governs them that leaf and blade, rain and drought, fruitful and barren years, food and drink, health and sickness, riches and poverty, (3) indeed, all things, come not by chance (4) but by His fatherly hand. (5)

(1) *Jer. 23:23, 24; Acts 17:24-28.* (2) *Heb. 1:3.* (3) *Jer. 5:24; Acts 14:15-17; John 9:3; Prov. 22:2.* (4) *Prov. 16:33.* (5) *Matt. 10:29.*

28. **What does it benefit us to know that God has created all things and still upholds them by His providence?**
We can be patient in adversity, (1) thankful in prosperity, (2) and with a view to the future we can have a firm confidence in our faithful God and Father

that no creature shall separate us from His love; [3] for all creatures are so completely in His hand that without His will they cannot so much as move. [4]

[1] *Job. 1:21, 22; Ps. 39:10; James 1:3.* [2] *Deut. 8:10; I Thess. 5:18.* [3] *Ps. 55:22; Rom. 5:3-5; 8:38, 39.* [4] *Job 1:12; 2:6; Prov. 21:1; Acts 17:24-28.*

LORD'S DAY 11

29. **Why is the Son of God called Jesus, that is, Saviour?**
Because He saves us from all our sins, [1] and because salvation is not to be sought or found in anyone else. [2]

[1] *Matt. 1:21; Heb. 7:25.* [2] *Is. 43:11; John 15:4, 5; Acts 4:11, 12; I Tim. 2:5.*

30. **Do those believe in the only Saviour Jesus who seek their salvation and well-being from saints, in themselves, or anywhere else?**
No. Though they boast of Him in words, they in fact deny the only Saviour Jesus. [1] For one of two things must be true: either Jesus is not a complete Saviour, or those who by true faith accept this Saviour must find in Him all that is necessary for their salvation. [2]

[1] *I Cor. 1:12, 13; Gal. 5:4.* [2] *Col. 1:19, 20; 2:10; I John 1:7.*

LORD'S DAY 12

31. **Why is He called Christ, that is, Anointed?**
Because He has been ordained by God the Father, and anointed with the Holy Spirit, [1] to be our chief Prophet and Teacher, [2] who has fully revealed to us the secret counsel and will of God concerning our redemption; [3] our only High Priest, [4] who by the one sacrifice of His body has redeemed us, [5] and who continually intercedes for us before the Father; [6] and our eternal King, [7]

who governs us by His Word and Spirit, and who defends and preserves us in the redemption obtained for us. [8]

[1] *Ps. 45:7 (Heb. 1:9); Is. 61:1 (Luke 4:18; Luke 3:21, 22).*
[2] *Deut. 18:15 (Acts 3:22).* [3] *John 1:18; 15:15.* [4] *Ps. 110:4 (Heb. 7:17).* [5] *Heb. 9:12; 10:11-14.* [6] *Rom. 8:34; Heb. 9:24; I John 2:1.* [7] *Zach. 9:9 (Matt. 21:5); Luke 1:33.*
[8] *Matt. 28:18-20; John 10:28; Rev. 12:10, 11.*

32. **Why are you called a Christian?**
Because I am a member of Christ by faith [1] and thus share in His anointing, [2] so that I may as prophet confess His Name, [3] as priest present myself a living sacrifice of thankfulness to Him, [4] and as king fight with a free and good conscience against sin and the devil in this life, [5] and hereafter reign with Him eternally over all creatures. [6]

[1] *I Cor. 12:12-27.* [2] *Joel 2:28 (Acts 2:17); I John 2:27.*
[3] *Matt. 10:32; Rom 10:9, 10; Heb. 13:15.* [4] *Rom. 12:1; I Pet. 2:5, 9.* [5] *Gal. 5:16, 17; Eph. 6:11; I Tim. 1:18, 19.*
[6] *Matt. 25:34; II Tim. 2:12.*

LORD'S DAY 33

33. **Why is He called God's only begotten Son, since we also are children of God?**
Because Christ alone is the eternal, natural Son of God. [1] We, however, are children of God by adoption, through grace, for Christ's sake. [2]

[1] *John 1:1-3, 14, 18; 3:16; Rom. 8:32; Heb. 1; I John 4:9.*
[2] *John 1:12; Rom. 8:14-17; Gal. 4:6; Eph. 1:5, 6.*

34. **Why do you call Him our Lord?**
Because He has ransomed us, body and soul, [1] from all our sins, not with silver or gold but with His precious blood, [2] and has freed us from all the power of the devil to make us His own possession. [3]

[1] *I Cor. 6:20; I Tim. 2:5, 6.* [2] *I Peter 1:18, 19.*
[3] *Col. 1:13, 14; Heb. 2:14, 15.*

LORD'S DAY 14

35. **What do you confess when you say: He was conceived by the Holy Spirit, born of the virgin Mary?**
The eternal Son of God, who is and remains true and eternal God, (1) took upon Himself true human nature from the flesh and blood of the virgin Mary, (2) through the working of the Holy Spirit. (3) Thus He is also the true seed of David, (4) and like His brothers in every respect, (5) yet without sin. (6)

(1) *John 1:1; 10:30-36; Rom. 1:3; 9:5; Col. 1:15-17; I John 5:20.*
(2) *Matt. 1:18-23; John 1:14; Gal. 4:4; Heb. 2:14.* (3) *Luke 1:35.*
(4) *II Sam. 7:12-16; Ps. 132:11; Matt. 1:1; Luke 1:32; Rom. 1:3.*
(5) *Phil. 2:7; Heb. 2:17.* (6) *Heb. 4:15; 7:26, 27.*

36. **What benefit do you receive from the holy conception and birth of Christ?**
He is our Mediator, (1) and with His innocence and perfect holiness covers, in the sight of God, my sin, in which I was conceived and born. (2)

(1) *I Tim. 2:5, 6; Heb. 9:13-15.* (2) *Rom. 8:3, 4; II Cor. 5:21; Gal. 4:4, 5; I Pet. 1:18, 19.*

LORD'S DAY 15

37. **What do you confess when you say that He suffered?**
During all the time He lived on earth, but especially at the end, Christ bore in body and soul the wrath of God against the sin of the whole human race. (1) Thus, by His suffering, as the only atoning sacrifice, (2) He has redeemed our body and soul from everlasting damnation, (3) and obtained for us the grace of God, righteousness, and eternal life. (4)

(1) *Is. 53; I Tim. 2:6; I Pet. 2:24; 3:18.* (2) *Rom. 3:25; I Cor. 5:7; Eph. 5:2; Heb. 10:14; I John 2:2; 4:10.* (3) *Rom. 8:1-4; Gal. 3:13; Col. 1:13; Heb. 9:12; I Pet 1:18, 19.* (4) *John 3:16; Rom. 3:24-26; II Cor. 5:21; Heb. 9:15.*

38. **Why did He suffer under Pontius Pilate as judge?**

Though innocent, Christ was condemned by an earthly judge, (1) and so He freed us from the severe judgment of God that was to fall on us. (2)

(1) *Luke 23:13-24; John 19:4, 12-16.*

(2) *Is. 53:4, 5; II Cor. 5:21; Gal. 3:13.*

39. **Does it have a special meaning that Christ was crucified and did not die in a different way?**

Yes. Thereby I am assured that He took upon Himself the curse which lay on me, for a crucified one was cursed by God. (1)

(1) *Deut. 21:23; Gal. 3:13.*

LORD'S DAY 16

40. **Why was it necessary for Christ to humble Himself even unto death?**

Because of the justice and truth of God (1) satisfaction for our sins could be made in no other way than by the death of the Son of God. (2)

(1) *Gen. 2:17.* (2) *Rom. 8:3; Phil. 2:8; Heb. 2:9, 14, 15.*

41. **Why was he buried?**

His burial testified that He had really died. (1)

(1) *Is. 53:9; John 19:38-42; Acts 13:29; I Cor. 15:3,4.*

42. **Since Christ has died for us, why do we still have to die?**

Our death is not a payment for our sins, but it puts an end to sin and is an entrance into eternal life. (1)

(1) *John 5:24; Phil. 1:21-23; I Thess. 5:9, 10.*

43. **What further benefit do we receive from Christ's sacrifice and death on the cross?**

Through Christ's death our old nature is crucified, put to death, and buried with Him, (1) so that the evil desires of the flesh may no longer reign in us, (2) but that we may offer ourselves to Him as a sacrifice of thankfulness. (3)

(1) *Rom. 6:5-11; Col. 2:11, 12.* (2) *Rom. 6:12-14.*

(3) *Rom. 12:1; Eph. 5:1, 2.*

44. **Why is there added: He descended into hell?**

In my greatest sorrows and temptations I may be assured and comforted that my Lord Jesus Christ, by His unspeakable anguish, pain, terror, and agony, which He endured throughout all His sufferings [(1)] but especially on the cross, has delivered me from the anguish and torment of hell. [(2)]

[(1)] *Ps. 18:5, 6; 116:3; Matt. 26:36-46; 27:45, 46; Heb. 5:7-10.* [(2)] *Is. 53.*

LORD'S DAY 17

45. **How does Christ's resurrection benefit us?**

First, by His resurrection He has overcome death, so that He could make us share in the righteousness which He had obtained for us by His death. [(1)] Second, by His power we too are raised up to a new life. [(2)] Third, Christ's resurrection is to us a sure pledge of our glorious resurrection. [(3)]

[(1)] *Rom. 4:25; I Cor. 15:16-20; I Pet. 1:3-5.* [(2)] *Rom. 6:5-11; Eph. 2:4-6; Col. 3:1-4.* [(3)] *Rom. 8:11; I Cor. 15:12-23; Phil. 3:20, 21.*

LORD'S DAY 18

46. **What do you confess when you say: He ascended into heaven?**

That Christ, before the eyes of His disciples, was taken up from the earth into heaven, [(1)] and that He is there for our benefit [(2)] until He comes again to judge the living and the dead. [(3)]

[(1)] *Mark 16:19; Luke 24:50, 51; Acts 1:9-11.* [(2)] *Rom. 8:34; Heb. 4:14; 7:23-25; 9:24.* [(3)] *Matt. 24:30; Acts 1:11.*

47. **Is Christ, then, not with us until the end of the world, as He has promised us?** [(1)]

Christ is true man and true God. With respect to His human nature He is no longer on earth, [(2)] but with respect to His divinity, majesty, grace, and Spirit He is never absent from us. [(3)]

[(1)] *Matt. 28:20.* [(2)] *Matt. 26:11; John 16:28; 17:11; Acts 3:19-21; Heb. 8:4.* [(3)] *Matt. 28:18-20; John 14:16-19; 16:13.*

48. **But are the two natures in Christ not separated from each other if His human nature is not present wherever His divinity is?**
Not at all, for His divinity has no limits and is present everywhere. [(1)] So it must follow that His divinity is indeed beyond the human nature which He has taken on and nevertheless is within this human nature and remains personally united with it. [(2)]

[(1)] *Jer. 23:23, 24; Acts 7:48, 49.* [(2)] *John 1:14; 3:13; Col. 2:9.*

49. **How does Christ's ascension into heaven benefit us?**
First, He is our Advocate in heaven before His Father. [(1)] Second, we have our flesh in heaven as a sure pledge that He, our Head, will also take us, His members, up to Himself. [(2)] Third, He sends us His Spirit as a counter-pledge, [(3)] by whose power we seek the things that are above, where Christ is, seated at the right hand of God, and not the things that are on earth. [(4)]

[(1)] *Rom. 8:34; I John 2:1.* [(2)] *John 14:2; 17:24; Eph. 2:4-6.*
[(3)] *John 14:16; Acts 2:33; II Cor. 1:21, 22; 5:5.* [(4)] *Col. 3:1-4.*

LORD'S DAY 19

50. **Why is it added, And sits at the right hand of God?**
Christ ascended into heaven to manifest Himself there as Head of His Church, [(1)] through whom the Father governs all things. [(2)]

[(1)] *Eph. 1:20-23; Col. 1:18.* [(2)] *Matt. 28:18; John 5:22, 23.*

51. **How does the glory of Christ, our Head, benefit us?**
First, by His Holy Spirit He pours out heavenly gifts upon us, His members. [(1)] Second, by His power He defends and preserves us against all enemies. [(2)]

[(1)] *Acts 2:33; Eph. 4:7-12.* [(2)] *Ps. 2:9; 110:1, 2; John 10:27-30; Rev. 19:11-16.*

52. **What comfort is it to you that Christ will come to judge the living and the dead?**
In all my sorrow and persecution I lift up my head and eagerly await as judge from heaven the very same person who before has submitted Himself to the judgment of God for my sake, and has removed all the curse from me. [(1)] He

will cast all His and my enemies into everlasting condemnation, but He will take me and all His chosen ones to Himself into heavenly joy and glory. (2)

(1) *Luke 21:28; Rom. 8:22-25; Phil. 3:20,21; Tit. 2:13, 14.*

(2) *Matt. 25:31-46; I Thess. 4:16, 17; II Thess. 1:6-10.*

LORD'S DAY 20

53. What do you believe concerning the Holy Spirit?

First, He is, together with the Father and the Son, true and eternal God. (1) Second, He is also given to me, (2) to make me by true faith share in Christ and all His benefits, (3) to comfort me, (4) and to remain with me forever. (5)

(1) *Gen. 1:1, 2; Matt. 28:19; Acts 5:3, 4; I Cor. 3:16.* (2) *I Cor. 6:19; II Cor. 1:21, 22; Gal. 4:6; Eph. 1:13.* (3) *Gal. 3:14; I Pet. 1:2.* (4) *John 15:26; Acts 9:31.* (5) *John 14:16, 17; I Pet. 4:14.*

LORD'S DAY 21

54. What do you believe concerning the holy catholic Christian church?

I believe that the Son of God, (1) out of the whole human race, (2) from the beginning of the world to its end, (3) gathers, defends, and preserves for Himself, (4) by His Spirit and Word, (5) in the unity of the true faith, (6) a church chosen to everlasting life. (7) And I believe that I am (8) and forever shall remain a living member of it. (9)

(1) *John 10:11; Acts 20:28; Eph. 4:11-13; Col. 1:18.* (2) *Gen. 26:4; Rev. 5:9.* (3) *Is. 59:21; I Cor. 11:26.* (4) *Ps. 129:1-5; Matt. 16:18; John 10:28-30.* (5) *Rom. 1:16; 10:14-17; Eph. 5:26.* (6) *Acts 2:42-47; Eph. 4:1-6.* (7) *Rom. 8:29; Eph. 1:3-14.* (8) *I John 3:14, 19-21.* (9) *Ps. 23:6; John 10:27, 28; I Cor. 1:4-9; I Pet. 1:3-5.*

55. What do you understand by the communion of saints?

First, that believers, all and everyone, as members of Christ have communion with Him and share in all His treasures and gifts. (1) Second, that everyone is duty-bound to use his gifts readily and cheerfully for the benefit and well-being of the other members. (2)

(1) *Rom. 8:32; I Cor. 6:17; 12:4-7, 12, 13; I John 1:3.*

(2) *Rom. 12:4-8; I Cor. 12:20-27; 13:1-7; Phil. 2:4-8.*

56. **What do you believe concerning the forgiveness of sins?**
I believe that God, because of Christ's satisfaction, will no more remember my sins, (1) nor my sinful nature, against which I have to struggle all my life, (2) but He will graciously grant me the righteousness of Christ, that I may never come into condemnation. (3)

(1) *Ps. 103:3, 4, 10, 12; Mic. 7:18, 19; II Cor. 5:18-21; I John 1:7; 2:2.*

(2) *Rom. 7:21-25.* (3) *John 3:17, 18; 5:24; Rom. 8:1, 2.*

LORD'S DAY 22

57. **What comfort does the resurrection of the body offer you?**
Not only shall my soul after this life immediately be taken up to Christ, my Head, (1) but also this my flesh, raised by the power of Christ, shall be reunited with my soul and made like Christ's glorious body. (2)

(1) *Luke 16:22; 23:43; Phil. 1:21-23.* (2) *Job 19:25, 26; I Cor. 15:20, 42-46, 54; Phil. 3:21; I John 3:2.*

58. **What comfort do you receive from the article about the life everlasting?**
Since I now already feel in my heart the beginning of eternal joy, (1) I shall after this life possess perfect blessedness, such as no eye has seen, nor ear heard, nor the heart of man conceived—a blessedness in which to praise God forever. (2)

(1) *John 17:3; Rom. 14:17; II Cor. 5:2, 3.* (2) *John 17:24; I Cor. 2:9.*

LORD'S DAY 23

59. **But what does it help you now that you believe all this?**
In Christ I am righteous before God and heir to life everlasting. (1)

(1) *Hab. 2:4; John 3:36; Rom. 1:17; 5:1, 2.*

60. **How are you righteous before God?**

Only by true faith in Jesus Christ. [(1)] Although my conscience accuses me that I have grievously sinned against all God's commandments, have never kept any of them, [(2)] and am still inclined to all evil, [(3)] yet God, without any merit of my own, [(4)] out of mere grace, [(5)] imputes to me the perfect satisfaction, righteousness, and holiness of Christ. [(6)] He grants these to me as if I had never had nor committed any sin, and as if I myself had accomplished all the obedience which Christ has rendered for me, [(7)] if only I accept this gift with a believing heart. [(8)]

[(1)] *Rom. 3:21-28; Gal. 2:16; Eph. 2:8, 9; Phil. 3:8-11.* [(2)] *Rom. 3:9, 10.* [(3)] *Rom. 7:23.* [(4)] *Deut. 9:6; Ezek. 36:22; Tit. 3:4, 5.* [(5)] *Rom. 3:24; Eph. 2:8.* [(6)] *Rom. 4:3-5; II Cor. 5:17-19; I John 2:1, 2.* [(7)] *Rom. 4:24, 25; II Cor. 5:21.* [(8)] *John 3:18; Acts 16:30, 31; Rom. 3:22.*

61. **Why do you say that you are righteous only by faith?**

Not that I am acceptable to God on account of the worthiness of my faith, for only the satisfaction, righteousness, and holiness of Christ is my righteousness before God. [(1)] I can receive this righteousness and make it mine my own by faith only. [(2)]

[(1)] *I Cor. 1:30, 31; 2:2.* [(2)] *Rom. 10:10; I John 5:10-12.*

LORD'S DAY 24

62. **But why can our good works not be our righteousness before God, or at least a part of it?**

Because the righteousness which can stand before God's judgment must be absolutely perfect and in complete agreement with the law of God, [(1)] whereas even our best works in this life are all imperfect and defiled with sin. [(2)]

[(1)] *Deut. 27:26; Gal. 3:10.* [(2)] *Is. 64:6.*

63. **But do our good works earn nothing, even though God promises to reward them in this life and the next?**

This reward is not earned [(1)]; it is a gift of grace. [(2)]

[(1)] *Matt. 5:12; Heb. 11:6.* [(2)] *Luke 17:10; II Tim. 4:7, 8.*

64. **Does this teaching not make people careless and wicked?**
No. It is impossible that those grafted into Christ by true faith should not bring forth fruits of thankfulness. [1]
[1] *Matt. 7:18; Luke 6:43-45; John 15:5.*

LORD'S DAY 25

65. **Since then faith alone makes us share in Christ and all His benefits, where does this faith come from?**
From the Holy Spirit, [1] who works it in our hearts by the preaching of the gospel, [2] and strengthens it by the use of the sacraments. [3]
[1] *John 3:5; I Cor. 2:10-14; Eph. 2:8; Phil. 1:29.*
[2] *Rom. 10:17; I Pet. 1:23-25.* [3] *Matt. 28:19, 20; I Cor. 10:16.*

66. **What are the sacraments?**
The sacraments are holy, visible signs and seals. They were instituted by God so that by their use He might the more fully declare and seal to us the promise of the gospel. [1] And this is the promise: that God graciously grants us forgiveness of sins and everlasting life because of the one sacrifice of Christ accomplished on the cross. [2]
[1] *Gen. 17:11; Deut. 30:6; Rom. 4:11*
[2] *Matt. 26:27, 28; Acts 2:38; Heb. 10:10.*

67. **Are both the Word and the sacraments then intended to focus our faith on the sacrifice of Jesus Christ on the cross as the only ground of our salvation?**
Yes, indeed. The Holy Spirit teaches us in the gospel and assures us by the sacraments that our entire salvation rests on Christ's one sacrifice for us on the cross. [1]
[1] *Rom. 6:3; I Cor. 11:26; Gal. 3:27.*

68. **How many sacraments has Christ instituted in the new covenant?**
Two: holy baptism and the holy supper. [1]
[1] *Matt. 28:19, 20; I Cor. 11:23-26.*

LORD'S DAY 26

69. **How does holy baptism signify and seal to you that the one sacrifice of Christ on the cross benefits you?**
In this way: Christ instituted this outward washing [1] and with it gave the promise that, as surely as water washes away the dirt from the body, so certainly His blood and Spirit wash away the impurity of my soul, that is, all my sins. [2]

[1] *Matt. 28:19.* [2] *Matt. 3:11; Mark 16:16; John 1:33; Acts 2:38; Rom. 6:3, 4; I Pet. 3:21.*

70. **What does it mean to be washed with Christ's blood and Spirit?**
To be washed with Christ's blood means to receive forgiveness of sins from God, through grace, because of Christ's blood, poured out for us in His sacrifice on the cross. [1] To be washed with His Spirit means to be renewed by the Holy Spirit and sanctified to be members of Christ, so that more and more we become dead to sin and lead a holy and blameless life. [2]

[1] *Ez. 36:25; Zech. 13:1; Eph. 1:7; Heb. 12:24; I Pet. 1:2; Rev. 1:5; 7:14.*
[2] *John 3:5-8; Rom. 6:4; I Cor. 6:11; Col. 2:11, 12.*

71. **Where has Christ promised that He will wash us with His blood and Spirit as surely as we are washed with the water of baptism?**
In the institution of baptism, where He says: Go therefore and make disciples of all nations, baptizing them in the name of the Father and of the Son and of the Holy Spirit. [1] He who believes and is baptized will be saved, but he who does not believe will be condemned. [2] This promise is repeated where Scripture calls baptism the washing of regeneration and the washing away of sins. [3]

[1]*Matthew 28:19.* [2] *Mark 16:16.* [3] *Titus 3:5; Acts 22:16.*

LORD'S DAY 27

72. **Does this outward washing with water itself wash away sins?**
No, only the blood of Jesus Christ and the Holy Spirit cleanse us from all sins. [1]

[1] *Matt. 3:11; I Pet. 3:21; I John 1:7.*

73. **Why then does the Holy Spirit call baptism the washing of regeneration and the washing away of sins?**
God speaks in this way for a good reason. He wants to teach us that the blood and Spirit of Christ remove our sins just as water takes away dirt from the body. (1) But, even more important, He wants to assure us by this divine pledge and sign that we are as truly cleansed from our sins spiritually as we are bodily washed with water. (2)

(1) *I Cor. 6:11; Rev. 1:5; 7:14.* (2) *Mark 16:16; Acts 2:38; Rom. 6:3, 4; Gal. 3:27.*

74. **Should infants, too, be baptized?**
Yes. Infants as well as adults belong to God's covenant and congregation. (1) Through Christ's blood the redemption from sin and the Holy Spirit, who works faith, are promised to them no less than to adults. (2) Therefore, by baptism, as sign of the covenant, they must be grafted into the Christian church and distinguished from the children of unbelievers. (3) This was done in the old covenant by circumcision, (4) in place of which baptism was instituted in the new covenant. (5)

(1) *Gen. 17:7; Matt. 19:14.* (2) *Ps. 22:11; Is. 44:1-3; Acts 2:38, 39; 16:31.* (3) *Acts 10:47; I Cor. 7:14.* (4) *Gen. 17:9-14.* (5) *Col. 2: 11-13.*

LORD'S DAY 28

75. **How does the Lord's Supper signify and seal to you that you share in Christ's one sacrifice on the cross and in all His gifts?**
In this way: Christ has commanded me and all believers to eat of this broken bread and drink of this cup in remembrance of Him. With this command He gave these promises: (1) First, as surely as I see with my eyes the bread of the Lord broken for me and the cup given to me, so surely was His body offered for me and His blood poured out for me on the cross. Second, as surely as I receive from the hand of the minister and taste with my mouth the bread and the cup of the Lord as sure signs of Christ's body and blood, so surely does

He Himself nourish and refresh my soul to everlasting life with His crucified body and shed blood.

(1) *Matt. 26:26-28; Mark 14:22-24; Luke 22:19, 20; I Cor. 11:23-25.*

76. What does it mean to eat the crucified body of Christ and to drink His shed blood?

First, to accept with a believing heart all the suffering and the death of Christ, and so receive forgiveness of sins and life eternal. (1) Second, to be united more and more to His sacred body through the Holy Spirit, who lives both in Christ and in us. (2) Therefore, although Christ is in heaven (3) and we are on earth, yet we are flesh of His flesh and bone of His bones, (4) and we forever live and are governed by one Spirit, as the members of our body are by one soul. (5)

(1) *John 6:35, 40, 50-54.* (2) *John 6:55, 56; I Cor. 12:13.* (3) *Acts 1:9-11; 3:21; I Cor. 11:26; Col. 3:1.* (4) *I Cor. 6:15, 17; Eph. 5:29, 30; I John 4:13.* (5) *John 6:56-58; 15:1-6; Eph. 4:15, 16; I John 3:24.*

77. Where has Christ promised that He will nourish and refresh believers with His body and blood as surely as they eat of this broken bread and drink of this cup?

In the institution of the Lord's supper: The Lord Jesus on the night when He was betrayed took bread, and when He had given thanks, He broke it and said, "This is my body which is for you. Do this in remembrance of me." In the same way also the cup, after supper, saying, "Do this, as often as you drink it, in remembrance of me." For as often as you eat this bread and drink the cup, you proclaim the Lord's death until He comes. (1) This promise is repeated by Paul where he says: The cup of blessing which we bless, is it not a participation in the blood of Christ? The bread which we break, is it not a participation in the body of Christ? Because there is one bread, we who are many are one body, for we all partake of the one bread. (2)

(1) *I Corinthians 11:23-26.* (2) *I Corinthians 10:16, 17.*

LORD'S DAY 29

78. **Are then the bread and wine changed into the real body and blood of Christ?**

No. Just as the water of baptism is not changed into the blood of Christ and is not the washing away of sins itself but is simply God's sign and pledge, (1) so also the bread in the Lord's supper does not become the body of Christ itself, (2) although it is called Christ's body (3) in keeping with the nature and usage of sacraments. (4)

(1) *Eph. 5:26; Tit. 3:5.* (2) *Matt. 26:26-29.* (3) *I Cor. 10:16, 17; 11:26-28.*
(4) *Gen. 17:10, 11; Ex. 12:11, 13; I Cor. 10:3, 4; I Pet. 3:21.*

79. **Why then does Christ call the bread His body and the cup His blood, or the new covenant in His blood, and why does Paul speak of a participation in the body and blood of Christ?**

Christ speaks in this way for a good reason: He wants to teach us by His supper that as bread and wine sustain us in this temporal life, so His crucified body and shed blood are true food and drink for our souls to eternal life. (1) But, even more important, He wants to assure us by this visible sign and pledge, first, that through the working of the Holy Spirit we share in His true body and blood as surely as we receive with our mouth these holy signs in remembrance of Him, (2) and, second, that all His suffering and obedience are as certainly ours as if we personally had suffered and paid for our sins. (3)

(1) *John 6:51, 55.* (2) *I Cor. 10:16, 17; 11:26.* (3) *Rom. 6:5-11.*

LORD'S DAY 30

80. **What difference is there between the Lord's supper and the papal mass?**

The Lord's supper testifies to us, first, that we have complete forgiveness of all our sins through the one sacrifice of Jesus Christ, which He Himself accomplished on the cross once for all; (1) and, second, that through the Holy Spirit we are grafted into Christ, (2) who with His true body is now in heaven at the right hand of the Father, (3) and this is where He wants to be worshipped. (4) But the mass teaches, first, that the living and the dead do not have forgiveness of sins through the suffering of Christ unless He is still offered for them daily by the priests; and, second, that Christ is bodily present in the form of bread and wine, and there is to be worshipped. Therefore the mass is basically nothing but a denial of the one sacrifice and suffering of Jesus Christ, and an accursed idolatry.

(1) *Matt. 26:28; John 19:30; Heb. 7:27; 9:12, 25, 26; 10:10-18.*
(2) *I Cor. 6:17; 10:16, 17.* (3) *Joh. 20:17; Acts 7:55, 56; Heb. 1:3; 8:1.*
(4) *John 4:21-24; Phil. 3:20; Col. 3:1; I Thess. 1:10.*

81. **Who are to come to the table of the Lord?**
Those who are truly displeased with themselves because of their sins and yet trust that these are forgiven them and that their remaining weakness is covered by the suffering and death of Christ, and who also desire more and more to strengthen their faith and amend their life. But hypocrites and those who do not repent eat and drink judgment upon themselves. [1]

(1) *I Cor. 10:19-22; 11:26-32.*

82. **Are those also to be admitted to the Lord's supper who by their confession and life show that they are unbelieving and ungodly?**
No, for then the covenant of God would be profaned and His wrath kindled against the whole congregation. [1] Therefore, according to the command of Christ and His apostles, the Christian church is duty-bound to exclude such persons by the keys of the kingdom of heaven, until they amend their lives.

(1) *Ps. 50:16; Is. 1:11-17; I Cor. 11:17-34.*

LORD'S DAY 31

83. **What are the keys of the kingdom of heaven?**
The preaching of the holy gospel and church discipline. By these two the kingdom of heaven is opened to believers and closed to unbelievers. [1]

(1) *Matt. 16:19; John 20:21-23.*

84. **How is the kingdom of heaven opened and closed by the preaching of the gospel?**
According to the command of Christ, the kingdom of heaven is opened when it is proclaimed and publicly testified to each and every believer that God has

really forgiven all their sins for the sake of Christ's merits, as often as they by true faith accept the promise of the gospel. The kingdom of heaven is closed when it is proclaimed and testified to all unbelievers and hypocrites that the wrath of God and eternal condemnation rest on them as long as they do not repent. According to this testimony of the gospel, God will judge both in this life and in the life to come. (1)

(1) *Matt. 16:19; John 3:31-36; 20:21-23.*

85. **How is the kingdom of heaven closed and opened by church discipline?**
According to the command of Christ, people who call themselves Christians but show themselves to be unchristian in doctrine or life are first repeatedly admonished in a brotherly manner. If they do not give up their errors or wickedness, they are reported to the church, that is, to the elders. If they do not heed also their admonitions, they are forbidden the use of the sacraments, and they are excluded by the elders from the Christian congregation, and by God Himself from the kingdom of Christ. (1) They are again received as members of Christ and of the church when they promise and show real amendment. (2)

(1) *Matt. 18:15-20; I Cor. 5:3-5; 11-13; II Thess. 3:14, 15.*

(2) *Luke 15:20-24; II Cor. 2:6-11.*

PART III: GRATITUDE

LORD'S DAY 32

86. **Since we have been delivered from our misery by grace alone through Christ, without any merit of our own, why must we yet do good works?**
Because Christ, having redeemed us by His blood, also renews us by His Holy Spirit to be His image, so that with our whole life we may show ourselves thankful to God for His benefits, (1) and He may be praised by us. (2) Further, that we ourselves may be assured of our faith by its fruits, (3) and that by our godly walk of life we may win our neighbours for Christ. (4)

(1) *Rom. 6:13; 12:1, 2; I Pet. 2:5-10.* (2) *Matt. 5:16; I Cor. 6:19, 20.*

(3) *Matt. 7:17, 18; Gal. 5:22-24; II Pet. 1:10, 11.*

(4) *Matt. 5:14-16; Rom. 14:17-19; I Pet. 2:12; 3:1, 2.*

87. **Can those be saved who do not turn to God from their ungrateful and impenitent walk of life?**

By no means. Scripture says that no unchaste person, idolater, adulterer, thief, greedy person, drunkard, slanderer, robber, or the like shall inherit the kingdom of God. (1)

(1) *I Cor. 6:9, 10; Gal. 5:19-21; Eph. 5:5, 6; I John 3:14.*

LORD'S DAY 33

88. **What is the true repentance or conversion of man?**

It is the dying of the old nature and the coming to life of the new. (1)

(1) *Rom. 6:1-11; I Cor. 5:7; II Cor. 5:17; Eph. 4:22-24; Col. 3:5-10.*

89. **What is the dying of the old nature?**

It is to grieve with heartfelt sorrow that we have offended God by our sin, and more and more to hate it and flee from it. (1)

(1) *Ps. 51:3, 4, 17; Joel 2:12, 13; Rom. 8:12, 13; II Cor. 7:10.*

90. **What is the coming to life of the new nature?**

It is a heartfelt joy in God through Christ, (1) and a love and delight to live according to the will of God in all good works. (2)

(1) *Ps. 51:8, 12; Is. 57:15; Rom. 5:1; 14:17.* (2) *Rom. 6:10, 11; Gal. 2:20.*

91. **But what are good works?**

Only those which are done out of true faith, (1) in accordance with the law of God, (2) and to His glory, (3) and not those based on our own opinion or on precepts of men. (4)

(1) *Joh. 15:5; Rom. 14:23; Heb. 11:6.* (2) *Lev. 18:4; I Sam. 15:22; Eph. 2:10.* (3) *I Cor. 10:31.* (4) *Deut. 12:32; Is. 29:13; Ezek. 20:18, 19; Matt. 15:7-9.*

LORD'S DAY 34

92. **What is the law of the LORD?**

God spoke all these words, saying: I am the LORD your God, who brought you out of the land of Egypt, out of the house of slavery. You shall have no other gods before Me. You shall not make for yourself a graven image, or any likeness of anything that is in heaven above, or that is in the earth beneath, or that is in the water under the earth; you shall not bow down to them or serve them; for I the LORD your God am a jealous God, visiting the iniquity of the fathers upon the children to the third and fourth generation of those who hate Me, but showing steadfast love to thousands of those who love Me and keep My commandments. You shall not take the Name of the LORD your God in vain; for the LORD will not hold him guiltless who takes His Name in vain. Remember the sabbath day, to keep it holy. Six days you shall labour, and do all your work; but the seventh day is a sabbath to the LORD your God; in it you shall not do any work, you, or your son, or your daughter, your manservant, or your maidservant, or your cattle, or the sojourner who is within your gates; for in six days the LORD made heaven and earth, the sea, and all that is in them, and rested the seventh day; therefore the LORD blessed the sabbath day and hallowed it. Honour your father and your mother, that your days may be long in the land which the LORD your God gives you. You shall not kill. You shall not commit adultery. You shall not steal. You shall not bear false witness against your neighbour. you shall not covet your neighbour's house; you shall not covet your neighbour's wife, 10. or his manservant, or his maidservant, or his ox, or his ass, or anything that is your neighbour's. (1)

(1) *Ex. 20:1-17; Deut. 5:6-21.*

93. **How are these commandments divided?**

Into two parts. The first teaches us how to live in relation to God; the second, what duties we owe our neighbour. (1)

(1) *Matt. 22:37-40.*

94. **What does the LORD require in the first commandment?**

That for the sake of my very salvation I avoid and flee all idolatry, (1) witchcraft, superstition, (2) and prayer to saints or to other creatures. (3) Further, that I rightly come to know the only true God. (4) trust in Him alone, (5) submit to Him with all humility (6) and patience, (7) expect all good from Him only, (8) and love,[9] fear,[10] and honour Him[11] with all my heart. In short, that I forsake all creatures rather than do the least thing against His will.[12]

[1] *I Cor. 6:9, 10; 10:5-14; I John 5:21.* [2] *Lev. 19:31; Deut. 18:9-12.* [3] *Matt. 4:10; Rev. 19:10; 22:8, 9.* [4] *John 17:3.* [5] *Jer. 17:5, 7.* [6] *I Pet. 5:5, 6.* [7] *Rom. 5:3, 4; I Cor. 10:10; Phil. 2:14; Col. 1:11; Heb. 10:36.* [8] *Ps. 104:27, 28; Is. 45:7; James 1:17.* [9] *Deut. 6:5; (Matt. 22:37).* [10] *Deut. 6:2; Ps. 111:10; Prov. 1:7; 9:10; Matt. 10:28; I Pet. 1:17.* [11] *Deut. 6:13; (Matt. 4:10); Deut. 10:20.* [12] *Matt. 5:29, 30; 10:37-39; Acts 5:29.*

95. **What is idolatry?**
Idolatry is having or inventing something in which to put our trust instead of, or in addition to, the only true God who has revealed Himself in His Word.[1]

[1] *I Chron. 16:26; Gal. 4:8, 9; Eph. 5:5; Phil. 3:19.*

LORD'S DAY 35

96. **What does God require in the second commandment?**
We are not to make an image of God in any way,[1] nor to worship Him in any other manner than He has commanded in His Word.[2]

[1] *Deut. 4:15-19; Is. 40:18-25; Acts 17:29; Rom. 1:23.*
[2] *Lev. 10:1-7; Deut. 12:30; I Sam. 15:22, 23; Matt. 15:9; John 4:23, 24.*

97. **May we then not make any image at all?**
God cannot and may not be visibly portrayed in any way. Creatures may be portrayed, but God forbids us to make or have any images of them in order to worship them or to serve God through them.[1]

[1] *Ex. 34:13, 14, 17; Num. 33:52; II Kings 18:4, 5; Is. 40:25.*

98. **But may images not be tolerated in the churches as "books for the laity"?**
No, for we should not be wiser than God. He wants His people to be taught not by means of dumb images[1] but by the living preaching of His Word.[2]

[1] *Jer. 10:8; Hab. 2:18-20.* [2] *Rom. 10:14, 15, 17; II Tim. 3:16, 17; II Pet. 1:19.*

LORD'S DAY 36

99. What is required in the third commandment?

We are not to blaspheme or to abuse the Name of God by cursing, [1] perjury, [2] or unnecessary oaths, [3] nor to share in such horrible sins by being silent bystanders. [4] In short, we must use the holy Name of God only with fear and reverence, [5] so that we may rightly confess Him, [6] call upon Him, [7] and praise Him in all our words and works. [8]

(1) *Lev. 24:10-17.* (2) *Lev. 19:12* (3) *Matt. 5:37; James 5:12.*
(4) *Lev. 5:1; Prov. 29:24.* (5) *Ps. 99:1-5; Is. 45:23; Jer. 4:2.*
(6) *Matt. 10:32, 33; Rom. 10:9, 10.* (7) *Ps. 50:14, 15; I Tim. 2:8.*
(8) *Rom. 2:24; Col. 3:17; I Tim. 6:1.*

100. Is the blaspheming of God's Name by swearing and cursing such a grievous sin that God is angry also with those who do not prevent and forbid it as much as they can?

Certainly, [1] for no sin is greater or provokes God's wrath more than the blaspheming of His Name. That is why He commanded it to be punished with death. [2]

(1) *Lev. 5:1.* (2) *Lev. 24:16.*

LORD'S DAY 37

101. But may we swear an oath by the Name of God in a godly manner?

Yes, when the government demands it of its subjects, or when necessity requires it, in order to maintain and promote fidelity and truth, to God's glory and for our neighbour's good. Such oath-taking is based on God's Word [1] and was therefore rightly used by saints in the Old and the New Testament. [2]

(1) *Deut. 6:13; 10:20; Jer. 4:1, 2; Heb. 6:16.* (2) *Gen. 21:24; 31:53; Josh. 9:15; I Sam. 24:22; I Kings 1:29, 30; Rom. 1:9; II Cor. 1:23.*

102. May we also swear by saints or other creatures?

No. A lawful oath is a calling upon God, who alone knows the heart, to bear witness to the truth, and to punish me if I swear falsely. (1) No creature is worthy of such honour. (2)

(1) *Rom. 9:1; II Cor. 1:23.* (2) *Matt. 5:34-37; 23:16-22; James 5:12.*

LORD'S DAY 38

103. What does God require in the fourth commandment?

First, that the ministry of the gospel and the schools be maintained (1) and that, especially on the day of rest, I diligently attend the church of God (2) to hear God's Word, (3) to use the sacraments, (4) to call publicly upon the LORD, (5) and to give Christian offerings for the poor. (6) Second, that all the days of my life I rest from my evil works, let the LORD work in me through His Holy Spirit, and so begin in this life the eternal sabbath. (7)

(1) *Deut. 6:4-9; 20-25; I Cor. 9:13, 14; II Tim. 2:2; 3:13-17; Tit. 1:5.*
(2) *Deut. 12:5-12; Ps. 40:9, 10; 68:26; Acts 2:42-47; Heb. 10:23-25.*
(3) *Rom. 10:14-17; I Cor. 14:26-33; I Tim. 4:13.* (4) *I Cor. 11:23, 24.*
(5) *Col. 3:16; I Tim. 2:1.* (6) *Ps. 50:14; I Cor. 16:2; II Cor. 8 and 9.*
(7) *Is. 66:23; Heb. 4:9-11.*

LORD'S DAY 39

104. What does God require in the fifth commandment?

That I show all honour, love, and faithfulness to my father and mother and to all those in authority over me, submit myself with due obedience to their good instruction and discipline, (1) and also have patience with their weaknesses and shortcomings, (2) since it is God's will to govern us by their hand. (3)

(1) *Ex. 21:17; Prov. 1:8; 4:1; Rom. 13:1, 2; Eph. 5:21, 22; 6:1-9; Col. 3:18-4:1.* (2) *Prov. 20:20; 23:22; I Pet.2:18.* (3) *Matt. 22:21, Rom. 13:1-8; Eph. 6:1-9; Col. 3:18-21.*

LORD'S DAY 40

105. What does God require in the sixth commandment?

I am not to dishonour, hate, injure, or kill my neighbour by thoughts, words, or gestures, and much less by deeds, whether personally or through another; (1) rather, I am to put away all desire of revenge. (2) Moreover, I am not to harm or recklessly endanger myself. (3) Therefore, also, the government bears the sword to prevent murder. (4)

(1) *Gen. 9:6; Lev. 19:17, 18; Matt. 5:21, 22; 26:52.*
(2) *Prov. 25:21, 22; Matt. 18:35; Rom. 12:19; Eph. 4:26.*
(3) *Matt. 4:7; 26:52; Rom. 13:11-14.* (4) *Gen. 9:6; Ex. 21:14; Rom. 13:4.*

106. But does this commandment speak only of killing?

By forbidding murder God teaches us that He hates the root of murder, such as envy, hatred, anger, and desire of revenge, (1) and that He regards all these as murder. (2)

(1) *Prov. 14:30; Rom. 1:29; 12:19; Gal. 5:19-21; James 1:20; I John 2:9-11.* (2) *I John 3:15.*

107. Is it enough, then, that we do not kill our neighbour in any such way?

No. When God condemns envy, hatred, and anger, He commands us to love our neighbour as ourselves, (1) to show patience, peace, gentleness, mercy, and friendliness toward him, (2) to protect him from harm as much as we can, and to do good even to our enemies. (3)

(1) *Matt. 7:12; 22:39; Rom. 12:10.* (2) *Matt. 5:5; Luke 6:36; Rom. 12:10, 18; Gal. 6:1, 2; Eph. 4:2; Col. 3:12; I Pet. 3:8.*
(3) *Ex. 23:4, 5; Matt. 5:44, 45; Rom. 12:20.*

LORD'S DAY 41

108. What does the seventh commandment teach us?

That all unchastity is cursed by God. (1) We must therefore detest it from the heart (2) and live chaste and disciplined lives, both within and outside of holy marriage. (3)

(1) *Lev. 18:30; Eph. 5:3-5.* (2) *Jude 22, 23.*
(3) *I Cor. 7:1-9; I Thess. 4:3-8; Heb. 13:4.*

109. Does God in this commandment forbid nothing more than adultery and similar shameful sins?

Since we, body and soul, are temples of the Holy Spirit, it is God's will that we keep ourselves pure and holy. Therefore He forbids all unchaste acts, gestures, words, thoughts, desires, (1) and whatever may entice us to unchastity. (2)

(1) *Matt. 5:27-29; I Cor. 6:18-20; Eph. 5:3, 4.* (2) *I Cor. 15:33; Eph. 5:18.*

LORD'S DAY 42

110. What does God forbid in the eighth commandment?

God forbids not only outright theft and robbery (1) but also such wicked schemes and devices as false weights and measures, deceptive merchandising, counterfeit money, and usury; (2) we must not defraud our neighbour in any way, whether by force or by show of right. (3) In addition God forbids all greed (4) and all abuse or squandering of His gifts. (5)

(1) *Ex. 22:1; I Cor. 5:9, 10; 6:9, 10.* (2) *Deut. 25:13-16; Ps. 15:5; Prov. 11:1; 12:22; Ezek. 45:9-12; Luke 6:35.*
(3) *Mic. 6:9-11; Luke 3:14; James 5:1-6.* (4) *Luke 12:15; Eph. 5:5.*
(5) *Prov. 21:20; 23:20, 21; Luke 16:10-13.*

111. What does God require of you in this commandment?

I must promote my neighbour's good wherever I can and may, deal with him as I would like others to deal with me, and work faithfully so that I may be able to give to those in need. (1)

(1) *Is. 58:5-10; Matt. 7:12; Gal. 6:9, 10; Eph. 4:28.*

LORD'S DAY 43

112. **What is required in the ninth commandment?**

I must not give false testimony against anyone, twist no one's words, not gossip or slander, nor condemn or join in condemning anyone rashly and unheard. (1) Rather, I must avoid all lying and deceit as the devil's own works, under penalty of God's heavy wrath. (2) In court and everywhere else, I must love the truth, (3) speak and confess it honestly, and do what I can to defend and promote my neighbour's honour and reputation. (4)

(1) *Ps. 15; Prov. 19:5, 9; 21:28; Matt. 7:1; Luke 6:37; Rom. 1:28-32.*
(2) *Lev. 19:11, 12; Prov. 12:22; 13:5; John 8:44; Rev. 21:8.*
(3) *I Cor. 13:6; Eph. 4:25.* (4) *I Pet. 3:8, 9; 4:8.*

LORD'S DAY 44

113. **What does the tenth commandment require of us?**

That not even the slightest thought or desire contrary to any of God's commandments should ever arise in our heart. Rather, we should always hate all sin with all our heart, and delight in all righteousness. (1)

(1) *Ps. 19:7-14; 139:23, 24; Rom. 7:7, 8.*

114. **But can those converted to God keep these commandments perfectly?**

No. In this life even the holiest have only a small beginning of this obedience. (1) Nevertheless, with earnest purpose they do begin to live not only according to some but to all the commandments of God. (2)

(1) *Eccles. 7:20; Rom. 7:14, 15; I Cor. 13:9; I John 1:8.*
(2) *Ps. 1:1, 2; Rom. 7:22-25; Phil. 3:12-16.*

115. **If in this life no one can keep the ten commandments perfectly, why does God have them preached so strictly?**

First, that throughout our life we may more and more become aware of our sinful nature, and therefore seek more eagerly the forgiveness of sins and righteousness in Christ. (1) Second, that we may be zealous for good deeds and constantly pray to God for the grace of the Holy Spirit, that He may more and more renew us after God's image, until after this life we reach the goal of perfection. (2)

(1) *Ps. 32:5; Rom. 3:19-26; 7:7, 24, 25; I John 1:9.*

(2) *I Cor. 9:24; Phil. 3:12-14; I John 3:1-3.*

LORD'S DAY 45

116. Why is prayer necessary for Christians?

Because prayer is the most important part of the thankfulness which God requires of us. (1) Moreover, God will give His grace and the Holy Spirit only to those who constantly and with heartfelt longing ask Him for these gifts and thank Him for them. (2)

(1) *Ps. 50:14, 15; 116:12-19; I Thess. 5:16-18.*

(2) *Matt. 7:7, 8; Luke 11:9-13.*

117. What belongs to a prayer which pleases God and is heard by Him?

First, we must from the heart call upon the one true God only, who has revealed Himself in His Word, for all that He has commanded us to pray. (1) Second, we must thoroughly know our need and misery, so that we may humble ourselves before God. (2) Third, we must rest on this firm foundation that, although we do not deserve it, God will certainly hear our prayer for the sake of Christ our Lord, as He has promised us in His Word. (3)

(1) *Ps. 145:18-20; John 4:22-24; Rom. 8:26, 27; James 1:5; I John 5:14, 15; Rev. 19:10.* (2) *II Chron. 7:14; 20:12; Ps. 2:11; 34:18; 62:8; Is. 66:2; Rev. 4.* (3) *Dan. 9:17-19; Matt. 7:8; John 14:13, 14; 16:23; Rom. 10:13; James 1:6.*

118. What has God commanded us to ask of Him?

All the things we need for body and soul, (1) as included in the prayer which Christ our Lord Himself taught us.

(1) *Matt. 6:33; James 1:17.*

119. What is the Lord's prayer?

Our Father who art in heaven, Hallowed be Thy Name. Thy kingdom come, Thy will be done, On earth as it is in heaven. Give us this day our daily bread;

And forgive us our debts, As we also have forgiven our debtors; And lead us not into temptation, But deliver us from the evil one. For Thine is the kingdom, and the power, and the glory, for ever. Amen. [(1)]

[(1)] *Matt. 6:9-13; Luke 11:2-4.*

LORD'S DAY 46

120. **Why has Christ commanded us to address God as Our Father?**

To awaken in us at the very beginning of our prayer that childlike reverence and trust toward God which should be basic to our prayer: God has become our Father through Christ and will much less deny us what we ask of Him in faith than our fathers would refuse us earthly things. [(1)]

[(1)] *Matt. 7:9-11; Luke 11:11-13. 121.*

121. **Why is there added, Who art in heaven?**

These words teach us not to think of God's heavenly majesty in an earthly manner, [(1)] and to expect from His almighty power all things we need for body and soul. [(2)]

[(1)] *Jer. 23:23, 24; Acts 17:24, 25.* [(2)] *Matt. 6:25-34; Rom. 8:31, 32.*

LORD'S DAY 47

122. **What is the first petition?**

Hallowed be Thy Name. That is: Grant us first of all that we may rightly know Thee, [(1)] and sanctify, glorify, and praise Thee in all Thy works, in which shine forth Thy almighty power, wisdom, goodness, righteousness, mercy, and truth. [(2)] Grant us also that we may so direct our whole life—our thoughts, words, and actions—that Thy Name is not blasphemed because of us but always honoured and praised. [(3)]

[(1)] *Jer. 9:23, 24; 31: 33, 34; Matt. 16:17; John 17:3.*

[(2)] *Ex. 34:5-8; Ps. 145; Jer. 32:16-20; Luke 1:46-55, 68-75; Rom. 11: 33-36.* [(3)] *Ps. 115:1; Matt. 5:16.*

LORD'S DAY 48

123. What is the second petition?

Thy kingdom come. That is: So rule us by Thy Word and Spirit that more and more we submit to Thee. (1) Preserve and increase Thy church. (2) Destroy the works of the devil, every power that raises itself against Thee, and every conspiracy against Thy holy Word. (3) Do all this until the fulness of Thy kingdom comes, wherein Thou shalt be all in all. (4)

(1) *Ps. 119:5, 105; 143:10; Matt. 6:33.* (2) *Ps. 51:18; 122:6-9; Matt. 16:18; Acts 2:42-47.* (3) *Rom. 16:20; I John 3:8.* (4) *Rom. 8:22, 23; I Cor. 15:28; Rev. 22: 17, 20.*

LORD'S DAY 49

124. What is the third petition?

Thy will be done, on earth as it is in heaven. That is: Grant that we and all men may deny our own will, and without any murmuring obey Thy will, for it alone is good. (1) Grant also that everyone may carry out the duties of his office and calling (2) as willingly and faithfully as the angels in heaven. (3)

(1) *Matt. 7:21; 16:24-26; Luke 22:42; Rom. 12:1, 2; Tit. 2:11, 12.* (2) *I Cor. 7:17-24; Eph. 6:5-9.* (3) *Ps. 103:20, 21.*

LORD'S DAY 50

125. What is the fourth petition?

Give us this day our daily bread. That is: Provide us with all our bodily needs (1) so that we may acknowledge that Thou art the only fountain of all good, (2) and that our care and labour, and also Thy gifts, cannot do us any good without Thy blessing. (3) Grant therefore that we may withdraw our trust from all creatures, and place it only in Thee. (4)

(1) *Ps. 104:27-30; 145:15, 16; Matt. 6:25-34.* (2) *Acts 14:17; 17:25; James 1:17.* (3) *Deut. 8:3; Ps. 37:16; 127:1, 2; I Cor. 15:58.* (4) *Ps. 55:22; 62; 146; Jer. 17:5-8; Heb. 13:5, 6.*

LORD'S DAY 51

126. **What is the fifth petition?**

And forgive us our debts, as we also have forgiven our debtors. That is: For the sake of Christ's blood, do not impute to us, wretched sinners; any of our transgressions, nor the evil which still clings to us, (1) as we also find this evidence of Thy grace in us that we are fully determined wholeheartedly to forgive our neighbor. (2)

(1) *Ps. 51:1-7; 143:2; Rom. 8:1; I John 2:1, 2.*
(2) *Matt. 6:14, 15; 18:21-35.*

LORD'S DAY 52

127. **What is the sixth petition?**

And lead us not into temptation, but deliver us from the evil one. That is: In ourselves we are so weak that we cannot stand even for a moment. (1) Moreover, our sworn enemies—the devil, (2) the world, (3) and our own flesh (4)—do not cease to attack us. Wilt Thou, therefore, uphold and strengthen us by the power of Thy Holy Spirit, so that in this spiritual war (5) we may not go down to defeat, but always firmly resist our enemies, until we finally obtain the complete victory. (6)

(1) *Ps. 103:14-16; John 15:1-5.* (2) *II Cor. 11:14; Eph. 6:10-13; I Pet. 5:8.* (3) *John 15:18-21.* (4) *Rom. 7:23; Gal. 5:17.*
(5) *Matt. 10:19, 20; 26:41; Mark 13:33; Rom. 5:3-5.*
(6) *I Cor. 10:13; I Thess. 3:13; 5:23.*

128. **How do you conclude your prayer?**

For Thine is the kingdom, and the power, and the glory, for ever. That is: All this we ask of Thee because, as our King, having power over all things, Thou art both willing and able to give us all that is good, (1) and because not we but Thy holy Name should so receive all glory for ever. (2)

(1) *Rom. 10:11-13; II Pet 2:9.* (2) *Ps. 115:1; Jer. 33:8, 9; John 14:13.*

129. **What does the word Amen mean?**
Amen means: It is true and certain. For God has much more certainly heard my prayer than I feel in my heart that I desire this of Him. (1)

(1) *Is. 65:24; II Cor. 1:20; II Tim. 2:13.* ▪

Westminster Shorter Catechism

Having defined exactly what they believed in the Westminster Confession of 1646, the Westminster Assembly turned to teaching the rising generations of Christians. In 1647 the Assembly wrote two catechisms—a larger and a shorter. The Larger Catechism was highly detailed and intended to be used by ministers. But the Shorter Catechism was written for children and families, and was meant to be memorized.

The English Parliament approved the two catechisms in 1648, and the Scottish Parliament did so in 1649. But along with the Westminster Confession, the Westminster Catechisms lost their status in the English church when Catholic-leaning Charles II was restored to the throne in 1660. Nevertheless, like their companion confession, the catechisms continued to be monumental to Reformed Christians throughout the world, even to the present day.

---

1. **What is the chief end of man?**
   Man's chief end is to glorify God,[(1)] and to enjoy him for ever.[(2)]
   [(1)] *I Cor. 10:31; Rom. 11:36.* [(2)] *Ps. 73:25-28.*

2. **What rule hath God given to direct us how we may glorify and enjoy him?**
   The word of God, which is contained in the scriptures of the Old and New Testaments,[(1)] is the only rule to direct us how we may glorify and enjoy him.[(2)]
   [(1)] *II Tim. 3:16; Eph. 2:20.* [(2)] *I John 1:3-4.*

3. **What do the scriptures principally teach?**
   The scriptures principally teach what man is to believe concerning God, and what duty God requires of man.[(1)]
   [(1)] *II Tim. 1:13; 3:16.*

4. **What is God?**

God is a Spirit,(1) infinite,(2) eternal,(3) and unchangeable,(4) in his being,(5) wisdom,(6) power,(7) holiness,(8) justice, goodness, and truth.(9)

(1) *John 4:24.* (2) *Job 11:7-9.* (3) *Ps. 90:2.* (4) *James 1:17.* (5) *Exod. 3:14.* (6) *Ps. 147:5.* (7) *Rev. 4:8.* (8) *Rev. 15:4.* (9) *Exod. 34:6-7.*

5. **Are there more Gods than one?**

There is but One only, the living and true God.(1)

(1) *Deut. 6:4; Jer. 10:10.*

6. **How many persons are there in the Godhead?**

There are three persons in the Godhead; the Father, the Son, and the Holy Ghost; and these three are one God the same in substance, equal in power and glory.(1)

(1) *I John 5:7; Matt. 28:19.*

7. **What are the decrees of God?**

The decrees of God are, his eternal purpose, according to the counsel of his will, whereby, for his own glory, he hath foreordained whatsoever comes to pass.(1)

(1) *Eph. 1:4, 11; Rom. 9:22-23.*

8. **How doth God execute his decrees?**

God executeth his decrees in the works of creation and providence.

9. **What is the work of creation?**

The work of creation is, God's making all things of nothing, by the word of his power, in the space of six days, and all very good.(1)

(1) *Gen. 1; Heb. 11:3.*

10. **How did God create man?**

God created man male and female, after his own image, in knowledge, righteousness, and holiness, with dominion over the creatures.(1)

(1) *Gen. 1:26-28; Col. 3:10; Eph. 4:24.*

11. **What are God's works of providence?**

God's works of providence are, his most holy,[1] wise,[2] and powerful preserving[3] and governing all his creatures, and all their actions.[4]

[1] *Ps. 145:17.* [2] *Ps. 104:24; Isa. 28:29.* [3] *Heb. 1:3.*

[4] *Ps. 103:19; Matt. 10:29-31.*

12. **What special act of providence did God exercise towards man in the estate wherein he was created?**

When God had created man, he entered into a covenant of life with him, upon condition of perfect obedience; forbidding him to eat of the tree of the knowledge of good and evil, upon the pain of death.[1]

[1] *Gal. 3:12; Gen. 2:17.*

13. **Did our first parents continue in the estate wherein they were created?**

Our first parents, being left to the freedom of their own will, fell from the estate wherein they were created, by sinning against God.[1]

[1] *Gen. 3:6-8, 13; Eccles. 7:29.*

14. **What is sin?**

Sin is any want of conformity unto, or transgression of, the law of God.[1]

[1] *I John 3:4.*

15. **What was the sin whereby our first parents fell from the estate wherein they were created?**

The sin whereby our first parents fell from the estate wherein they were created, was their eating the forbidden fruit.[1]

[1] *Gen. 3:6, 12.*

16. **Did all mankind fall in Adam's first transgression?**

The covenant being made with Adam, not only for himself, but for his posterity; all mankind, descending from him by ordinary generation, sinned in him, and fell with him, in his first transgression.[1]

[1] *Gen. 2:16-17; Rom. 5:12; I Cor. 15:21-22.*

17. **Into what estate did the fall bring mankind?**
The fall brought mankind into an estate of sin and misery.[1]

(1) *Rom. 5:12.*

18. **Wherein consists the sinfulness of that estate whereinto man fell?**
The sinfulness of that estate whereinto man fell, consists in the guilt of Adam's first sin, the want of original righteousness, and the corruption of his whole nature, which is commonly called Original Sin; together with all actual transgressions which proceed from it.[1]

(1) *Rom. 5:12, 19; 5:10-20; Eph. 2:1-3; James 1:14-15; Matt. 15:19.*

19. **What is the misery of that estate whereinto man fell?**
All mankind by their fall lost communion with God,[1] are under his wrath and curse,[2] and so made liable to all miseries in this life, to death itself, and to the pains of hell for ever.[3]

(1) *Gen. 3:8, 10, 24.* (2) *Eph. 2:2-3, Gal. 3:10.*
(3) *Lam. 3:39; Rom. 6:23, Matt. 25:41, 46.*

20. **Did God leave all mankind to perish in the estate of sin and misery?**
God having, out of his mere good pleasure, from all eternity, elected some to everlasting life,[1] did enter into a covenant of grace, to deliver them out of the estate of sin and misery, and to bring them into an estate of salvation by a Redeemer.[2]

(1) *Eph. 1:4.* (2) *Rom. 3:20-22; Gal. 3:21-22.*

21. **Who is the Redeemer of God's elect?**
The only Redeemer of God's elect is the Lord Jesus Christ,[1] who, being the eternal Son of God, became man,[2] and so was, and continueth to be, God and man in two distinct natures, and one person, for ever.[3]

(1) *I Tim. 2:5-6.* (2) *John 1:14; Gal. 4:4.*
(3) *Rom. 9:5; Luke 1:35; Col. 2:9; Heb. 7:24-25.*

22. How did Christ, being the Son of God, become man?

Christ, the Son of God, became man, by taking to himself a true body,(1) and a reasonable soul,(2) being conceived by the power of the Holy Ghost, in the womb of the Virgin Mary, and born of her,(3) yet without sin.(4)

(1) *Heb. 2:14, 16; 10:5.* (2) *Matt. 26:38.*

(3) *Luke 1:27, 31, 35, 42; Gal. 4:4.* (4) *Heb. 4:15; 7:26.*

23. What offices doth Christ execute as our Redeemer?

Christ, as our Redeemer, executeth the offices of a prophet, of a priest, and of a king, both in his estate of humiliation and exaltation.(1)

(1) *Acts 3:21-22; Heb. 12:25. Cf. II Cor. 13:3; Heb. 5:5-7; 7:25; Ps. 2:6; Isa. 9:6-7; Matt. 21:5; Ps. 2:8-11.*

24. How doth Christ execute the office of a prophet?

Christ executeth the office of a prophet, in revealing to us, by his word and Spirit, the will of God for our salvation.(1)

(1) *John 1:18; I Peter 1:10-12; John 15:15; 20:31.*

25. How doth Christ execute the office of a priest?

Christ executeth the office of a priest, in his once offering up of himself a sacrifice to satisfy divine justice,(1) and reconcile us to God,(2) and in making continual intercession for us.(3)

(1) *Heb. 9:14, 28.* (2) *Heb. 2:17.* (3) *Heb. 7:24-25.*

26. How doth Christ execute the office of a king?

Christ executeth the office of a king, in subduing us to himself,(1) in ruling(2) and defending us,(3) and in restraining and conquering all his and our enemies.(4)

(1) *Acts 15:14-16.* (2) *Isa. 33:22.* (3) *Isa. 32:1-2.* (4) *I Cor. 15:25, Ps. 110.*

27. Wherein did Christ's humiliation consist?

Christ's humiliation consisted in his being born, and that in a low condition,(1) made under the law,(2) undergoing the miseries of this life,(3) the wrath of

God,[4] and the cursed death of the cross;[5] in being buried,[6] and continuing under the power of death for a time.[7]

[1] *Luke 2:7.* [2] *Gal. 4:4.* [3] *Heb. 12:2-3; Isa. 53:2-3.* [4] *Luke 22:44; Matt. 27:46.* [5] *Phil. 2:8.* [6] *I Cor. 15:3-4.* [7] *Acts 2:24-27, 31.*

28. Wherein consisteth Christ's exaltation?

Christ's exaltation consisteth in his rising again from the dead on the third day,[1] in ascending up into heaven,[2] in sitting at the right hand of God the Father,[3] and in coming to judge the world at the last day.[4]

[1] *I Cor. 15:4.* [2] *Mark 16:19.* [3] *Eph. 1:20.* [4] *Acts 1:11; 17:31.*

29. How are we made partakers of the redemption purchased by Christ?

We are made partakers of the redemption purchased by Christ, by the effectual application of it to us[1] by his Holy Spirit.[2]

[1] *John 1:11-12.* [2] *Titus 3:5-6.*

30. How doth the Spirit apply to us the redemption purchased by Christ?

The Spirit applieth to us the redemption purchased by Christ, by working faith in us,[1] and thereby uniting us to Christ in our effectual calling.[2]

[1] *Eph. 1:13-14; John 6:37, 39; Eph. 2:8.* [2] *Eph. 3:17, I Cor. 1:9.*

31. What is effectual calling?

Effectual calling is the work of God's Spirit,[1] whereby, convincing us of our sin and misery,[2] enlightening our minds in the knowledge of Christ,[3] and renewing our wills,[4] he doth persuade and enable us to embrace Jesus Christ, freely offered to us in the gospel.[5]

[1] *II Tim. 1:9; II Thess. 2:13-14.* [2] *Acts 2:37.* [3] *Acts 26:18.* [4] *Ezek. 36:26-27.* [5] *John 6:44-45; Phil. 2:13.*

32. What benefits do they that are effectually called partake of in this life?

They that are effectually called do in this life partake of justification,[1] adoption,[2] and sanctification, and the several benefits which in this life do either accompany or flow from them.[3]

[1] *Rom. 8:30.* [2] *Eph. 1:5.* [3] *I Cor. 1:26, 30.*

33. **What is justification?**

Justification is an act of God's free grace, wherein he pardoneth all our sins,(1) and accepteth us as righteous in his sight,(2) only for the righteousness of Christ imputed to us,(3) and received by faith alone.(4)

(1) *Rom. 3:24-25; 4:6-8.* (2) *II Cor. 5:19, 21.*
(3) *Rom. 5:17-19.* (4) *Gal. 2:16; Phil. 3:9.*

34. **What is adoption?**

Adoption is an act of God's free grace,(1) whereby we are received into the number, and have a right to all the privileges of the Sons of God.(2)

(1) *I John 3:1.* (2) *John 1:12; Rom. 8:17.*

35. **What is sanctification?**

Sanctification is the work of God's free grace,(1) whereby we are renewed in the whole man after the image of God,(2) and are enabled more and more to die unto sin, and live unto righteousness.(3)

(1) *II Thess. 2:13.* (2) *Eph. 4:23-24.* (3) *Rom. 6:4, 6.*

36. **What are the benefits which in this life do accompany or flow from justification, adoption, and sanctification?**

The benefits which in this life do accompany or flow from justification, adoption, and sanctification, are, assurance of God's love, peace of conscience,(1) joy in the Holy Ghost,(2) increase of grace,(3) and perseverance therein to the end.(4)

(1) *Rom. 5:1-2, 5.* (2) *Rom. 14:17.* (3) *Prov. 4:18.* (4) *I John 5:13; I Pet. 1:5.*

37. **What benefits do believers receive from Christ at death?**

The souls of believers are at their death made perfect in holiness,(1) and do immediately pass into glory;(2) and their bodies, being still united to Christ,(3) do rest in their graves(4) till the resurrection.(5)

(1) *Heb. 12:23.* (2) *II Cor. 5:1, 6, 8; Phil. 1:23; Luke 23:43.*
(3) *I Thess. 4:14.* (4) *Isa. 57:2.* (5) *Job 19:26-27.*

38. What benefits do believers receive from Christ at the resurrection?

At the resurrection, believers being raised up in glory,[1] shall be openly acknowledged and acquitted in the day of judgment,[2] and made perfectly blessed in the full enjoying of God[3] to all eternity.[4]

(1) *I Cor. 15:43.* (2) *Matt. 25:23; 10:32.*

(3) *I John 3:2; I Cor. 13:12.* (4) *I Thess. 4:17-18.*

39. What is the duty which God requireth of man?

The duty which God requireth of man, is obedience to his revealed will.[1]

(1) *Micah 6:8; I Sam. 15:22.*

40. What did God at first reveal to man for the rule of his obedience?

The rule which God at first revealed to man for his obedience, was the moral law.[1]

(1) *Rom. 2:14-15; 10:5.*

41. Where is the moral law summarily comprehended?

The moral law is summarily comprehended in the ten commandments.[1]

(1) *Deut. 10:4.*

42. What is the sum of the ten commandments?

The sum of the ten commandments is, To love the Lord our God with all our heart, with all our soul, with all our strength, and with all our mind; and our neighbor as ourselves.[1]

(1) *Matt. 22:37-40.*

43. What is the preface to the ten commandments?

The preface to the ten commandments is in these words, I am the Lord thy God, which have brought thee out of the land of Egypt, out of the house of bondage.[1]

(1) *Exod. 20:2.*

44. **What doth the preface to the ten commandments teach us?**

The preface to the ten commandments teacheth us, That because God is the Lord, and our God, and Redeemer, therefore we are bound to keep all his commandments.[(1)]

(1) *Luke 1:74-75; I Pet. 1:15-19.*

45. **Which is the first commandment?**

The first commandment is, Thou shalt have no other gods before me.[(1)]

(1) *Exod. 20:3.*

46. **What is required in the first commandment?**

The first commandment requireth us to know and acknowledge God to be the only true God, and our God;[(1)] and to worship and glorify him accordingly.[(2)]

(1) *I Chron. 28:9; Deut. 26:17.* (2) *Matt. 4:10; Ps. 29:2.*

47. **What is forbidden in the first commandment?**

The first commandment forbiddeth the denying,[(1)] or not worshipping and glorifying the true God as God,[(2)] and our God;[(3)] and the giving of that worship and glory to any other, which is due to him alone.[(4)]

(1) *Ps. 14:1.* (2) *Rom. 1:21.* (3) *Ps. 81:10-11.* (4) *Rom. 1:25-26.*

48. **What are we specially taught by these words, "before me," in the first commandment?**

These words "before me" in the first commandment teach us, That God, who seeth all things, taketh notice of, and is much displeased with, the sin of having any other God.[(1)]

(1) *Ezek. 8:5-18.*

49. **Which is the second commandment?**

The second commandment is, Thou shalt not make unto thee any graven image, or any likeness of any thing that is in heaven above, or that is in the earth beneath, or that is in the water under the earth: Thou shalt not bow down thyself to them, nor serve them: for I the Lord thy God am a jealous God, visiting the iniquity of the fathers upon the children unto the third and fourth generation of them that hate me; and showing mercy unto thousands of them that love me, and keep my commandments.(1)

(1) *Exod. 20:4-6.*

50. **What is required in the second commandment?**

The second commandment requireth the receiving, observing, and keeping pure and entire, all such religious worship and ordinances as God hath appointed in his word.(1)

(1) *Deut. 32:46; Matt. 28:20; Acts. 2:42.*

51. **What is forbidden in the second commandment?**

The second commandment forbiddeth the worshipping of God by images,(1) or any other way not appointed in his word.(2)

(1) *Deut. 4:15-19; Exod. 32:5, 8.* (2) *Deut. 12:31-32.*

52. **What are the reasons annexed to the second commandment?**

The reasons annexed to the second commandment are, God's sovereignty over us,(1) his propriety in us,(2) and the zeal he hath to his own worship.(3)

(1) *Ps. 95:2-3, 6.* (2) *Ps. 45:11.* (3) *Exod. 34:13-14.*

53. **Which is the third commandment?**

The third commandment is, Thou shalt not take the name of the Lord thy God in vain: for the Lord will not hold him guiltless that taketh his name in vain.(1)

(1) *Exod. 20:7.*

54. **What is required in the third commandment?**

The third commandment requireth the holy and reverend use of God's names,(1) titles,(2) attributes,(3) ordinances,(4) word,(5) and works.(6)

(1) *Matt. 6:9; Deut. 28:58.* (2) *Ps. 68:4.* (3) *Rev. 15:3-4.*
(4) *Mal. 1:11, 14.* (5) *Ps. 138:1-2.* (6) *Job 36:24.*

55. **What is forbidden in the third commandment?**

The third commandment forbiddeth all profaning or abusing anything whereby God maketh himself known.(1)

(1) *Mal. 1:6-7, 12; 2:2; 3:14.*

56. **What is the reason annexed to the third commandment?**
The reason annexed to the third commandment is, That however the breakers of this commandment may escape punishment from men, yet the Lord our God will not suffer them to escape his righteous judgment.(1)
(1) *I Sam. 2:12, 17, 22, 29; 3:13; Deut. 28:58-59.*

57. **Which is the fourth commandment?**
The fourth commandment is, Remember the sabbath-day, to keep it holy. Six days shalt thou labour, and do all thy work: but the seventh day is the sabbath of the Lord thy God: in it thou shalt not do any work, thou, nor thy son, nor thy daughter, thy man-servant, nor thy maid-servant, nor thy cattle, nor thy stranger that is within thy gates: For in six days the Lord made heaven and earth, the sea, and all that in them is, and rested the seventh day: wherefore the Lord blessed the sabbath day, and hallowed it.(1)
(1) *Exod. 20:8-11.*

58. **What is required in the fourth commandment?**
The fourth commandment requireth the keeping holy to God such set times as he hath appointed in his word; expressly one whole day in seven, to be a holy sabbath to himself.(1)
(1) *Deut. 5:12-14.*

59. **Which day of the seven hath God appointed to be the weekly sabbath?**
From the beginning of the world to the resurrection of Christ, God appointed the seventh day of the week to be the weekly sabbath; and the first day of the week ever since, to continue to the end of the world, which is the Christian sabbath.(1)
(1) *Gen. 2:2-3; I Cor. 16:1-2; Acts 20:7.*

60. **How is the sabbath to be sanctified?**
The sabbath is to be sanctified by a holy resting all that day,(1) even from such worldly employments and recreations as are lawful on other days;(2) and spending the whole time in the publick and private exercises of God's

worship,[3] except so much as is to be taken up in the works of necessity and mercy.[4]

[1] *Exod. 20:8, 10; 16:25-28.* [2] *Neh. 13:15-19, 21-22.*

[3] *Luke 4:16; Acts 20:7; Ps. 92 title; Isa. 66:23.* [4] *Matt. 12:1-31.*

61. **What is forbidden in the fourth commandment?**

The fourth commandment forbiddeth the omission or careless performance of the duties required,[1] and the profaning the day by idleness,[2] or doing that which is in itself sinful,[3] or by unnecessary thoughts, words, or works, about our worldly employments or recreations.[4]

[1] *Ezek. 22:26; Amos 8:5; Mal. 1:13.* [2] *Acts 20:7, 9.* [3] *Ezek. 23:38.* [4] *Jer. 17:24-26; Isa. 58:13.*

62. **What are the reasons annexed to the fourth commandment?**

The reasons annexed to the fourth commandment are, God's allowing us six days of the week for our own employments,[1] his challenging a special propriety in the seventh, his own example, and his blessing the sabbath-day.[2]

[1] *Exod. 20:9.* [2] *Exod. 20:11.*

63. **Which is the fifth commandment?**

The fifth commandment is, Honour thy father and thy mother; that thy days may be long upon the land which the Lord thy God giveth thee.[1]

[1] *Exod. 20:12.*

64. **What is required in the fifth commandment?**

The fifth commandment requireth the preserving the honour, and performing the duties, belonging to every one in their several places and relations, as superiors,[1] inferiors,[2] or equals.[3]

[1] *Eph. 5:21.* [2] *I Pet. 2:17.* [3] *Rom. 12:10.*

65. **What is the forbidden in the fifth commandment?**

The fifth commandment forbiddeth the neglecting of, or doing anything against, the honour and duty which belongeth to every one in their several places and relations.[1]

[1] *Matt. 15:4-6; Ezek. 34:2-4; Rom. 13:8.*

66. **What is the reason annexed to the fifth commandment?**
The reason annexed to the fifth commandment, is a promise of long life and prosperity (as far as it shall serve for God's glory and their own good) to all such as keep this commandment.(1)

(1) *Deut. 5:16; Eph. 6:2-3.*

67. **Which is the sixth commandment?**
The sixth commandment is, Thou shalt not kill.(1)

(1) *Exod. 20:13.*

68. **What is required in the sixth commandment?**
The sixth commandment requireth all lawful endeavours to preserve our own life,(1) and the life of others.(2)

(1) *Eph. 5:28-29.* (2) *I Kings 18:4.*

69. **What is forbidden in the sixth commandment?**
The sixth commandment forbiddeth the taking away of our own life, or the life of our neighbour unjustly, or whatsoever tendeth thereunto.(1)

(1) *Acts 16:28; Gen. 9:6.*

70. **Which is the seventh commandment?**
The seventh commandment is, Thou shalt not commit adultery.(1)

(1) *Exod. 20:14.*

71. **What is required in the seventh commandment?**
The seventh commandment requireth the preservation of our own and our neighbor's chastity, in heart, speech, and behaviour.(1)

(1) *I Cor. 7:2-3, 5, 34, 36; Col. 4:6; I Pet. 3:2.*

72. **What is forbidden in the seventh commandment?**
The seventh commandment forbiddeth all unchaste thoughts, words, and actions.(1)

(1) *Matt. 15:19; 5:28; Eph. 5:3-4.*

73. Which is the eighth commandment?

The eighth commandment is, Thou shalt not steal.[1]

[1] *Exod. 20:15.*

74. What is required in the eighth commandment?

The eighth commandment requireth the lawful procuring and furthering the wealth and outward estate of ourselves and others.[1]

[1] *Gen. 30:30; I Tim. 5:8; Lev. 25:35; Deut. 22:1-5; Exod. 23:4-5; Gen. 47:14, 20.*

75. What is forbidden in the eighth commandment?

The eighth commandment forbiddeth whatsoever doth or may unjustly hinder our own or our neighbour's wealth or outward estate.[1]

[1] *Prov. 21:17; 23:20-21; 28:19; Eph. 4:28.*

76. What is the ninth commandment?

The ninth commandment is, Thou shalt not bear false witness against thy neighbour.[1]

[1] *Exod. 20:16.*

77. What is required in the ninth commandment?

The ninth commandment requireth the maintaining and promoting of truth between man and man,[1] and of our own and our neighbour's good name,[2] especially in witness-bearing.[3]

[1] *Zech. 8:16.* [2] *III John 12.* [3] *Prov. 14:5, 25.*

78. What is forbidden in the ninth commandment?

The ninth commandment forbiddeth whatsoever is prejudicial to truth, or injurious to our own or our neighbour's good name.[1]

[1] *I Sam. 17:28; Lev. 19:16; Ps. 15:3.*

79. Which is the tenth commandment?

The tenth commandment is, Thou shalt not covet thy neighbour's house, thou shalt not covet thy neighbour's wife, nor his manservant, nor his maidservant, nor his ox, nor his ass, nor any thing that is thy neighbour's.[1]

[1] *Exod. 20:17.*

80. **What is required in the tenth commandment?**

The tenth commandment requireth full contentment with our own condition,(1) with a right and charitable frame of spirit toward our neighbour, and all that is his.(2)

(1) *Heb. 13:5; I Tim. 6:6.* (2) *Job 31:29; Rom. 12:15; I Tim. 1:5; I Cor. 13:4-7.*

81. **What is forbidden in the tenth commandment?**

The tenth commandment forbiddeth all discontentment with our own estate,(1) envying or grieving at the good of our neighbour,(2) and all inordinate motions and affections to any thing that is his.(3)

(1) *I Kings 21:4; Esther 5:13; I Cor. 10:10.*
(2) *Gal. 5:26; James 3:14, 16.* (3) *Rom. 7:7-8; 13:9; Deut. 5:21.*

82. **Is any man able perfectly to keep the commandments of God?**

No mere man since the fall is able in this life perfectly to keep the commandments of God,(1) but doth daily break them in thought, word, and deed.(2)

(1) *Eccles. 7:20; I John 1:8, 10; Gal. 5:17.*
(2) *Gen. 6:5; 8:21; Rom. 3:9-21; James 3:2-13.*

83. **Are all transgression of the law equally heinous?**

Some sins in themselves, and by reason of several aggravations, are more heinous in the sight of God than others.(1)

(1) *Ezek. 8:6, 13, 15; I John 5:16; Ps. 78:17, 32, 56.*

84. **What doth every sin deserve?**

Every sin deserveth God's wrath and curse, both in this life, and that which is to come.(1)

(1) *Eph. 5:6; Gal. 3:10; Lam. 3:39; Matt. 25:41.*

85. **What doth God require of us, that we may escape his wrath and curse due to us for sin?**

To escape the wrath and curse of God due to us for sin, God requireth of us faith in Jesus Christ, repentance unto life,(1) with the diligent use of all the outward means whereby Christ communicateth to us the benefits of redemption.[2]

[1] *Acts. 20:21.* [2] *Prov. 2:1-5; 8:33-36; Isa. 55:3.*

86. **What is faith in Jesus Christ?**
Faith in Jesus Christ is a saving grace,[1] whereby we receive and rest upon him alone for salvation, as he is offered to us in the gospel.[2]

[1] *Heb. 10:39.* [2] *John 1:12; Isa. 26:3-4; Phil. 3:9; Gal. 2:16.*

87. **What is repentance unto life?**
Repentance unto life is a saving grace,[1] whereby a sinner, out of a true sense of his sin,[2] and apprehension of the mercy of God in Christ,[3] doth, with grief and hatred of his sin, turn from it unto God,[4] with full purpose of, and endeavour after, new obedience.[5]

[1] *Acts. 11:18.* [2] *Acts. 2:37-38.* [3] *Joel 2:12; Jer. 3:22.*
[4] *Jer. 31:18-19; Ezek. 36:31.* [5] *II Cor. 7:11; Isa. 1:16-17.*

88. **What are the outward means whereby Christ communicateth to us the benefits of redemption?**
The outward and ordinary means whereby Christ communicateth to us the benefits of redemption, are his ordinances, especially the word, sacraments, and prayer; all which are made effectual to the elect for salvation.[1]

[1] *Matt. 28:19-20; Acts 2:42, 46-47.*

89. **How is the word made effectual to salvation?**
The Spirit of God maketh the reading, but especially the preaching of the word, an effectual means of convincing and converting sinners, and of building them up in holiness and comfort, through faith, unto salvation.[1]

[1] *Neh. 8:8; I Cor. 14:24-25; Acts 26:18; Ps. 19:8; Acts 20:32; Rom. 15:4; II Tim. 3:15-17; Rom. 10:13-17; 1:16.*

90. How is the word to be read and heard, that it may become effectual to salvation?

That the word may become effectual to salvation, we must attend thereunto with diligence,[1] preparation,[2] and prayer;[3] receive it with faith and love,[4] lay it up in our hearts,[5] and practice it in our lives.[6]

[1] *Prov. 8:34.* [2] *I Pet. 2:1-2.* [3] *Ps. 119:18.*
[4] *Heb. 4:2; II Thess. 2:10.* [5] *Ps. 119:11.* [6] *Luke 8:15; James 1:25.*

91. How do the sacraments become effectual means of salvation?

The sacraments become effectual means of salvation, not from any virtue in them, or in him that doth administer them; but only by the blessing of Christ,[1] and the working of his Spirit in them that by faith receive them.[2]

[1] *I Pet. 3:21; Matt. 3:11; I Cor. 3:6-7.* [2] *I Cor. 12:13.*

92. What is a sacrament?

A sacrament is an holy ordinance instituted by Christ, wherein, by sensible signs, Christ, and the benefits of the new covenant, are represented, sealed, and applied to believers.[1]

[1] *Gen. 17:7, 10; Exod. 12; I Cor. 11:23, 26.*

93. Which are the sacraments of the New Testament?

The sacraments of the New Testament are, Baptism,[1] and the Lord's supper.[2]

[1] *Matt. 28:19.* [2] *Matt. 26:26-28.*

94. What is baptism?

Baptism is a sacrament, wherein the washing with water in the name of the Father, and of the Son, and of the Holy Ghost,[1] doth signify and seal our ingrafting into Christ, and partaking of the benefits of the covenant of grace, and our engagement to be the Lord's.[2]

[1] *Matt. 28:19.* [2] *Rom. 6:4; Gal. 3:27.*

95. To whom is baptism to be administered?

Baptism is not to be administered to any that are out of the visible church, till they profess their faith in Christ, and obedience to him;(1) but the infants of such as are members of the visible church are to be baptized.(2)

(1) *Acts 8:36-37; 2:38.*

(2) *Acts 2:38-39; Gen. 17:10. Cf. Col. 2:11-12; I Cor. 7:14.*

96. What is the Lord's supper?

The Lord's Supper is a sacrament, wherein, by giving and receiving bread and wine, according to Christ's appointment, his death is showed forth; and the worthy receivers are, not after a corporal and carnal manner, but by faith, made partakers of his body and blood, with all his benefits, to their spiritual nourishment, and growth in grace.(1)

(1) *I Cor. 11:23-26; 10:16.*

97. What is required to be the worthy receiving of the Lord's supper?

It is required of them that would worthily partake of the Lord's supper, that they examine themselves of their knowledge to discern the Lord's body,(1) of their faith to feed upon him,(2) of their repentance,(3) love,(4) and new obedience;(5) lest, coming unworthily, they eat and drink judgment to themselves.(6)

(1) *I Cor. 11:28-29.* (2) *II Cor. 13:5.* (3) *I Cor. 11:31.*

(4) *I Cor. 10:16-17.* (5) *I Cor. 5:7-8.* (6) *I Cor. 11:28-29.*

98. What is prayer?

Prayer is an offering up of our desires unto God,(1) for things agreeable to his will,(2) in the name of Christ,(3) with confession of our sins,(4) and thankful acknowledgment of his mercies.(5)

(1) *Ps. 62:8.* (2) *I John 5:14.* (3) *John 16:23.*

(4) *Ps. 32:5-6; Dan. 9:4.* (5) *Phil. 4:6.*

99. **What rule hath God given for our direction in prayer?**

The whole word of God is of use to direct us in prayer;[12] but the special rule of direction is that form of prayer which Christ taught his disciples, commonly called The Lord's prayer.[2]

[1] *I John 5:14.* [2] *Matt. 6:9-13. Cf. Luke 11:2-4.*

100. **What doth the preface of the Lord's prayer teach us?**

The preface of the Lord's prayer (which is, Our Father which art in heaven)[1] teacheth us to draw near to God with all holy reverence and confidence, as children to a father, able and ready to help us;[2] and that we should pray with and for others.[3]

[1] *Matt. 6:9.* [2] *Rom. 8:15; Luke 11:13.* [3] *Acts. 12:5; I Tim. 2:1-2.*

101. **What do we pray for in the first petition?**

In the first petition (which is, Hallowed be thy name)[1] we pray, That God would enable us and others to glorify him in all that whereby he maketh himself known;[2] and that he would dispose all things to his own glory.[3]

[1] *Matt. 6:9.* [2] *Ps. 67:2-3.* [3] *Ps. 83.*

102. **What do we pray for in the second petition?**

In the second petition (which is, Thy kingdom come)[1] we pray, That Satan's kingdom may be destroyed;[2] and that the kingdom of grace may be advanced,[3] ourselves and others brought into it, and kept in it;[4] and that the kingdom of glory may be hastened.[5]

[1] *Matt. 6:10.* [2] *Ps. 68:1, 18.* [3] *Rev. 12:10-11.*
[4] *II Thess. 3:1; Rom. 10:1; John 17:9, 20.* [5] *Rev. 22:20.*

103. **What do we pray for in the third petition?**

In the third petition (which is, Thy will be done in earth, as it is in heaven)[1] we pray, That God, by his grace, would make us able and willing to know, obey, and submit to his will in all things,[2] as the angels do in heaven.[3]

[1] *Matt. 6:10.* [2] *Ps. 67; 119:36; Matt. 26:39; II Sam. 15:25; Job 1:21.*
[3] *Ps. 103:20-21.*

104. What do we pray for in the fourth petition?

In the fourth petition (which is, Give us this day our daily bread)[1], we pray, That of God's free gift we may receive a competent portion of the good things of this life, and enjoy his blessing with them.[2]

[1] *Matt. 6:11.* [2] *Prov. 30:8-9; Gen. 28:20; I Tim. 4:4-5.*

105. What do we pray for in the fifth petition?

In the fifth petition (which is, And forgive us our debts, as we forgive our debtors)[1] we pray, That God, for Christ's sake, would freely pardon all our sins;[2] which we are the rather encouraged to ask, because by his grace we are enabled from the heart to forgive others.[3]

[1] *Matt. 6:12.* [2] *Ps. 51:1-2, 7, 9; Dan. 9:17-19.*
[3] *Luke 11:4, Matt. 18:35.*

106. What do we pray for in the sixth petition?

In the sixth petition (which is, And lead us not into temptation, but deliver us from evil)[1] we pray, that God would either keep us from being tempted to sin,[2] or support and deliver us when we are tempted.[3]

[1] *Matt. 6:13.* [2] *Matt. 26:41.* [3] *II Cor. 12:7-8.*

107. What doth the conclusion the Lord's prayer teach us?

The conclusion of the Lord's prayer (which is, For thine is the kingdom, and the power, and the glory, for ever, Amen)[1] teacheth us to take our encouragement in prayer from God only,[2] and in our prayers to praise him, ascribing kingdom, power, and glory to him.[3] And, in testimony of our desire, and assurance to be heard, we say, Amen.[4]

[1] *Matt. 6:13.* [2] *Dan. 9:4, 7-9, 16-19.*
[3] *I Chron. 29:10-13.* [4] *I Cor. 14:16; Rev. 22:20-21.* ▪

Keach's Catechism

The Second London Baptist Confession was first written in secret in 1677. That same year, two of its framers wrote a Reformed Baptist catechism to accompany the confession and teach its precepts to the church's children. That catechism has usually been known as Keach's Catechism, named for Benjamin Keach, who is traditionally credited as the writer. But it is now thought likely that the first draft of the catechism was actually written by William Collins, who had helped Keach write the second London confession.

With the "Glorious Revolution" of 1688, religious persecution ended for the Nonconformists of Britain, including the Reformed Baptists. Now that it was safe, the Reformed Baptist leaders reassembled in London and publicly released the Second London Baptist Confession in 1689. Keach's Catechism, also known as the Baptist Catechism, was published shortly afterward in 1693.

Just as the Second London Baptist Confession very closely resembles the Westminster Confession on all points except baptism, Keach's Catechism is much like the Westminster and Heidelberg catechisms except where baptism is concerned.

---

1. **Who is the first and best of beings?**
   God is the first and best of beings.
   (Isaiah 44:6; Psalm 8:1; 97:9)

2. **What is the chief end of man?**
   Man's chief end is to glorify God and to enjoy Him forever.
   (1 Cor. 10:31; Psalm 73:25-26)

3. **How do we know there is a God?**

The light of nature in man, and the works of God, plainly declare that there is a God; but His Word and Spirit only, do effectually reveal Him unto us for our salvation.

(Rom. 1:18-20; Psalm 19:1, 2; 2 Tim. 3:15; 1 Cor. 1:21-24; 1 Cor. 2:9, 10)

4. **What is the Word of God?**

The Scriptures of the Old and New Testaments, being given by divine inspiration, are the Word of God, the only infallible rule of faith and practice.

(2 Peter 1:21; 2 Timothy 3:16, 17; Isaiah 8:20)

5. **How do we know that the Bible is the Word of God?**

The Bible evidences itself to be God's Word by the heavenliness of its doctrine, the unity of its parts, its power to convert sinners and to edify saints; but the Spirit of God only, bearing witness by and with the Scriptures in our hearts, is able fully to persuade us that the Bible is the Word of God.

(1 Cor. 2:6, 7, 13; Ps. 119:18, 129; Acts 10:43, 26:22; Acts 18:28; Heb 4:12; Ps. 19:7-9; Rom. 15:4; John 16:13, 14; 1 John 2:20-27; 2 Cor. 3:14-17)

6. **May all men make use of the Scriptures?**

All men are not only permitted, but commanded and exhorted, to read, hear, and understand the Scriptures.

(John 5:39; Luke 16:29; Acts 8:28-30; 17:11)

7. **What do the Scriptures principally teach?**

The Scriptures principally teach what man is to believe concerning God and what duty God requires of man.

(2 Tim. 3:16, 17; John 20:31; Acts 24:14; 1 Cor. 10:11; Eccles. 12:13)

8. **What is God?**

God is a Spirit, infinite, eternal, and unchangeable in His being, wisdom, power, holiness, justice, goodness and truth.

(John 4:24; Ps. 147:5; Ps. 90:2; James 1:17; Rev. 4:8; Ps. 89:14; Exod. 34:6, 7; 1 Tim. 1:17)

9. **Are there more gods than one?**
There is but one only, the living and true God.
(Deut. 6:4; Jeremiah 10:10)

10. **How many persons are there in the Godhead?**
There are three persons in the Godhead, the Father, the Son, and the Holy Spirit; and these three are one God, the same in essence, equal in power and glory.
(1 Cor. 8:6; John 10:30; John 14:9; Acts 5:3, 4; Matt. 28:19; 2 Cor. 13:14)

11. **What are the decrees of God?**
The decrees of God are His eternal purpose, according to the counsel of His will, whereby for His own glory, He has fore-ordained whatsoever comes to pass.
(Eph. 1:11; Rom. 11:36; Dan. 4:35)

12. **How does God execute His decrees?**
God executes His decrees in the works of creation and providence.
(Gen. 1:1; Rev. 4:11; Matt. 6:26; Acts 14:17)

13. **What is the work of creation?**
The work of creation is God's making all things of nothing, by the Word of His power, in the space of six days, and all very good.
(Gen. 1:1; Heb. 11:3; Ex. 20:11; Gen. 1:31)

14. **How did God create man?**
God created man male and female, after His own image, in knowledge, righteousness, and holiness, with dominion over the creatures.
(Gen. 1:27; Col. 3:10; Eph. 4:24; Gen. 1:28)

15. **What are God's works of providence?**
God's works of providence are His most holy, wise, and powerful preserving and governing all His creatures, and all their actions.
(Neh. 9:6; Col. 1:17; Heb. 1:3; Ps. 103:19; Matt. 10:29, 30)

16. **What special act of providence did God exercise towards man, in the estate wherein he was created?**
When God had created man, He entered into a covenant of works with him, upon condition of perfect obedience, forbidding him to eat of the tree of the knowledge of good and evil, upon pain of death.
(Gen. 2:16, 17; Gal. 3:12; Rom. 5:12)

17. **Did our first parents continue in the estate wherein they were created?**
Our first parents, being left to the freedom of their own will, fell from the estate wherein they were created, by sinning against God.
(Gen. 3:6; Eccles. 7:29; Rom. 5:12)

18. **What is sin?**
Sin is any want of conformity unto, or transgression of, the law of God.
(1 John 3:4; Rom. 5:13)

19. **What was the sin whereby our first parents fell from the estate wherein they were created?**
The sin whereby our first parents fell from the estate wherein they were created, was their eating the forbidden fruit.
(Gen. 3:6, 12, 13)

20. **Did all mankind fall in Adam's first transgression?**
The covenant being made with Adam, not only for himself but for his posterity, all mankind, descending from him by ordinary generation, sinned in him, and fell with him in his first transgression.
(1 Cor. 15:21, 22; Rom. 5:12, 18, 19)

21. **Into what estate did the fall bring mankind?**
The fall brought mankind into an estate of sin and misery.
(Ps. 51:5; Rom. 5:18, 19: Is. 64:6)

22. **Wherein consists the sinfulness of that estate whereunto man fell?**
The sinfulness of that estate whereunto man fell, consists in the guilt of Adam's first sin, the want of original righteousness, and the corruption of

his whole nature, which is commonly called original sin, together with all actual transgressions which proceed from it.

(Rom. 5:19; 3:10; Eph. 2:1; Is. 53:6; Ps. 51:5; Matt. 15:19)

23. **What is the misery of that estate whereunto man fell?**
All mankind, by their fall, lost communion with God, are under His wrath and curse, and made liable to all the miseries of this life, to death itself, and to the pains of hell forever.

(Gen. 3:8, 24; Eph. 2:3; Gal. 3:10; Rom. 6:23; Matt. 25:41-46; Ps. 9:17)

24. **Did God leave all mankind to perish in the estate of sin and misery?**
God, out of His mere good pleasure, from all eternity, having chosen a people to everlasting life, did enter into a covenant of grace, to deliver them out of the estate of sin and misery, and to bring them into an estate of salvation, by a Redeemer.

(Eph. 1:3, 4; 2 Thess. 2:13; Rom. 5:21; Acts 13:8; Jer. 31:33)

25. **Who is the Redeemer of God's elect?**
The only Redeemer of God's elect is the Lord Jesus Christ, who, being the eternal Son of God, became man, and so was and continues to be God and man, in two distinct natures and one person, forever.

(Gal. 3:13; 1 Tim. 2:5; John 1:14; 1 Tim. 3:16; Rom. 9:5; Col. 2:9)

26. **How did Christ, being the Son of God, become man?**
Christ, the Son of God became man by taking to himself a true body and a reasonable soul; being conceived by the power of the Holy Spirit in the womb of the Virgin Mary and born of her, yet without sin.

(Heb. 2:14; Matt. 26:38; Luke 2:52; John 12:27; Luke 1:31, 35; Heb. 4:15; 7:26)

27. **What offices does Christ execute as our Redeemer?**
Christ, as our Redeemer, executes the offices of a prophet, of a priest, and of a king, both in His estate of humiliation and exaltation.

(Acts 3:22; Heb. 5:6; Ps. 2:6)

28. **How does Christ execute the office of a prophet?**
Christ executes the office of a prophet, in revealing to us, by this Word and Spirit, the will of God for our salvation.
(John 1:18; 14:26; 15:15)

29. **How does Christ execute the office of a priest?**
Christ executes the office of a priest, in His once offering up of Himself, a sacrifice to satisfy divine justice, and reconcile us to God, and in making continual intercession for us.
(1 Peter 2:24; Heb. 9:28; Eph. 5:2; Heb. 2:17; 7:25; Rom. 8:34)

30. **How does Christ execute the office of a king?**
Christ executes the office of a king, in subduing us to Himself, in ruling and defending us, and in restraining and conquering all His and our enemies.
(Ps. 110:3; Matt. 2:6; 1 Cor. 15:25)

31. **Wherein did Christ's humiliation consist?**
Christ's humiliation consisted in His being born, and that in a low condition, made under the law, undergoing the miseries of this life, the wrath of God, and the cursed death of the cross, in being buried, and continuing under the power of death for a time.
(Luke 2:7; Gal. 4:4; Is. 53:3; Luke 22:44; Matt. 27:46; Phil. 2:8; Matt. 12:40; Mark 15:45, 46)

32. **Wherein consists Christ's exaltation?**
Christ's exaltation consists in His rising again from the dead on the third day, in ascending up into heaven, in sitting at the right hand of God the Father, and in coming to judge the world at the last day.
(1 Cor. 15:4; Acts 1:11; Mark 16:19; Acts 17:31)

33. **How are we made partakers of the redemption purchased by Christ?**
We are made partakers of the redemption purchased by Christ, by the effectual application of it to us, by His Holy Spirit.
(John 3:5, 6; Titus 3:5, 6)

34. **How does the Spirit apply to us the redemption purchased by Christ?**
The Spirit applies to us the redemption purchased by Christ, by working faith in us, and thereby uniting us to Christ in our effectual calling.
(Eph. 2:8; 3:17)

35. **What is effectual calling?**
Effectual calling is the work of God's Spirit, whereby, convincing us of our sin and misery, enlightening our minds in the knowledge of Christ, and renewing our wills, He does persuade and enable us to embrace Jesus Christ, freely offered to us in the Gospel.
(2 Tim. 1:9; John 16:8-11; Acts 2:37; 26:18; Ezekiel 36:26; John 6:44, 45; 1 Cor. 12:3)

36. **What benefits do they that are effectually called, partake of in this life?**
They that are effectually called, do in this life partake of justification, adoption, sanctification, and the several benefits which in this life do either accompany or flow from them.
(Rom. 8:30; Gal. 3:26; 1 Cor. 6:11; Rom. 8:31, 32; Eph. 1:5; 1 Cor. 1:30)

37. **What is justification?**
Justification is an act of God's free grace, wherein He pardons all our sins, and accepts us as righteous in His sight, only for the righteousness of Christ imputed to us, and received by faith alone.
(Rom. 3:24; Eph. 1:7; 2 Cor. 5:21; Rom. 5:19; Phil. 3:9; Gal. 2:16)

38. **What is adoption?**
Adoption is an act of God's free grace, whereby we are received into the number, and have a right to all the privileges of the sons of God.
(1 John 3:1; John 1:12; Rom. 8:16, 17)

39. **What is sanctification?**
Sanctification is a work of God's free grace whereby we are renewed in the whole man after the image of God, and are enabled more and more to die unto sin, and live unto righteousness.
(2 Thess. 2:13; Eph. 4:23, 24; Rom. 6:11)

40. What are the benefits which in this life do accompany or flow from justification, adoption, and sanctification?
The benefits which in this life do accompany or flow from justification, adoption, and sanctification, are, assurance of God's love, peace of conscience, joy in the Holy Spirit, increase of grace, and perseverance therein to the end.
(Rom. 5:1-5; 14:17; Prov. 4:18; 1 Peter 1:5; 1 John 5:13)

41. What benefits do believers receive from Christ at death?
The souls of believers are at death made perfect in holiness, and do immediately pass into glory, and their bodies, being still united to Christ, do rest in their graves till the resurrection.
(Heb. 12:23; Phil. 1:23; 2 Cor. 5:8; Luke 23:43; 1 Thess 4:14; Is. 57:2; Job 19:26)

42. What benefits do believers receive from Christ at the Resurrection?
At the resurrection, believers become raised up in glory, shall be openly acknowledged and acquitted in the day of judgment, and made perfectly blessed in the full enjoyment of God to all eternity.
(Phil. 3:20, 21; 1 Cor. 15:42, 43; Matt. 10:32; 1 John 3:2; 1 Thess. 4:17)

43. What shall be done to the wicked at death?
The souls of the wicked shall at death, be cast into the torments of hell, and their bodies lie in their graves till the resurrection and judgement of the great day.
(Luke 16:22-24; Ps. 49:14)

44. What shall be done to the wicked at the day of judgement?
At the day of judgement, the bodies of the wicked, being raised out of their graves, shall be sentenced, together with their souls, to unspeakable torments with the devil and his angels forever.
(Dan. 12:2; John 5:28, 29; 2 Thess. 1:9; Matt. 25:41)

45. What is the duty which God requires of man?
The duty which God requires of man, is obedience to His revealed will.
(Micah 6:8; Eccles. 12:13; Ps. 119:4; Luke 10:26-28)

46. **What did God at first reveal to man for the rule of his obedience?**
The rule which God at first revealed to man for his obedience was the moral law.
(Rom. 2:14, 15; 5:13, 14)

47. **Where is the moral law summarily comprehended?**
The moral law is summarily comprehended in the Ten Commandments.
(Deut. 10:4; Matt. 19:17)

48. **What is the sum of the Ten Commandments?**
The sum of the Ten Commandments is, to love the Lord our God, with all our heart, with all our soul, with all our strength, and with all our mind; and our neighbor as ourselves.
(Matt. 22:36-40; Mark 12:28-33)

49. **What is the preface to the Ten Commandments?**
The preface to the Ten Commandments is, I am the Lord thy God, which have brought thee out of the land of Egypt, out of the house of bondage.
(Exodus 20:2)

50. **What does the preface to the Ten Commandments teach us?**
The preface to the Ten Commandments teaches us, that because God is the Lord, and our God and Redeemer, therefore we are bound to keep all His commandments.
(Deut 11:1)

51. **Which is the first commandment?**
The first commandment is, Thou shalt have no other gods before me.
(Exodus 20:3)

52. **What is required in the first commandment?**
The first commandment requires us to know and acknowledge God to be the only true God, and our God, and to worship and glorify Him accordingly.
(Joshua 24:15; 1 Chron. 28:9; Deut. 26:17; Ps. 29:2; Matt. 4:10)

53. **What is forbidden in the first commandment?**

The first commandment forbids the denying, or not worshipping and glorifying the true God, as God and our God; and the giving that worship and glory to any other, which is due unto Him alone.

(Joshua 24:27; Rom. 1:20, 21; Ps. 14:1; Rom. 1:25)

54. **What are we especially taught by these words, "before me," in the first commandment?**

These words, "before me," in the first commandment, teach us, that God, who sees all things, takes notice of, and is much displeased with the sin of having any other God.

(Deut.30:17, 18; Ps. 44:20, 21; Ps. 90:8)

55. **Which is the second commandment?**

The second commandment is, Thou shalt not make unto thee any graven image, or any likeness of any thing that is in heaven above, or that is in the earth beneath, or that is in the water under the earth. Thou shalt not bow down thyself to them, nor serve them; for I the Lord thy God am a jealous God, visiting the iniquity of the fathers upon the children, unto the third and fourth generation of them that hate me: and showing mercy unto thousands of them that love me and keep my commandments.

(Exodus 20:4-6)

56. **What is required in the second commandment?**

The second commandment requires the receiving, observing, and keeping pure and entire, all such religious worship and ordinances, as God has appointed in His Word.

(Deut. 32:46; Matt. 28:20; Deut. 12:32)

57. **What is forbidden in the second commandment?**

The second commandment forbids the worshipping of God by images, or any other way not appointed in His Word.

(Rom. 1:22, 23; Deut. 4:15,16; Matt. 15:9; Col. 2:18)

58. **What are the reasons annexed to the second commandment?**

The reasons annexed to the second commandment, are, God's sovereignty over us, His propriety in us, and the zeal He has for His own worship.

(Ps. 45:11; Ex. 34:14; 1 Cor. 10:22)

59. **Which is the third commandment?**

The third commandment is, Thou shalt not take the name of the Lord thy God in vain: for the Lord will not hold him guiltless that taketh his name in vain.

(Exodus 20:7)

60. **What is required in the third commandment?**

The third commandment requires the holy and reverent use of God's names, titles, attributes, ordinances, words, and works.

(Ps. 29:2; Deut. 32:1-4; Deut. 28:58, 59; Ps. 111:9; Matt. 6:9, Eccles. 5:1; Ps. 138:2, Job 36:24; Rev. 15:3, 4; Rev. 4:8)

61. **What is forbidden in the third commandment?**

The third commandment forbids all profaning and abusing of any thing whereby God makes Himself known.

(Malachi 1:6, 7; Lev. 20:3; 19:12; Matt. 5:34-37; Isa. 52:5)

62. **What is the reason annexed to the third commandment?**

The reason annexed to the third commandment is, that howsoever the breakers of this commandment may escape punishment from men, yet the Lord our God will not suffer them to escape His righteous judgment.

(Deut. 28:58, 59; Malachi 2:2)

63. **Which is the fourth commandment?**

The fourth commandment is, Remember the Sabbath day to keep it holy. Six days shalt thou labor and do all thy work; but the seventh day is the Sabbath of the Lord thy God: in it thou shalt not do any work, thou, nor thy son, nor thy daughter, thy manservant, nor thy maid servant, nor your cattle, nor your stranger who is within thy gates: for in six days the Lord made heaven and earth, the sea, and all that in them is, and rested the seventh day: wherefore the Lord blessed the Sabbath day and hallowed it.

(Exodus 20:8-11)

64. **What is required in the fourth commandment?**

The fourth commandment requires the keeping holy to God such set times as He has appointed in His Word, expressly one whole day in seven to be a holy Sabbath to Himself.

(Lev. 19:30; Deut. 5:12)

65. **Which day of the seven has God appointed to be the weekly Sabbath?**

From the creation of the world to the resurrection of Christ, God appointed the seventh day of the week to be the weekly Sabbath; and the first day of the week ever since, to continue to the end of the world, which is the Christian Sabbath.

(Gen. 2:3; John 20:19; Acts 20:7; 1 Cor. 16:1, 2; Rev. 1:10)

66. **How is the Sabbath to be sanctified?**

The Sabbath is to sanctified by a holy resting all that day, even from such worldly employments and recreations as are lawful on other days, and spending the time in the public and private exercises of God's worship, except so much as is to be taken up in the works of necessity and mercy.

(Lev. 23:3; Isa. 58:13, 14; Isa. 66:23; Matt. 12:11, 12)

67. **What is forbidden in the fourth commandment?**

The fourth commandment forbids the omission or careless performance of the duties required, and the profaning the day by idleness, or doing that which is in itself sinful, or by unnecessary thoughts, words, or works, about worldly employments or recreations.

(Ezekiel 22:26; 23:38; Jer. 17:21; Neh. 13:15, 17; Acts 20:7)

68. **What are the reasons annexed to the fourth commandment?**
The reasons annexed to the fourth commandment are, God's allowing us six days of the week for our own employments, His challenging a special propriety in the seventh, His own example and His blessing the Sabbath day.
(Exodus 34:21; 31:16, 17; Gen. 2:2, 3)

69. **Which is the fifth commandment?**
The fifth commandment is, Honor thy father and thy mother, that thy days may be long upon the land which the Lord thy God giveth thee.
(Exodus 20:12)

70. **What is required in the fifth commandment?**
The fifth commandment requires preserving the honor, and performing the duties, belonging to every one in their several places and relations, as superiors, inferiors, or equals.
(Lev. 19:32; 1 Peter 2:17; Rom. 13:1; Eph. 5:21, 22; Eph. 6:1, 5, 9; Col. 3:19-22; Rom. 12:10)

71. **What is forbidden in the fifth commandment?**
The fifth commandment forbids the neglecting of, or doing anything against the honor and duty which belongs to every one in their several places and relations.
(Prov. 30:17; Rom. 13:7, 8)

72. **What is the reason annexed to the fifth commandment?**
The reason annexed to the fifth commandment is a promise of long life and prosperity (as far as it shall serve God's glory and their own good), to all such as keep this commandment.
(Eph. 6:2, 3; Prov. 4:3-6; 6:20-22)

73. **Which is the sixth commandment?**
The sixth commandment is, Thou shalt not kill.
(Exodus 20:13)

74. **What is required in the sixth commandment?**
The sixth commandment requires all lawful endeavors to preserve our own life and the life of others.
(Eph. 5:29, 30; Ps. 82:3, 4; Prov. 24:11, 12; Act 16:28)

75. **What is forbidden in the sixth commandment?**
The sixth commandment forbids the taking away our own life, or the life of our neighbor unjustly, or whatsoever tends thereto.
(Gen. 4:10, 11; 9:6; Matt. 5:21-26)

76. **Which is the seventh commandment?**
The seventh commandment is, Thou shalt not commit adultery.
(Exodus 20:14)

77. **What is required in the seventh commandment?**
The seventh commandment requires the preservation of our own and our neighbor's chastity, in heart, speech, and behavior.
(1 Cor. 6:18; 7:2; 2 Tim. 2:22; Matt. 5:28; 1 Peter 3:2)

78. **What is forbidden in the seventh commandment?**
The seventh commandment forbids all unchaste thoughts, words, and actions.
(Matt. 5:28-32; Job 31:1; Eph. 5:3, 4; Rom. 13:13; Col. 4:6)

79. **Which is the eighth commandment?**
The eighth commandment is, Thou shalt not steal.
(Exodus 20:15)

80. **What is required in the eighth commandment?**
The eighth commandment requires the lawful procuring and furthering the wealth and outward state of ourselves and others.
(Prov. 27:23; Lev. 25:35; Deut. 15:10; 22:14)

81. **What is forbidden in the eighth commandment?**
The eighth commandment forbids whatsoever does or may unjustly hinder our own or our neighbor's wealth or outward state.
(1 Tim. 5:8; Prov. 28:19; 23:20, 21; Eph. 4:28)

82. **Which is the ninth commandment?**
The ninth commandment is, Thou shalt not bear false witness against thy neighbor.
(Exodus 20:16)

83. **What is required in the ninth commandment?**
The ninth commandment requires the maintaining and promoting of truth between man and man, and of our own and our neighbor's good name, especially in witness bearing.
(Zech. 8:16; Acts 25:10; Eccles. 7:1; 3 John 12; Prov. 14:5, 25)

84. **What is forbidden in the ninth commandment?**
The ninth commandment forbids whatsoever is prejudicial to truth, or injurious to our own, or our neighbor's good name.
(Eph. 4:25; Ps. 15:3; 2 Cor. 8:20, 21)

85. **Which is the tenth commandment?**
The tenth commandment is, Thou shalt not covet thy neighbor's house. Thou shalt not covet thy neighbor's wife, nor his man servant, nor his maid servant, nor his ox, nor his ass, nor anything that is thy neighbor's.
(Exodus 20:17)

86. **What is required in the tenth commandment?**
The tenth commandment requires full contentment with our own condition, with a right and charitable frame of spirit towards our neighbor, and all that is his.
(Heb. 13:5; 1 Tim. 6:6; Rom. 12:15; 1 Cor. 13:4-7; Lev. 19:18)

87. **What is forbidden in the tenth commandment?**
The tenth commandment forbids all discontentment with our own estate, envying or grieving at the good of our neighbor, and all inordinate motions and affections to anything that is his.
(1 Cor. 10:10; James 5:9; Gal. 5:26; Col. 3:5)

88. **Is any man able perfectly to keep the commandments of God?**
No mere man, since the fall, is able in this life, perfectly to keep the commandments of God, but daily breaks them in thought, word, and deed.
(Eccles. 7:20; Gen. 6:5; Gen. 8:21; 1 John 1:8; James 3:8; James 3:2; Rom. 3:23)

89. **What then is the purpose of the law since the fall?**
The purpose of the law, since, the fall, is to reveal the perfect righteousness of God, that His people may know his will for their lives and the ungodly, being convicted of their sin, may be restrained therein and brought to Christ for salvation.
(Ps. 19:7-11; Rom. 3:20, 31; 7:7; 12:2; Titus 2:12-14; Gal. 3:22, 24; 1 Tim. 1:8)

90. **Are all transgressions of the law equally heinous?**
Some sins in themselves and by reason of several aggravations, are more heinous in the sight of God than others.
(Ezekiel 8:13; John 19:11; 1 John 5:16)

91. **What does every sin deserve?**
Every sin deserves God's wrath and curse, both in this life, and in that which is to come.
(Eph. 5:6; Gal. 3:10; Prov. 3:33; Ps. 11:6; Rev. 21:8)

92. **What does God require of us, that we may escape His wrath and curse, due to us for sin?**
To escape the wrath and curse of God due to us for sin, God requires of us faith in Jesus Christ, repentance unto life, with the diligent use of all the outward and ordinary means whereby Christ communicates to us the benefits of redemption.
(Acts 20:21; Acts 16:30, 31; 17:30)

93. **What is faith in Jesus Christ?**
Faith in Jesus Christ is a saving grace, whereby we receive and rest upon Him alone for salvation, as He is offered to us in the Gospel.
(Heb. 10:39; John 1:12; Phil. 3-9; Gal. 2:15, 16)

94. **What is repentance unto life?**
Repentance unto life is a saving grace, whereby a sinner, out of a true sense of his sin, and apprehension of the mercy of God in Christ, does, with grief and hatred of his sin, turn from it unto God, with full purpose of, and endeavor after, new obedience.
(Acts 2:37; Joel 2:13; Jer. 31:18, 19: 2 Cor. 7:10,11; Rom. 6:18)

95. **What are the outward and ordinary means whereby Christ communicates to us the benefits of redemption?**
The outward and ordinary means whereby Christ communicates to us the benefits of redemption are His ordinances, especially the Word, Baptism, the Lord's Supper, and Prayer; all which are made effectual to the elect for salvation.
(Rom. 10:17; James 1:18; 1 Cor. 3:5; Acts 14:1; 2:41, 42)

96. **How is the Word made effectual to salvation?**
The Spirit of God makes the reading, but especially the preaching of the Word an effectual means of convincing and converting sinners, and of building them up in holiness and comfort, through faith unto salvation.
(Ps. 119:11, 18; 1 Thess. 1:6; 1 Peter 2:1, 2; Rom. 1:16; Ps. 19:7)

97. **How is the Word to be read and heard that it may become effectual to salvation?**
That the Word may become effectual to salvation we must attend thereunto with diligence, preparation and prayer, receive it in faith and love, lay it up in our hearts, and practice it in our lives.
(Prov. 8:34; 1 Peter 2:1, 2; 1 Tim. 4:13; Heb. 2:1, 3; Heb. 4:2; 2 Thess. 2:10; Ps. 119:11; James 1:21, 25)

98. How do Baptism and the Lord's Supper become effectual means of salvation?

Baptism and the Lord's Supper become effectual means of salvation, not from any virtue in them or in him that administers them, but only by the blessing of Christ and the working of His Spirit in them that by faith receive them.

(1 Peter 3:21; 1 Cor. 3:6, 7; 1 Cor. 12:13)

99. Wherein do Baptism and the Lord's Supper differ from the other ordinances of God?

Baptism and the Lord's Supper differ from the other ordinances of God in that they were specially instituted by Christ to represent and apply to believers the benefits of the new covenant by visible and outward signs.

(Matt. 28:19; Acts 22:16; Matt. 26:26-28; Rom. 6:4)

100. What is Baptism?

Baptism is an holy ordinance, wherein the washing with water in the name of the Father, the Son, and the Holy Spirit, signifies our ingrafting into Christ and partaking of the benefits of the covenant of grace, and our engagement to be the Lord's.

(Matt. 28:19; Rom. 6:3-5; Col. 2:12; Gal. 3:27)

101. To whom is Baptism to be administered?

Baptism is to be administered to all those who actually profess repentance towards God, faith in, and obedience to our Lord Jesus Christ; and to none other.

(Acts 2:38; Matt. 3:6; Mark 16:16; Acts 8:12, 36; Acts 10:47, 48)

102. Are the infants of such as are professing believers to be baptized?

The infants of such as are professing believers are not to be baptized; because there is neither command nor example in the Holy Scriptures, or certain consequence from them, to baptize such.

103. **How is Baptism rightly administered?**

Baptism is rightly administered by immersion, or dipping the whole body of the person in water, in the name of the Father, and of the Son, and of the Holy Spirit.

(Matt. 3:16; John 3:23; Acts 8:38, 39)

104. **What is the duty of those who are rightly baptized?**

It is the duty of those who are rightly baptized to give up (join) themselves to some visible and orderly church of Jesus Christ, that they may walk in all the commandments and ordinances of the Lord blameless.

(Acts 2:46, 47; Acts 9:26; 1 Peter 2:5; Heb. 10:25; Rom. 16:5)

105. **What is the visible church?**

The visible church is the organized society of professing believers, in all ages and places, wherein the Gospel is truly preached and the ordinances of Baptism and the Lord's Supper rightly administered.

(Acts 2:42; 20:7; Acts 7:38; Eph. 4:11, 12)

106. **What is the invisible church?**

The invisible church is the whole number of the elect, that have been, are, or shall be gathered into one under Christ the head.

(Eph. 1:10; 1:22, 23; John 10:16; 11:52)

107. **What is the Lord's Supper?**

The Lord's Supper is a holy ordinance, wherein, by giving and receiving bread and wine, according to Christ's appointment, His death is showed forth, and the worthy receivers are, not after a corporeal and carnal manner, but by faith, made partakers of His body and blood, with all His benefits, to their spiritual nourishment, and growth in grace.

(1 Cor. 11:23-26; 10:16)

108. **What is required to the worthy receiving of the Lord's Supper?**

It is required of them that would worthily (that is, suitably) partake of the Lord's Supper, that they examine themselves, of their knowledge to discern the Lord's body; of their faith to feed upon Him; of their repentance, love, and new obedience: lest, coming unworthily, they eat and drink judgment to themselves.

(1 Cor. 11:27-31; 1 Cor. 5:8; 2 Cor. 13:5)

109. **What is Prayer?**

Prayer is an offering up of our desires to God, for things agreeable to His will, in the name of Christ, with confession of our sins and thankful acknowledgment of His mercies.

(1 John 5:14; 1 John 1:9; Phil. 4:6; Ps. 10:17; 145:19; John 14:13, 14)

110. **What rule has God given for our direction in prayer?**

The whole Word of God is of use to direct us in prayer, but the special rule of direction is that prayer which Christ taught His disciples, commonly called the Lord's Prayer.

(Matt. 6:9-13; 2 Tim. 3:16, 17)

111. **What does the preface of the Lord's Prayer teach us?**

The preface of the Lord's Prayer, which is, Our Father, which art in heaven, teaches us to draw near to God, with all holy reverence and confidence, as children to a father, able and ready to help us, and that we should pray with and for others.

(Matt. 6:9; Luke 11:13; Rom. 8:15; Acts 12:5; 1 Tim. 2:1-3)

112. **What do we pray for in the first petition?**

In the first petition, which is, Hallowed be thy name, we pray that God would enable us and others to glorify Him in all that whereby He makes Himself known, and that He would dispose all things to His own glory.

(Matt. 6:9; Ps. 67:1-3; Rom. 11:36; Rev. 4:11)

113. **What do we pray for in the second petition?**

In the second petition, which is, Thy kingdom come, we pray that Satan's kingdom may be destroyed, and that the kingdom of grace may be advanced;

ourselves and others brought into it, and kept in it, and that the kingdom of glory may be hastened.

(Matt. 6:10; Ps. 68:1-18; Rom. 10:1; 2 Thess. 3:1; Matt. 9:37, 38; Rev. 22:20)

114. **What do we pray for in the third petition?**

In the third petition, which is, Thy will be done in earth as it is in heaven, we pray that God by His grace, would make us able and willing to know, obey, and submit to His will in all things, as the angels do in heaven.

(Matt. 6:10; Ps. 103:20, 21; Ps. 25:4, 5; Ps. 119:26)

115. **What do we pray for in the fourth petition?**

In the fourth petition, which is, Give us this day our daily bread, we pray that of God's free gift, we may receive a competent portion of the good things of this life and enjoy His blessing with them.

(Matt. 6:11; Prov. 30:8, 9; 1 Tim. 6:6-8; 4:4, 5)

116. **What do we pray for in the fifth petition?**

In the fifth petition, which is, And forgive us our debts, as we forgive our debtors, we pray that God, for Christ's sake, would freely pardon all our sins; which we are the rather encouraged to ask, because by His grace we are enabled from the heart to forgive others.

(Matt. 6:12; Ps. 51:1, 3, 7; Mark 11:25; Matt. 18:35)

117. **What do we pray for in the sixth petition?**

In the sixth petition, which is, And lead us not into temptation, but deliver us from evil, we pray that God would either keep us from being tempted to sin, or support and deliver us when we are tempted.

(Matt. 6:13; 26:41; Ps. 19:13; 1 Cor. 10:13; John 17:15)

118. **What does the conclusion of the Lord's Prayer teach us?**

The conclusion of the Lord's Prayer, which is, For thine is the kingdom, and the power, and the glory, forever, Amen, teaches us to take our encouragement in prayer from God only, and in our prayers to praise Him, ascribing kingdom, power, and glory to Him; and in testimony of our desire, and assurance to be heard, we say, AMEN.

(Matt. 6:13; Dan. 9:18, 19; 1 Chron. 29:11-13; 1Cor. 14:16; Phil. 4:6; Rev. 22:20) ▪

COVENANTS

AT VARIOUS TIMES in Church history, Christians felt the need to sit down together with open Bibles and determine precisely what they believed. Those times produced the creeds and confessions. But after they left their synods and assemblies, our spiritual forebears had to face the consequences of whatever they had written—and more often than not, that meant persecution.

In the face of their trials, Christians entered into agreements with each other to defend the truths they had already confessed. These agreements were written covenants between similar-minded Christians who collectively confessed that the Bible is the only true rule for life, and who then publicly and formally promised each another that they would be faithful to that confession against whatever enemies there might be at the time. Indeed, as with the confessions, the most common reason Christians covenanted with each other was because their allegiance to Christ *was* threatened. Consequently, the signers of these covenants often suffered or died for their stand—but they suffered together, as brothers and sisters, as they had covenanted to do.

While creeds and confessions bring clarity of doctrine, covenants bring accountability and brotherhood of action. Confessions avow what is true, and covenants shape the Christians' witness to the world. Creeds and confessions ask, "Christians, what do we believe?" Covenants declare, "Christians, we know what we believe. And here is what we're going to do about it—together." ▪

A NOTE ON THE COLONIAL COVENANTS

The first several covenants featured in the following section are from the earliest settlements in America. In the early 17th century, groups of Christians began to migrate from the Old World to the New World. Their newly planted settlements emerged in the area known as New England, particularly in the Massachusetts Bay region. A great many of these incoming settlers were Puritans, from the same theological stock as many of the men who would later sit in the Westminster Assembly back in England.

Though some settlers came to the New World's shores seeking wealth and worldly opportunity, the Puritans and other Christian settlers like them were looking for new ground to build on. They wished to leave behind the corrupt government and religious persecution they had known in Europe. They dreamed of growing a social structure that would honor King Jesus as its head, and His Word as its law. As they founded towns and established congregations, the Puritans sometimes wrote covenants to formally bind themselves to that dream.

Several of the colonial churches that wrote these covenants still exist, but in the centuries since their Puritan fathers established them, almost all of them have completely abandoned orthodox Christianity. But their founding covenants still stand as memorials of what their churches were supposed to believe and practice. May God remind them of their heritage, and bring them to repentance.

Watertown Covenant

In June 1630, eleven ships full of Puritans under the leadership of John Winthrop arrived at Salem in the Massachusetts Bay Colony. As soon as they landed, the settlers dispersed to establish new towns and congregations. One of the groups of colonists, led by George Philips and Richard Saltonstall, obtained land along the Charles River, and there they founded Watertown and a congregational church.

Watertown's founders signed a covenant on July 30, 1630, which may have been written by George Philips, who was also the first pastor of the new Congregational Church. The Watertown Covenant was a declaration before God that the Puritans intended to honor God in their colonizing enterprise.

We whose Names are hereto subscribed, having through God's Mercy escaped out of Pollutions of the World, and been taken into the Society of his People, with all Thankfulness do hereby both with Heart and Hand acknowledge, That his Gracious Goodness, and Fatherly Care, towards us: And for further and more full Declaration thereof, to the present and future Ages, have undertaken (for the promoting of his Glory and the Churches Good, and the Honor of our Blessed Jesus, in our more full and free subjecting of our selves and ours, under his Gracious Government, in the practice of, and Obedience unto all his Holy Ordinances and Orders, which he Hath pleased to Prescribe and impose upon us) a long and hazardous Voyage from East to West, from Old England in Europe, to New England in America that we may walk before him, and serve him, without Fear in Holiness and Righteousness, all the Days of our Lives: And being safely arrived here, and thus far onwards peaceably preserved by his special Providence, that we bring forth our Intentions into Actions, and perfect our Resolutions, in the Beginnings of some Just and Meet Executions; We have separated the Day above written from all other Services, and Dedicated it wholly to the Lord in Divine employments, for a Day of Afflicting our

Souls, and humbling our selves before the Lord, to seek him, and at his Hands, a Way to walk in, by Fasting and Prayer, that we might know what was Good in his Sight: And the Lord was entreated of us.

For in the End of the Day, after the finishing of our Public Duties, we do all, before we depart, solemnly and with all our Hearts, personally, Man by Man for our selves and others (charging them before Christ and his Elect Angels, even them that are not here with us this Day, or are yet unborn, That they keep the Promise unblameably and faithfully unto the coming of our Lord Jesus) Promise, and enter into a sure Covenant with the Lord our God, and before him with one another, by Oath and serious Protestation made, to renounce all Idolatry and Superstition, Will-Worship, all Humane Traditions and Inventions whatsoever, in the Worship of God; and forsaking all Evil Ways, do give ourselves wholly unto the Lord Jesus, to do him faithful Service, observing and keeping all his Statutes, Commands, and Ordinances, in all Matters concerning our Reformation; his Worship, Administrations, Ministry, and Government; and in the Carriage of our selves among our selves, and one another towards another, as he hath prescribed in his Holy Word. Further swearing to cleave unto that alone, and the true Sense and meaning thereof to the utmost of our Power, as unto the most clear Light and infallible Rule, and All-sufficient Canon, in all things that concern us in this our Way. In Witness of all, we do ex Animo, and in the presence of God, hereto set our Names, or Marks, in the Day and Year above written. ▪

Covenant of the First Church in Boston

In 1630, a fleet of eleven ships carried John Winthrop and at least seven hundred Puritan settlers to Salem in Massachusetts Bay. When they arrived, these settlers set about building new towns and official congregations. John Winthrop's group settled in Charlestown, where they met under a tree to establish their church—the First Church, with John Wilson as minister—and signed a covenant on August 27, 1630. Three months after signing their covenant, the congregation moved from Charlestown to a village which they renamed Boston, so their covenant is known as the Covenant of the First Church of Boston, or the Covenant of the Charles-Boston Church.

In the Name of our Lord Jesus Christ, and in Obedience to his holy Will and Divine Ordinance, We whose Names are here under written, being by his most wise and good providence brought together into this part of America in the Bay of Massachusetts, and desirous to unite ourselves into one Congregation or Church under the Lord Jesus Christ our Head, in such sort as becometh all those whom he hath redeemed, and sanctified to himself, do hereby solemnly and religiously (as in his most holy Presence) promise and bind ourselves, to walk in all our ways according to the Rule of the Gospel, and in all sincere Conformity to his holy Ordinances, and in mutual Love and Respect each to other, so near as God shall give us Grace.

At Charlestown, August 27, 1630.

John Winthrop, Governor
Thomas Dudley, Deputy Governor
Isaac Johnson
John Wilson
Increase Nowell
Parnell Nowell, the wife of Increase Nowell
Thomas Sharpe
Simon Bradstreete
Willyam Gager

Willyam Colborne
Margery Colborne, the wife of Willyam Colborne
Willyam Aspinall
Elizabeth Aspinall, the wife of Willyam Aspinall
Christian Beecher
Robert Harding
Robert Hayle
John Hall
Dorothy Dudley, the wife of Thomas Dudley
Anne Bradstreete, the wife of Simon Bradstreete
Margarett Hoames
John Sale
Henry Kingsbury and Margarett, his wife
Henry Harwood and Elizabeth, his wife
Gregory Nash
John Waters and Frances, his wife
Henry Gosnell and Mary, his wife
James Penne and Katherine, his wife
John Milles and Susan, his wife
Edmund Belcher
James Browne
Edward Ransford
John Edmundes
Willyam Waterbury and Alice, his wife
John Ruggle
Frances, the wife of John Ruggle
Willyam Baulstone and Elizabeth, his wife
Phillip Hammond's widow
Richard Maurice and his wife
Edward Converse
Willyam Hudson
Abram Palmer and his wife
John Haukins
Nicholis Stowers
John Dillingham
Ralph Mousall and Alice, his wife
Samuell Cole and Anne, his wife
Willyam Cheesborough and Anne, his wife
Sarah Cheesborough
Willyam Frothingham and Anne, his wife
Gregory Taylor
Edward Bendall
Thomas Alcocke
Sarah Converse
Richard Sprage
Ezechiel Richardson and his wife
Miles Reading
Thomas Squire
Margarette, the wife of Jeffery Ruggle
Henry Bright
Thomas Matson, received by Communion of Churches from a Church in London
Mary Morton
Bithea Joanes
Isabell Brett

Richard Wright
John Cranwell
Edward Deekes
John Gage
Elizabeth Welden
Willyam Coddington
Thomas Howlett
Thomas Hutchinson
George Hutchinson
Francis Hesseldon
Richard Garret
Anthony Chaulby
John Boswell
Willyam Dady
Susan Hudson
Henry and Susan Peas
John Baker and Charity, his wife
Thomas French
Margarett Cooke
Martha Winthrop
Robert Walker
Thomas Oliver and Anne, his wife
John Underhill
Sarah Woolrich
Willyam Talmige
Joseph Reading
Garret Haddon
John Bigges
Zacheus Bosworth
Margarett Wright
Anne Needham
Thomas Faireweather
Ralph Sprage and Joan, his wife
Anne Peeters, received from the Church of Salem
Richard Palsgrave and Anne, his wife
John Perkins and Judith, his wife
Ryce Cole
John Elliot
Anne, the wife of John Elliot
Margaret Winthrop
John and Jane Willisse
Robert Roys
Thomas Beecher
Edward Gibbons
Margarett Gibbons
Jacob Elliott
John Clarke
John Audley
Amy Chambers
Anna Swanson
Alice French
Elizabeth Wing
Richard Brackitt
John Sampfort
Magery Chauner
Gyles Firmin, Jr.
Mary, the wife of Samuel Dudley
Bridgett Gyver
Thomas and Elizabeth James
James and Lydia Pennyman
Isaack Perry
Elizabeth Webbe
John Winthrop, Jr.
Willyam Pierce. ▪

Salem Covenants

The settlement of Salem took root in the Massachusetts colony in 1626. Its first official congregation was formed in 1629, the First Church of Salem, a Congregationalist Church under the leadership of Reverend Samuel Skelton as pastor and Reverend Francis Higginson as "Teacher." On August 6, 1629, the congregation gathered to sign a covenant together, which had been written by Reverend Higginson. Though the congregation degenerated into Unitarian-Universalist heresy centuries ago, the original Salem Covenant is still recited weekly by the First Church of Salem.

In 1636, the congregation of the First Church of Salem gathered to elaborate and reaffirm their covenant with God and one another. Their own opening remarks, seen below, explain their reasons very well.

THE SALEM COVENANT OF 1629

We Covenant with the Lord and one with another; and do bind our selves in the presence of God, to walk together in all his ways, according as he is pleased to reveal himself unto us in his Blessed word of truth.

THE ENLARGED SALEM COVENANT OF 1636

"Gather my Saints together unto me that have made a Covenant with me by sacrifice." — Psalm 50:5

We whose names are here underwritten, members of the present Church of Christ in Salem, having found by said experience how dangerous it is to sit loose to the Covenant we make with our God: and how apt we are to wander into by-paths, even to the loosing of our first aims in entering into church fellowship: Do therefore solemnly, in the presence of the Eternal God, both for our own comforts, and those which shall or may be joined unto us, renew that Church Covenant we find this Church bound unto at their first beginning, viz: That,

We covenant with our Lord, and one with another; and we do bind our selves in the presence of God, to walk together in all his ways, according as he is pleased to reveal himself unto us in his blessed word of truth; and do explicitly, in the name and fear of God, profess and protest to walk as followeth, through the power and grace of our Lord, Jesus Christ.

We avouch the Lord to be our God, and our selves to be his people, in the truth and simplicity of our spirits.

We give our selves to the Lord Jesus Christ, and the word of his grace for the teaching, ruling and sanctifying of us in matters of worship and conversion, resolving to cleave unto him alone for life and glory, and to reject all contrary ways, canons, and constitutions of men in his worship.

We promise to walk with our brethren, with all watchfulness and tenderness, avoiding jealousies and suspicions, back-bitings, censurings, provokings, secret risings of spirit against them; but in all offences to follow the rule of our Lord Jesus, and to bear and forbear, give and forgive, as he hath taught us.

In public or private, we will willingly do nothing to the offence of the church; but willing to take advice for our selves and ours, as occasion shall be presented.

We will not in the congregation be forward either to show our own gifts and parts in speaking or scrupling, or there discover the weakness or failings of our brethren; but attend an orderly call thereunto, knowing how much the Lord may be dishonored, and his gospel, and the profession of it, slighted by our distempers and weaknesses in public.

We bind our selves to study the advancement of the gospel in all truth and peace; both in regard of those that are within or without; no way slighting our sister churches, but using their counsel, as need shall be; not laying a stumbling-block before any, no, not the Indians, whose good we desire to promote; and so to converse, as we may avoid the very appearance of evil.

We do hereby promise to carry our selves in all lawful obedience to those that are over us, in Church or Commonwealth, knowing how well pleasing it will be to the Lord, that they should have encouragement in their places, by our not grieving their spirits through our irregularities.

We resolve to approve our selves to the Lord in our particular callings; shunning idleness as the bane of any stake; nor will we deal hardly or oppressingly with any, wherein we are the Lord's stewards.

Promising also unto our best ability to teach our children and servants the knowledge of God, and of His Will, that they may serve Him also; and all this not by any strength of our own, but by the Lord Jesus Christ; whose blood we desire may sprinkle this our Covenant made in his name. ▪

Dedham Covenant

In 1635, colonists began to fear that the settlements in the Massachusetts Bay Area were too close together. The Massachusetts General Court called for new settlements to be formed. Among others who left to accomplish that, thirty Puritan families from Watertown and Roxbury set out on the Charles River to find a new home.

They founded Dedham (originally called Contentment) and signed a covenant that would structure their new town and church to the glory of God. The Dedham Covenant was first signed on August 15, 1636 by eighteen men. After a few decades, 125 men had set their names to the covenant.

The Society Covenant in these terms, viz.

1. We whose names are hereunto subscribed do, in the fear and reverence of our Almighty God, mutually and severally promise amongst ourselves and each other to profess and practice one truth according to that most perfect rule, the foundation whereof is everlasting love.

2. That we shall by all means labor to keep off from us all such as are contrary minded, and receive only such unto us as may be probably of one heart with us, as that we either know or may well and truly be informed to walk in a peaceable conversation with all meekness of spirit, for the edification of each other in the knowledge and faith of the Lord Jesus, and the mutual encouragement unto all temporal comforts in all things, seeking the good of each other out of which may be derived true peace.

3. That if at any time differences shall rise between parties of our said town, that then such party or parties shall presently refer all such differences unto some one, two or three others of our said society to be fully accorded and determined without any further delay, if it possibly may be.

4. That every man may now, or at any time hereafter shall have lots in our said town shall pay his share in all such rates of money and charges as shall be imposed upon him rateably in proportion with other men, as also become freely subject unto all such orders and constitutions as shall be necessarily had or made now or at any time hereafter from this day forward as well for loving and comfortable society in our said town as also for the prosperous and thriving condition of our said fellowship, especially respecting the fear of God, in which we desire to begin and continue whatsoever we shall by his loving favour take in hand.

5. And for the better manifestation of our true resolution herein, every man so received into the town is to subscribe hereunto his name, thereby obliging both himself and his successors after him forever, as we have done.

Robert Feke	Francis Austen	Thomas Fisher
Edward Alleyn	Ezekiell Holleman	Joseph Kingsberye
Samuel Morse	Joseph Shawe	John Batchelor
Philemon Dalton	William Bearstowe	Nathaniell Coaleburne
John Dwight	John Haward	John Roper
Lambert Generye	Thomas Bartlett	Martin Philips
Richard Euered [Everett]	Ferdinandoe Adams	Henry Smyth
	Daniell Morse	John Fraerye
Ralph Shepheard	Joseph Morse	Thomas Hastings
John Huggin	John Ellice	Francis Chickering
Ralph Wheelock	Jonathan Fairbanks	Thomas Alcock
Thomas Cakebread	John Eaton	William Bullard
Henry Phillips	Michaell Metcalfe	Jonas Humphery
Timothie Dalton	John Morse	Edward Kempe
Thomas Carter	John Allin	John Hunting
Abraham Shawe	Anthony Fisher	Tymothie Dwight
John Coolidge	Thomas Wight	Henry Deengaine
Nicholas Phillips	Eleazer Lusher	Henry Brocke
John Gaye	Robert Hinsdell	James Hering
John Kingsbery	John Luson	Nathan Aldus
John Rogers	John Fisher	Edward Richards

Michaell Powell
John Elderkine
Michaell Bacon
Robert Onion
Samuell Milles
Edward Colver
Thomas Bayes
George Bearstowe
John Bullard
Thomas Leader
Joseph Moyes
Jeffery Mingeye
James Allin
Richard Barber
Thomas Jordan
Joshua Fisher
Christopher Smith
John Thurston
Joseph Clarke
Thomas Eames
Peter Woodward

Thwaits Strickland
John Guild
Samuell Bulleyne
Robert Gowen
Hugh Stacey
George Barber
James Jordan
Nathaniell Whiteing
Beniamine Smith
Richard Ellice
Austen Kalem
Robert Ware
Thomas Fuller
Thomas Payne
John Fayerbanke
Henry Glover
Thomas Hering
John Plimption
George Fayerbanke
Tymoth Dwight
Andr. Duein

Joseph Ellice
Ralph Freeman
Joh: Rice
Danll. Ponde
John Houghton
Jonathan Fayerbank Jr.
James Vales
Thomas Metcalfe
Robert Crossman
William Avery
John Aldus
John Mason
Isaac Bullard
Cornelus Fisher
John Partridge
James Draper
James Thorpe
Samuell Fisher
B. Benjamin Bullard
Ellice W. Woode
Thomas Fisher ▪

Scottish National Covenant

Ever since the Scottish Parliament ratified the Scots Confession in 1560, the Scottish Kirk had been Reformed and Presbyterian. But by the end of the century, the Scots were growing increasingly wary of the Roman Catholic Counter-Reformation efforts infesting Scotland. Certain nobles who were close to James VI, king of Scotland, were openly Roman Catholic. James was making changes to the Kirk—such as introducing bishops—that were too suggestive of Roman Catholicism for Reformed Scots to stomach.

As a precaution, in 1580 the Presbyterian leaders wrote the Second Scots Confession (also called the Negative Confession, or the King's Confession) to make it clear that no papist practices would be tolerated in their churches. Though it goes by other names, this confession was essentially the first National Covenant. It was signed by James VI and his court (hence "King's Confession"), and then signed by the vast majority of the Scottish people in 1581. In 1590, it was reaffirmed and generally signed again.

But King James was not faithful to his signature. In 1603, James inherited the English throne also—thus uniting Scotland, which had been Presbyterian for half a century, and England, which had been establishing the Anglican Church with episcopal government since 1534. In 1618, King James caused the five Articles of Perth to be written, which imposed certain episcopalian practices on the Presbyterians.

James' son, Charles I, inherited the United Kingdom in 1624 with his French Roman Catholic queen at his side. Taking up his father's mission, he began systematically forcing episcopal church government and practices on the Scottish Kirk. Above all, as Henry VIII had done, Charles I maintained that, as king of the realm, he was also Head of the Church by Divine Right and could dictate what the church would teach and how it would worship.

Scottish Presbyterians staunchly rejected Charles I's imposition of the Book of Common Prayer on the worship and doctrine of the church. They considered aspects of the episcopal liturgy to be far too reminiscent of Roman Catholicism, and declared that Charles was usurping the crown rights of the Redeemer, King Jesus, over his Kirk.

In 1638, the Scottish Presbyterians commissioned Presbyterian pastor Alexander Henderson, and Archibald Johnston, the Lord Wariston to write a covenant that would do two things: First, reaffirm the Reformed theology that the Scots had long accepted, and second, rebuke the notion that the king was Head of the Church, while still affirming that the king indeed had God-given authority over the State.

Henderson and Lord Wariston framed a covenant in three sections: The first section reprinted the Second Scots Confession of 1580-81. The second section, by Lord Wariston, cited and applied past Acts of Parliament that had condemned Roman Catholicism. The third section, by Henderson, protested against the popish practices being smuggled back into the Scottish Kirk.

This new National Covenant was accepted in Greyfriars Kirk in Edinburgh on February 28, 1638. After being prayed over and read aloud, it was laid on a tombstone to be signed. It was said that 60,000 people crowded in to sign it—nobles, clergy, and common people of all ranks. Beside their name, some wrote, "until death." Some pricked their finger and signed with their blood. Afterward, copies of the National Covenant were carried to villages throughout the Lowlands, gathering more signatures wherever they went.

The confession of faith of the Kirk of Scotland, subscribed at first by the King's Majesty and his household in the year of God 1580; thereafter by persons of all ranks in the year 1581, by ordinance of the lords of the secret council, and acts of the general assembly; subscribed again by all sorts of persons in the year 1590, by a new ordinance of council, at the desire of the general assembly; with a general band for the maintenance of the true religion, and the King's person, and now subscribed in the year 1638, by us noblemen, barons, gentlemen, burgesses, ministers, and commons under subscribing; together with our resolution and promises for the causes after specified, to maintain the said true religion, and the King's Majesty, according to the confession aforesaid, and Acts of Parliament; the tenure whereof here followeth.

[1][We all, and every one of us underwritten, do protest, that after long and due examination of our own consciences in matters of true and false religion, we are now thoroughly resolved of the truth, by the word and spirit of God; and therefore we believe with our hearts, confess with our mouths, subscribe with our hands, and constantly affirm before God and the whole world, that this only is the true Christian faith and religion, pleasing God, and bringing salvation to man, which now is by the mercy of God revealed to the world by the preaching of the blessed evangel, and received, believed, and defended by many and sundry notable kirks[2] and realms, but chiefly by the Kirk of Scotland, the King's Majesty, and three estates of this realm, as God's eternal truth and only ground of our salvation; as more particularly is expressed in the confession of our faith, established and publicly confirmed by sundry Acts of Parliament; and now of a long time hath been openly professed by the King's Majesty, and whole body of this realm, both in burgh and land. To the which confession and form of religion we willingly agree in our consciences in all points, as unto God's undoubted truth and verity, grounded only upon His written Word; and therefore we abhor and detest all contrary religion and doctrine, but chiefly all kind of papistry in general and particular heads, even as they are now damned and confuted by the Word of God and Kirk of Scotland. But in special we detest and refuse the usurped authority of that Roman Antichrist upon the Scriptures of God, upon the Kirk, the civil magistrate, and consciences of men; all his tyrannous laws made upon indifferent things against our Christian liberty; his erroneous doctrine against the sufficiency of the written Word, the perfection of the law, the office of Christ and His blessed evangel; his corrupted doctrine concerning original sin, our natural inability and rebellion to God's law, our justification by faith only, our imperfect sanctification and obedience to the law, the nature, number, and use of the holy sacraments; his five bastard sacraments, with all his rites, ceremonies, and false doctrine, added to the ministration of the true sacraments, without the Word of God; his cruel judgments against infants departing without the sacrament; his absolute necessity of baptism; his blasphemous opinion of transubstantiation or real presence of Christ's body in the elements, and receiving of the same by the wicked,

1 From this bracket to the next (see page 414) is the first of the three sections. This was the original Second Scots Confession (or King's Confession).
2 That is, churches.

or bodies of men; his dispensations, with solemn oaths, perjuries, and degrees of marriage, forbidden in the Word; his cruelty against the innocent divorced; his devilish mass; his blasphemous priesthood; his profane sacrifice for the sins of the dead and the quick; his canonization of men, calling upon angels or saints departed, worshipping of imagery, relics, and crosses; dedicating of kirks, altars, days, vows to creatures; his purgatory, prayers for the dead, praying or speaking in a strange language; with his processions and blasphemous litany, and multitude of advocates or mediators; his manifold orders, auricular confession; his desperate and uncertain repentance; his general and doubtsome faith; his satisfactions of men for their sins; his justification by works, opus operatum, works of supererogation, merits, pardons, peregrinations and stations; his holy water, baptizing of bells, conjuring of spirits, crossing, saning,[3] anointing, conjuring, hallowing of God's good creatures, with the superstitious opinion joined therewith; his worldly monarchy and wicked hierarchy; his three solemn vows, with all his shavelings[4] of sundry sorts; his erroneous and bloody decrees made at Trent, with all the subscribers and approvers of that cruel and bloody band conjured against the Kirk of God. And finally, we detest all his vain allegories, rites, signs, and traditions, brought in the Kirk without or against the Word of God, and doctrine of this true reformed Kirk. To which we join ourselves willingly, in doctrine, religion, faith, discipline, and life of the holy sacraments, as lively members of the same, in Christ our head, promising and swearing, by the great name of the Lord our God, that we shall continue in the obedience of the doctrine and discipline of this Kirk, and shall defend the same according to our vocation and power all the days of our lives, under the pains contained in the law, and danger both of body and soul in the day of God's fearful judgment. And seeing that many are stirred up by Satan and that Roman Antichrist, to promise, swear, subscribe, and for a time use the holy sacraments in the Kirk, deceitfully against their own consciences, minding thereby, first under the external cloak of religion, to corrupt and subvert secretly God's true religion within the Kirk; and afterwards, when time may serve, to become open enemies and persecutors of the same, under vain hope of the Pope's dispensation, devised

3 Also spelled "saining." This is referring to the Roman Catholic practice of making the sign of the cross.
4 "Shaveling" was a nickname for priests and their tonsured (partially-shaved) heads.

against the Word of God, to his great confusion, and their double condemnation in the day of the Lord Jesus.

We therefore, willing to take away all suspicion of hypocrisy, and of such double dealing with God and His Kirk, protest and call the Searcher of all hearts for witness, that our minds and hearts do fully agree with this our confession, promise, oath, and subscription: so that we are not moved for any worldly respect, but are persuaded only in our consciences, through the knowledge and love of God's true religion printed in our hearts by the Holy Spirit, as we shall answer to Him in the day when the secrets of all hearts shall be disclosed. And because we perceive that the quietness and stability of our religion and Kirk doth depend upon the safety and good behaviour of the King's Majesty, as upon a comfortable instrument of God's mercy granted to this country for the maintenance of His Kirk, and ministration of justice among us, we protest and promise with our hearts under the same oath, hand-writ, and pains, that we shall defend his person and authority with our goods, bodies, and lives, in the defence of Christ His evangel, liberties of our country, ministration of justice, and punishment of iniquity, against all enemies within this realm or without, as we desire our God to be a strong and merciful defender to us in the day of our death, and coming of our Lord Jesus Christ; to Whom, with the Father and the Holy Spirit, be all honour and glory eternally.]

Like as many Acts of Parliament not only in general do abrogate, annul, and rescind all laws, statutes, acts, constitutions, canons civil or municipal, with all other ordinances and practick[5] penalties whatsoever, made in prejudice of the true religion, and professors thereof, or of the true Kirk discipline, jurisdiction, and freedom thereof; or in favours of idolatry and superstition; or of the papistical kirk (as Act 3. Act 31. Parl. I. Act 23. Parl. 11. Act 114. Parl. 12, of K. James VI), that papistry and superstition may be utterly suppressed, according to the intention of the Acts of Parliament reported in Act 5. Parl. 20. K. James VI. And to that end they ordained all papists and priests to be punished by manifold civil and ecclesiastical pains, as adversaries to God's true religion preached, and by law established within this realm (Act. 24. Parl. 11. K. James VI) as common enemies to all Christian government (Act 18. Parl. 16. K. James VI), as rebellers and gainstanders of our

5 A term in Scottish law, meaning "the ancient reported decision of the Court of Session used to show the customary practices and law." (From the modern *Merriam-Webster* dictionary)

Sovereign Lord's authority (Act 47. Parl. 3. K. James VI), and as idolaters (Act 104. Parl. 7. K. James VI), but also in particular (by and attour[6] the confession of faith) do abolish and condemn the Pope's authority and jurisdiction out of this land, and ordains the maintainers thereof to be punished (Act 2. Parl. 1. Act. 51. Parl. 3. Act 106. Parl. 7. Act 114. Parl. 12. of K. James VI); do condemn the Pope's erroneous doctrine, or any other erroneous doctrine repugnant to any of the Articles of the true and Christian religion publicly preached, and by law established in this realm; and ordains the spreaders or makers of books or libels, or letters or writs of that nature, to be punished (Act 46. Parl. 3. Act 106. Parl. 7. Act 24. Parl. 11. K.James VI); do condemn all baptism conform to the Pope's kirk, and the idolatry of the Mass; and ordains all sayers, willful hearers, and concealers of the Mass, the maintainers and resetters of the Priests, Jesuits, trafficking Papists, to be punished without exception or restriction (Act 5. Parl. I. Act 120. Parl. 12. Act 164. Parl. 13. Act 193. Parl. 14. Act. I. Parl. 19. Act 5. Parl. 20 K. James VI); do condemn all erroneous books and writs containing erroneous doctrine against the religion presently professed, or containing superstitious rights and ceremonies papistical, whereby the people are greatly abused; and ordains the home-bringers of them to be punished (Act 25. Parl. 11. K. James VI); do condemn the monuments and dregs of bygone idolatry, as going to crosses, observing the festival days of saints, and such other superstitious and papistical rites, to the dishonour of God, contempt of true religion, and fostering of great errors among the people, and ordains the users of them to be punished for the second fault as idolaters (Act 104. Parl. 7. K. James VI).

Like as many Acts of Parliament are conceived for maintenance of God's true and Christian religion, and the purity thereof in doctrine and sacraments of the true Church of God, the liberty and freedom thereof in her national synodal assemblies, presbyteries, sessions, policy, discipline, and jurisdiction thereof, as that purity of religion and liberty of the Church was used, professed, exercised, preached, and confessed according to the reformation of religion in this realm. (As for instance: Act 99. Parl. 7. Act 23. Parl. 11. Act 114. Parl. 12. Act 160. Parl. 13. K. James VI, ratified by Act 4. K. Charles.) So that Act 6. Parl. I. and Act 68. Parl. 6. of K. James

6 A Scottish word meaning "over."

VI, in the year of God 1579, declares the ministers of the blessed evangel, whom God of His mercy had raised up or hereafter should raise, agreeing with them that then lived in doctrine and administration of the sacraments, and the people that professed Christ as He was then offered in the evangel, and doth communicate with the holy sacraments (as in the reformed Kirks of this realm they were presently administered) according to the confession of faith to be the true and holy Kirk of Christ Jesus within this realm, and discerns and declares all and sundry, who either gainsays the word of the evangel, received and approved as the heads of the confession of faith, professed in Parliament in the year of God 1560, specified also in the first Parliament of K. James VI, and ratified in this present Parliament, more particularly do specify; or that refuses the administration of the holy sacraments as they were then ministrated, to be no members of the said Kirk within this realm and true religion presently professed, so long as they keep themselves so divided from the society of Christ's body. And the subsequent Act 69. Parl. 6. K. James VI, declares that there is no other face of Kirk, nor other face of religion than was presently at that time by the favour of God established within this realm, which therefore is ever styled God's true religion, Christ's true religion, the true and Christian religion, and a perfect religion, which by manifold Acts of Parliament all within this realm are bound to profess to subscribe the Articles thereof, the confession of faith, to recant all doctrine and errors repugnant to any of the said Articles (Act 4 and 9. Parl. 1. Act 45. 46. 47. Parl. 3. Act 71. Parl. 6. Act 106. Parl. 7. Act 24. Parl. 11. Act 123. Parl. 12. Act 194 and 197. Parl. 14 of K. James VI). And all magistrates, sheriffs, &c., on the one part, are ordained to search, apprehend, and punish all contraveners (for instance, Act 5. Parl. I. Act 104. Parl. 7. Act 2 5. Parl. 11. K. James VI). And that, notwithstanding of the King's Majesty's licences on the contrary, which are discharged and declared to be of no force, in so far as they tend in any ways to the prejudice and hindrance of the execution of the Acts of Parliament against Papists and adversaries of the true religion (Act 106. Parl. 7. K. James VI). On the other part, in Act 47. Parl. 3. K. James VI, it is declared and ordained, seeing the cause of God's true religion and His Highness's authority are so joined as the hurt of the one is common to both; and that none shall be reputed as loyal and faithful subjects to our Sovereign Lord or his authority, but be punishable as rebellers and gainstanders of the same, who shall not give their confession and make profession of the said true religion; and that they, who after defection shall give the confession of their faith of new, they shall promise to continue therein in time coming, to maintain our Sovereign Lord's authority, and at the uttermost of their power to fortify, assist, and maintain the true preachers and professors of Christ's religion, against whatsoever enemies and gainstanders of the same; and namely, against all such of whatsoever nation, estate, or degree they be of, that have joined or bound themselves, or have assisted or assists to set forward and execute the cruel decrees of Trent, contrary to the preachers and true professors of the Word of God, which is repeated word by word in the Articles of Pacification at Perth, the 23rd of Feb., 1572, approved by Parliament the last of April 1573, ratified in Parliament 1578, and related Act 123. Parl. 12. of K. James VI, with this addition, that they are bound to resist all treasonable uproars and hostilities raised against the true religion, the King's Majesty and the true professors.

Like as all lieges are bound to maintain the King's Majesty's royal person and authority, the authority of Parliaments, without which neither any laws or lawful judicatories can be established (Act 130. Act 131. Parl. 8. K. James VI), and the subjects' liberties, who ought only to live and be governed by the King's laws, the common laws of this realm allanerly[7] (Act 48. Parl. 3. K. James I, Act 79. Parl. 6. K. James VI, repeated in Act 131. Parl. 8. K. James VI), which if they be innovated or prejudged the commission anent the union of the two kingdoms of Scotland and England, which is the sole Act of 17 Parl. James VI, declares such confusion would ensue as this realm could be no more a free monarchy; because by the fundamental laws, ancient privileges, offices, and liberties of this kingdom, not only the princely authority of His Majesty's royal descent hath been these many ages maintained, also the people's security of their lands, livings, rights, offices, liberties and dignities preserved. And therefore for the preservation of the said true religion, laws and liberties of this kingdom, it is statute by Act 8. Parl. 1. repeated in Act 99. Parl. 7. ratified in Act 23. Parl. 11 and 14. Act of K. James VI and 4 Act of K. Charles, that all Kings and Princes at their coronation and reception of their princely authority, shall make their faithful promise by their solemn oath in the presence of the Eternal God, that during the whole time of their lives they shall

7 A Scottish word meaning "only."

serve the same Eternal God to the utmost of their power, according as He hath required in His most Holy Word, contained in the Old and New Testaments, and according to the same Word shall maintain the true religion of Christ Jesus, the preaching of His Holy Word, the due and right ministration of the sacraments now received and preached within this realm (according to the confession of faith immediately preceding); and shall abolish and gainstand all false religion contrary to the same; and shall rule the people committed to their charge according to the will and commandment of God revealed in His foresaid Word, and according to the laudable laws and constitutions received in this realm, no ways repugnant to the said will of the Eternal God; and shall procure to the utmost of their power, to the Kirk of God, and whole Christian people, true and perfect peace in all time coming; and that they shall be careful to root out of their Empire all heretics and enemies to the true worship of God, who shall be convicted by the true Kirk of God of the aforesaid crimes. Which was also observed by His Majesty at his Coronation in Edinburgh, 1633, as may be seen in the Order of the Coronation. In obedience to the commands of God, conform to the practice of the godly in former times, and according to the laudable example of our worthy and religious progenitors, and of many yet living amongst us, which was warranted also by act of council, commanding a general band to be made and subscribed by His Majesty's subjects of all ranks for two causes: one was, for defending the true religion, as it was then reformed, and is expressed in the confession of faith above written, and a former large confession[8] established by sundry acts of lawful general assemblies and of Parliament, unto which it hath relation, set down in public catechisms, and which had been for many years with a blessing from heaven preached and professed in this Kirk and kingdom, as God's undoubted truth grounded only upon His written Word. The other cause was for maintaining the King's Majesty, his person and estate; the true worship of God and the King's authority being so straitly joined, as that they had the same friends and common enemies, and did stand and fall together. And finally, being convinced in our minds, and confessing with our mouths, that the present and succeeding generations in this land are bound to keep the aforesaid national oath and subscription inviolable:

8 Likely referring to the Scots Confession of 1560.

We noblemen, barons, gentlemen, burgesses, ministers, and commons under subscribing, considering divers times before, and especially at this time, the danger of the true reformed religion, of the King's honour, and of the public peace of the kingdom, by the manifold innovations and evils generally contained and particularly mentioned in our late supplications, complaints, and protestations, do hereby profess, and before God, His angels and the world, solemnly declare, that with our whole hearts we agree and resolve all the days of our life constantly to adhere unto and to defend the aforesaid true religion, and forbearing the practice of all novations already introduced in the matters of the worship of God, or approbation of the corruptions of the public government of the Kirk, or civil places and power of kirkmen, till they be tried and allowed in free assemblies and in Parliaments, to labour by all means lawful to recover the purity and liberty of the Gospel as it was established and professed before the aforesaid novations; and because, after due examination, we plainly perceive and undoubtedly believe that the innovations and evils contained in our supplications, complaints, and protestations have no warrant of the Word of God, are contrary to the articles of the aforesaid confessions, to the intention and meaning of the blessed reformers of religion in this land, to the above-written Acts of Parliament, and do sensibly tend to the re-establishing of the popish religion and tyranny, and to the subversion and ruin of the true reformed religion, and of our liberties, laws and estates; we also declare that the aforesaid confessions are to be interpreted, and ought to be understood of the aforesaid novations and evils, no less than if every one of them had been expressed in the aforesaid confessions; and that we are obliged to detest and abhor them, amongst other particular heads of papistry abjured therein; and therefore from the knowledge and conscience of our duty to God, to our King and country, without any worldly respect or inducement so far as human infirmity will suffer, wishing a further measure of the grace of God for this effect, we promise and swear by the great name of the Lord our God to continue in the profession and obedience of the aforesaid religion; that we shall defend the same, and resist all these contrary errors and corruptions according to our vocation, and to the utmost of that power that God hath put into our hands, all the days of our life. And in like manner, with the same heart we declare before God and men, that we have no intention or desire to attempt anything that may turn to the dishonour of God or the diminution of the King's greatness and authority; but on the contrary we promise and swear that we shall to the utmost of our power, with our means and lives, stand to the defence of our dread Sovereign the King's Majesty, his person and authority, in the defence and preservation of the aforesaid true religion, liberties and laws of the kingdom; as also to the mutual defence and assistance every one of us of another, in the same cause of maintaining the true religion and His Majesty's authority, with our best counsels, our bodies, means and whole power, against all sorts of persons whatsoever; go that whatsoever shall be done to the least of us for that cause shall be taken as done to us all in general, and to every one of us in particular; and that we shall neither directly or indirectly suffer ourselves to be divided or withdrawn by whatsoever suggestion, combination, allurement or terror from this blessed and loyal conjunction; nor shall cast in any let or impediment that may stay or hinder any such resolution as by common consent shall be found to conduce for so good ends; but on the contrary shall by all lawful means labour to further and promote the same; and if any such dangerous and divisive motion be made to us by word or writ, we and every one of us shall either suppress it or (if need be) shall incontinently make the same known, that it may be timously[9] obviated. Neither do we fear the foul aspersions of rebellion, combination or what else our adversaries from their craft and malice would put upon us, seeing what we do is so well warranted, and ariseth from an unfeigned desire to maintain the true worship of God, the majesty of our King, and the peace of the kingdom, for the common happiness of ourselves and posterity. And because we cannot look for a blessing from God upon our proceedings, except with our profession and subscription, we join such a life and conversation as beseemeth Christians who have renewed their covenant with God; we therefore faithfully promise, for ourselves, our followers, and all other under us, both in public, in our particular families and personal carriage, to endeavour to keep ourselves within the bounds of Christian liberty, and to be good examples to others of all godliness, soberness and righteousness, and of every duty we owe to God and man; and that this our union and conjunction may be observed without violation we call the living God, the searcher of our hearts to witness, who knoweth this to be our sincere desire

---

9 Also spelled "timeously." This is a Scottish word that means "early, in good time."

and unfeigned resolution, as we shall answer to Jesus Christ in the great day, and under the pain of God's everlasting wrath, and of infamy, and of loss of all honour and respect in this world; most humbly beseeching the Lord to strengthen us by His Holy Spirit for this end, and to bless our desires and proceedings with a happy success, that religion and righteousness may flourish in the land, to the glory of God, the honour of our King, and peace and comfort of us all.

In witness whereof we have subscribed with our hands all the premises, &c. ▪

Solemn League & Covenant

In 1642, after having willfully ignored Parliament for eleven years, King Charles I of the United Kingdom finally called for Parliament to meet—only to discover that at least a third of the Members of Parliament were against him, mainly Puritan men who had long suffered persecution under him. They were known as the Parliamentarians, while those loyal to tyrannical Charles and his Roman Catholic queen were called Royalists. This polarized meeting of the Long Parliament, as it was nicknamed, soon erupted into the English Civil Wars.

One of the first things the Long Parliament did was call for the Westminster Assembly. The Parliamentarians were in dire need of Scotland's help if they were to win the civil war against the Royalists. One of the Westminster Assembly's first tasks, then, was to arrange an agreement with the Scots. In general, the English MPs wanted the agreement to be purely political, but the Scots proposed for it to have a broader scope: the Parliamentarians would get sorely needed military help against the Royalists, and the Scots would get protection for their Presbyterian Kirk, which Charles had long been attacking. They got their way, and ended up with not just a political league, but a theological covenant.

Alexander Henderson and Archibald Johnston, the Lord Wariston—both Scottish delegates in the Westminster Assembly—had co-written the Scottish National Covenant five years before, and now they were called upon to write this new, broader covenant. Their Solemn League and Covenant was accepted by the Kirk of Scotland in August 1643, and then by Parliament and the Westminster Assembly in September. Copies of the covenant were carried throughout England and Scotland to be signed by the people.

In 1649, the English Parliament under Oliver Cromwell executed Charles I. Their Scottish allies saw this as a violation of the Solemn League and Covenant and were up in arms at the betrayal. Scots Presbyterians believed Oliver Cromwell had willfully ignored the covenant and shown himself to be no friend of Presbyterians. Meanwhile, Charles I's son and heir to the throne, Charles II, shrewdly signed both the National Covenant and the Solemn League and Covenant "several times" in 1650–51, hoping to secure Presbyterian support. English Parliamentarians turned on their erstwhile Scottish allies and the Second Civil War ensued. When the dust settled and Charles II was restored to the throne in 1660, he repudiated the covenants and implemented horrific persecution against the Covenanters in the Scottish Kirk.

Beleaguered Scottish Covenanters banded together in their faithfulness to King Jesus. In the bloody years until the "Glorious Revolution" of 1688, their rallying cry was, "For Christ's Crown and Covenant!"

The Solemn League and Covenant, for Reformation and Defense of Religion, the Honor and Happiness of the King, and the Peace and Safety of the Three Kingdoms of Scotland, England, and Ireland.

Taken and Subscribed several times by King Charles II, and by all ranks in the said three kingdoms.

With an Act of the General Assembly 1643 and an Act of Parliament 1644, Ratifying and Approving the Said League and Covenant.

> "Come, and let us join ourselves to the Lord in a perpetual Covenant that shall not be forgotten." — Jer. 50:5
>
> "Take away the wicked from before the king, and his throne shall be established in righteousness." — Prov. 25:5
>
> "And all Judah rejoiced at the oath; for they had sworn with all their heart." — 2 Chron. 15:15
>
> "Though it be but a man's covenant, yet if it be confirmed by an oath, no man disannulleth or addeth thereto." — Gal. 3:15

Assembly at Edinburgh, August 17, 1643. Sess. 14. The General Assembly's Approbation of the Solemn League and Covenant.

The Assembly having recommended unto a Committee appointed by them to join with the Committee of the Honourable Convention of Estates, and the Commissioners of the Honourable Houses of the Parliament of England, for bringing the kingdoms to a more near conjunction and union, received from the foresaid Committees the Covenant after mentioned, as the result of their consultations: and having taken the same, as a matter of so publick concernment and so deep importance doth require, unto their gravest consideration, did, with all their hearts, and with the beginnings of the feelings of that joy, which they did find in go great measure upon the renovation of the National Covenant of this kirk and kingdom, All with one voice approve ad embrace the same, as the most powerful mean, by the blessing of God, for settling and preserving the true Protestant religion with perfect peace in his Majesty's dominions, and propagating the same to other nations, and for establishing his Majesty's throne to all ages and generations. And therefore, with their best affections, recommend the same to the Honourable Convention of Estates, that, being examined and approved by them, it may be sent with all diligence to the kingdom of England, that, being received and approven there the same may be, with publick humiliation, and all religious and answerable solemnity, sworn and subscribed by all true professors of the reformed religion, an all his Majesty's good subjects in both kingdoms.

A. Johnstoun.

Charles I. Parl. 3. Sess. 1. Act 5. Act anent the Ratification of the calling of the Convention, Ratification of the League and Covenant, Articles of Treaty betwixt the Kingdoms of Scotland and England, and remanent Acts of the Convention of Estates, and Committee thereof. At Edinburgh, July 15, 1644.

The Estates of Parliament, presently convened by virtue of the last act of the last Parliament, holden by his Majesty, and the three Estates, in anno 1641, considering, that the Lords of his Majesty's Privy Council, and Commissioners for conserving the articles of the treaty, having, according to their interests and trust committed to them by his Majesty and Estates of Parliament, used all means, by supplications, remonstrances, and sending of Commissioners, for securing the peace of this kingdom, and removing the unhappy distractions betwixt his Majesty and his subjects in England, in such a way as might serve most for his Majesty's honour, and good of both kingdoms; and their humble and dutiful endeavours for so good ends having proven ineffectual, and their offer of mediation and intercession being refused by his Majesty; and thereby finding the weight and difficulty of affairs, and the charge lying on them to be greater than they could bear; did therefore, in the month of May 1643, meet together with the Commissioners for the common burdens, that, by joint advice, some resolution might be taken therein; and in respect of the danger imminent to the true Protestant religion, his Majesty's honour, and peace of their kingdoms, by the multitude of Papists and their adherents in arms in England and Ireland, and of many other publick and important affairs, which could not admit delay, and did require the advice of the representative body of the kingdom; appointed and caused indict a meeting of the Convention of Estates (his Majesty having formerly refused their humble desires for a Parliament) to be on the 22d of June following; which diet being frequently kept by the Noblemen, commissioners of shires and burghs, and they finding these dangers against this kirk and state still increasing, resolved, after serious deliberation and advice of the General Assembly, and joint concurrence of the Commissioners authorized by the Parliament of England, that one of the chiefest remedies for preventing of these ad the like dangers, for preservation of religion, and both kingdoms, from ruin and destruction, and for procuring of peace, That both kingdoms should, for these ends, enter into Covenant; which was accordingly drawn up, and cheerfully embraced and allowed. And at last a treaty was agreed unto by both kingdoms, concerning the said Covenant, and assistance craved from this kingdom b the kingdom of England, in pursuance of the ends expressed therein:—And the Estates being still desirous to use all good means, that, without the effusion of more blood, there may be such a blessed pacification betwixt his Majesty and his subjects, as may tend to the good of religion, his Majesty's true honour and safety, and happiness of his people, did therefore give commission to John Earl of Loudoun, Lord Chancellor, Lord Maitland, Lord Waristoun, and Mr. Robert Barclay, to repair to England, and endeavour the effectuating of these ends contained in the covenant of treaties, conform to their instructions.

And the said Estates having taken the proceedings above written to their consideration, do find and declare, That the Lords of council, and conservers of peace, did behave themselves as faithful counsellors, loyal subjects, and good patriots, in tendering their and in calling the Commissioners for the common burdens, and, by joint advice, appointing the late meeting of Convention, wherein they have approven themselves answerable to the duty of their places, and that trust committed to them; and therefore ratifies and approves their whole proceedings therein, and declares the said Convention was lawfully called, and also full and free in itself, consisting of all the members thereof, as any Convention hath been at any time bygone; and ratifies and approves the several acts made by them, or their committee, for enjoining the Covenant. And also, the said estates of Parliament (but prejudice of the premises, and of the general ratification above mentioned) ratify, approve, and confirm the foresaid mutual League and Covenant, concerning the reformation and defence of religion, the honour and happiness of the King, and the peace a safety of the three kingdoms of Scotland, England, and Ireland; together with the acts of the Kirk an Estate authorizing the same League and Covenant; together also with the foresaid articles of treaty and the Commissioners of both the Houses of Parliament of England, concerning the said Solemn League and Covenant. And the said Estates ordain the same acts, with the League and Covenant above specified, acts authorizing the same, and the articles of treaty foresaid, to have the full force and strength of perfect laws and acts of Parliament, and to be observed by all his Majesty's lieges, conform to the tenors thereof respective. Of the which League and Covenant, the tenor follows:

The Solemn League and Covenant, for reformation and defence of religion, the honour and happiness of the King, and the peace and safety of the three kingdoms of Scotland, England, and Ireland; agreed upon by Commissioners from the Parliament and Assembly of Divines in England, with Commissioners of the Convention of Estates and General Assembly of the Church of Scotland; approved by the General Assembly of the Church of Scotland, and by both Houses of Parliament, and the Assembly of Divines in England, and taken and subscribed by them anno 1643; and thereafter, by the said authority, taken and subscribed by all ranks in Scotland and England the same year; and ratified by act of the Parliament of Scotland anno 1644. (And again renewed in Scotland, with an acknowledgement of sins and engagements to duties, by all ranks, anno 1648, and by Parliament, 1649; and taken and subscribed by King Charles II, at Spey, June 23, 1650; and at Scoon, January 1, 1651.)

We, noblemen, barons, knights, gentlemen, citizens, burgesses, ministers of the Gospel, and commons of all sorts, in the kingdoms of Scotland, England, and Ireland, by the providence of God living under one king, and being of one reformed religion, having before our eyes the glory of God, and the advancement of the kingdom of our Lord and Saviour Jesus Christ, the honour and happiness of the king's majesty and his posterity, and the true public liberty, safety, and peace of the kingdom, wherein every one's private condition is included: and calling to mind the treacherous and bloody plots, conspiracies, attempts, and practices of the enemies of God, against the true religion and professors thereof in all places, especially in these three kingdoms, ever since the reformation of religion; and how much their rage, power, and presumption, are of late, and at this time, increased and exercised, whereof the deplorable state of the Church and kingdom of Ireland, the distressed state of the Church and kingdom of England, and the dangerous state of the Church and kingdom of Scotland, are present and public testimonies: we have now at last (after other means of supplication, remonstrance, protestation, and sufferings), for the preservation of ourselves and our religion from utter ruin and destruction, according to the commendable practice of these kingdoms in former times, and the example of God's people in other nations, after mature deliberation, resolved and determined to enter into a Mutual and Solemn League and Covenant, wherein we all subscribe, and each one of us for himself, with our hands lifted up to the Most High God, do swear,

I. That we shall sincerely, really, and constantly, through the grace of God, endeavor, in our several places and callings, the preservation of the reformed religion in the Church of Scotland, in doctrine, worship, discipline, and government, against our common enemies; the reformation of religion in the kingdoms of England and Ireland, in doctrine, worship, discipline, and government, according to the Word of God, and the example of the best reformed Churches; and shall endeavour to bring the Churches of God in the three kingdoms to the nearest conjunction and uniformity in religion, Confession of Faith, Form of Church Government, Directory for Worship and Catechising; that we, and our posterity after us, may, as brethren, live in faith and love, and the Lord may delight to dwell in the midst of us.

II. That we shall, in like manner, without respect of persons, endeavour the extirpation of Popery, Prelacy (that is, Church government by archbishops, bishops, their chancellors and commissioners, deans, deans and chapters, archdeacons, and all other ecclesiastical officers depending on that hierarchy), superstition, heresy, schism, profaneness, and whatsoever shall be found contrary to sound doctrine and the power of Godliness; lest we partake in other men's sins, and thereby be in danger to receive of their plagues; and that the Lord may be one, and his mane one, in the three kingdoms.

III. We shall, with the same sincerity, reality, and constancy, in our several vocations, endeavour, with our estates and lives, mutually to preserve the rights and privileges of the Parliaments, and the liberties of the kingdoms; and to preserve and defend the king's majesty's person and authority, in the preservation and defence of the true religion and liberties of the kingdoms; that the world may bear witness with our consciences of our loyalty, and that we have no other thoughts or intentions to diminish his majesty's just power and greatness.

IV. We shall also, with all faithfulness, endeavour the discovery of all such as have been or shall be incendiaries, malignants, or evil instruments, be hindering the reformation of religion, dividing the king from his people, or one of the kingdoms from another, or making any faction or parties among the people, contrary to this League and Covenant; that they may be brought to public trial, and receive condign punishment, as the degree of their offences shall require or deserve, or the supreme judicatories of both kingdoms respectively, or others having power from them for that effect, shall judge convenient.

V. And whereas the happiness of a blessed peace between these kingdoms, denied in former times to our progenitors, is, by the good providence of God, granted unto us, and hath been lately concluded and settled by both Parliaments; we shall, each one of us, according to our place and interest, endeavour that they may remain conjoined in a firm peace and union to all posterity; and that justice may be done upon the willful opposers thereof, in manner expressed in the precedent article.

VI. We shall also, according to our places and callings, in this common cause of religion, liberty, and peace of the kingdoms, assist and defend all those that enter into this League and Covenant, in the maintaining and pursuing thereof; and shall not suffer ourselves, directly or indirectly, by whatsoever combination, persuasion, or terror, to be divided or withdrawn from this blessed union and conjunction, whether to make defection to the contrary part, or to give ourselves to a detestable indifferency or neutrality in this cause, which so much concerneth the glory of God, the good of the kingdom, and honour of the king; but shall, all the days of our lives, zealously and constantly continue therein against all opposition, and promote the same, according to our power, against all lets and impediments whatsoever; and what we are not able ourselves to suppress or overcome, we shall reveal and make known, that it may be timely prevented or removed: All which we shall do as in the sight of God.

And, because these kingdoms are guilty of many sins and provocations against God, and his Son Jesus Christ, as is too manifest by our present distresses and dangers, the fruits thereof; we profess and declare, before God and the world, our unfeigned desire to be humbled for our own sins, and for the sins of these kingdoms; especially that we have not, as we ought, valued the inestimable benefit of the Gospel; that we have not laboured for the purity and power thereof; and the we have not endeavoured to receive Christ in our hearts, not to walk worthy of him in our lives; which are the causes of other sins and transgression so much abounding amongst us: and our true and unfeigned purpose, desire, and endeavour, for ourselves, and all others under our power and charge, both in public and private, in all duties we owe to God and man, to amend our lives, and each one to go before another in the example of a real reformation; that the Lord may turn away his wrath and heavy indignation, and establish these Churches and kingdoms in truth and peace. And this Covenant we make in the presence of Almighty God, the Searcher of all hearts, with a true intention to perform the same, as we shall answer at that great day, when the secrets of all hearts shall be disclosed; most humbly beseeching the Lord to strengthen us by his Holy Spirit for this end, and to bless our desires and proceedings with such success, as may be deliverance and safety to his people, and encouragement to other Christian Churches, groaning under, or in danger of the yoke of antichristian tyranny, to join in the same or like association and covenant, to the glory of God, the enlargement of the kingdom of Jesus Christ, and the peace and tranquillity of Christian kingdoms and commonwealths. ▪

The Children's Bond

In 1638, tens of thousands of Scots had signed the Scottish National Covenant to band together in defense of true, biblical, Reformed faith. In 1646, the Scots renewed that bond when they signed the Solemn League and Covenant with the English Puritans. The Scottish Christians who signed these covenants, and proved their allegiance with their lives, became known as Covenanters.

But when King Charles II was restored to the throne in 1660, twenty-eight years of bloody persecution followed for Covenanters across Scotland's Lowlands. First, Covenanting ministers were driven from their own churches and replaced with the king's favorites. But the congregations followed their beloved pastors, and worshiped in the hills at secret meetings called "conventicles." Charles II declared that such conventicles were illegal and punishable, but that did not stop the Covenanters from faithfully meeting anyway. If they were caught, they could be massacred by the king's men, as many of them were. Their ministers were constantly hunted, and usually caught and executed. Covenanters often saw their farms burned, their lands confiscated, and their families abused or murdered. But they were willing to endure all this for the sake of the pure gospel of King Jesus.

Covenanter children who were born into this persecution grew up on rich spiritual food. In 1683, fifteen girls in Pentland, Scotland held a meeting. At least one of them, Beatrix Umpherston, was only ten years old. They were daughters of Covenanters, and from their birth they had worshiped alongside their elders in the valley of the shadow of death. A childhood under persecution had filled these little girls' hearts with the same resoluteness that filled their parents and grandparents. At this meeting in 1683, they wrote a covenant of their very own, The Children's Bond.

This is a Covenant made between the Lord and us, with our whole hearts, and to give up ourselves freely to Him without reserve, soul and body, hearts and affections, to be His children and Him to be our God and Father; if it please the Lord to send His gospel to the land again, that we stand to this Covenant which we have written, between the Lord and us, as we shall answer at that great day. That we shall never break this Covenant which we have made with the Lord and us, that we shall stand to this Covenant which we have made; and if not, it shall be a witness against us in the great day when we shall stand before the Lord and His holy angels. O Lord give us real grace in our hearts this day to mind Zion's breaches which are in such low case this day: and make us to mourn with her, for Thou hast said them that mourn with her in the time of trouble shall rejoice when she rejoiceth, when the Lord shall bring back the captivity of Zion, when he shall deliver her out of her enemies' hand, when her King shall come and raise her from the dust, in spite of all her enemies that oppose her, either devils or men. That thus, they have banished their King, Christ out of the land, yet he will arise and avenge His children's blood at her enemies' hands, which cruel murderers have shed.

Them that will not stand to every article of this Covenant which we have made betwixt the Lord and us, that they shall not go to the Kirk to hear any of those soul-murdering curates we will neither speak nor converse with them. Any that break this Covenant, they shall never come into our Society. We shall declare before the Lord that have bound ourselves in Covenant, to be covenanted with Him all the days of our life, to be His children and Him to be our Covenanted Father.

We subscribe with our hands these presents—

Beatrix Umpherston	Helen Clark	Margaret Brown
Helen Moutray	Marion Swan	Janet Brown
Helen Straiton	Janet Swan	Marion M'Morren
Margaret Galloway	Isobel Craig	Christian Laurie
Janet Brown	Martha Logan	Agnes Aitken ▪

AFTERWORD

The Confessing Church Is Still Alive

IN THIS VOLUME, we have focused on the creeds, confessions, catechisms, and covenants from long-ago centuries of Church history. But we want to leave you with a reminder that the Body of Christ is still alive and active, being sanctified day by day, and resolutely fighting back against the gates of hell until our Lord returns to finish the fight.

This means that confessions and covenants and the like are not just things of the past. There are a number of very young ones, in fact, and more will surely be made. We have not included these modern confessions in this book due to copyrights and limited page space, but we list a few of them here for your consideration and further study.

THEOLOGICAL DECLARATION OF BARMEN

Signed in 1934 by 139 Church leaders in Barmen, Germany, who had gathered to affirm biblical Christianity, which was under attack in Nazi Germany. The Barmen Declaration rebukes the Third Reich's heretical "German Christianity," which scrapped the Old Testament, taught Aryanism, and demanded that the church be subservient to the government.

LAUSANNE COVENANT

Undertaken in 1974 by Church leaders who met in the First International Congress on World Evangelization in Lausanne, Switzerland. The congress spanned many denominations and united over its allegiance to Scripture and its passion for "the whole Church to take the whole gospel to the whole world."

CHICAGO STATEMENT ON BIBLICAL INERRANCY

Accepted in Chicago, Illinois, in 1978 by over 200 Church leaders gathered at Summit I of the International Council on Biblical Inerrancy (ICBI). Its signers represented several denominations, who united to defend the supremacy and trustworthiness of Scripture.

CHICAGO STATEMENT ON BIBLICAL HERMENEUTICS

Accepted in Chicago, Illinois, in 1982 by Summit II of the ICBI. It was written as a sequel to the Statement on Biblical Inerrancy, on the belief that we can only defend Biblical inerrancy if we understand the Bible.

CHICAGO STATEMENT ON BIBLICAL APPLICATION

Accepted in Chicago, Illinois, in 1986 by Summit III of the ICBI. This is the final Statement in the trilogy, and it applies the doctrines of the first two statements to the Church's interactions with the modern world.

DANVERS STATEMENT

Published in 1988 by the Council on Biblical Manhood and Womanhood, this statement affirms the biblical, traditional, complementarian roles of men and women.

NASHVILLE STATEMENT

Written in Nashville, Tennessee, in 2017 by the Council on Biblical Manhood and Womanhood to affirm a biblical view of marriage and rebuke all forms of perversion and immorality. The statement was signed by over 150 Church leaders from various denominations. ▪

www.ingramcontent.com/pod-product-compliance
Lightning Source LLC
Chambersburg PA
CBHW070049030426
42335CB00016B/1838